VIRGINIA DOMESTIC RELATIONS HANDBOOK

Third Edition

MARGARET F. BRINIG
Professor of Law
George Mason University
School of Law

MICHIE
Law Publishers
CHARLOTTESVILLE, VIRGINIA

TABLE OF CONTENTS

TABLE OF CONTENTS

TABLE OF CONTENTS

xiv

CHAPTER 1

Introduction

This book was written to aid Virginia practitioners who occasionally or often handle cases dealing with family relationships.

Despite the fears of some family lawyers in the nineteen eighties, domestic relations practice has changed dramatically. It has become at once more complicated and more lucrative. The low status family lawyers bore because of the problems with fault divorce is a thing of the past. The work family practitioners do now resembles corporate practice: much more is accomplished through contracts and negotiation. Since emotions are almost always involved, however, and children take center stage in most families, dissolution of families, whether through termination of parental rights or divorce, isn't exactly like winding up a business partnership.

Though most family law, in this state and others, begins with statutes, courts still exercise their equitable powers. Judges continue to wrestle with the discretion they are given to determine which custodial arrangement will be in a child's best interest and how much property should equitably be awarded to each spouse. Increasingly, their task involves expert testimony, whether about valuing pensions, closely held corporations, or deciding whether a parent or the state has proven child abuse.

As I prepare this edition, many of the assumptions of the past twenty years are being rethought. Virginia, with other states, is reconsidering no-fault divorce, custody arrangements, parental rights, and the basis for alimony. The changes contemplated are not minor tinkering; they will have real consequences for the citizens of the state. In contrast to earlier editions of this book, this volume has citations to authorities that may be helpful in making these important public policy choices.

Additionally, there are increasing opportunities for attorneys dealing with cases involving status. For example, Virginia has abolished interspousal immunity, and has engrafted many exceptions onto the rule prohibiting suits between parent and child. Although there are no longer actions in the common law field of "heartbalm actions," a cause of action is available for parents who have emotional distress as the result of being deprived of the custody or visitation with their children. Increasingly,

1

individuals in status relationships such as parent and child or husband and wife are being granted court recognition of their individual rights.

CHAPTER 2

Contracts Between Unmarried Cohabitants

§ 2-1. Introduction.

Before the Married Women's Property Acts, Va. Code §§ 55-35 to 55-47.1, contracts made by a married woman were ineffective, since by marrying, she went under her husband's protection or coverture. See, e.g., *Virginia R. & P. Co. v. Gorsuch,* 20 Va. 655, 662, 91 S.E. 632, 634 (1917); *Wynn v. Southan's Adm'r & Heirs,* 86 Va. 946, 11 S.E. 878 (1890). The parties owned everything together, and the husband was the only one who could act to bind the parties. The woman lacked capacity to contract. *Wynn,* 86 Va. at 949, 11 S.E. at 879.

Contracts between a man and a woman living together who were not married were also invalid. If they thought that they were married, but the marriage was void, the parties' agreement did not amount to a contract because it was presumed to have been undertaken out of love and affection rather than hope of a pecuniary gain. *Alexander v. Kuykendall,* 192 Va. 8, 10, 11, 63 S.E.2d 746, 747 (1951). Many of the services that might be performed by a married couple would obviously not be the subject of a separate contract because of the promises the spouses made to each other through their wedding vows. They were in any event not dealing with each other at arms' length. If they knew that they were not married, the contract was not valid either because the relationship's illegality tainted it, or because there was no legal consideration, since payment in sexual services outside marriage was invalid. See, e.g., *Grant v. Butt,* 198 S.C. 298, 17 S.E.2d 689 (1941); *Restatement, Contracts* § 589; 6A *Corbin on Contracts* § 1476 (1962).

Today these positions have changed. Married women can contract with the same efficacy as all other persons. Va. Code § 55-36. Husbands and wives generally contract between themselves; this will be discussed further in Chapter 9. Va. Code § 55-36; *Moreland v. Moreland,* 108 Va. 93, 60 S.E. 730 (1908) (contract after separation); *Capps v. Capps,* 216 Va. 378, 219 S.E.2d 901 (1975) (contract after marriage).

3

If one (or both) of the parties to a void marriage thinks in good faith that the marriage is valid, there are several ways in which relief may be sought.

(1) *Tort action in fraud and deceit.* In *Alexander v. Kuykendall,* 192 Va. 8, 63 S.E.2d 746 (1951), a woman gave up her employment and moved in order to marry a man who was, unknown to her, already married. When she discovered the truth, she sued in contract to recover the value of the services she performed while the two lived together, and in tort for damages for fraud and deceit. The Virginia Supreme Court denied her contractual relief since she thought she was married, and therefore did not bargain for financial remuneration at arm's length. However, she recovered in tort, for she had suffered damage as the result of his intentional misrepresentation.[1]

Similarly, in *Allen v. Jackson,* 9 Va. Cir. 60 (Nottoway Co. 1987), Mrs. Jackson placed George Jackson's name on a deed as co-owner of her separate property, thinking they had been validly married when in fact he was still married to another woman. George died intestate, leaving his daughter, the plaintiff, as his survivor. Both Mr. and Mrs. Jackson contributed to the construction of the house. The trial court found that Mrs. Jackson would not have purchased or put property in his name if she had known that he was not divorced from his prior wife, and proceeded to invalidate the deed on grounds of fraud.

(2) *Common law marriage.* Virginia does not recognize common law marriages contracted within the state. Va. Code § 20-13; *Offield v. Davis,* 100 Va. 250, 263, 40 S.E. 910, 914 (1902). However, if parties entered into a common law marriage valid in another state, it will be recognized even though an attempted ceremonial marriage occurred in Virginia. For example, in *Metropolitan Life Ins. Co. v. Holding,* 293 F. Supp. 854 (E.D. Va. 1968), a serviceman, relying upon his wife's attorney's erroneous statement that their divorce was final, married another woman in France. The couple lived in various places abroad during the man's career in the Armed Forces and foreign service, but travelled through the

---

1. This action would lie despite the statutory invalidation of actions involving breach of promise to marry and seduction, since both of these actions involve a sexual performance that is knowingly unlawful. Va. Code § 8.01-220. In *Kuykendall,* the action involved a totally innocent party, so that the action existed because "a woman so induced has changed her status from that of a virtuous single woman and has been forced to live meretriciously with defendant, to her humiliation, disgrace and mental anguish." 192 Va. at 12, 63 S.E.2d at 748.

common law marriage jurisdictions of Florida and Ohio when they were on leave in the United States. When the husband died in Virginia, the French woman was able to recover insurance money as a surviving spouse since she had never known of the invalidity of the ceremonial marriage and the couple had agreed to and ratified a common law marriage recognizable in Virginia.

(3) *Estoppel.* Although there are no Virginia cases on point, cases from other jurisdictions frequently allow a dependent would-be spouse relief on grounds of estoppel, if there was a change in position based upon a bona fide reliance upon the validity of a marriage (or a prior divorce).[2] *Alexander v. Kuykendall,* supra, may be read in part as a protection of the putative wife's change in position. Virginia recognizes the efficacy of the doctrine of estoppel generally. See 7 Michie's Jurisprudence *Estoppel* § 14.

(4) *Putative spouse.* Several important states,[3] following a civil law formulation, allow recovery for persons who mistakenly believe that they are validly married. They are permitted the share of property to which they would have been entitled had the marriage been valid. This doctrine is not available to plaintiffs in Virginia, and would not be absent a legislative change.

(5) *Support following annulment.* If the parties went through a marriage ceremony and the dependent spouse can show need and lack of fault, there may be recovery under the general spousal support and maintenance statute unless the marriage was void ab initio. *Bray v. Landergren,* 161 Va. 699, 706, 172 S.E. 252, 254 (1933) (dictum). In *Fulton v. Fulton,* Chancery No. 87732 (1985), the supposed husband was wed to another before he took part in a marriage ceremony with the plaintiff. When plaintiff amended her annulment action to include a count for equitable distribution under Va. Code § 20-107.3, the Circuit Court sustained defendant's demurrer on the grounds that a marriage, at least a voidable marriage, must have existed in order for distribution to take place. See

---

2. *See, e.g.,* Spellens v. Spellens, 49 Cal. 2d 210, 317 P.2d 613 (1957); Poor v. Poor, 381 Mass. 392, 409 N.E.2d 758 (1980); Rosen v. Sitner, 274 Pa. Super. 445, 418 A.2d 490 (1980). *See generally* Restatement, Conflict of Laws (Second) § 74; 24 Am. Jur. 2d *Divorce and Separation* §§ 971, 972; 27B C.J.S. *Divorce* §§ 364-366.

3. These states include California, Cal. Civ. Code § 4452; Illinois, Ill. Rev. Stat. ch. 40, § 305; and Texas, Hupp v. Hupp, 235 S.W.2d 753 (Tex. Civ. App. 1950). Both the Illinois formulation, enacted in 1977, and that occurring in Michigan, Mich. Stat. Ann. § 26-190.1, enacted in 1978, have occurred through legislative action.

also *Mato v. Mato*, 12 Va. Cir. 153 (Spotsylvania Co. 1988) (substantially the same facts as in *Fulton*). The case for disallowing support was even stronger in *Kleinfield v. Veruki*, 7 Va. App. 183, 372 S.E.2d 407 (1988), where the alleged wife had a preexisting marriage. She had married a would-be immigrant in order to keep him from being deported, and had the marriage annulled only after her marriage to defendant, making this second marriage bigamous and void.

(6) *No recovery absent a contract.* In the case of *Cooper v. Spencer*, 218 Va. 541, 238 S.E.2d 805 (1977), a man and a woman mistakenly believed that their prior marriages had ended in divorce. They went through a marriage ceremony and lived together for many years, supporting the family in large part through an egg and poultry business called Jo-Bets farm (an acronym made of portions of each party's first name). When the relationship ended, and the parties discovered that they were not married, the woman attempted to sue the man for some of the farm's assets. The Supreme Court disallowed relief, because the woman did not sufficiently prove a partnership. If there were no partnership, an implied contract would not lie since the woman believed herself married and therefore acted out of love and affection rather than the hope of pecuniary gain. Although the court did not take note of the landmark California decision in *Marvin v. Marvin*, 18 Cal. 3d 660, 134 Cal. Rptr. 815, 557 P.2d 106 (1976), even if an action were allowed for express contract, the result would be the same. There was no proof that a business relationship between the man and woman had been established, and therefore all that remained was the presumed affectionate relationship between them. *Cooper v. Spencer*, 218 Va. at 543-44, 238 S.E.2d at 806-07.

A recently reported circuit court case used an implied contract to allow a putative wife to recover reasonable compensation for her services. In *Paxton v. Paxton*, 29 Va. Cir. 496 (Craig Co. 1977), the woman believed in good faith that she was married to decedent, performing various services for him and receiving support and maintenance from him. The court did not mention *Cooper v. Spencer*, but permitted the woman to recover the difference between the value of services rendered and the support and maintenance paid by the supposed husband before he died.

If the parties know that they are not married, but nevertheless live together, a growing number of jurisdictions allow relief on the basis of an express contract.[4] Although there will be no recovery based upon the illicit exchange of sexual favors, the decisions state that there is no reason that the other forms of consideration, such as performance of household tasks, work in the other's business, or entertainment of business friends, cannot be a valid exchange for a promise of support. In other words, the fact that the parties to a contract are living together in an unmarried relationship will not invalidate an otherwise valid contract. However, it may be difficult to prove that other forms of consideration are involved. In a recent West Virginia case, *Thomas v. LaRosa,* 400 S.E.2d 809 (W. Va. 1990), a woman who lived for some years with a man she knew to be already married was not permitted to recover under an alleged oral contract under which he agreed to provide her with financial security for her lifetime and to educate her children. The contract was found to be unenforceable because it was explicitly and inseparably founded on illegal sexual services. In that state, cohabitation outside marriage is illegal.

The states not following the majority position, which finds express agreements enforceable, reason that heterosexual nonmarital living arrangements are illegal. See, e.g., *Hewitt v. Hewitt,* 77 Ill. 2d 49, 394 N.E.2d 1204 (1979); *Merrill v. Davis,* 100 N.M. 552, 673 P.2d 1285 (1983); *Roach v. Buttons,* 6 Fam. L. Rep. (BNA) 2355 (Tenn. Ch. App. 1980). Additionally, to recognize financial repercussions from such relationships would be, in effect, to create a type of common law marriage, abolished as difficult to prove and tending towards collusion many years ago. See, e.g., *Hewitt v. Hewitt,* 77 Ill. 2d 49, 63, 394 N.E.2d 1204, 1209-10 (1979); *Merrill v. Davis,* 100 N.M. 552, 554, 673 P.2d 1285, 1287 (1983); cf. *Morone v. Morone,* 50 N.Y.2d 481, 488, 596, 407 N.E.2d 438, 442, 413 N.E.2d 1154, 1156, 429 N.Y.S.2d 592 (1980) (relief allowed for express contracts only). Further, the extramarital relationship, because it allows participants to escape many of the duties and responsibilities of marriage, might become so popular as to threaten the institution of marriage, at the heart of the fabric of society. *Hewitt v. Hewitt,* 77 Ill. 2d 49, 58, 394 N.E.2d 1204, 1207 (1979); *Merrill v. Davis,* 100 N.M. 552, 554, 673 P.2d 1285, 1287 (1983).

---

4. *See, e.g.,* Mason v. Rostad, 476 A.2d 662 (D.C. App. 1984) (quasi-contract); Morone v. Morone, 50 N.Y.2d 481, 407 N.E.2d 438, 413 N.E.2d 1154, 429 N.Y.S.2d 592 (1980) (express contract); Crowe v. De Gioia, 90 N.J. 126, 447 A.2d 173 (N.J. 1982); *see generally* Hunter, *An Essay on Contract and Status: Race, Marriage and the Meretricious Spouse,* 64 VA. L. REV. 1039 (1978); Comment, 30 STAN. L. REV. 359 (1978).

§ 2-2. The Virginia position.

The Virginia fornication statute was successfully challenged in the case of *Doe v. Duling,* 603 F. Supp. 960 (E.D. Va. 1985). However, on appeal, the Fourth Circuit found that the plaintiffs did not have standing, and so vacated the lower court opinion. *Doe v. Duling,* 782 F.2d 1202 (4th Cir. 1986). Lewd and lascivious cohabitation remains a misdemeanor under Va. Code § 18.2-345, and adultery is made criminal by Va. Code § 18.2-365. There is therefore a basis for arguing the minority position. However, unlike Illinois at the time of *Hewitt v. Hewitt,* 77 Ill. 2d 49, 394 N.E.2d 1204 (1979), Virginia recognizes no-fault divorce and does not provide the alternative relief of the putative spouse doctrine. Although it appears from an analysis of *Cooper v. Spencer,* 218 Va. 541, 238 S.E.2d 805 (1977), that an express contract will be necessary, the older *Alexander v. Kuykendall,* 192 Va. 8, 63 S.E.2d 746 (1951), would cast doubt upon the availability of recovery in any case. The question really becomes whether the parties lacked the arms' length necessary for a valid transaction. It could certainly be argued that the difference between *Cooper* and *Alexander* and the modern cohabitation case is the express intent not to be married in the latter. The counterargument would be that the feelings of affection noted in *Cooper* and *Alexander* are just as likely to be present where a couple contemplates a meretricious relationship. The desire not to be entangled with the complex of rights and duties that arises from the marital status should arguably be sufficient to keep the same sort of financial responsibilities from being incurred.

However, there is lower court support for the contrary view, allowing recovery without an express contract in a situation where the supposed husband had died. In *Paxton v. Paxton,* 29 Va. Cir. 496 (Craig Co. 1977), the court cited a North Carolina case and permitted the woman to recover the difference between the reasonable value of the services she had performed before the man's death and the support and maintenance she had received from him.

If the Virginia Supreme Court were to recognize such a contract, the attorney would have to prove: (1) the parties were not married; (2) they knew they were not married; (3) they contracted at arms' length and expressly for the service arrangement; and (4) sexual favors were not the major part of the consideration. Recovery would be possible if factors (1) and (2) could not be proven. It would not be possible if (3) or (4) were not susceptible of proof.

In the first Virginia Supreme Court case to consider the question of the division of property of cohabitants, *Tiller v. Owen,* 243 Va. 176, 413 S.E.2d 51 (1992), Tiller purchased property in her own name while the couple lived together. She used $23,000 obtained from Owen for the down payment, but was the sole purchaser named in the real estate contract and the only party obligated on the note that secured the deed of trust on the property. Owen was married to another woman during this whole time, but furnished Tiller with sufficient money to make each mortgage payment from October 1987 until June 1989, when their relationship ended. At that point Tiller moved out of the home since Owen refused to leave. He continued making mortgage payments directly, and asked the trial court to declare a resulting trust on the property in his favor since he had delivered to Tiller both the money for the down payment and the monthly mortgage payments. The Supreme Court reversed the trial court's imposition of a resulting trust, finding that Owen had not obligated himself to purchase all or part of the property in question. When he delivered the checks to Tiller, therefore, he was not acting in satisfaction of any obligation he had regarding purchase of the property, so a resulting trust could not arise.

CHAPTER 3

Antenuptial Contracts

§ 3-1. Historical perspective.

For many years, Virginia, like most common law jurisdictions, did not recognize antenuptial contracts. This was because such agreements might promote or facilitate divorce, and they might attempt to affect the incidents of marriage. 2 A. Lindey, *Separation Agreements and Ante-Nuptial Contracts* § 90, at 90-93 (1979). Additionally, persons contemplating marriage have always been held to be in a confidential relationship. *Batleman v. Rubin,* 199 Va. 156, 160, 98 S.E.2d 519, 522 (1957). Since in many cases the husband to be was the dominant partner in this relationship, he might too easily take advantage of his fiancee who would then be left without viable means of support. *Volid v. Volid,* 6 Ill. App. 3d 386, 286 N.E.2d 42, 46 (1972).

Virginia abandoned any reluctance to accept antenuptial agreements before most other states, *Cumming v. Cumming,* 127 Va. 16, 102 S.E. 572 (1920), and now recognizes that antenuptial contracts tend to promote rather than discourage marital stability. *Gillinan v. Gillinan,* 406 N.E.2d 981 (Ind. App. 1980); 12B Michie's Jurisprudence *Marriage Contracts and Settlements* § 2; cf. *Capps v. Capps,* 216 Va. 378, 219 S.E.2d 901 (1975) (agreement between spouses after their marriage).

In 1985, Virginia became the first state to adopt the Uniform Premarital Agreement Act, codified after ratification by the 1986 General Assembly in Va. Code § 20-147 et seq. The Act applies to any premarital agreement executed on or after July 1, 1986, and codifies the case law as developed in this chapter.

11

§ 3-2. Reasons for antenuptial contracts.

Although, as previously mentioned, Virginia has recognized antenuptial agreements for many years, they have become increasingly popular recently for several reasons.

The first is the relatively high divorce rate. Since many divorced persons marry again, there may be families from a first marriage to support, or a reluctance to risk further dividing scarce resources should the second marriage fail. See, e.g., *Posner v. Posner,* 233 So. 2d 381, 384 (Fla. 1970).

The second reason is the social trend toward marrying later in life, when substantial assets have already been accumulated. Since women are very frequently employed outside the home, there is an increased probability that the wife as well as the husband will have substantial personal assets, or will at least have the capacity to be self-supporting by the time the marriage takes place. This reason relates to the general tendency toward private ordering of married life that began in the nineteen seventies. Private ordering allows spouses to tailor marriage, at least in part, to their own specifications.

A final reason that the antenuptial agreement should be considered is the equitable distribution statute, which, absent a contract entered into prior to or during the marriage, will require all marital property to be divided in cases of divorce. As we will see in Chapter 22, the law presumes that any property acquired during marriage is marital. After a lengthy marriage, even separately acquired property may take on the character of marital assets.

The careful attorney might advise a contract before marriage if: (1) the client has been previously married, particularly if there is another family to support; or (2) if the client is older and has already accumulated a substantial estate. See the facts in *Batleman v. Rubin,* 199 Va. 156, 98 S.E.2d 519 (1957), where the husband was a 54-year-old widower with two children and successfully engaged in real estate ventures and a storage business.

§ 3-3. Subjects of a valid agreement.

The antenuptial agreement may clearly regulate the disposition of the parties' property upon death or divorce. Va. Code § 20-150(3). However, it will not be enforceable if it attempts to regulate the central incidents of marriage, such as the duty to support the spouse, *Cumming v. Cumming,*

127 Va. 16, 30, 102 S.E. 572 (1920); *In re Marriage of Higgason,* 10 Cal. 3d 476, 516 P.2d 289, 110 Cal. Rptr. 897 (1973), or the conduct of intimate relations between the parties, *Favot v. Burns,* 332 So. 2d 873 (La. App. 1976) (sexual relations); cf. *Matthews v. Matthews,* 2 N.C. App. 143, 162 S.E.2d 697 (1968) (contract void when wife agreed not to leave husband in exchange for all his property should he ever leave her).

There is also a clear prohibition against encouraging divorce. *Cumming v. Cumming,* 127 Va. 16, 25, 102 S.E. 572, 574 (1920):

> The public policy rendering such agreements void is the policy to foster and protect marriage, to encourage the parties to live together, and to prevent separation, marriage being the foundation of the family and of society, without which there would be neither civilization nor progress.

Shelton v. Stewart, 193 Va. 162, 166, 67 S.E.2d 841, 843 (1951) (separation agreement).

In *Cumming,* the husband and wife married to legitimize the child of the parties who had been born before the marriage. The only condition under which the husband would marry was the execution of an agreement, which provided that each party was to retain separate property and the husband was to pay the wife a trivial sum for her and the child's support. The husband never intended to live with the wife and in fact never did so. The wife later sued for divorce based upon his desertion and sought alimony pendente lite and child support. The antenuptial agreement was found void since it was made to encourage or facilitate a separation after the marriage. 127 Va. at 25, 102 S.E. at 574 (citing 1 Bishop on *Marriage, Divorce and Separation* § 1277 (1891)). The contract was distinguished from bona fide antenuptial agreements not made with the specific object of providing a contractual limitation of the support obligation. *Id.* at 30, 102 S.E. at 576. See also *Schmidt v. Schmidt,* 9 Va. Cir. 273 (City of Richmond, 1988).

The prohibition against contracts facilitating divorce and separation would also exclude agreements whose language limited the duration of the marriage or specified grounds for divorce. For example, where before their separation at the instigation of the husband, a contract was drawn between husband and wife giving her $6000 and some personal property and relieving the husband of any further duties of support, the agreement was void as contrary to public policy because "any contract between the parties having for its object the dissolution of the marriage or facilitating that result is void as contra bonos mores." *Arrington v. Arrington,* 196 Va. 86, 94, 82 S.E.2d 548 (1954) (postnuptial agreement) (citing 1 Bishop on *Marriage, Divorce and Separation* § 1261 (1891)); cf. *In re Marriage of Dawley,* 17 Cal. 3d 342, 131 Cal. Rptr. 3, 551 P.2d 323 (1976).

However, the parties may validly contract regarding support should the marriage fail. Va. Code § 20-150(4). The parties in *Schmidt v. Schmidt,* 12 Va. Cir. 313 (City of Richmond, 1988), had a prenuptial agreement limiting the wife's right to support following divorce. When the matter was litigated in their divorce proceedings, res judicata barred the wife's later claim that during the marriage the husband had promised to always take care of her. There are limits to the ability to contract out of alimony, however. In *Davis v. Davis,* 239 Va. 657, 391 S.E.2d 255 (1990), a valid antenuptial agreement provided that each spouse would keep property separate and waive any property interests that might accrue in the future by operation of law. After the husband shot and paralyzed the wife, she filed for divorce and obtained support pendente lite. On the day before the divorce hearing, the husband conveyed his real property to a friend. The circuit court awarded the wife a divorce, and found that the husband was in arrears by $9,000. The Supreme Court agreed with the wife that the agreement did not preclude her obtaining spousal support, so that the judgment against him was valid. The deed was set aside as fraudulent, and was subject to her lien.

The most obvious candidate for inclusion in an agreement continues to be parties' property. In two cases, the parties' antenuptial agreement provided that each would keep separate property and that there would be no equitable distribution of property upon divorce. Such provisions do not prevent a divorce court from awarding spousal support in appropriate circumstances. *Bracken v. Bracken,* 1993 Va. App. LEXIS 582; *Hankins v. Hankins,* 1993 Va. App. LEXIS 317. In another variation, after the spouses in *Schmidt v. Schmidt,* 9 Va. Cir. 273 (City of Richmond, 1988), executed an antenuptial contract and married, the Virginia Code was amended to allow equitable distribution of a married spouse's pension. Mrs. Schmidt could not later claim that she was entitled to an equitable share in her husband's pension and retirement funds when she had been represented by counsel when the antenuptial agreement was prepared, and when the husband had filed a financial statement reflecting more assets than he really owned.

§ 3-4. Formalities.

Although no specific form must be used, the antenuptial agreement must be in writing and signed by both parties. Va. Code § 20-147. This eliminates many problems of proof, see, e.g., *Hannon v. Hounihan*, 85 Va. 429, 434-35, 12 S.E. 157, 158-59 (1888), and satisfies the statute of frauds. Va. Code §§ 11-1 and 11-2. The subsequent marriage would not otherwise take the contract out of the statute. 85 Va. at 435, 12 S.E. at 158.

However, in one famous case, *T. v. T.*, 216 Va. 867, 224 S.E.2d 148 (1976), the parties agreed orally that if the woman, who was pregnant by another, did not go to New York and put the child up for adoption, the man would marry her and support the child as if it were his. The woman in fact gave up prospects of a job in New York, married the man, and gave birth. The man was named as the child's father on the birth certificate, and claimed the child as his on income tax returns until the couple divorced. The contract was upheld although not in writing because not only had the marriage taken place, but also because the wife had terminated her employment plans and reconsidered her decision to place the baby for adoption. These changes in the lives of both mother and child constituted part performance, as did the husband's marriage and acceptance of her services as a housewife. The partial performance took the case out of the statute of frauds, and the husband's promises to the wife, in reliance upon which she changed her position, acted to her detriment, so that when she substantially performed her obligations, he was estopped from pleading the statute of frauds.

§ 3-5. Mutuality of agreement.

Where the consideration for the promise of one party is a promise, there must be absolute mutuality of agreement, so that each has the right to hold the other to a positive agreement. *Capps v. Capps*, 216 Va. 378, 219 S.E.2d 901 (1975) (agreement made between married couple in which the wife agreed that she would relinquish her interest in property held in joint names should she file any matrimonial action in return for a release on the mortgage note). See also *Osborne v. Osborne*, 384 Mass. 591, 428 N.E.2d 810 (1981).

Part of the consideration for an antenuptial agreement is the marriage itself. When the husband called off the wedding after execution of a premarital agreement, although the parties eventually married nearly a year later, the agreement did not govern the terms of their divorce. The court of appeals agreed with the trial court that the contract had been repudiated and no subsequent mutual consent of the parties had been given to revitalize it. *Hurt v. Hurt,* 16 Va. App. 792, 433 S.E.2d 493 (1993).

If the agreement was formulated according to foreign laws, it will be enforceable in Virginia if it satisfies existing Virginia law pertaining to prenuptial agreements. *Carpenter v. Carpenter,* 19 Va. App. 147, 449 S.E.2d 502 (1994). Each spouse must be reasonably and fairly provided for, or, in the alternative, there must be full and fair disclosure to the wife of the husband's worth before she signs. A contract called a *nikah nama* prepared before the parties' 1982 Pakistan marriage was not enforceable according to *Chaudhary v. Ali,* 1994 Va. App. LEXIS 759 (not designated for publication).

§ 3-6. Capacity to contract.

The usual rules relating to the parties' capacity to contract will apply to antenuptial agreements. The parties must be acting voluntarily and without duress. Va. Code § 20-151(1), (2). They must be of sufficient age and mental condition to make such an important disposition of their affairs. See, e.g., *Osborne v. Osborne,* 384 Mass. 591, 428 N.E.2d 810 (1981).

§ 3-7. Equality of bargaining position.

Courts continue to invalidate antenuptial agreements where the parties do not possess equal bargaining positions. One component of equality is complete information about the financial resources and income of the other. Va. Code § 20-151(2)(i). Each party should have knowledge about what might normally accrue upon death or divorce. *Batleman v. Rubin,* 199 Va. 156, 160, 98 S.E.2d 519, 522 (1957). In *Batleman,* husband and wife agreed before their marriage that in lieu of all marital rights, husband would leave wife $25,000 in his will. At the time of the antenuptial contract, husband was worth $250,000. The agreement was void because the husband did not make any disclosure to his intended wife of the value of the property, nor did she know it. The wife agreed to less than one-third of the value of her rights, if married, in the property. The evidence raised a presumption, since the amount received was dispropor-tionate, that there had not been full disclosure. The husband was unable to rebut the presumption. *Id.* at 161, 98 S.E.2d at 523-24.

McIntyre v. McIntyre, 1995 Va. App. LEXIS 719, is a modern equivalent of *Batleman*. Here the husband, but not the wife, brought significant assets into the marriage without disclosing the extent of these holdings to her. He drafted the antenuptial agreement and had her sign a waiver of alimony and of her marital rights to any interest in her holdings, and seventeen years later, sued her for divorce.

However, where the husband underestimated his financial condition but had no intent to conceal property from his wife, the misstatement did not invalidate an otherwise valid antenuptial agreement. Nor could the contract be voided because, in hindsight, there existed a better opportunity for the wife. *Schmidt v. Schmidt*, 9 Va. Cir. 273 (City of Richmond, 1988).

See generally 12B Michie's Jurisprudence *Marriage Contracts and Settlements* § 3.

§ 3-8. General sources.

For further reading, see Lenore Weitzman, *The Marriage Contract* (1981); Howard Hunter, *An Essay on Contract and Statutes: Race, Marriage, and the Meretricious Spouse,* 64 Va. L. Rev. 1039 (1978); Marjorie Macguire Schultz, *Contractual Ordering of Marriage: A New Model for State Policy,* 70 Calif. L. Rev. 707 (1982); Elizabeth Scott, *Rational Decisionmaking About Marriage and Divorce,* 76 Va. L. Rev. 9 (1990); Peter Swisher, *Divorce Planning in Antenuptial Agreements: Towards a New Objectivity,* 13 U. Rich. L. Rev. 175 (1979); Homer Clark, *The New Marriage,* 12 Willamette L.J. 441 (1976); Comment, *Marital Contracts for Support and Services: Constitutionality Begins at Home,* 49 N.Y.U. L. Rev. 1161 (1974); 12B Michie's Jurisprudence *Marriage Contracts and Settlements;* 26 Am. Jur. *Husband and Wife* § 277; West Digest, *Husband and Wife* Key No. 29(9).

CHAPTER 4

Unmarried Parents and Their Children

§ 4-1. Introduction.

At common law, the illegitimate child was *nullius filius*, no one's son. *Brown v. Commonwealth*, 218 Va. 40, 45, 235 S.E.2d 325, 329 (1977). This meant that he could not inherit, *Bond v. Bond*, 16 Va. L. Reg. 411 (1910), nor generally advance in society, since tainted by his parents' meretricious relationship. See *Goodman v. Goodman*, 150 Va. 42, 45, 142 S.E. 412, 413 (1928). See generally Lasoh, *Virginia Bastardy Laws: A Burdensome Heritage*, 9 Wm. & Mary L. Rev. 402 (1967).

Because the fate of the illegitimate was so harsh, the law has provided several avenues of relief. These include: (1) the presumption of legitimacy; (2) statutory legitimation following void marriage, Va. Code § 64-1.7; see *Henderson v. Henderson*, 187 Va. 121, 46 S.E.2d 10 (1948); (3) legitimacy if parents are later wedded, Va. Code § 20-31.1, and the father acknowledges the child, *Hoover v. Hoover*, 131 Va. 522, 105 S.E. 91 (1921); and (4) the paternity proceeding allowing support from the unwed father. Va. Code § 20-61.1 et seq.

In more recent times, much of the stigma has passed from the illegitimate child and his parents. Fit fathers of illegitimate children must be given the right to refuse consent to their child's adoption, *Stanley v. Illinois*, 405 U.S. 645 (1972); support is due since provided for by statute for legitimate children, *Gomez v. Perez*, 409 U.S. 535 (1973); Va. Code § 20-61.1; *Brown v. Commonwealth*, 218 Va. 40, 235 S.E.2d 325 (1977), and custody may be granted to the father if in the child's best interests. Compare *Caban v. Mohammed*, 441 U.S. 380 (1979), with *Commonwealth v. Hayes*, 215 Va. 49, 205 S.E.2d 644 (1974). A variety of United

States Supreme Court decisions have allowed illegitimate children to recover under workman's compensation laws, *Weber v. Aetna Cas. & Sur. Co.,* 406 U.S. 164 (1972), and wrongful death statutes, see *Levy v. Louisiana,* 391 U.S. 68 (1968); *Carroll v. Sneed,* 211 Va. 640, 179 S.E.2d 620 (1971) (where child can prove damages), and have clarified inheritance under the intestacy laws, *Labine v. Vincent,* 401 U.S. 532 (1971) (distinguishing between classes of illegitimate children constitutional) all on constitutional grounds. See generally Krause, *Equal Protection for the Illegitimate,* 65 Mich. L. Rev. 402 (1967); Lasoh, *Virginia Bastardy Laws: A Burdensome Heritage,* 9 Wm. & Mary L. Rev. 402 (1967).

§ 4-2. Presumption of legitimacy.

Because of the ancient problems of proof and the societal preference for the marital status, it was conclusively presumed that a child born during the mother's marriage was that of her husband. In fact, the spouse was frequently unable to testify at all due to the evidentiary maxim called Lord Mansfield's Rule. *Stegall v. Stegall,* 22 F. Cas. 1226 (C.C. Va. 1825). See *Bowles v. Bingham,* 16 Va. (2 Munf.) 442 (1811) (quoting 2 Blackstone's *Commentaries* 466). See generally McCormick *Evidence* § 343, 9 Wigmore, *Evidence* § 21537. This continues to remain the rule in some states, and was recently upheld against due process challenges by the Supreme Court. *Michael H. v. Gerald D.,* 491 U.S. 110 (1989).

Gradually it became possible in paternity proceedings, where the parties had never entered into a marriage, to show nonaccess by the husband during the period of likely conception. See, e.g., *Smith v. Perry,* 80 Va. 563, 569 (1885) (if beyond the seas, etc.); *Scott v. Hillenberg,* 85 Va. 245, 7 S.E. 377 (1888) (not overcome where husband was a soldier in the Confederate Army who frequently deserted and returned home); see generally 3 Michie's Jurisprudence *Bastardy* § 6.

In *Gibson v. Gibson,* 207 Va. 821, 153 S.E.2d 189 (1967), the wife gave birth to a son 314 days after the husband and she had last cohabited together, according to evidence adduced at their divorce hearing. The wife alleged that they had resumed cohabitation only after the child was born, and in fact denied that she was pregnant less than three months before his birth. The Virginia Supreme Court allowed the husband's appeal from a support order, stating that "[i]mprobability of known access by the husband merely of itself is not sufficient to repel the presumption; but when the evidence forces the conclusion of non-access beyond all reasonable doubt, it is sufficient to repel the presumption." *Id.* at 825, 153 S.E.2d at 192 (citing 3 Michie's Jurisprudence *Bastardy* § 7, at 132, 10 C.J.S. *Bastards* § 3, at 25 et seq., § 5(a) at 30-31; 10 Am. Jur. 2d *Bastards* § 15, at 855). The burden, therefore, is upon the person claiming illegitimacy. *Scott v. Hillenberg,* 85 Va. 245, 7 S.E. 377 (1888). See generally Friend, *The Law of Evidence in Virginia* § 129 (2d ed. 1983). When the juvenile and domestic relations district court ruled that blood test results had not been timely filed, the Division of Child Support Enforcement was a proper party to appeal. *Jones v. Division of Child Support Enforcement,* 19 Va. App. 184, 450 S.E.2d 172 (1994). However, the notice of appeal must be filed by the Division's attorney. Because the rules for appeal were not followed, the circuit court never acquired jurisdiction over the appeal.

More recently, the Human Leukocyte Antigen (H.L.A.) blood test has been available to show to a very high degree of certainty that a child could not be that of the husband in question (or that it most probably is his). See Va. Code §§ 20-61.1(5) and 20-61.2. There may still be problems with introducing evidence following a divorce proceeding, however.

In *Slagle v. Slagle,* 11 Va. App. 341; 398 S.E.2d 346 (1990), the wife told the husband prior to their marriage that she was pregnant with his child. After the child was born, the parties married and lived together for more than a year. They separated, and the wife was awarded $600 per month in pendente lite support. A final divorce was granted several years later, and the wife was given child custody, while the husband was ordered to pay $250 in child support and $350 in spousal support. After the decree was entered, the husband obtained blood tests conclusively establishing that he could not be the father of the child. The juvenile court, which had ordered the blood tests performed at the husband's request, abated his child support payments, but continued his spousal support obligation and ordered payment of support arrearages. Both parties appealed. The circuit court found that the final decree of divorce constituted a final adjudication of the husband's paternity and thus was not subject to collateral attack. The court of appeals agreed that the husband was collaterally estopped from challenging the support obligation established by the final divorce decree, which stated that the child was born of the marriage. See also *Comer v. Comer*, 1996 Va. App. LEXIS 277.

A child born more than ten months after a parent's death shall not be recognized as the parent's child for intestacy purposes. Va. Code § 2-164

(1994). Although a child is presumed to be the child of his or her married mother's husband, the presumption may be rebutted by a preponderance of the evidence of the paternity of another man or the impossibility or improbability of conception by the husband. Va. Code § 63.1-220.3(D). The presumptive father must give consent to adoption under Va. Code § 63.1-220.3(C).

§ 4-3. Support of children born out of wedlock.

Beginning in 1576, the English Poor Laws provided that the parish should be responsible for the maintenance of children born out of wedlock, with the power to punish both parents and to make orders for the upkeep of the illegitimate by charging the mother or the father with payment. 18 Eliz. 1, c. 3; Comment, *Support of Children Born Out of Wedlock: Virginia at the Crossroads,* 18 Wash. & Lee L. Rev. 343 (1961). The Virginia equivalent was found in L. 1769, 8 Hening 374. The brunt of illicit sexual relations was to be borne by the mother and the child through indenture into service or the workhouse. However, in *Mc-Claugherty v. McClaugherty,* 180 Va. 51, 21 S.E.2d 761 (1942), the Virginia Supreme Court stated that support was due even in the absence of statute where a child sued the father to collect support. The parents had gone through a secret ceremonial marriage and then lived together for twenty years, after which they separated and the father eventually married another, *id.* at 65, 21 S.E.2d at 767 (citing 1 Minor's *Institutes* 405). *McClaugherty* did not signal a trend, however. A later case with less compelling facts stated that the father was under no legal obligation to support or to contribute to the support to his illegitimate offspring. *Brown v. Brown,* 183 Va. 353, 32 S.E.2d 79 (1944). This lack of a legal obligation continued until Virginia adopted its paternity statute, Va. Code § 61.1. See generally Comment, *Support of Children Born Out of Wedlock: Virginia at the Crossroads,* 18 Wm. & Mary L. Rev. 343 (1961). More recently, the Supreme Court has compelled such a result since legitimate children are provided for by statute. *Gomez v. Perez,* 409 U.S. 535 (1973); Va. Code § 20-61.1; *Brown v. Commonwealth,* 218 Va. 40, 235 S.E.2d 325 (1977).

In *T. v. T.,* 216 Va. 867, 224 S.E.2d 148 (1976), an unwed pregnant woman gave up employment prospects in New York and plans to put the child up for adoption upon a man's oral agreement that he would marry her and support the child as if it were his own. The husband's name was placed as father on the birth certificate, and the husband claimed the child on income tax returns until the couple divorced. Although the agreement was oral, it was upheld despite the statute of frauds on grounds of estoppel and partial performance. See also *Dunnaville v. Department of Social Servs.,* 1995 Va. App. LEXIS 222 (husband required to pay unless he could demonstrate fraud). Similarly, where the husband refused to make court-ordered child support payments in contempt of the divorce order, he was later refused equitable relief to recover whatever payments he did make or any withheld tax funds, despite the fact that H.L.A. testing revealed that he could not be the child's father. *Stover v. Stover,* 31 Va. Cir. 484 (City of Roanoke 1990).

When the parties agreed during their deposition that the husband would acknowledge paternity of a child born during the marriage and would support that child, and the divorce decree recited that there were five children of the marriage, "including one infant child born during the marriage," the decree was a valid, conclusive judgment. *Rose v. Rose,* 1993 Va. App. LEXIS 375. The husband was therefore obligated to pay support. However, a separation agreement that acknowledged that the husband was not the father of his wife's child, born during the marriage, waived her right to enforce express promises made prior to and after the birth to support the child as if it were his own. The agreement allowed the wife to remain in the marital residence for a year and have $6,500 to cover the birth expenses and care of the infant. *Mills v. Mills,* 36 Va. Cir. 351 (Fairfax Co. 1995).

Likewise, the unwed father in *Lawson v. Murphy,* 36 Va. Cir. 465 (Wise Co. 1995), was unable to enforce a contract according to which he agreed to pay the child's mother $7,500 to replace all child support. The mother received AFDC payments and the father had to reimburse the state.

A sworn declaration of paternity is not res judicata of paternity and does not collaterally estop the putative father from adjudicating the issue of paternity, when he never had a hearing to litigate the issue. The putative father in *Dunbar v. Hogan,* 16 Va. App. 667, 432 S.E.2d 16 (1993), was therefore able to introduce H.L.A. tests excluding the possibility that he was the child's biological father in support proceedings brought by the child's mother.

A father was responsible for paying child support although he maintained that the mother had seduced him, refused to obtain an abortion, and refused to place the child for adoption. *Hur v. Department of Social Servs.,* 13 Va. App. 54, 409 S.E.2d 454 (1991). The court of appeals quoted from a New York case, *L. Pamela P. v. Frank S.,* 59 N.Y.2d 1, 6-7, 449 N.E.2d 713, 715-16, 462 N.Y.S.2d 819, 821-22 (1983):

> [The father] seeks to have his choice regarding procreation fully respected by other individuals and effectuated to the extent that he should be relieved of his obligation to support a child that he did not voluntarily choose to have. But [the father's] constitutional entitlement to avoid procreation does not encompass a right to avoid a child support obligation simply because another private person has not fully respected his desires in this regard. However unfairly [the father] may have been treated by [the mother's] failure to allow him an equal voice in the decision to conceive a child, such a wrong does not rise to the level of a constitutional violation.

The court expressly rejected the father's argument that the mother's intentional conduct deprived him of a right to decide whether to father a child. The trial court had correctly found that Hur had not shown any seduction on the part of the child's mother and that he was voluntarily underemployed, so that imputation of an income was appropriate. However, the court of appeals reversed the ruling that Hur was not entitled to visitation.

§ 4-4. Custody of children of unwed parents.

At common law, custody of illegitimate children rested with their mothers. See, e.g., *State ex rel. Bennett v. Anderson,* 129 W. Va. 671, 41 S.E.2d 241 (1946). This was in contrast to legitimate children, who were under their father's governance. In part this was because of problems of proof of paternity.

Since the Supreme Court case of *Stanley v. Illinois,* 405 U.S. 645 (1972), unwed fathers must be given an opportunity to demonstrate their fitness before an adoption of their child will be granted. This does not, however, mean that a putative unwed father must give his consent to adoption. In *Commonwealth v. Hayes,* 215 Va. 49, 205 S.E.2d 644 (1974), the trial court found that the father had been "guilty of anti-social, immoral and illegal conduct," *Id.* at 53, 205 S.E.2d at 648, and allowed an adoption despite the "refreshing" desire of the father to have custody. He had never offered any financial assistance to the mother, seen the child, or even inquired about her. His plans were so speculative and unsatisfactory that the court wrote they deserved no comment. *Id.* at 52,

205 S.E.2d at 647. *Hayes* further noted that under Va. Code § 64.1-6, the father's consent was unnecessary since the mother had relinquished the child, in contrast to the involuntary event of the mother's death that produced the custody dispute in *Stanley*. *Id.* at 52-53, 205 S.E.2d at 647.

If the children have been legitimated because their parents' marriage was void and the husband acknowledged the children under Va. Code § 64-7, their custody will be decided on the same basis as children born during wedlock. *Henderson v. Henderson,* 187 Va. 121, 46 S.E.2d 10 (1948). Recognition of the child by the natural father will suffice to revoke a prior interlocutory order for adoption. *Harmon v. D'Adamo,* 195 Va. 125, 77 S.E.2d 318 (1953).

§ 4-5. Children of void marriages.

One of the earliest American statutes lessening the harsh treatment of the illegitimate child, enacted as c. 60 in 1785, Va. Code § 64.1-7 makes children of marriages deemed null at law or dissolved by courts legitimate and therefore capable of inheriting under the intestate statute. This help was extended to children of common law marriages in *McClaugherty v. McClaugherty,* 180 Va. 51, 21 S.E.2d 761 (1942). See also *Murphy v. Holland,* 237 Va. 212, 377 S.E.2d 363 (1989) (attempted common law marriage legitimated children for inheritance purposes). Even a bigamous second marriage will legitimize a child under the statute. *Stones v. Keeling,* 9 Va. (5 Call.) 143 (1804):

> But if it were otherwise, if the legislature should even be supposed to consider every second marriage, living a first husband or wife [sic], as criminal, wherefore should they visit the sins of the parents upon the innocent and unoffending offspring?

See also *Brown v. Commonwealth,* 218 Va. 40, 235 S.E.2d 325 (1977); *Kasey v. Richardson,* 331 F. Supp. 580 (W.D. Va. 1971).

For example, in *Brown v. Commonwealth,* 218 Va. 40, 235 S.E.2d 325 (1977), a child was conceived after the parties to a bigamous marriage ceased cohabiting together as man and wife, but following a period when they were seeing each other for extended periods nearly every day. The mother was not required to prove paternity under the strict standards of Va. Code § 20-61.1 as she would need to in cases involving a meretricious relationship where the parties had never entered into marriage, but rather could claim support under Va. Code § 64.1-7. *Id.* at 43-44, 235

S.E.2d at 327-28. The child should not be deprived of her rights because of statutes affecting the marital status of her parents. *Id.* at 44, 235 S.E.2d at 328.

§ 4-6. Inheritance.

Illegitimate children, by statute, Va. Code § 64.1-5, inherit from their mothers and may transmit inheritance on her part as if born in lawful wedlock. For inheritance from fathers, the children must be legitimated by subsequent marriage of their parents and recognition by the father, or by specific bequest under the father's will.

The child has the burden of proving recognition. *Hoover v. Hoover,* 131 Va. 522, 526, 105 S.E. 91, 92 (1921), *reh'g granted,* 109 S.E. 424 (1921). Although in *Hoover* the putative father married the mother after the child's birth since he had been unable to satisfy a seduction prosecution against him, he never had intercourse with her after the marriage and consistently denied that the child was his. *Id.* at 534, 105 S.E. at 94. The child was not legitimated by the mere fact of the marriage, for his acknowledgment must be plain and unequivocal. *Id.* at 540, 105 S.E. at 96. However, upon rehearing the court found that because of the presumption in favor of legitimacy, Hoover's silence when he should have spoken to deny his paternity, and some of his conduct and words, Hoover recognized the child. *Id.* at 545, 109 S.E. at 425.

A child born out of wedlock may establish paternity for inheritance purposes by clear and convincing evidence, which may include cohabitation with the mother during the ten months immediately prior to birth of the child, consent to entry of his name as the father on the birth records of the child, allowance of his surname by a general course of conduct, claiming of the child as his on any government document signed by him, admission before any court having jurisdiction over such matters that he is the child, voluntary admission of paternity in writing and under oath, a judgment for support entered against the man as if the child were born during marriage, the results of medically reliable genetic blood grouping tests, or medical or anthropological evidence relating to the alleged parentage performed by experts. The last two indications of paternity were added to Va. Code § 64.1-5.2 in 1991. See *Hart v. Posey,* 31 Va. Cir. 284 (Stafford Co. Cir. Ct. 1993) (clear and convincing evidence shown when alleged father placed his name on the child's birth certificate and later appeared before a notary to have the spelling of his name changed).

Even though an unwed father posted no appeal bond from a juvenile and domestic relations court finding of contempt, the Circuit Court had jurisdiction to hear his appeal. The court found that he was not in arrears, and this decision was affirmed by the court of appeals. *Commonwealth v. Walker*, 1996 Va. App. LEXIS 244, 468 S.E.2d 695.

§ 4-7. Children conceived through artificial means.

According to statute, Va. Code § 64-7, children conceived by a wife after written permission of her husband through artificial insemination by a third party donor are legitimate, and able to inherit from and through the married couple. Va. Code § 32.1-257. There are also out-of-state cases holding that even absent such a statute, the husband owes the duty of support under a theory of estoppel. See, e.g., *Gursky v. Gursky,* 39 Misc. 2d 1083, 242 N.Y.S.2d 406 (1963); *People v. Sorensen,* 68 Cal. 2d 280, 66 Cal. Rptr. 7, 437 P.2d 495 (1968).

Children conceived through the in vitro method of fertilization would be legitimate so long as both the sperm and ovum were obtained from the married couple, and the wife was implanted with the resulting embryo. Presumably if a third party's sperm were utilized instead of the husband's, Va. Code § 64-7 would apply. This would not be true if the embryo were implanted in a woman other than the wife. The "biological" mother would then be different from the "genetic" mother.

The case of *In re Baby M,* 109 N.J. 396, 537 A.2d 1227 (1988), demonstrates many of the problems posed by agreements attempting to regularize surrogate parenthood. The lower court specifically enforced a contract, awarding the biological mother, who had agreed to give up her child, the $10,000 promised in the contract, terminating her parental rights, and allowing the wife of the natural father to adopt the child. The New Jersey Supreme Court found that the surrogate contract conflicted with state laws prohibiting use of money in connection with adoptions, requiring proof of parental unfitness or abandonment before termination of parental rights, and making surrender of custody and consent to adoption revocable in private placement adoptions. Although the contract was void, custody of the infant was awarded to the natural father and his wife on the usual standards of best interest of the child, with the natural mother awarded visitation.

In 1991, the legislature enacted Va. Code §§ 20-156 through 20-165, providing that contracts for surrogate motherhood, whether the pregnancy is naturally or artificially created, are enforceable so long as there is compliance with a detailed set of requirements including a home study, and there is no payment of fees to the mother beyond reimbursement for medical care. See § 7-6, *infra*.

In *Baby Doe v. John & Mary Doe,* 15 Va. App. 292, 421 S.E.2d 913 (1992), the court of appeals reversed the district court's denial of a continuance sought by the guardian ad litem of an infant born to a surrogate mother in a declaratory judgment action brought by her genetic parents. The genetic parents sought to have an original birth certificate listing themselves as the infant's parents issued to replace one listing the surrogate mother. The trial court had terminated the infant's relationship with her birth mother and had directed that an original birth certificate issue with the genetic parents listed as the infant's parents. The guardian ad litem argued successfully that the trial court abused its discretion in denying her motion for a continuance because the summary proceedings prejudiced and impaired Baby Doe's due process rights.

When a child is born after artificial conception, the birth certificate shall name the mother's husband as the father and the gestational mother as the mother of the child. Donors of sperm or ova do not have any parental rights or duties for such child. Va. Code § 32.1-257(D) [amended 1994].

See generally Richard Epstein, *Surrogacy: The Case for Full Contractual Enforcement*, 81 Va. L. Rev. 2305 (1995); Margaret Friedlander Brinig, *A Maternalistic Approach to Surrogacy: Comment on Richard Epstein's Surrogacy: The Case for Full Contractual Enforcement*, 81 Va. L. Rev. 2377 (1995).

§ 4-8. Paternity proceedings.

Virginia Code § 20-49.1 provides that the circuit courts and juvenile and domestic relations district courts shall have concurrent original jurisdiction of cases involving paternity. According to Va. Code § 20-61.1 et seq., a child, suing through a next friend, Va. Code § 20-64, may bring an action to declare that a man is the natural father in Juvenile and Domestic Relations Court. Va. Code § 20-67. This action may be brought at any time after the child's birth. Paternity proceedings in some ways resemble criminal actions, since the person convicted of nonsupport may be sentenced to jail or workhouse. Va. Code § 20-62. Under new Va. Code § 8.01-328.1(8)(iii), personal jurisdiction may be asserted over a person alleged by affidavit to have conceived or fathered a child in this

Commonwealth, but only upon proof of personal service on a nonresident pursuant to Va. Code § 8.01-320.

In recent years, many recipients of Aid for Dependent Children or public housing have been required to sign statements naming the fathers of their children so that the agencies may be reimbursed. This is apparently constitutional as a condition of receiving government largesse. *Edelman v. Jordan,* 415 U.S. 651 (1974); *King v. Smith,* 392 U.S. 309 (1968). See generally 3A Michie's Jurisprudence *Bastardy* §§ 11-20.

The party seeking to prove paternity must do so by clear and convincing evidence if there has been no admission by the alleged father. Va. Code §§ 20-49.1 et seq. See, e.g., *Wellington v. Broadwater,* 1994 Va. App. LEXIS 736 (H.L.A. testing showed probability of over 99% that Wellington was the father, and he had access to the mother during the period of time when the child was conceived). See also *Commonwealth v. Overby,* 1996 Va. App. LEXIS 273. The putative father may have the right to a free blood test if he is indigent and has the right to cross-examine witnesses called to testify for the plaintiff. Va. Code § 20-48. The clear and convincing standard of proof required under § 20-49.1, which became effective in 1988, is appropriate even though the child in question was born (and juvenile court proceedings begun) when repealed Code § 20-61.1, requiring proof beyond a reasonable doubt, was still in effect. *Wyatt v. Virginia Dep't of Social Services,* 11 Va. App. 225, 397 S.E.2d 412 (1990).

Results of scientifically reliable genetic tests, including blood tests, are admissible to prove paternity. Va. Code §§ 20-49.1 and 20-49.4. The genetic blood grouping tests were made mandatory by 1989 amendments to Va. Code § 20-49.3, which provides that upon its own motion or upon motion of either party, where child support is in issue, the court *shall* direct the parties to submit to such tests. The uncorroborated testimony of the mother will not be sufficient to establish paternity. Blood tests may be ordered upon motion of either party, and the court, in its discretion, may require the person requesting such blood grouping tests to pay the cost. In order to be admissible, the results must be filed with the clerk of the court at least fifteen days prior to the hearing. An expert personally appearing to make his or her analysis may, upon motion of either party, be required to appear as a witness and be subject to cross-examination provided that such motion is made within not less than seven days prior to the trial. Va. Code § 20-71.2, as amended in 1988. Code § 20-49.1 et seq. provides for procedures in proceedings to determine paternity, including admission of blood grouping tests, clear and convincing evidence as the standard of proof, and proceedings to establish paternity or enforce support of minor parents aged fourteen to eighteen. If a putative father fails to appear after having been personally served with notice, the court may proceed in hearing the evidence in the case, according to Code § 20-61.3. Putative fathers between the ages of fourteen and eighteen who are represented by a guardian ad litem may testify pursuant to Code § 20-61.1. However, a guardian ad litem need not be appointed for the child in paternity proceedings. *Rowland v. Shurbutt,* 1993 Va. App. LEXIS 353.

Amendments to Va. Code § 20-49.1 allow establishment of paternity by a written sworn statement of the father and mother acknowledging paternity or by blood testing that affirms at least a ninety-eight percent probability of paternity. Without either the acknowledgement or the strong indication of paternity through blood testing, paternity may be established as described above. Va. Code § 20-49.1B. However, the sworn statement of paternity will not provide the same res judicata effect as the hearings. Thus a putative father may introduce evidence in a support proceeding that shows he could not be the child's father even though he previously executed a sworn declaration of paternity. *Dunbar v. Hogan,* 16 Va. App. 667, 432 S.E.2d 16 (1993). Because the true identity of the father became a substantial issue in *Myers v. Brolin,* 1995 Va. App. LEXIS 560, the trial court should have required him to verify two relevant and material facts: his identity and his employment.

Section 20-49.8 now allows equitable apportionment of the expenses incurred for the child in establishing paternity. These may be recovered by the natural parent or by any other person or agency incurring the expenses.

Res judicata will not bar a finding of nonpaternity as far as a child is concerned, although his mother may be barred by the findings in the prior proceeding, since the child and mother's interests are not the same. *Commonwealth ex rel. Gray v. Johnson,* 7 Va. App. 614, 376 S.E.2d 787 (1989). On the other hand, a prior finding that a man was the father of a child in a divorce proceeding acts to collaterally estop him from establishing through conclusive blood testing that he was not the biological parent. *Slagle v. Slagle,* 11 Va. App. 341; 398 S.E.2d 346 (1990).

CHAPTER 5

Marriages

§ 5-1. Introduction.

Marriage in theory is a status created by the interaction of three parties — husband, wife and the state. *Maynard v. Hill,* 125 U.S. 190, 205 (1888). The fact that the relationship is created by contract requires such factors as agreement between the parties, legality of the union as within public policy, and capacity to contract, all of which will be considered in the next chapter. See generally 12B Michie's Jurisprudence *Marriage* § 2. The fact that status is involved and that therefore the state is interested means that in addition various statutory formalities must be observed or the marriage will not be valid. See *Boddie v. Connecticut,* 401 U.S. 371, 376 (1971):

> It is not surprising, then, that the States have seen fit to oversee many aspects of that institution. Without a prior judicial imprimatur, individuals may fully enter into and rescind commercial contracts, for example, but we are unaware of any jurisdiction where private citizens may covenant for or dissolve marriages without state approval.

See also *Cramer v. Commonwealth,* 214 Va. 561, 565, 202 S.E.2d 911, 915 (1974).

When a question arises about the validity of a marriage, the following questions should be asked: (1) Was a valid license obtained? (2) Was a ceremony performed by one authorized to do so by statute? (3) Was the marriage performed in a jurisdiction where neither party was domiciled, to which the parties travelled to evade Virginia public policy? and (4) Did a common law marriage arise in some state other than Virginia?

31

If the answers to the foregoing questions do not prove helpful, the annulment chapter, following, should also be consulted.

§ 5-2. Common law marriages.

At common law, marriages could begin by an agreement between a man and woman to be husband and wife that was made in words of the present tense. *Offield v. Davis,* 100 Va. 250, 40 S.E. 910 (1902); see 12B Michie's Jurisprudence *Marriage* § 8. In order to demonstrate objectively that this agreement had taken place and to show that in fact a marriage contract had been made, it was also necessary for the couple to live together as man and wife and to have the reputation of being man and wife in the community. See *Pickens v. O'Hara,* 120 W. Va. 751, 200 S.E. 746 (1938) (common law marriage not shown where man later ceremonially married another, although relationship with woman continued for forty-one years). Since a contract was involved, the parties needed the capacity to become married at the time of the agreement. See generally Note, *Common Law Marriage and Annulment,* 15 Vill. L. Rev. 134 (1969).

Virginia has not recognized common law marriages created within the state for many years. *Offield v. Davis,* 100 Va. 250, 253, 40 S.E. 910, 914 (1902) (no dower rights created by nonceremonial "marriage.") However, because of the mobility of the population, it may be necessary to consider such marriages even if both husband and wife currently live in Virginia. This is because once a marriage has validly been created, it will be valid everywhere unless grossly against public policy. *Greenhow v. James' Executor,* 80 Va. 636, 640 (1885) (marriage void and children not legitimate when white man married black woman in District of Columbia and returned to Virginia). Where a husband and wife married according to the common law in a foreign country, or even in such neighboring jurisdictions as the District of Columbia or Pennsylvania, they will retain their status in Virginia. 12B Michie's Jurisprudence *Marriage* § 8.

Once a common law marriage has been created, the relationship will be the exact equivalent of a ceremonial marriage. In order to remarry, the parties must divorce. Dower and curtesy exist if they would for any other married couple, husband and wife inherit exactly the same way other married persons do, their children are legitimate, and the same privileges and duties flow between them as for other married couples.

Most of the recent Virginia cases involving common law marriages are concerned not with their consequences, since that is settled law, but rather

Most of the recent Virginia cases involving common law marriages are concerned not with their consequences, since that is settled law, but rather with whether or not the marital status was in fact created. One recurring problem is whether a common law marriage arises after the impediment to a valid ceremonial marriage is removed. *Travers v. Reinhardt,* 205 U.S. 423 (1907).

For example, in *Metropolitan Life Insurance Co. v. Holding,* 293 F. Supp. 854 (E.D. Va. 1968), the man had been married to another woman for many years when he met a French woman while serving in the Armed Forces. He was informed by his first wife's attorney that a divorce of his first marriage was final, and married in a ceremony. In fact the divorce did not become final until after the ceremony. When his tour of duty ended, he became employed as a foreign service officer, so that for most of their relationship the couple lived abroad, in places not recognizing common law marriages. From time to time, while on leave, the couple visited friends and relatives in the United States, spending as much as a month in the states of Florida and Ohio, both of which recognize common law marriage. Finally the man died in Virginia, to which the couple had moved when he retired. The second wife was allowed to recover insurance proceeds as a surviving spouse, although the ceremonial marriage had not resulted in a valid union, because of the time the couple had spent living together as man and wife and holding themselves out as such in Florida and Ohio. Compare *Goldin v. Goldin,* 48 Md. App. 154, 426 A.2d 410 (1981), where a couple cohabited in Virginia but never married because the man, who had been previously married and divorced, and the woman, who had her first marriage annulled, would not go through a ceremony for religious reasons. Although the couple lived together for many years, had two children, and were regarded by many as husband and wife, a common law marriage was not created when they frequently vacationed in Pennsylvania, since they never really had the intent to be married.

Courts will be apt to recognize a common law marriage where the parties, or at least one of them, has acted in good faith, compare *McPherson v. Steamship South African Pioneer,* 321 F. Supp. 42 (E.D. Va. 1971) (no common law marriage where both parties knew that wife's divorce was not final) and there are no innocent third parties, such as surviving first spouses or children of a prior marriage, who will be hurt. This policy is particularly true when all possible objections to the validity of the union have ceased: in *Holding,* for example, by the death of the husband.

See generally Stein, *Common-Law Marriage: Its History and Certain Contemporary Problems,* 9 J. Fam. L. 271 (1970).

§ 5-3. Persons who may perform marriages.

The interest of the state is not only in marriage as an institution, but in the contract between the parties who marry, and in the proper memorializing of the entry into, and execution of, such a contract. In the proper exercise of its legislative power it can require that the person who performs a marriage ceremony be certified or licensed.

Cramer v. Commonwealth, 214 Va. 561, 567, 202 S.E.2d 911, 914 (1974).

The Virginia Code recognizes the classes of persons who may perform marriages. Va. Code §§ 20-23, 20-25 and 20-26 (clergymen, public officials, and members of religious groups not having clergy). Va. Code § 20-25 was amended in 1987 to allow retired as well as sitting judges and justices to perform marriages.

In *In re Application of Ginsburg,* 236 Va. 165, 372 S.E.2d 387 (1988), the Supreme Court determined that the Clerk of a Quaker Meeting was a minister authorized to perform marriages without posting bond according to Va. Code § 20-23. The Clerk meets with members of the Meeting for weekly worship and "performs such ministerial duties in meeting for worship and meeting for business as are consistent with Quaker discipline," including the performance of marriages.

In contrast, *Cramer v. Commonwealth,* 214 Va. 561, 202 S.E.2d 911 (1974), involved an action rescinding the authority to perform marriages for six ministers of the Universal Life Church, ordained without instruction for a "free will offering," and holding no particular dogma. Everyone belonging to the church was encouraged to become a minister. The court found that the organization in fact had no "minister" within the contemplation of Va. Code § 20-23, which referred to the head of a religious congregation, society, or order. At that time there was still the paramount and compelling duty of returning the completed certificate within five days after the ceremony. The rescission was therefore consistent with the Code section.

The question remains whether marriages will be valid despite the fact that the person performing the ceremony did not fall into the categories named in the statutes. Generally speaking, if the parties to the marriage acted in good faith, not realizing that the persons marrying them had no authority to do so, the marriage will nevertheless be valid. Va. Code § 20-31; *Stanley v. Rasnick,* 137 Va. 415, 119 S.E. 76 (1923). In such cases, the person performing the ceremony may be subject to punishment. Va. Code § 20-28. The reason for the directory nature of the statute is that the clergyman or official performing the ceremony is really acting in the nature of a witness: the vows or contractual agreements are exchanged by the parties. *Cramer v. Commonwealth,* 214 Va. 561, 567, 202 S.E.2d 911, 914 (1974).

Virginia courts will not recognize a proxy marriage performed in England, which itself does not recognize proxy marriages. In *Farah v. Farah,* 16 Va. App. 225, 429 S.E.2d 626 (1993), both parties resided in the United States, and their marriage had been solemnized by proxy in London. The parties then traveled to the bride's native Pakistan where her father held a reception to symbolize the sending away of the bride with her husband. The parties then returned to Virginia, purchased a house jointly titled in both names, and lived together for about one year. The parties then separated, and the man sought to have the marriage declared void. The woman filed for divorce and equitable distribution. The court of appeals held that the trial judge erred in granting a divorce and by equitably distributing the parties' property because the marriage was not valid in England where celebrated. The court reasoned that because Virginia does not recognize common law marriages where the relationship is created in the state, the parties never entered into a valid marriage. There could therefore be no divorce and no distribution of the parties' property.

§ 5-4. Requirement of a license.

Va. Code § 20-13 provides that in order for a marriage to be valid, a license must first be obtained. However, if the couple in good faith marries in a ceremony performed by one authorized to do so with an invalid license, or an expired license, Va. Code § 20-41, the marriage will still be valid. Va. Code § 20-31.2. In 1988, Va. Code § 20-16.1 was added, allowing the clerk to amend marriage records on his own authority, upon application under oath and submission of evidence deemed by the clerk to be adequate and sufficient, and directing him to forward a certified copy of the corrected marriage record to the State Registrar. The person performing the ceremony may be subject to punishment. Va. Code § 20-28. This is because the license requirements are largely to avoid later problems of proof or possible collusion, and do not really affect the contract.

In *Stanley v. Rasnick,* 137 Va. 415, 119 S.E. 76 (1923), a father sued for loss of the services of his daughter, who obtained a license and married without his permission. She was sixteen at the time and therefore above the age of consent (twelve years). The marriage was valid despite the defect in the license and the incidental loss of services to the father brought about by the change in the daughter's status.

Despite this trend upholding the validity of the marriage despite defects in licensing, in *Davis v. Davis,* 29 Va. Cir. 110 (Accomac Co. 1992), the court held that a religious ceremony performed in Virginia using a Maryland license was not effective. The license was returned to Maryland and stated that the marriage ceremony took place in that state. The parties lived together in Virginia as husband and wife for seven years after the ceremony. The court found that the Virginia marriage statutes were mandatory rather than directory, citing a West Virginia case decided under a similar statute. Compare *Carabetta v. Carabetta,* 182 Conn. 344, 438 A.2d 109 (1980) (marriage without license following religious ceremony).

§ 5-5. Blood tests.

Although blood tests for syphilis have not been required since Va. Code § 20-1 was repealed in 1984, the 1987 legislature revised Code § 20-14.2, requiring that each applicant for a marriage license receive information on acquired immunodeficiency syndrome and the availability of testing for this disease, in addition to information concerning genetic disorders and contraceptive measures. As with the old blood test requirement, if the license was issued without complying with the code, the marriage would nevertheless be valid under Va. Code § 20-31.

§ 5-6. Necessity for domicile.

As will be seen in the chapter on annulments, it is not necessary for persons to be domiciled in a state to be married there. The problems occur when couples leave Virginia to be married in another state in order to evade particular Virginia laws, such as those involving marriage between persons under age, *Needam v. Needam,* 183 Va. 681, 688, 33 S.E.2d 288 (1945) (provision for parental consent at that time was directory and preventive rather than prohibitive of the consummation of the marriage contract), or, in earlier days, those prohibiting interracial marriages, *Naim v. Naim,* 197 Va. 80, 87 S.E.2d 749 (1955); *Greenhow v. James' Executor,* 80 Va. 636 (1885); *Kenney v. Commonwealth,* 71 Va. (30 Gratt.) 858 (1871). If such a marriage would be against Virginia public policy, and is mentioned in Va. Code § 20-38.1 (bigamy and incest), it will be void under the Virginia anti-evasion statute, Va. Code § 20-40, and the parties will be subject to punishment.

§ 5-7. Proof of ceremonial marriage.

Marriage may be proved by evidence of reputation, *McClaugherty v. McClaugherty,* 180 Va. 51, 60, 21 S.E.2d 761, 764 (1942); *Eldred v. Eldred,* 97 Va. 606, 34 S.E. 477 (1899); civil records, Va. Code § 32-1.272B (prima facie evidence), or the testimony of witnesses to the marriage ceremony. There is a strong presumption in cases of ceremonial marriage that the parties living as husband and wife are in the legitimate state of matrimony. *Newsom v. Fleming,* 165 Va. 89, 181 S.E. 393 (1935); *Eldred v. Eldred,* 97 Va. 606, 625, 34 S.E. 477 (1899) (marriage not proved). However, the presumption of validity was overcome where the woman, a patient with Alzheimer's Disease, shook her head from left to right when asked if she wanted to marry the man and otherwise remained mute throughout the ceremony. The ceremony was witnessed only by the minister, a longtime friend of the man, who was told to keep the marriage a secret. The man also forged her signature to a spurious common law marriage "contract" after the ceremony. *Nicely v. Gardner,* 12 Va. Cir. 216 (City of Roanoke 1988).

There is also a strong presumption, in cases where there have been two marriages by one of the parties, that the first marriage ended in divorce so that the second one is valid. *Parker v. American Lumber Corp.,* 190 Va. 181, 185, 56 S.E.2d 214, 217 (1949).

CHAPTER 6

Annulments

§ 6-1. Introduction.

For religious reasons it was not possible for Christians to divorce until the time of Henry VIII. In order to escape from unhappy relationships and to be free to marry again, it was sometimes permissible for the ecclesiastical court to declare that the marriage had never taken place. This nullification procedure developed into a most complex set of grounds. It was the sole form of relief for many years, and even after the advent of divorce in the nineteenth century, in many cases (since adultery and desertion for five years were the only causes of action for divorce), the only practical means of severing the relationship. *Bailey v. Bailey,* 62 Va. (21 Gratt.) 43 (1871) (divorce from bed and board only). As the phenomenon of separation, annulment, and remarriage became increasingly popular, more and more grounds for annulment were added, and those existing were more leniently applied. This trend continued until absolute divorce rules were relaxed in Virginia in the 1940s.

As opposed to the problems concerning requisites for marital status discussed in the prior chapter, annulments involve problems in the contract between man and woman that normally would result in a marriage. Unlike divorce, solely a creature of statute, annulment rests within the inherent power of equity inherited from the English ecclesiastical courts. *Pretlow v. Pretlow*, 177 Va. 524, 548-49, 14 S.E.2d 381, 383-84 (1941).

§ 6-2. Reasons for modern annulments.

Although there are very few annulments today because of the relative ease of no-fault divorces, they should be considered for some clients. The most common reason that a modern client may elect an annulment is that his or her religion prohibits remarriage following divorce. In particular, the fact that a civil annulment was obtained may be an aid to the client who also wishes a canon law annulment.

A second reason is that, at least in the case of void marriages, there is apparently no duty to support the person who shared an annulled marriage, *Bray v. Landergren*, 161 Va. 699, 172 S.E. 252 (1933); Va. Code § 20-107.1; see also *Mato v. Mato*, 12 Va. Cir. 153 (Spotsylvania Co. 1988); nor, absent some written contract, an obligation to divide marital property under § 20-107.3, since no marriage ever existed. *Id.; Fulton v. Fulton*, Chancery No. 87732 (Fairfax Co. 1984).

A corollary is that, at least in cases of void marriages, there may be a resumption of prior benefits that were lost upon marriage, such as insurance or alimony from a first spouse. *McConkey v. McConkey*, 216 Va. 106, 215 S.E.2d 640 (1975).

Finally, there may be some psychological reason for legally declaring that a marriage never existed. The parties, especially when the mistake was youthful and the relationship of short duration, can declare themselves "single" with a clear conscience. See *Crouch v. Wartenberg*, 91 W. Va. 91, 112 S.E. 234 (1922).

§ 6-3. Jurisdiction in annulment cases.

Although it is appropriate for an annulment to be brought in the state where the ceremony occurred, it may also be brought in the place where a party is domiciled.

There is case law from other jurisdictions that would support the theory that personal jurisdiction must be obtained in annulment cases. *Sacks v. Sacks*, 47 Misc. 2d 1050, 263 N.Y.S.2d 891 (1965); *Flaxman v. Flaxman*, 57 N.J. 458, 273 A.2d 567 (1971); cf. *Whealton v. Whealton*, 67 Cal. 2d 656, 432 P.2d 979, 63 Cal. Rptr. 291 (1967) (although no domicile of either party, in personam jurisdiction over both is sufficient to confer jurisdiction for annulment). Virginia follows the minority position in requiring only that one party be domiciled in the state, with constructive or substituted service if the other cannot be personally served. Va. Code § 20-104. This is the same requirement as in divorce cases, which are in essence status adjudications. *Williams v. North Carolina,* 317 U.S. 287 (1942). New amendments to Va. Code § 20-97 provide jurisdiction for annulment to persons in the United States armed forces or their spouses who have been stationed in and resided in the Commonwealth for a period of six months or more preceding separation, and for service persons domiciled in Virginia for the six months prior to being stationed in a foreign country or territory. Unlike a suit for divorce or legal separation, the person in the armed forces or the spouse apparently need not continue to reside in Virginia until the complaint is filed.

If more than the annulling of the relationship is involved, personal service will clearly be required. This may be by service upon the party within Virginia or by use of the long-arm statute, Va. Code § 8.01-328.1(9), where appropriate in child support or child custody matters. The contacts of the absent party with Virginia and the due process aspects of notice must both be satisfied in such cases. Service of process in annulment cases will be governed by the rules of the Supreme Court or statute (§ 8.01-328 et seq.), as appropriate. Va. Code § 16.1-263(F).

In its 1993 reconvened session, the Virginia Legislature enacted Chapter 929 of the Virginia Acts of Assembly, which created a statewide system of family courts that were to replace the juvenile and domestic relations district courts in 1995. The new legislation provided that the family courts will assume the powers and territorial jurisdiction on January 1, 1996 (§ 16.1-69.8(2)). The new family court will also have exclusive original jurisdiction to annul or affirm marriages. Va. Code §§ 16.1-241(S) and 20-96. The new family court will be a "court not of record" similar to the general district court. The method of trials and appeals for the court will be governed by applicable statutes and rules of court. Va. Code § 16.1-69.5(a).

Venue will be in the family court in the county or city in which judgment was rendered or a proceeding is pending. Transfer of venue in suits for annulment or affirmation of marriage will be governed by § 8.01-257 et seq. as these provisions relate to circuit court.

Counsel may be appointed to represent the child in cases involving annulment or affirmation of marriage as provided in § 8.01-9 (§ 16.1-

266(D)). In cases involving the status of marriage, confidentiality of the cases is governed by § 20-124.

Procedures governing fees will be found in § 14.1-135.1.

For any issue arising in a suit for annulment or affirmation of marriage, the judge shall consider whether to refer the parties to mediation, and, on its own motion or one of the parties, may refer the issue to mediation. Upon referral, the parties must attend one session in which the parties and the mediator assess the case and decide whether to continue the mediation or to proceed to adjudication. Further participation in the mediation shall be by consent of all parties, and attorneys for any party may attend mediation sessions. Va. Code § 16.1-272.1. When the court refers parties to mediation, it shall set a return date. The parties shall notify the court in writing if the dispute is resolved prior to this return date. In its discretion, the court may incorporate any mediated agreement into the terms of a final decree. Only if the order is entered incorporating the mediated agreement will the terms of the voluntary settlement agreement affect any outstanding court order.

Most cases heard by the family court will be disposed of in accordance with existing procedures for annulment contained in Title 20. Appeals from final orders or judgments of the family court in cases of annulment shall be to the court of appeals as provided in § 17-116.05:5. Final orders involving the division or transfer of real property between the parties incident to divorce or annulment, or following a foreign divorce, shall be transmitted to the circuit court named in the order or decree for docketing on the judgment lien index, if the decree so directs. Va. Code § 20-107.3.

§ 6-4. The complaint.

As in cases of divorce, the complaint for annulment is brought in the circuit court. The complaint should allege jurisdiction through domicile of the complainant, the fact that a ceremony occurred on some date and in a particular place, the grounds for relief, and the fact that no ratification occurred after the defect was discovered in cases of voidable marriage.

If the prayers for relief involve more than annulment, personal jurisdiction must also be alleged. Of course, the relief sought should be listed. In addition to declaring the marriage void ab initio, a female complainant may wish to resume her maiden name, and any plaintiff may seek support for self or children, division of property held jointly, and resolution of custody or visitation matters. If the incidents of the relationship can be resolved in writing between the parties beforehand, their agreement can be made a part of the complaint by incorporation. Courts may make child support or custody orders and decrees in suits for annulment or separate maintenance. Va. Code Ann. § 20-107.2 [amended 1996].

Most cases heard by the family court will be disposed of in accordance with existing procedures for annulment contained in Title 20. Appeals from final orders or judgments of the family court in cases of annulment shall be to the court of appeals as provided in § 17-116.05:5. Final orders involving the division or transfer of real property between the parties incident to divorce or annulment, or following a foreign divorce, shall be transmitted to the circuit court named in the order or decree for docketing on the judgment lien index, if the decree so directs. Va. Code § 20-107.3.

§ 6-5. Parties to annulment actions.

Obviously the most usual parties to an action declaring a marriage void ab initio are the man and woman involved. Either may initiate suits under Va. Code § 20-89.1(a) for void marriages and voidable marriages except those for impotency, felony conviction, pregnancy by another, or fathering a child by another. The latter actions may only be brought by the innocent party.

However, in cases of bigamous or incestuous marriages, any third party can bring an action. In cases of marriages annulled for nonage, the parents of the child involved may bring an action on his or her behalf. This was not the case before the statute made such marriage void. *Kirby v. Gilliam,* 182 Va. 111, 28 S.E.2d 40 (1943). In cases of insanity or mental retardation, the guardian or committee of the incompetent may bring an action.

§ 6-6. Void and voidable marriages.

Two types of marriages may be annulled. The most obvious group consists of void marriages, which require no legal action to declare that the marriage never existed. Grounds are listed in Va. Code § 20-38.1. Void marriages have always included bigamous, *Toler v. Oakwood Smokeless Coal Corp.,* 173 Va. 425, 4 S.E.2d 364 (1939), and incestuous relationships. Until the Supreme Court case of *Loving v. Virginia,* 388 U.S. 1 (1967), interracial marriages also fell within the relationships that were prohibited because they were considered grossly against public policy. Va. Code § 20-50 et seq. (now repealed); see *Naim v. Naim,* 197

Va. 80, 87 S.E.2d 749 (1955). More recently, marriages of people below the statutory age have been deemed void. Although there has been no Virginia case on the subject, it is also quite clear that a marriage requires a man and a woman, each acting as such. Homosexual marriages also violate Virginia criminal laws. See *Doe v. Commonwealth's Attorney for Richmond,* 403 F. Supp. 1199 (E.D. Va. 1975), *aff'd mem.,* 425 U.S. 901 (1976). Other void marriages are generally illegal (except in cases of the Enoch Arden rule).

The other type of annullable marriages are those with contractual defects other than illegality and offense to public policy. These are listed in Va. Code § 20-89.1. Voidable marriages require court action to dissolve, and therefore possess the indicia of status until that time. See, e.g., *Cornwall v. Cornwall,* 160 Va. 183, 190-91, 168 S.E. 439, 442 (1933). In Virginia, such marriages include those where there has been lack of capacity through insanity or mental defect; marriages procured through fraud, coercion or duress; marriages where there is no intent to assume the consequences of marital status, including sham and joke marriages; and those where the spouse has concealed pregnancy, prior prostitution, conviction of a felony or infection with venereal disease.

> A void marriage confers no legal rights, and, when it is determined that the marriage is void, it is as if no marriage had ever been performed.... A voidable marriage differs from a void marriage in that it may be afterwards ratified by the parties and become valid and usually is treated as a valid marriage until it is decreed void. [Toler v. Oakwood Smokeless Coal Corp., 173 Va. 425, 4 S.E.2d 364 (1939)]. A void marriage is a mere nullity and its validity may be impeached in any court, whether the question arises directly or indirectly, and whether the parties be living or dead. *Alexander v. Kuykendall,* 192 Va. 8, 10, 63 S.E.2d 746, 748 (1951).

The topic is discussed at length in Margaret F. Brinig & Michael V. Alexeev, *Fraud in Courtship: Divorce and Annulment,* 2 Eur. J. Law & Econ 45 (1995). In brief, the idea is that discoverable fraud (like a false identity or a bogus fortune) will not be grounds for annulment. On the other hand, fraud that requires the parties to be married before it can be discovered (like the intention never to have children, or not to practice the religion that was supposedly the foundation of the parties' marriage) will be grounds. In the article, the different types of fraud are compared to "search goods" (which one buys after examination) and "experience goods" (which must be opened or consumed before one knows their quality).

§ 6-7. Homosexual marriages.

Marriages in Virginia must be between persons of the opposite sex. Va. Code § 20-45.2. This is required as well by the state public policy that continues to declare homosexual intercourse a criminal offense. *Doe v. Commonwealth's Attorney for Richmond,* 403 F. Supp. 1199 (E.D. Va. 1975), *aff'd mem.,* 425 U.S. 901 (1976). See also *Baker v. Nelson,* 291 Minn. 310, 191 N.W.2d 185 (1971), and *Dean v. District of Columbia,* 653 A.2d 307 (D.C. App. 1995), which held that the legislature never intended to sanction same-sex marriages, nor did it intend the Human Rights Act to change the fundamental definition of marriage. The court wrote:

> There is no constitutional basis under the due process clause to find that the fundamental right of heterosexual couples to marry is extended to same-sex partners: Even without reference to *Hardwick*'s constitutional approval of statutes criminalizing consensual sodomy, we cannot say that same-sex marriage is deeply rooted in this Nation's history and tradition. Indeed, the District of Columbia marriage statute reflects an altogether different tradition.
>
> An attempted marriage between two persons of the same sex would be absolutely void even though not mentioned in the statutes listing grounds for annulment. See *Anonymous v. Anonymous,* 67 Misc. 2d 982, 325 N.Y.S.2d 499 (1971) (Plaintiff married defendant mistakenly believing that he was a woman. The parties separated and never resumed cohabitation after the wedding night. The plaintiff did not have to pay support nor medical expenses even before the marriage was annulled).

For additional discussions of marriage by same-sex couples, see Andrew Sullivan, *Virtually Normal: An Argument about Homosexuality* (Alfred A. Knopf, 1995); William Eskridge, *A History of Same-Sex Marriage,* 79 Va. L. Rev. 1419 (1993); and Judith McDaniel, *Lesbian Couples' Guide* (Harper, 1995).

§ 6-8. Bigamous marriages.

Marriages contracted by parties when one has a living spouse are void. Va. Code §§ 20-38.1(a)(1) and 20-43. Some are also punishable criminally. The marriage will be found void despite the fact that one party was unaware of the impediment to a valid marriage because of concealment by the other or honest mistake regarding the validity of a prior divorce or death of a former spouse.

The fact that a person believes he is validly divorced from a first spouse does not preclude a subsequent criminal conviction for bigamy as opposed to a mere finding that he had violated § 20-38.1 by entering into a prohibited marriage. *Stuart v. Commonwealth,* 11 Va. App. 216, 397 S.E.2d 533 (1990).

The customary relief for innocent bigamous spouses is the so-called Enoch Arden rule. After a spouse has been missing and presumed dead for seven years, Va. Code § 64.1-105, the other spouse may remarry without fear of a criminal bigamy prosecution. *Simpson v. Simpson,* 162 Va. 621, 175 S.E. 320 (1934); see also *Toler v. Oakwood Smokeless Coal Corp.,* 173 Va. 425, 435, 4 S.E.2d 364, 368 (1939). Should the missing spouse reappear, however, the second marriage would still be absolutely void. *Toler v. Oakwood Smokeless Coal Corp.,* 173 Va. 425, 435, 4 S.E.2d 364, 368 (1939); Va. Code § 18.2-364. See generally Fenton & Kaufman, *Enoch Arden Revisited,* 13 J. Fam. L. 245 (1973). The prudent attorney in such cases would secure a no-fault divorce before a remarriage took place. See *Simpson v. Simpson,* 162 Va. 621, 175 S.E. 320 (1934). The problem is then one of proving that the absent spouse at some time was aware of his spouse's desire, or had himself formed the intent to separate. *Hooker v. Hooker,* 215 Va. 415, 211 S.E.2d 34 (1975).

The section on defenses should be consulted, however, regarding the applicability of estoppel and res judicata.

§ 6-9. Incestuous marriages.

Marriage between close relatives is prohibited by Va. Code § 20-38.1, which lists nephews and nieces, uncles and aunts, grandparents and, of course, parents and siblings or half-siblings. There are two reasons that incestuous marriages are void and subject to criminal penalty. Va. Code § 18.2-366. One is that there may be genetic problems in the offspring of incestuous couples. The second is that if such marriages were permitted, great strains would be placed upon families, particularly in those where stepfathers and young daughters were concerned. The first reason indicates that even if the man and woman have not been raised in the same household, and even if one has been adopted, the marriage cannot take place. See *State v. H.*, 429 A.2d 1321 (Del. Super. 1981); *In re Marriage of Flores*, 96 Ill. App. 3d 279, 421 N.E.2d 393 (1981). The second is the rationale for including stepparents and adopted children in the statute, although obviously they are not related by blood. *Simpson v. Simpson*, 162 Va. 621, 175 S.E. 320 (1934).

§ 6-10. Marriages of persons under the statutory age.

Marriages below the age of consent have always been void and against public policy. *Needam v. Needam*, 183 Va. 681, 33 S.E.2d 288 (1945); *Kirby v. Gilliam*, 182 Va. 111, 28 S.E.2d 40 (1943); see *Stanley v. Rasnick*, 137 Va. 415, 119 S.E. 76 (1923). In the years of adolescence, however, parental consent has been required since 1975. Va. Code § 20-89.1. Before that time, if the man and woman chose to live together after reaching majority, the marriage was still valid. If the minor has been emancipated, no parental consent shall be required. Va. Code § 20-49 (new in 1993).

In *Needam v. Needam*, 183 Va. 681, 33 S.E.2d 288 (1945), two young people, without their parents' knowledge or consent, left Virginia and proceeded to Maryland, where they were married. They immediately returned to Virginia, where they lived together for some time. The marriage was valid although they could not have married in Virginia without parental approval since they were above the age of consent (twelve) and the marriage would have therefore merely been voidable. *Id.* at 688, 33 S.E.2d at 291. Parental consent was required not only to aid the couple in making a rational decision but also to protect the father's right to his children's services.

In modern times, youthful marriages have more and more frequently ended in divorce. The legislature has therefore made such marriages absolutely void unless obtained with parental consent, Va. Code § 20-45.1, although the nonminor spouse may not bring suit. Va. Code § 20-89.1(d). Marriages are allowed, however, in cases of teenaged pregnancy where criminal charges are pending under Va. Code § 18.2-66.

In *Pifer v. Pifer*, 12 Va. Cir. 448 (Frederick Co. 1975), the circuit court upheld the validity of an underage marriage similar to that of *Needam*. Complainant, who was seventeen, married a nineteen-year-old high school graduate in Hagerstown, Maryland after the man applied for a Maryland license, falsely stating that she was eighteen and failing to obtain the parental approval required for underage marriages in both Virginia and Maryland. The two wished to marry because the complainant suspected she was pregnant. After the wedding, they continued to live at their respective parents' homes. When the complainant's parents learned of the marriage, they took her to an obstetrician who confirmed the pregnancy. It was the doctor's opinion that she would shortly have a miscarriage. The miscarriage in fact occurred two days later, and shortly thereafter the complainant's mother filed for annulment. Because the complainant had participated in the false application, she could not claim the benefits of her minority. Nor could she complain of mistake, for the marriage would have been upheld on grounds of public policy even if she had not been pregnant in the first place. Finally, there was no duress because, all things considered, she preferred the course that she took.

§ 6-11. Insanity and mental defect.

Where one of the parties was unable to give a valid consent to marriage because he was incurably insane or mentally defective at the time of the ceremony, see *Counts v. Counts,* 161 Va. 768, 771-72, 172 S.E. 248, 249 (1933). An annulment may be obtained by the sane partner or by the committee or guardian of the incompetent. Va. Code §§ 20-45.1 and 20-89.1. Insanity may also, if acquired after the marriage, be the basis for separate grounds for divorce under Va. Code § 20-45.1. Spousal support may not be awarded to the defendant incompetent when the marriage is found void on these grounds. *Somers-Shiflet v. Shiflet,* 29 Va. Cir. 206 (Fairfax Co. 1992), even though the defendant's guardian sought to have the support awarded before entry of the final decree of nullity.

A woman with Alzheimer's Disease did not give her consent when she moved her head from right to left in response to the question whether she wished to marry Gardner during a ceremony performed by a minister in a car, with no other witnesses present. The only thing she did during the ceremony, according to the minister, was to try to get out of the car, whereupon the groom locked the door. *Nicely v. Gardner,* 12 Va. Cir. 216 (City of Roanoke 1988).

Although there are no Virginia cases on point, case law from other jurisdictions indicates that where one party was involuntarily intoxicated by the other so that during the marriage ceremony there was no capacity for knowing consent, and there was no cohabitation following the ceremony, the marriage was voidable. *Thomas v. Thomas,* 111 Ill. App. 3d 1032, 444 N.E.2d 826 (1983).

§ 6-12. Fraud.

If one spouse procures the other's consent only through fraud going to some matter essential to the marriage relationship, see *Jacobs v. Jacobs,* 184 Va. 281, 296, 35 S.E.2d 119, 125 (1945) ("There must be some evidence that the appellant did not intend before the marriage or at the time of the marriage to become in truth and fact the wife of the appellee"), the resulting marriage is voidable and may be annulled by the innocent spouse if there is no cohabitation after the defect is discovered. Va. Code § 20-89.1(c).

Falsehoods relating to wealth or social status will not render a marriage voidable, since the spouse received the person bargained for, *Francis v. Francis* (V.I. Territorial Ct. 1985); *McKee v. McKee,* 262 So. 2d 111 (La. App. 1972); *Emmons v. Emmons,* 34 A.D.2d 725, 312 N.Y.S.2d 117 (1970). However, marriages are voidable where there was a misstatement of a desire to have children, *Heup v. Heup,* 45 Wis. 2d 71, 172 N.W.2d 334 (1969) (no fraud found on facts); *Ciarochi v. Ciarochi,* 194 Va. 313, 73 S.E.2d 402 (1952) (question not decided although alleged by wife's testimony), or to ever engage in sexual intercourse. *Pretlow v. Pretlow,* 177 Va. 524, 14 S.E.2d 381 (1941). See Note, 28 Va. L. Rev. 305 (1941). There was no fraud when the woman herself acquiesced in the application process, falsely stating that she was over eighteen. *Pifer v. Pifer,* 12 Va. Cir. 448 (Frederick Co. 1975).

Another type of fraud that has been recognized in recent cases is misleading as to the existence of a prior spouse, or that spouse's continued life, to a person who for religious reasons cannot marry one who is divorced while the former spouse still lives. See, e.g., *Wolfe v. Wolfe,* 62 Ill. App. 3d 498, 378 N.E.2d 1181 (1978), and cases cited therein. Compare *State Compensation Fund v. Foughty,* 13 Ariz. App. 381, 476 P.2d 902 (1970) (false assurance that had deep religious convictions made voidable a marriage to a devout Protestant). Fraud regarding pregnancy will not render marriage voidable in Virginia, although concealment of pregnancy by another will be grounds of annulment. Va. Code § 20-89.1. Misrepresentation as to prior marital status will not invalidate a marriage. *Sanderson v. Sanderson,* 212 Va. 537, 186 S.E.2d 84 (1972) (wife alleged one prior marriage and divorce, but had been married and divorced five times).

However, duress is not involved when a pregnant young woman, who under other circumstances might have greatly preferred to delay marriage by some months, considering all things, preferred marrying. *Pifer v. Pifer,* 12 Va. Cir. 448 (Frederick Co. 1975).

There must be a clear setting forth of the facts upon which the alleged fraud is based in the complaint, and the alleged fraud must be clearly proved. *Ciarochi v. Ciarochi,* 194 Va. 313, 73 S.E.2d 402 (1952).

See generally Margaret F. Brinig & Michael V. Alexeev, *Fraud in Courtship: Divorce and Annulment,* 2 Eur. J. Law & Econ 45 (1995).

§ 6-13. Duress and coercion.

Some older cases involve parents of young women who literally hold a gun to the young man's head in order to get him to marry. Such "shotgun" marriages are voidable. See *Copeland v. Copeland,* 2 Va. Dec. 81, 21 S.E. 241 (1895) (marriage not shown in this case to be product of duress, but rather the result of a prosecution for seduction).

See generally Kingsley, *Duress as a Ground for Annulment of Marriage,* 33 S. Cal. L. Rev. 1 (1959).

§ 6-14. Sham or joke marriages.

A marriage may be valid regardless of the purpose for which the parties contracted it, so long as they intended to assume a marital status. *Mpiliris v. Hellenic Lines, Ltd.,* 323 F. Supp. 865 (S.D. Tex. 1969). If, however, the parties did not intend to acquire the rights and obligations of married persons, the marriage is voidable as a sham. *Faustin v. Lewis,* 85 N.J. 507, 427 A.2d 1105 (1981), cf. *Boyter v. Commissioner,* 668 F.2d 1382 (4th Cir. 1981).

In *Aboulhosen v. Elawar,* 12 Va. Cir. 157 (Henrico Co. 1988), plaintiff sought to annul a marriage on the grounds that it had been entered into without any intent to live together. The court found that the plaintiff did not carry her burden of proof that the man had always intended it to be a lark.

Sham marriages occur most frequently in cases involving spouses who marry in part to gain lawful United States residence. In *Dao v. Nguyen,* 1995 Va. App. LEXIS 820, however, although the parties married for these reasons, they actually lived together and conceived a child. Thus the marriage was one for which the wife could be awarded spousal support.

If the marriage is entered into in a spirit of joke or jest, it is likewise annullable. See *Crouch v. Wartenberg,* 91 W. Va. 91, 112 S.E. 234 (1922), where the parties went through a marriage ceremony only in order to alleviate their embarrassment but never lived together, and *Meredith v. Shakespeare,* 96 W. Va. 229, 122 S.E. 520 (1924), where the parties married as a joke in a spirit of great exuberance and fun, but never lived together nor intended to be married. In neither of these cases was there a meeting of the minds in good faith nor any intent to assume the duties and obligations of the marital relationship. See generally 1 J. Bishop, *Marriage and Divorce* §§ 296, 298, 339, 366 et seq.

§ 6-15. Miscellaneous grounds.

Some grounds for annulment are also grounds for divorce. These include impotency, conviction for an infamous offense, prostitution, pregnancy by another, or fathering another's child. Va. Code § 20-89.1. Virginia courts will not recognize a proxy marriage performed in England, which itself does not recognize proxy marriages. In *Farah v. Farah,* 16 Va. App. 225, 429 S.E.2d 626 (1993), both parties resided in the United States, and their marriage had been solemnized by proxy in London. The parties then traveled to the bride's native Pakistan, where her father held a reception to symbolize the sending away of the bride with her husband. The parties then returned to Virginia, purchased a house jointly titled in both names, and lived together for about one year. The parties then separated, and the man sought to have the marriage declared void. The woman filed for divorce and equitable distribution. The court of appeals held that the trial judge erred in granting a divorce and by equitably distributing the parties' property because the marriage was not valid in England where celebrated. The court reasoned that because Virginia does not recognize common law marriages where the relationship is created in the state, the parties never entered into a valid marriage. There could therefore be no divorce and no distribution of the parties' property.

§ 6-16. Defenses.

The usual defenses to annulment action include: (1) lack of jurisdiction; (2) lack of proof that the alleged grounds occurred; (3) estoppel; (4) ratification of a voidable marriage by continued or renewed cohabitation after the defect was discovered, Va. Code § 20-89.1(c); (5) res judicata;

(6) expiration of more than two years after the ceremony, Va. Code § 20-89.1(c) (voidable marriages only); and (7) laches.

The estoppel cases do not make the marriage valid, but merely state that the innocent party who did not know of the defect and relied upon it to his or her detriment should be able to receive financial remunerations as though the marriage were valid and the parties were now divorcing. See, e.g., *Poor v. Poor,* 381 Mass. 392, 409 N.E.2d 758 (1980); *Rosen v. Sitner,* 274 Pa. Super. 445, 418 A.2d 490 (1980); 24 Am. Jur. 2d *Divorce and Separation* §§ 971, 972; 27B C.J.S. *Divorce* §§ 364-366; Restatement, Conflict of Laws § 112; Clark, *Estoppel Against Jurisdictional Attack on Decrees of Divorce,* 70 Yale L.J. 45 (1960). Compare *George v. King,* 208 Va. 136, 156 S.E.2d 615 (1967), where the husband was not allowed to annul his marriage when he sought to collaterally attack the wife's divorce from a prior marriage, since he had no interest adversely affected at the time of the prior divorce.

Apparently in Virginia the defense of "unclean hands" will be unavailable in cases of void marriages. See *Heflinger v. Heflinger,* 136 Va. 289, 118 S.E. 316 (1923) (husband who remarried before first divorce was effective could bring an action to have second marriage annulled as bigamous).

Res judicata becomes a defense if a prior Virginia proceeding found that a marriage existed. This may be a prior spousal support and maintenance proceeding, see, e.g., *Hosier v. Hosier,* 221 Va. 827, 273 S.E.2d 564 (1981); *Psaroudis v. Psaroudis,* 27 N.Y.2d 527, 312 N.Y.S.2d 998, 261 N.E.2d 108 (1970), or a prior finding that a first divorce was valid. See, e.g., *Kessler v. Fauquier Nat'l Bank,* 195 Va. 1095, 81 S.E.2d 440 (1954) (right to share as surviving spouse in distribution of former wife's estate).

If the impediment to a void or voidable marriage is removed, a valid common law marriage, which requires a divorce to dissolve, may result. See, e.g., *Metropolitan Life Ins. Co. v. Holding,* 293 F. Supp. 854 (E.D. Va. 1968).

Laches was claimed as a defense in *Pretlow v. Pretlow,* 177 Va. 524, 14 S.E.2d 381 (1941), and *Counts v. Counts,* 161 Va. 768, 172 S.E. 248 (1933), but was not substantiated in either case. Laches was found in *Robinson v. Robinson,* 33 Va. Cir. 351 (Fairfax Co. Cir. Ct. 1994) (delay of nearly three years after wife knew of West Virginia divorce proceedings).

§ 6-17. Effects of annulment.

Before an annulment is granted, especially in cases of voidable marriages, the usual incidents of marital status exist. This would include the marital privilege for confidential communications or exemption from testifying, compare *People v. Godines,* 17 Cal. App. 2d 721, 727, 62 P.2d 787, 790 (1936) (voidable marriage; communication protected), with *People v. Mabry,* 71 Cal. 2d 430, 78 Cal. Rptr. 655, 455 P.2d 759 (1969) (no privilege where marriage void); interspousal immunity from suit, *Gordon v. Pollard,* 207 Tenn. 45, 336 S.W.2d 25 (1960) (the immunity is now abolished in Virginia by Va. Code § 8-220.1) and legitimacy of children, *Cornwall v. Cornwall,* 160 Va. 183, 191, 168 S.E. 439, 442 (1933). See also *Henderson v. Henderson,* 187 Va. 121, 46 S.E.2d 10 (1948); Va. Code § 64-7. Dower would also exist where otherwise applicable unless the marriage were annulled.

In many ways, annulments resemble divorces. Child custody, see, e.g., *Brown v. Kittle,* 225 Va. 451, 303 S.E.2d 864 (1983), and support, *Henderson v. Henderson,* 187 Va. 121, 46 S.E.2d 10 (1948), must still be dealt with if children were born of the relationship. These principles were incorporated into Virginia statutes in 1996, when Va. Code Ann. § 20-107.2 added annulment to the list of times child custody and support matters could be determined.

Spousal support is more questionable. Pendente lite awards may be given under Va. Code § 20-103, and support appears to be available under § 20-107.2 in cases of dissolution of the marriage as well as divorce. One older Virginia case, *Bray v. Landergren,* 161 Va. 699, 172 S.E. 252 (1933), indicates in dicta that if the marriage is absolutely void, there is no status upon which to base the duty of support. Similarly, in *Mato v. Mato,* 12 Va. Cir. 153 (Spotsylvania Co. 1988), the wife sued the husband for divorce, and during depositions the attorneys for both parties discovered that the husband was still married to someone else at the time; the marriage was undoubtedly void. No alimony would be given, nor could there be distribution of property. See also *Fulton v. Fulton,* Chancery No. 87732 (Fairfax Co. 1984), which noted that the court did not have jurisdiction to distribute property under Va. Code § 20-107.3 when the parties had gone through a marriage ceremony before the man's prior marriage was dissolved. Partition may be made in another action. When her husband contracted a bigamous second marriage and bought property with the alleged wife as tenants by the entirety with the right of survivorship, the legitimate (first) wife was not entitled to a dower interest in the property because the couple in fact held the property as joint tenants with right of survivorship. When the husband died, the property passed to his companion by survivorship, so that his widow acquired no interest. *Funches v. Funches,* 243 Va. 26, 413 S.E.2d 44 (1992).

In *Farah v. Farah,* 16 Va. App. 225, 429 S.E.2d 626 (1993), the court of appeals held that the trial judge erred by granting the parties a divorce and by equitably distributing their property since their proxy marriage was not valid in England where celebrated. Because Virginia does not recognize common law marriages where the relationship is created in the state, the parties never entered into a valid marriage. There could therefore be no divorce and no distribution of the parties' property.

However, *Henderson v. Henderson,* 187 Va. 121, 46 S.E.2d 10 (1948), indicates that child support, and impliedly spousal support, actions are found in the same paragraph of a statute talking about divorce and annulment. *Id.* at 127, 46 S.E.2d at 130. In Maryland, a similar problem was solved by reasoning that support is no longer really alimony, which did require the continued existence of a valid marriage. *Clayton v. Clayton,* 231 Md. 74, 188 A.2d 550 (1963). Support (misnamed alimony) may now be granted even where the marriage is absolutely dissolved by divorce. Since a spouse in many cases can receive either an annulment or a divorce, see Va. Code § 20-89.1, and support is authorized in cases of divorce, support should also follow annulments.

Following an annulment for a void marriage, it may be possible to recover some monetary benefit that ceased upon the marriage ceremony. One case indicates that this consequence does not adhere to marriages that are voidable only, *McConkey v. McConkey,* 216 Va. 106, 215 S.E.2d 640 (1975), since the former spouse has a right to change his position upon the remarriage of a dependent spouse. *Id.* at 108, 215 S.E.2d at 641. Compare *Stegall v. Stegall,* 2 Brock. 256, F. Cas. No. 1335 (C.C. Va. 1825), where the wife's gross misconduct in leaving her husband and living with another disqualified her from claiming a dower interest in the husband's estate. There may still be recovery from a fund, such as Social Security, however. See *Johnson County Nat'l Bank & Trust Co. v. Bach,* 189 Kan. 291, 369 P.2d 231 (1962); cf. *Flaxman v. Flaxman,* 57 N.J. 458, 273 A.2d 567 (1971), where a revival of alimony was not allowed after a voidable marriage was annulled but Social Security would have been. There may also be recovery in tort for fraud and deceit. *Alexander v. Kuykendall,* 192 Va. 8, 63 S.E.2d 746 (1951). See generally Comment, *The Aftereffects of Annulment: Alimony, Property Division, Provision for Children,* 1968 Wash. U.L.Q. 148.

CHAPTER 7

Adoption

§ 7-1. Historical perspective and introduction.

Adoption was unknown at common law, *Fletcher v. Flanary,* 185 Va. 409, 411, 38 S.E.2d 433, 434 (1946), although in Roman times it was customary for childless men to choose adult heirs by adopting them.

Adoption is therefore a creature of statute, *Clarkson v. Bliley,* 185 Va. 82, 92, 38 S.E.2d 22, 26 (1946), and the Virginia procedures and statutes may be quite different from those followed in other states.

What occurs in adoption is the creation of status: a new parent-child relationship. Because of its importance and the complex of privileges and duties flowing from it, the state has an interest in adoption. In addition, the state is concerned because in most cases a minor child, over which the state exercises parens patriae authority, is the adoptee. See generally Rendleman, *Parens Patriae: From Chancery to the Juvenile Court,* 23 S.C.L.Q. 205 (1971); Zainaldin, *The Emergence of a Modern American Family Law 1796-1851,* 72 Nw. U.L. Rev. 1083 (1979). See Va. Code § 63.1-222 for a discussion of adoption of adults.

§ 7-2. Termination of natural parents' rights and creation of new ones.

An adoption case has two parts. In the first, the natural parents' rights are severed. In most cases, this is done with the consent of the parents. If a voluntary termination, as this is called, takes place, the concerns are largely contractual: was the consent freely, knowingly and voluntarily given? Va. Code § 63.1-221. On other occasions, the parents' rights are involuntarily terminated because of parental unfitness that cannot be remedied.

The fundamental nature of the parent's right to raise the child requires that due process be afforded the parent before rights are terminated involuntarily. This may involve appointing counsel for the indigent parent or the child, and certainly involves notice and a hearing in most cases. *Armstrong v. Manzo,* 380 U.S. 545 (1965).

The second step in the adoption proceeding involves a state inquiry into whether adoption by the prospective parents will be in the child's best interests. Va. Code § 63.1-223. Such factors as emotional attachment of the child, age of the parents, their sexual orientation and religious preference, their social stability and ability to care for and nurture the child will all be considered, as well as the child's preference. Va. Code § 63.1-225B.

§ 7-3. Voluntary placement.

In many cases, consent is given by the natural parents to adoption by another. This cannot be effective unless given more than ten days after the child's birth. Va. Code § 63.1-225A. The legislature has significantly revised the procedures governing voluntary surrender for adoption. New Code § 63.1-220.2 provides, among other things, that the consent of a parent less than eighteen years of age shall be deemed fully competent. The father of a child born out of wedlock need not sign an entrustment agreement if his identity is not known or reasonably ascertainable, or if he has been given notice by mail at his last known address and fails to object within twenty-one days. An affidavit of the mother that the identity of the father is not reasonably ascertainable shall be sufficient evidence of this fact if there is no contradictory evidence before the court, and "reasonably ascertainable" is defined as what is reasonable under the circumstances, taking into account the relative interests of the child, the mother, and the father. Va. Code § 63.1-220.3(C)(2). The entrustment agreement is revocable until the child has reached the age of twenty-five days and fifteen days have elapsed from the date of execution of the agreement, or until the child has been placed in an adoptive home. The agreement may also be invalidated in court if fraud or duress is shown and a decree nisi for adoption of the child has not been entered.

Virginia Code § 63.1-220.3 provides for direct placement of children by the birth parent or legal guardian. Placement under this section may be with adoptive parents of choice, but only after a valid consent is executed before a juvenile and domestic relations district court. For the consent to be valid, the court must determine that the birth parents are aware of alternatives to adoption, that their consent is informed and uncoerced, that a licensed or duly authorized child-placing agency has counseled the prospective parents with regard to adoption procedures, that the birth parents and adoptive parents have exchanged identifying information and relevant medical and other records, that any financial agreement or exchange of property or fees for placement have been disclosed, that the parties are aware that no binding contract regarding placement or adoption exists, and that a home study has been conducted by a licensed or duly authorized child-placing agency that has been provided to the court. This section also applies when a licensed agency or local board of public welfare accepts custody for placement with adoptive parents chosen by the birth parents. Va. Code § 63.1-220.2 [amended 1990]. However, consent need not be executed in court in the presence of prospective adoptive parents when a child has been placed by the birth parents with the child's grandparents, adult brother or sister, or adult uncle or aunt. In such cases, the court may accept written consent that has been signed and duly acknowledged. Va. Code § 63-220.3(C)(5).

Donors of sperm or ova to assist reproduction have no parental rights or duties when the child is born of a married woman and was conceived with the written consent of her husband. Such a child is deemed to be the natural child of the woman and her husband. Va. Code § 32.1-257. Consent from surrogate mothers is discussed in § 7-6.

In some cases, the parents will already have placed the child with an adoption agency, or will have died. Consent must then be obtained from the agency. See Va. Code §§ 63.1-204C(1) and 63.1-225B(3).

§ 7-4. Fraud, duress, and coercion.

Consent may be revoked prior to the final adoption decree if there was fraud, duress, or coercion in procuring the consent. Va. Code § 63.1-225.

Fraud might involve collusion by one parent with the person arranging for the adoption that was unknown by the other parent, as in the case of *Huebert v. Marshall,* 132 Ill. App. 2d 793, 270 N.E.2d 464 (1971).

There may also be fraud on the part of the prospective adoptive parent, such as in *In re Adoption of Robin,* 571 P.2d 850 (Okla. 1977), where the adoptive mother, the child's step-grandmother, had children taken from her in the past, had assaulted several men including her present husband, and had failed to disclose the known whereabouts of the child's father, who had married the natural mother.

Coercion, although it usually must be more than embarrassment or financial pressure, see, e.g., *In re K.,* 31 Ohio Misc. 218, 282 N.E.2d 370 (1969); *Regenold v. Baby Fold, Inc.,* 68 Ill. 2d 419, 369 N.E.2d 858 (1977); *Bidwell v. McSorley,* 194 Va. 135, 72 S.E.2d 245 (1952), might involve such facts as a group of hostile relatives accusing a young, unwed mother of causing her mother's illness and death, as in *In re Adoption of Susko,* 363 Pa. 78, 69 A.2d 132 (1949).

Virginia Code § 63.1-220.2 provides that valid entrustment agreements terminating all parental rights and responsibilities to the child shall be revocable by either of the birth parents until the child has reached the age of twenty-five days and fifteen days have elapsed from the date of execution of the agreement. This implies that the entrustment agreement is not valid unless executed after the child's birth. A ten-day age requirement is imposed by § 63.1-220.3, which governs direct placement of children by birth parents.

Even though parental rights and responsibilities have been terminated by an entrustment agreement, these rights may be restored to the birth parents and the child by court order prior to entry of a final order of adoption upon proof of fraud or duress, according to Va. Code § 63.1-220.2.

"For good cause shown," however, "means more than the simple changing of the mind by the parent who has given consent for adoption." *Bidwell v. McSorley*, 194 Va. 135, 140, 72 S.E.2d 245, 249 (1952).

§ 7-5. Time for consent.

By statute, Virginia has provided that consent may be revoked until twenty-five days following the child's birth. Va. Code § 63.1-204C(1). This delay is primarily required to prevent placement with prospective parents followed by a change of heart by a natural mother, who did not foresee her attachment to the child.

> [S]uch consents fail to allow for one of nature's strongest instincts. Who knows what the reaction will be of a mother once she sees *her* baby?... To deny the mother's natural desire to keep her baby is in derogation of the purpose of our statute to preserve the natural family relationship to the fullest extent possible. *Johnson v. Cupp,* 149 Ind. App. 611, 274 N.E.2d 411 (1971) (Buchanan, J., dissenting).

The rule also ensures that a hasty decision will not be made during the immediate postpartum period, when the natural mother may be taking medication or otherwise may be prevented from thinking through the entire situation. See, e.g., *Bidwell v. McSorley,* 194 Va. 135, 72 S.E.2d 245 (1952) (consent form effective when signed on day of child's birth, but no duress shown; statute then did not require ten-day period; but was amended two years later in Act of 1954, ch. 489).

Consent must be given in writing, Va. Code § 63.1-225A, before a judge of the juvenile and domestic relations court. Va. Code § 63.1-204C(2), except in cases of adoption by a close relative. Va. Code § 63-220.3(C)(5), which states that consent in such cases may be in writing duly acknowledged. Counselling must also be suggested before consent is obtained. Va. Code § 63.1-204C(1), (2). New Va. Code § 63.1-220.3(C)(2) provides, however, that execution of consent before the juvenile and domestic relations court (or, when operational, the family court) shall not be required of the father of a child born to an unmarried woman if he consents under oath and in writing to the adoption. In such cases, the father must provide the identifying information required in Va. Code § 63.1-220.3(B)(3) to the court, and the birth mother must give her consent in court in accordance with subsection A of the statute. The statutes also waive the requirements for consent if the mother swears under oath and in writing that she does not know the identity of the father or that he cannot be found, or if the putative father named by the mother denies paternity under oath and in writing.

Blanket consent forms, although administratively convenient, may not suffice to educate the parents of the irrevocability of the adoption decision. See generally *In re Holder,* 218 N.C. 136, 141, 10 S.E.2d 620, 622 (1940); 2 Am. Jur. 2d *Adoption* § 45.

§ 7-6. Contracts to adopt.

Contracts to adopt are illegal in Virginia if money is to be paid to a natural mother. See Va. Code § 63.1-223(d)(7), which requires notification by the investigating agency to the court of any fees paid to persons assisting in obtaining the child. The state has a strong policy against "baby selling" as well as a strong presumption that it is in most children's interests to be in the custody of their natural parents. See, e.g., *People v. Free Synagogue Child Adoption Comm.,* 194 Misc. 332, 337, 85 N.Y.S.2d 541, 546 (1949). In the first reported Virginia case involving surrogate contracts, *Baby Doe v. Doe,* 15 Va. App. 292, 421 S.E.2d 913 (1992), the court of appeals remanded a declaratory judgment action. The case was originally filed by the genetic parents of the child called Baby Doe, who was born to a surrogate mother. The trial court had terminated the infant's relationship with her birth mother and had directed the Virginia Registrar of Vital Records to issue an original birth certificate with the genetic parents listed as the infant's parents. The guardian ad litem for the child successfully appealed from this ruling, arguing that the trial court abused its discretion in denying her motion for a continuance because the summary proceedings prejudiced and impaired Baby Doe's due process rights.

Absent recent statutory changes, contracts with surrogate mothers would apparently fall within these guidelines, although if the father were to agree to raise the child, as is usually the case, he would not be "adopting" his own child. 704 S.W.2d 209 (Ky. 1986). In Virginia this argument would be unsuccessful for a married surrogate whose husband gave consent to the procedure because under Va. Code § 64.1-7.1, a child conceived through artificial insemination with the husband's consent "shall be presumed, for all purposes, the legitimate natural child of such woman and such husband the same as a natural child not conceived by means of artificial insemination." In the much publicized case of *In re Baby M.*, 217 N.J. Super. 313, 525 A.2d 1128 (1987), *aff'd in part* and *rev'd in part*, 109 N.J. 396, 537 A.2d 1227 (1988), the trial court awarded the child in question to the father and his wife, specifically enforcing the contractual arrangement between them and the surrogate. Although the Supreme Court found that the agreement was void because it went against public policy, the award of custody was upheld on the usual "best interests" test. In 1991, Virginia enacted legislation allowing such contracts effective July 1, 1992, but only where there was no payment of fees to the mother beyond reimbursement for medical care, when a home study has been made, and the arrangement has been judicially approved. The surrogate may revoke during the first six months of pregnancy, with a penalty as set forth in the agreement between parties. There may be few such agreements where there is no payment for the surrogate's services, and attempts to avoid this requirement are all but inevitable. The legislation specifically provides for penalties for providing brokerage services. Va. Code §§ 20-156 through 20-165 relate generally to assisted conception.

However, an attorney may ethically represent the prospective adoptive parents in drafting a contract providing for payment of the biological mother's medical and legal fees in consideration for her consent to adoption. Representation is permissible if the lawyer determines that such a contract is neither illegal nor against public policy. In such cases the attorney may handle the payment of the pregnant woman's medical and legal bills as the prospective adoptive parents' agent. Va. State Bar Ethics Opinion No. 1227, May 8, 1989.

Because the surrogate mother bears the child, she would presumably have a right to custody equal to that of any other natural mother at least where the parties did not have judicial approval. Custody would be decided, in cases of a dispute, on the basis of the best interest of the child rather than any contract the natural parents might have made. Other problems involving surrogates include the restriction of the surrogate mother's sexual behavior during the period of conception, submission to tests such as amniocentesis, with a view towards abortion of a fetus with genetic problems, limitations on the ingestion of alcohol and various drugs during gestation, and decisions regarding custody of a physically or mentally handicapped child. Those matters involving "clinical management of pregnancy" are left to the surrogate mother under the new statute. Va. Code § 20-163. A child born under an approved contract, since no longer deemed the child of the surrogate mother, is the responsibility of the natural father even if handicapped. *Id.*

Without judicial approval, surrogacy contracts would not be enforceable through specific performance because consent may not be given until after the child's birth. Va. Code § 63.1-204C(1). Where there has been judicial approval, the statute indicates that the wife of the biological father shall be treated as the child's mother. Consent after birth by the gestational mother does not appear to be required, as it usually would be under § 63.1-204C(1), although many of the usual biological reasons for requiring a waiting period would seem to be present. Such a contract was performed substantially by both parties and therefore was not considered on the merits in *Harry v. Fisher,* 216 Va. 530, 221 S.E.2d 118 (1976) (natural mother attempted to revoke consent executed eleven days after birth of child, pursuant to contract).

The exchange of fees or other consideration for the placement or referral of adoption does not necessarily invalidate the adoption, but under Va. Code § 63.1-220.4, results in commission of a Class 5 felony. Payment to a licensed or duly authorized child-placing agency for reasonable and customary services, reimbursement for the mother's medical expenses directly related to the pregnancy, payment for transportation necessary to execute consent or for intercounty placements, and usual and customary fees for legal services in adoption are not prohibited under this section.

See generally Comment, *Surrogate Mother Agreements: Contemporary Legal Aspects of a Biblical Notion,* 16 U. Rich. L. Rev. 467 (1982).

§ 7-7. Placement by third parties.

In Virginia, as in most states, it is illegal to act as a child welfare agency without obtaining a license. Va. Code § 63.1-215; see also Va. Code § 63.1-220.1. This would include taking a fee to place a child with a set of prospective adoptive parents. Placement involves any activity that provides assistance to a parent or guardian in locating an adoptive home or moving a child to an adoptive home. Va. Code § 63.1-195. Attorneys in particular should be cautioned to avoid even the appearance of acting as "baby brokers."

§ 7-8. Interstate compact on the placement of children.

Virginia, through Va. Code §§ 63.1-219.1 to 63.1-219.5, participates in the Interstate Compact on Child Placement. The policy of the Act, reflected in Va. Code § 63.1-219, is similar to the adoption policies of the state in general: assuring insofar as possible that a child coming to or from Virginia will be placed in an atmosphere with desirable care. In order to achieve this goal, the Act requires state agencies in both the receiving and sending states to make appropriate investigations regarding the child and his future placement. (Article III). Jurisdiction over the child's welfare is retained until the child is adopted, reaches majority, or is emancipated. (Article V). The Act does not apply to placement by close relations. (Article VIII).

§ 7-9. Foreign adoptions.

Adoptions of children that take place in foreign countries will be recognized in Virginia so long as the court rendering the adoption had jurisdiction to render the decree, and so long as the foreign country's laws of adoption do not violate the public policy of Virginia. *Doulgeris v. Bambacus,* 203 Va. 670, 127 S.E.2d 145 (1962) (Greek adoption not recognized for purposes of determining descent and distribution since Greek view of adoption was contrary to Virginia public policy).

§ 7-10. Revocation of consent.

An entrustment agreement under new Va. Code § 63.1-220.2 is revocable until the child has reached the age of twenty-five days and fifteen days have elapsed from the date of execution of the agreement, or until the child has been placed in an adoptive home. Even though parental rights and responsibilities have been terminated by an entrustment agreement, these rights may be restored to the birth parents and the child by court order prior to entry of a final order of adoption upon proof of fraud or duress. The revocation rules were clarified in 1995 by Va. Code § 63.1-220.3(D). Revocation of consent shall be in writing, and may be made for any reason for up to fifteen days from its execution. After the expiration of the fifteen-day period, any party may revoke consent prior to the final order of adoption where fraud or duress is shown. After placement of the child in an adoptive home, revocation occurs only upon written mutual consent of both the birth parents and the prospective adoptive parents.

Once there has been a voluntary relinquishment, which must be shown by clear and convincing evidence, the natural parents must bear the burden of showing that the change of custody to them is in the child's best interests. *Shortridge v. Deel,* 224 Va. 589, 299 S.E.2d 500 (1983). In *Shortridge,* the natural mother asked another woman to take her baby at some point during her pregnancy. Once the child was born, the natural mother did not remove her from the foster mother's home for seventeen months. The foster mother had taken custody only upon the assurance of the natural mother that she would not want the baby back, and had nourished him to good health. Although the natural parents had married and stabilized their lives by the time of trial, custody was not transferred since the child was thriving with the foster parents. See also *Harry v. Fisher,* 216 Va. 530, 221 S.E.2d 118 (1976); *Szemler v. Clements,* 214 Va. 639, 202 S.E.2d 880 (1974).

Revocation of consent after the petition for adoption has been filed does not divest the court of its jurisdiction. *Szemler v. Clements,* 214 Va. 639, 643, 202 S.E.2d 880, 884 (1974). Thus, the trial court was free to find that custody should be continued in the prospective adoptive parents since a change to the natural parents would be detrimental to the child, and an interlocutory order of adoption was correctly entered.

See generally Margaret F. Brinig, *The Effect of Transaction Costs on the Market for Babies,* 18 Seton Hall Legis. J. 553 (1994) (discussing the relationship between the length of the consent revocation period and the number of completed adoptions).

§ 7-11. Consent of minor parent.

Even though a natural parent is less than age eighteen, a valid consent may be given relinquishing a child for adoption and terminating all parental duties and rights. Va. Code § 63.1-204D.

§ 7-12. Procedural requirements for termination of parental rights.

Because the right of a child to its parents' custody is so strong and the privilege of being a parent so fundamental, involuntary termination of parental rights involves substantial substantive and procedural safeguards. *Weaver v. Roanoke Dep't of Human Resources,* 220 Va. 921, 926, 265 S.E.2d 692, 695 (1980); Va. Code § 61.1-283. Involuntary termination therefore requires clear and convincing proof, *Santosky v. Kramer,* 455 U.S. 745 (1982), that the natural parents' rights should be terminated due to their unfitness. *Rocka v. Roanoke County Dep't of Public Welfare,* 215 Va. 515, 211 S.E.2d 76 (1975). A specific finding of unfitness is not required, however, if one of the statutory factors is present. *Knox v. Lynchburg Division of Social Services,* 223 Va. 213, 288 S.E.2d 399 (1982). See also *Edwards v. County of Arlington,* 5 Va. App. 294, 361 S.E.2d 644 (1987), where the county's termination of an immigrant mother's parental rights was held not supported by clear and convincing evidence. The termination had been based upon a finding of mental illness on the mother's part. Language difficulties and problems with cultural acclimation significantly affected her ability to function properly. There was therefore no clear and convincing showing that her problems in parenting sprang from a "mental or emotional illness or mental deficiency of such severity that there is no reasonable expectation" that she would be able to care responsibly for the child. But see *Jenkins v. Winchester Dep't of Social Servs.,* 12 Va. App. 1178, 409 S.E.2d 16 (1991), where after eleven years of involvement with the Department, the mother had not progressed to a point where she was capable of functioning as an independent parent. It was appropriate for the county to remove the youngest child from her custody at age three months because "the child would be subjected to an imminent threat to life or health to the extent that severe or irreversible injury would be likely to result if the child were ... left in the custody of his parent." But see *Ferguson v. Stafford County Dep't of Social Servs.,* 14 Va. App. 333, 417 S.E.2d 1 (1992), where a father's parental rights were terminated after he was imprisoned for two years and finally sentenced to life imprisonment for first-degree murder on another charge. The court held that "while long-term incarceration does not, per se, authorize termination of parental rights or negate the Department's obligation to provide services, it is a valid and proper circumstance which, when combined with other evidence concerning the parent/child relationship, can support a court's finding by clear and convincing evidence that the best interests of the child will be served by termination."

Thus, unfitness must be proven by clear and convincing evidence according to *Bailes v. Sours,* 231 Va. 96, 100, 340 S.E.2d 824, 827 (1986), and according to the United States Supreme Court case of *Santosky v. Kramer,* 455 U.S. 745 (1982). For example, in *Kaywood v. Halifax County Dep't of Social Services,* 10 Va. App. 530, 394 S.E.2d

492 (1990), a father's parental rights were permanently terminated when it was not reasonably likely that the conditions resulting in the neglect of the child could be substantially corrected or eliminated so as to allow the child's return within a reasonable amount of time. Kaywood had been sentenced to a twenty-year penitentiary term for malicious wounding of his then ten-month-old son. There was no regular visitation between the father and son, and on those occasions when there were visits, the child became visibly upset and clung to the social worker as soon as he entered the room. The child was apparently prospering in foster care, and the father "has not demonstrated any increased ability, or desire" to fulfill his child's needs in the years since their separation. Likewise, in *Helen and Robert W. v. Fairfax County Dep't of Human Dev.,* 12 Va. App. 877, 407 S.E.2d 25 (1991), the parents' residual rights to their daughter were terminated after supervised visitation was fraught with conflict between the mother and the child's social workers while the father either would not participate or, when he did, was unable to alleviate the conflict. When allowed unsupervised visitation, the parents repeatedly violated the conditions placed on the visitation and removed the child to unknown locations. During one of these visits, the child, who was multiply-handicapped, inflicted serious injuries to herself. In addition, the parents refused to participate in recommended mental health treatment, in spite of requirements in the foster care service plan and court orders that they do so. Termination was found to be in her best interest. See also *Logan v. Fairfax County Dep't of Human Dev.,* 13 Va. App. 123, 409 S.E.2d 460 (1991) (failure to have child attend therapy and medical appointments, attend school conferences, or visit child in foster care except when threatened with termination of parental rights); *Edwards v. Fairfax County Dep't of Human Dev.,* 1993 Va. App. LEXIS 332 (girls unable to form attachments because they felt abandoned; mother not amenable to accepting services offered her); *Morris v. Fairfax County Dep't of Human Dev.,* 1993 Va. App. LEXIS 422 (mother failed to keep scheduled visits and only occasionally contacted children by phone, failed to plan for return of children after incarceration, and failed to request services available to her after her release); *Gray v. Commonwealth,* 1993 Va. App. LEXIS 496 (mother abusive; plaintiff father incarcerated and failed to comply with rehabilitative plan); *Gault v. Commonwealth,* 1994 Va. App. LEXIS 49 (failure to follow substance abuse program); *O'Dell v. Department of Social Servs. of Henrico County,* 1993 Va. App. LEXIS 380 (mother not able to provide adequate parenting for child, but could

only enjoy supervised visitation; child had suffered neglect and abuse from mother and was afraid he would be taken away from foster home); *Hughes v. Dep't of Soc. Serv., Arlington Co.*, 1996 Va. App. LEXIS 77 (termination appropriate when mother participated in Satanic cult that still existed at the time of hearings; child doing well in foster care and no longer showing signs of attachment disorder); *Jackson v. Alexandria Div. of Soc. Serv.*, 1995 Va. App. LEXIS 888 (parental rights should not have been terminated where mother had mastered substance abuse problem while maintaining an unbroken stream of visits with her daughter). Even though the custodial mother acted to alienate the children from their father, he may not act to terminate his own parental rights. *Willis v. Gamez*, 20 Va. App. 75, 455 S.E.2d 274 (1995). In any event, the proceeding should have been brought in juvenile and domestic relations district court, and only after filing of foster care plan. *Tallent v. Rosenbloom*, 32 Va. Cir. 61 (Fairfax Co. 1993).

The Virginia Department of Social Services has adopted a Protective Services Manual for use by its local departments. It contains guidelines interpreting Va. Code § 63.1-248.2A, which defines an abused or neglected child. In *Larry D. Jackson, Commissioner v. W.*, 14 Va. App. 391, 419 S.E.2d 385 (1992), these guidelines were upheld over a father's constitutional challenge. The terms "rejecting, intimidating, humiliating, ridiculing, chaotic, bizarre, violent, hostile, or excessively guilt-producing" were not too ambiguous when interpreting types of behavior constituting mental abuse. Nor was a finding that the child abuse charges were "founded" a disposition that required full due process hearings or the criminal standard of proof "beyond a reasonable doubt."

Unfitness may involve abandonment, Va. Code § 16.1-283D. Abandonment must be shown by clear, cogent, and convincing evidence. Because termination of parental rights is so final and serious, even if abandonment is found, termination may still not be appropriate. *Robinette v. Keene*, 2 Va. App. 578, 347 S.E.2d 156 (1986). In *In re Adoption of Slayton*, 13 Va. Cir. 511 (Henrico Co. 1982), a father placed his children in the custody of his uncle when the paternal grandparents, who had been caring for the children, became ill. The father consented to adoption. The mother, who was then incarcerated, objected, but the court allowed adoption by the uncle, noting that she had not sent any letters or cards nor provided or offered financial support during the eight years in question. The court found that broadening the mother-child relationship might well be disruptive to the child.

The burden of proof for a *temporary* showing of unfitness, sufficient to remove the child from the parental home and for placement in foster care, is a preponderance of the evidence. This is because the placement is only temporary and the risk of an improper placement can be corrected by later action. *Wright v. Arlington County Dep't of Social Services,* 9 Va. App. 411, 388 S.E.2d 477 (1990). For example, in *Accomack County Dep't of Social Services v. Muslimani,* 12 Va. App. 220, 403 S.E.2d 1 (1991), the trial court erred in not reopening a custody proceeding based upon contradictory evidence casting doubt upon the father's testimony. Finality is important, held the court, but the child's best interests are paramount. In *Muslimani,* the father had admitted to having sexual relations with his 11-year-old stepdaughter, whom he had eventually married.

In cases of temporary placement in foster care, written consent by the foster parents must usually be obtained in advance. However, in cases of emergency placement in a residential institution or shelter, verbal consent must be obtained within eight hours of the child's arrival, and written consent must be obtained within 24 hours. Va. Code § 63.1-56.

If he or she is of the age of discretion, the minor child must also be consulted before parental rights are terminated. *Deahl v. Winchester Dep't of Social Services,* 224 Va. 664, 299 S.E.2d 863 (1983). A juvenile court investigating alleged child abuse has the authority to appoint a guardian ad litem for the infant in question, according to one circuit court. *In re J.B.,* 19 Va. Cir. 158 (Fairfax Co. 1990). A validly appointed guardian may file a petition for termination of parental rights. *Stanley v. Fairfax County Dep't of Social Services,* 10 Va. App. 596, 395 S.E.2d 119 (1990), *aff'd,* 242 Va. 60, 405 S.E.2d 621 (1991). In *Stanley,* the court of appeals found insufficient evidence for terminating a mother's parental rights for one of her three children because the most recent foster care plan did not recommend termination. Termination was clearly and convincingly shown to be in the best interests of the other two children. This must be intentional. *In re Adoption of J.J.P.,* 175 N.J. Super. 420, 419 A.2d 1135 (1980). However, a presumption that when a child has been in continuous foster care for two years, it is in the child's best interest to be placed for adoption is constitutional even as to an incarcerated parent. *Keeney v. Prince George's County Dep't of Social Services,* 43 Md. App. 688, 406 A.2d 955 (1979). Virginia creates such a presumption after twelve months if the parent has failed to maintain contact with the child. Va. Code § 16.1-283C. The facts will be construed against abandonment, which must be the intention of giving up the child, never to resume or claim the right of interest in it. *Meyers v. State,* 124 Ga. App. 146, 183 S.E.2d 42 (1971) (mother did not abandon child when she placed the newborn in phone booth with money and a bottle and called the suicide "hotline"; and several days later, accompanied by her mother, came to get the baby back). Other forms of unfitness include nonsupport, neglect, or abuse. See Va. Code §§ 63.1-225(4) and 63.1-248.2.

In its 1993 reconvened session, the Virginia Legislature established a statewide system of family courts. The new legislation, Chapter 929 of the Virginia Acts of Assembly, provided that the family courts will assume the powers and territorial jurisdiction of the juvenile and domestic relations district courts on January 1, 1996 (§ 16.1-69.8(2)). However, the legislature still has not funded the court. When the plan is implemented, the court will also have jurisdiction over custody, visitation, support, control, or disposition of children who are neglected, abused, delinquent, or in need of supervision (§ 16.1-241). The family court will hear cases involving determination of custody, visitation or support, cases in which the child is the subject of an entrustment agreement or where parents desire to be relieved of care and custody, and cases where the termination of residual parental rights and responsibilities is sought. Complaints and the processing of petitions to initiate a case shall be the responsibility of the intake officer (§ 16.1-260). As with most matters within family court jurisdiction, the termination proceeding shall be commenced by filing of a petition.

In all cases, the judge shall consider whether to refer the parties to mediation concerning any issue arising out of a suit for termination of residual parental rights. The judge may do so sua sponte or on motion of one of the parties. Upon referral, the parties must attend one evaluation session during which the parties and the mediator assess the case and decide whether to continue with mediation or with adjudication. Further participation in the mediation shall be by consent of all parties, and attorneys for any party may be present during mediation. Va. Code § 16.1-272.1. When the parties are referred to mediation, the court shall set a return date. The parties shall notify the court in writing if the dispute is resolved prior to this return date. The court may, in its discretion, incorporate any mediated agreement into the terms of its final decree disposing of a case. Only if the order is entered incorporating the mediated agreement will the terms of the voluntary settlement agreement affect any outstanding court order. Appeals from a final order terminating parental rights may be taken to the circuit court within 10 days. Competent evidence by a physician makes a prima facie showing of abuse or neglect to justify temporary removal of a child from the parents' home. Va. Code § 63.1-248.15. Abuse and neglect are characterized by "willful act or omission or by refusal to provide any necessary care for the child's health" that "causes or permits the life or health of such child to be seriously injured." In addition to being cause for termination of parental rights, abuse and neglect are criminal conduct punishable as Class 5 felonies. Va. Code § 18.2-371.1. Virginia Code § 63.1-248.6:2 provides that tape recordings may be made of conversations between people who are the subjects of child abuse investigations and child protective services if all parties are aware that the conversation is to be recorded.

Failure to comply with the conditions leading to foster care placement, Va. Code § 16.1-283C, is another grounds for termination. This requires that the state agency put forth evidence showing that it made appropriate efforts to remedy the conditions. *Weaver v. Roanoke Dep't of Human Resources,* 220 Va. 921, 265 S.E.2d 692 (1980). See also *Babb v. Scott Co. Dept. of Soc. Services,* 1996 Va. App. LEXIS 41; *Rivenbank v. Fairfax Co. Dep't of Human Dev.,* 1995 Va. App. LEXIS 459. The very length of time children remain in foster care may indicate that termination would be in their best interests. For an example, see *Price v. Arlington Dep't of Human Servs.,* 1995 Va. App. LEXIS 902 (six years). The therapist certified that if "Ellie were to be taken from their home now, it's my opinion that she would be at risk to hurt others, hurt herself in very aggressive behaviors, and/or to withdraw from the world and become lost in a fantasy world, to lose her trust in the world and the safety and security of it."

Due process does not require in every case that a parent whose rights in a child may be terminated have an appointed attorney if indigent. *Lassiter v. Dep't of Social Services,* 452 U.S. 18 (1981). Some cases hold that a minor should also have independent counsel. See *New Jersey Division of Youth & Family Services v. Wandell,* 155 N.J. Super. 302, 382 A.2d 711 (1978); see Va. Code § 16.1-266. In Virginia the child must at least be asked his opinion at the hearing. *Deahl v. Winchester Dep't of Social Services,* 224 Va. 664, 299 S.E.2d 863 (1983) (thirteen-year-old was "of sufficient discretion"). These proceedings are held in an informal setting and are usually uncomplicated. *Lassiter v. Dep't of Social Services,* 452 U.S. at 29, 32-33 (1981). The parent and the parent's attorney must be given a copy of the social services' investigation report. Va. Code

§ 16.1-274. In a trial de novo in circuit court after appeal of a termination proceeding in juvenile and domestic relations court, it was error to place the burden of proving lack of unfitness upon the natural parents rather than upon the county. *Walker v. Dep't of Public Welfare,* 223 Va. 557, 290 S.E.2d 887 (1982).

The trial court is not required to bifurcate termination and custody proceedings, because "the issues of custody and termination of parental rights are so interrelated that to bifurcate the issues may well obfuscate both proceedings." *Etzold v. Loudoun County Dep't of Social Servs.,* 1993 Va. App. LEXIS 458, *7 (custody granted to county with goal of adoption although grandparents petitioned for custody). However, there must be a hearing on termination of parental rights in addition to an abuse and neglect proceeding. *Cogan v. Fairfax County Dep't of Human Dev.,* 1994 Va. App. LEXIS 87 (harmless error in this case).

Once a mother's parental rights were terminated, she could not have contact with the children following adoption. *Cage v. Harrisonburg Dep't of Social Servs.,* 13 Va. App. 246, 410 S.E.2d 405 (1991). Termination of parental rights and responsibilities under Code § 16.1-228 includes "all rights and responsibilities remaining with the parent after the transfer of legal custody and guardianship of the person, including but not limited to the right of visitation, consent to adoption, the right to determine religious affiliation and the responsibility for support." See also *Wright v. Alexandria Div. of Social Servs.,* 16 Va. App. 821, 433 S.E.2d 500 (child had standing, through her guardian, to raise issues on mother's behalf in termination proceeding, but not entitled as a constitutional matter to maintain some parent-child relationship after termination). Once a termination order has been entered, the natural parents no longer must give consent for adoption. *Shank v. Dep't of Social Services,* 217 Va. 506, 230 S.E.2d 454 (1976). A parent's rights may be terminated even though the parent objects that placement with the child's paternal grandmother might be possible. *Sauer v. Franklin County Dep't of Social Servs.,* 18 Va. App. 769, 446 S.E.2d 640 (1994).

See generally Levy, *Using "Scientific" Testimony to Prove Child Sexual Abuse,* 23 Fam. L.Q. 383 (1989); Sobelson, *Termination of Indigents' Parental Rights After Lassiter: Ignoring Complexity and Protecting the Best Interests of Psychological Parents,* 16 U. Rich. L. Rev. 731 (1982); Comment, *Termination of Parental Rights in Adoption Cases: Focusing on the Child,* 14 J. Fam. L. 547 (1975-1976); Comment,

Termination of Parental Rights — An Analysis of Virginia's Statute, 15 U. Rich. L. Rev. 213 (1981).

§ 7-13. Substantive standards for termination of parental rights.

Although the types of physical abuse we will see in Section 16-6 typify grounds for termination, this definition is at once over- and under-inclusive. Even if the court finds serious abuse has taken place, for termination to occur, the condition must be permanent as well as grave. The parent must not be able to remedy the situation, even with the help of social services. Parental rights are not terminated solely because of abuse. The state may act to permanently sever the parent-child bond when the child is abandoned or neglected as well.

For example, in *Edwards v. County of Arlington,* 5 Va. App. 294, 361 S.E.2d 644 (1987), the termination was based upon a finding of mental illness on the mother's part. Language difficulties and problems with cultural acclimation significantly affected her ability to function properly. There was thus no clear and convincing showing that her problems in parenting sprang from a "mental or emotional illness or mental deficiency of such severity that there is no reasonable expectation" that she would be able to care responsibly for the child. But see *Jenkins v. Winchester Dep't of Social Servs.,* 12 Va. App. 1178, 409 S.E.2d 16 (1991), where after eleven years of involvement with the Department, the mother had not progressed to a point where she was capable of functioning as an independent parent. It was appropriate for the county to remove the youngest child from her custody at age three months because "the child would be subjected to an imminent threat to life or health to the extent that severe or irreversible injury would be likely to result if the child were ... left in the custody of his parent." See also *Frye v. Winchester Dep't of Social Servs.,* 1993 Va. App. LEXIS 235 (termination upheld even though parents not at fault since mentally retarded); *Midgette v. City of Virginia Beach,* 1995 Va. App. LEXIS 216 (termination upheld even though children entered foster care only upon mother's voluntary hospitalization); and *Lecky v. Reed,* 20 Va. App. 306; 456 S.E.2d 538 (1995)(termination upheld where 14-year-old mother given reasonable time to correct unfitness).

The Virginia Department of Social Services has adopted a Protective Services Manual for use by its local departments. It contains guidelines interpreting Va. Code § 63.1-248.2A, which defines an abused or neglected child. In *Larry D. Jackson, Commissioner v. W.,* 14 Va. App.

391, 419 S.E.2d 385 (1992), these guidelines were upheld over a father's constitutional challenge. The terms "rejecting, intimidating, humiliating, ridiculing, chaotic, bizarre, violent, hostile, or excessively guilt-producing" were not too ambiguous when interpreting types of behavior constituting mental abuse.

Unfitness may involve abandonment. Va. Code § 16.1-283D. Abandonment must be shown by clear, cogent, and convincing evidence. And, because termination of parental rights is so final and serious, even if abandonment is found, termination may still not be appropriate. *Robinette v. Keene*, 2 Va. App. 578, 347 S.E.2d 156 (1986). However, in *In re Adoption of Slayton*, 13 Va. Cir. 511 (Henrico Co. 1982), a father placed his children in the custody of his uncle when the paternal grandparents, who had been caring for the children, became ill. The father consented to adoption. The mother, who was then incarcerated, objected, but the court allowed adoption by the uncle, noting that she had not sent any letters or cards nor provided or offered financial support during the eight years in question. The court found that broadening the mother-child relationship might well be disruptive to the child.

§ 7-14. Unwed fathers.

Consent of a father whose child was born out of wedlock must be sought where the father's identity and address are known or are readily ascertainable. Va. Code § 63.1-225B(2). For example, in *Unknown Father v. Division of Social Servs.*, 15 Va. App. 110, 422 S.E.2d 407 (1992), the mother said that she did not know which of several men was the father of her child. After publication of the date of the child's birth together with the woman's name, the unknown father's rights were terminated because the court found that his identity was not "reasonably ascertainable." The court contrasted this case with *Augusta County Dep't of Social Servs. v. Unnamed Mother*, 3 Va. App. 40, 348 S.E.2d 26 (1986), where the unwed mother knew but refused to reveal the identity of the father, and notice of termination proceedings by order of publication was required. The court noted that "protection of the privacy rights of the mother and the child under specific circumstances argue well for not requiring publication to notify a mere biological father so that his rights, if any, may be protected." See also new Va. Code § 63.1-220.3(C)(2). But the father's consent will not be required if the father is unfit, as where he had shown no interest in the child, not given any support, and failed to have a concrete plan for the child's care. *Commonwealth v. Hayes*, 215 Va. 49,

205 S.E.2d 644 (1974). See also *Quilloin v. Walcott,* 434 U.S. 246 (1978) and *Lyle v. Eskridge,* 14 Va. App. 874, 419 S.E.2d 863 (1992) (fifteen-year-old father; adoption not allowed). There can be no irrebuttable presumption that a natural father of an illegitimate child is unfit to have custody. *Stanley v. Illinois,* 405 U.S. 645 (1972). When a child's mother is married to a man not the child's father, consent from both the natural and legal father must be obtained. Va. Code § 16.1-225. The presumption is that the child is the legitimate child of the mother's husband, although this is rebuttable. See Section 4-2, *supra.*

Virginia Code § 63.1-220.3(C)(2) provides that the father of a child born to an unmarried woman shall not be required to consent before the juvenile and domestic relations court (or, when funded, the family court) if he consents under oath and in writing to the adoption. In such cases the father must provide to the court the identifying information required in Va. Code § 63.1-220.3(B)(3), and the birth mother must give her consent in court in accordance with subsection A of the statute.

See generally Weinhaus, *Substantive Rights of the Unwed Father: The Boundaries Are Defined,* 19 J. Fam. L. 445 (1981); Comment, *The Emerging Constitutional Protection of the Putative Father's Parental Rights,* 70 Mich. L. Rev. 1581 (1972).

§ 7-15. Dispensing with consent.

In some cases the parent's residual rights in a child are terminated by divorce. Va. Code § 63.1-225B(1). In these situations or when there has been a finding of unfitness, such parents need not consent to adoption for it to be effective. *Shank v. Dep't of Social Services,* 217 Va. 506, 230 S.E.2d 454 (1976) (Mother had abused children before parental rights were terminated, and the children were placed in a foster home; only defense to adoption was a showing that prospective adoptive parents were unfit. A dissenting opinion suggested that the natural mother should have the chance to demonstrate that she had been rehabilitated since the original order.).

In other cases, the unwed father's identity or whereabouts are unknown, and consent cannot be obtained. See Va. Code § 63.1-225B(2), saying only reasonable efforts must be made, considering the relative interests of child, mother, and father. Reasonable efforts under Va. Code § 8.01-317 include mailing a copy of the order of publication to the last known address of the party on whom service is sought in addition to posting the order on the courthouse door and publishing it in a newspaper.

Noncompliance will apparently be sufficient to vacate a final adoption order. *Carlton v. Paxton,* 14 Va. App. 105, 415 S.E.2d 600, *aff'd,* 15 Va. App. 265, 422 S.E.2d 423 (1992). Not only must the adoption be in the child's best interests, but a continuation of the relationship between the nonconsenting parent and the child must be detrimental to the child's welfare. *Knight v. Laney,* 1996 Va. App. LEXIS 4.

Obviously if both parents are deceased and the child has not yet been placed with an agency, consent is not required. Va. Code § 63.1-225.

§ 7-16. Adoption over objection of natural parent.

Va. Code § 63.1-225C provides that if the parent's consent is unreasonably withheld contrary to the best interests of the child, the judge may nevertheless order the adoption. A similar standard from the District of Columbia, D.C. Code § 16-304, was challenged in *Petition of L.,* 409 A.2d 1073 (D.C. 1979), but, since the stepfather withdrew his petition to adopt, was never resolved by the Supreme Court. 449 U.S. 989 (1981). Virginia not only requires unreasonableness, as the District does, but also that the withholding of adoption serves to harm the child. *Ward v. Faw,* 219 Va. 1120, 253 S.E.2d 658, 662 (1979); *Malpass v. Morgan,* 213 Va. 393, 399, 192 S.E.2d 794, 799 (1972). Cf. *In re Adoption of Morton,* 25 Va. Cir. 531 (Spotsylvania Co. 1991) (grandparents had custody for eight years; mother successfully objected to adoption). Va. Code § 63.1-231(B) requires that such a proceeding first be referred to the local Superintendent of Public Welfare, even though both natural parents would prefer to waive such a reference. *In re Adoption of Renaud,* 21 Va. Cir. 293 (Stafford Co. 1990). Due process does not require that a court-appointed social services investigator conduct a formal interview with the parent whose rights are subject to divestment, although it must make a "thorough investigation." *Key v. Beckstoffer,* 1994 Va. App. LEXIS 102 (parent incarcerated).

In cases where the parents of a child are not married, the consent of the father is not required if his identity is not reasonably ascertainable, or if he is known, is given notice by registered or certified mail to last known address, and fails to object to the proceeding. Va. Code § 63.1-220.3. The standard of what is reasonable under the circumstances controls, taking into account the relative interests of the child, the mother, and the father. The father need not be notified if convicted of rape or statutory rape that resulted in the child's conception. Virginia Code § 63.1-204. Va. Code § 63.1-220.3 was amended again in 1995 to clarify the various consent requirements.

In *Ward,* a mother had custody of the child after separation, and the father made regular support payments and sent cards and gifts. He had not seen the son, however, for three and one-half years. The child's stepfather was not allowed to adopt although he was unquestionably fit and loving. There was no finding that the natural father was unfit, nor that he had by legal action or conduct lost his rights to the child. See also *Doe v. Doe,* 222 Va. 736, 284 S.E.2d 799 (1981); *Cunningham v. Gray,* 221 Va. 792, 273 S.E.2d 562 (1981) (no evidence presented by natural mother or her new husband that continuation of the limited relationship, with only one face-to-face encounter in eight years, would be disruptive of her well-being); *Jolliff v. Crabtree,* 224 Va. 654, 299 S.E.2d 358 (1983) (father was unable to exercise visitation rights since he did not know mother's location, and had provided no support). But compare *Frye v. Spotte,* 4 Va. App. 530, 359 S.E.2d 315 (1987), where the father deserted his wife and daughters for another woman, taking all the food from the family home and disconnecting the electricity and water, intentionally leaving the family in such necessitous circumstances that his wife was forced to apply for public assistance. In addition, he failed to support the children regularly, and demonstrated recurring incidents of spousal and child abuse, including sexual abuse. The custodial mother whose husband sought to adopt the children therefore demonstrated that a continuing or expanded relationship with the children might well present a threat to their emotional, physical, and sexual well being. *Id.* at 537-38. See also *In re Adoption of Buchanan,* 13 Va. Cir. 53 (Washington Co. 1987) (no affirmative steps toward pursuing a father-son relationship; no relationship to continue); *In re Tabb,* 18 Va. Cir. 355 (Chesterfield Co. 1989). In *Linkous v. Kingery,* 10 Va. App. 45, 390 S.E.2d 188 (1990), the court allowed a stepparent adoption over the objection of a natural father who had been incarcerated for armed robbery and who had committed a further crime while incarcerated. The court noted that not only must the proposed adoption be in the best interests of the child, but also that the fit non-consenting parent must be shown to be "obstinately self-willed in refusing to consent" and "acting prejudicially to the child's interest."

In some cases, a natural parent who is homosexual wishes to prevent the adoption of the child. In *Doe v. Doe,* 222 Va. 736, 284 S.E.2d 799 (1981), the Virginia Supreme Court indicated that the natural mother's objection to adoption by the child's stepmother could prevent his adoption. This was in a case where the natural mother was not only fit but also according to all accounts was an extremely creative and loving parent who maintained an excellent relationship with her son. The court indicated that if custody as opposed to visitation were in question, or at some later point if the child's well-being were threatened by continued contact through visitation, the mother might have to cease living with her lover. Homosexuality does not per se make a parent unfit. *Id.* at 748, 284 S.E. at 806. Compare the decision in *Roe v. Roe,* 228 Va. 722, 324 S.E.2d 691 (1985), changing custody from a father who lived with his male lover because of the necessary adverse impact upon the child.

Since Virginia's focus is upon the *child's* rights as opposed to the parent's, the Virginia statute would better withstand constitutional challenge than that of the District of Columbia. The "rights of parents may not be lightly severed but are to be respected if at all consonant with the best interests of the child." *Malpass v. Morgan,* 213 Va. at 400, 192 S.E.2d at 799. See generally Wadlington, *The Divorced Parent and Consent for Adoption,* 36 U. Cinn. L. Rev. 196 (1967).

§ 7-17. Consent by state licensed agency.

When the natural parents have relinquished their child to a state licensed agency for adoptive placement, or when the parents' rights have been terminated because of their unfitness, the agency having custody of the child must give consent to adoption. Va. Code § 63.1-225.

§ 7-18. Equitable adoption.

Although some states recognize the concept of equitable adoption, see, e.g., *In re Estate of McConnell,* 268 F. Supp. 346 (D.C. 1967), and cases cited therein, Virginia does not. *Clarkson v. Bliley,* 185 Va. 82, 38 S.E.2d 22 (1946). Under the doctrine, when an adult agrees to take a child into the adult's home and adopt, but fails to acquire a judicial decree of adoption, the child may nevertheless recover as would an adopted child from the adult's estate. The action belongs to the child, and those inheriting through the child, not to the adult nor those inheriting through the adult.

However, a man who believed he had fathered a child and supported the infant after her birth and even after testing showed that he was not the biological father, had a legitimate interest in the child pursuant to Va. Code § 16.1-278.15, and was granted custody when the child's mother was found unfit. *In re Davis,* Shenandoah Cir. Ct., No. CH 94-275 (1995).

When children were entrusted to a couple who planned to adopt them but the adoption was never completed before the adoptive parents divorced, the husband had no legal obligation to continue supporting the child. *Schalton v. Schalton,* 31 Va. Cir. 47 (Fairfax Co. 1993) (distinguishing *T. v. T.,* found *infra* Section 16-1).

Equitable adoption has not been accepted in Virginia because, as in the case of common law marriages, allowing such a remedy would be to invite fraud and collusion. *Clarkson v. Bliley,* 185 Va. at 93-94, 38 S.E.2d at 27.

§ 7-19. Procedure for adoption.

A petition for adoption, in the name by which the child will be known, is filed in the circuit court. Attached must be the written consent by the natural parents or state licensed agency to the adoption. The petition will indicate the names and complete addresses of the couple wishing to adopt. Va. Code § 63.1-221. If necessary, a guardian ad litem will be appointed for the child. At this point an interlocutory order will be entered, Va. Code § 63-1.233, ordering further investigations over a ninety-day period.

Amendments to Va. Code § 63.1-223 mandate that where the child was placed by an agency in another state or in another country, the petition and all exhibits shall be forwarded to the local agency that performed the home study or provided supervision. If no Virginia agency provided such services, the petition and exhibits shall be forwarded to the local director of social services or superintendent of public welfare. Where a licensed child-placing agency has completed a home study, the petition and all exhibits shall be forwarded to the child-placing agency. The agency then reports to the court within 90 days. If the birth parent does not reside in Virginia, consent shall be given before a court having jurisdiction over child custody matters in the birth parent's state of residence.

Where the child is placed by the birth parents in the adoptive home, the petition shall be heard within ten days of filing or as soon thereafter as is practicable. Va. Code § 16.1-241(T). Hearings in these cases shall be commenced in the city or county where the child was born or where the birth parents or the adoptive parents reside. Va. Code § 16.1-243.

In its 1993 reconvened session, the Virginia Legislature established a statewide system of family courts. The new legislation, Chapter 929 of the Virginia Acts of Assembly, provided that the family courts would assume the powers and territorial jurisdiction of the juvenile and domestic relations district courts on January 1, 1996 (§ 16.1-69.8(2)). However, the new courts have not yet been funded, so the courts remain experimental in a few jurisdictions. After funding of the new court, judges of the juvenile and domestic relations district courts shall continue in office as family court judges until their terms of appointment or election expire, or until a vacancy occurs or a successor is appointed or elected (§ 16.1-69.9:01). Like the current juvenile and domestic relations district court judges, family court judges shall be prohibited from engaging in the practice of law. Va. Code § 16.1-12(c). General district court judges, substitute judges, and retired and recalled district court judges may serve on the family court, but only after completing the training program required by the Judicial Council of Virginia. (Va Code §§ 16.1-69.21, 16.1-69.22:1 and 16.1-69.36(8)). Family court jurisdiction extends to suits for adoption. Va Code § 16.1-241(V). Venue shall be in the family court in the county or city in which judgment was rendered or a proceeding is pending. Transfer of venue in suits for divorce, annulment or affirmation of marriage, separate maintenance, equitable distribution based on a foreign decree, and the award of an injunction shall be governed by §§ 8.01-257 et seq. as these provisions relate to circuit courts. Adoption cases shall be filed directly with the clerk of the family court. In adoption and birth record amendment cases, service of process shall be governed by the rules of the Supreme Court or by statute (§ 62.1-220) as appropriate. Va. Code § 16.1-263(F). In cases provided for in § 16.1-259, complaints and the processing of petitions to initiate a case shall be the responsibility of the intake officer. Va. Code § 16.1-260. Disposition, as with most cases heard by the family court, will be in accordance with existing procedures under Title 63.1. Appeals from most final orders or judgments of the family court may be taken to the circuit court within 10 days. Confidentiality of the cases is governed by §§ 63.1-235 and 63.1-236. Adoption records shall be retained permanently by the circuit court for adoptions filed prior to January 1, 1995, or thereafter by the family court in which the case was filed. Va. Code § 63.1-235.

At this point, the child's name will be changed to that of the adopting parents, and the adoption will be entered on the birth certificate. All records regarding the investigation and the natural parents will be sealed.

The former spouse of a parent may not petition to adopt her child despite the fact that the biological father gave his consent. *Sozio v. Thorpe*, 1996 Va. App. LEXIS 267. The adoption statutes, which must be strictly construed, require that an adoption petition filed by a married person be joined by the spouse, and Sozio's present wife had not joined in his petition.

§ 7-20. Inspection by state agency.

In all cases except where the child is to be adopted by a stepparent with the natural parent's permission, the Department of Social Services, a local child-placing agency or the Commissioner's Office of Adoption makes a study upon the order of reference by the court to determine whether the adoption will be in the child's best interests. A study is prepared before the child is placed in the home. After an interlocutory decree of adoption is entered, a probationary period of six months elapses before the adoption is final. The home is reinspected, so that the child can be observed as part of the new family unit. The Virginia statutes provide that adoptions will not be recognized without such investigations, even of children coming from or going to other states. Va. Code § 63.1-217. After such visitations a final report is submitted to the court.

Even in the cases of private placement adoptions, before placement the court is to ascertain whether the adoptive parents are in satisfactory physical and mental health to enable them to provide adequate care to the child. Va. Code §§ 63.1-204(C)(2); 63.1-221; 63.1-223(E). If the Commissioner disapproves of the pending adoption, he must so notify the court within twenty-one days of date of delivery or mailing of the report. Va. Code § 63.1-223. The reports filed by the agency performing the home study must include an inquiry as to whether the prospective adoptive parents are financially able, morally suitable, and in satisfactory physical and mental health to enable them to care for the child. Further, the report should reflect the physical and mental condition of the child, if known, the circumstances under which the child came to live, or will be living, in the home of the prospective adoptive family, what fees have been paid by the prospective adoptive family or on their behalf in connection with the adoption, and any other matters specified by the court. Va. Code § 63.1-220.3(B)(6). The social service agencies making investigations, visits, and reports may establish fee schedules for actual expenses incurred. Receipts for payment of these fees shall be provided to the court before entry of any final order. Va. Code § 63.1-236.

This home study is not required, however. Where the child is being adopted by close relatives: the child's grandparents, adult siblings, or adult uncle or aunt, consent by the natural parents for the adoption can be signed and acknowledged, and need not be executed in court in the presence of the adoptive parents. Va. Code § 63.1-220.3. A petition for adoption must be signed by both the prospective adoptive parents as well as by counsel of record. Where the statutes do not require referral for an investigation, the petition must be under oath. Va. Code § 63.1-221.

See generally Cynthia E. Cordle, *Open Adoption: The Need for Legislative Action*, 2 Va. J. Soc. Pol'y & L. 275 (1995).

§ 7-21. Adoption by foster parents.

By statute, Virginia has created a network of foster families. Va. Code §§ 16.1-281 and 16.1-282. In exchange for a monthly remission from the Department of Social Services, these families contract to accept children whose parents are unable to care for them on a temporary basis. This may be because the parents have voluntarily placed the custody of the children with a state agency, or because the children have been adjudicated dependent due to the parents' neglect or abuse.

Although the foster parents may have some liberty interest in the custody of the child, *Kyees v. County Dep't of Public Welfare*, 600 F.2d 693 (7th Cir. 1979), the overall objective of the program is to return the children as quickly as possible to their natural parents. In addition, the foster parents have contracted for the temporary nature of their custody, and are compensated for their care of the child. *Smith v. Organization of Foster Families for Equality & Reform (OFFER)*, 431 U.S. 816 (1977).

Except in cases where a relative acts as a foster parent, see, e.g., *Rivera v. Marcus*, 696 F.2d 1016 (2d Cir. 1982), the state agency retains the right, after hearing, to remove the child for placement with another foster family or for return to the natural parent. This removal may only take place upon court order. Va. Code § 63.1-206.1.

Of course, children as well as foster parents may develop psychological bonds, particularly after long residence together, that make it in the child's best interests to remain with the foster family. Some foster parents do end up adopting the children whose custody they have been given. See Va. Code § 63.1-221 for the requirements: (1) residence for eighteen months in foster home; (2) termination of natural parents' rights; and (3) investigation and report by agency not having custody of the child, in addition to the best interests of the child requirement. In *Carter v. Dinwiddie County Dep't of Social Servs.*, 1993 Va. App. LEXIS 149, the adopted child's natural mother placed him with the Carter family shortly after his birth in December of 1988. The Carters were officially recognized as foster parents in February 1989. When the natural mother terminated her parental rights in 1990, the Carters changed the goal of their foster care plan to adoption. The parties signed an Adoptive Homes Agreement approved by the Board of Public Welfare. Some time later, the child, who had "special needs," became difficult for the Carters to manage. After "several equivocal requests" for help with the child, the parties agreed to place him in a therapeutic foster home. During this placement, the child did well. The Department, after discussion with the Carters, decided not to return the child to them, and instead withdrew consent for adoption. Because the Carters did not appeal, the decision became final. The Carters subsequently filed a petition for custody pursuant to Va. Code § 16.1-241(A)(3), which allows petitions from "parties with a legitimate interest" in the custody of a child. The Carters alleged that as former potential adoptive parents they had standing to sue. On appeal, the court of appeals agreed, but found that they had not met their burden of showing that the best interests of the child would be served by changing his custody to them. There was ample credible evidence that he had caused stress in their household, while he had flourished in his new foster placement.

See generally Karoline S. Homer, *Program Abuse in Foster Care: A Search for Solutions*, 1 Va. J. Soc. Pol'y & L. 177 (1993); Musewicz, *The Failure of Foster Care: Federal Statutory Reform and the Child's Right to Permanence,* 54 S. Cal. L. Rev. 633 (1981); and Michael P. Kennedy, Comment, *In the Best Interest of the Child: Religious and Racial Matching in Foster Care*, 3 Geo. Mason U. Civ. Rts. L.J. 299 (1993).

§ 7-22. Care of children during trial period.

Before a decree of adoption becomes final, the inquiry becomes whether adoption by this particular family is in the child's best interest. At this juncture, the child is in the physical custody of prospective adoptive parents, while in most cases legal custody remains with the state agency in most cases. The prospective adoptive parents are responsible for the child's support, education, and care during this interim period, when strong psychological bonds may also form.

Once the child has been placed in the adoptive home, removal from the home is governed by Va. Code § 63.1-220.5, and may occur only upon consent of the adoptive parents, upon order of the juvenile and domestic relations district court or circuit court, pursuant to Va. Code § 63-1.211, or upon order of the court that accepted consent when such consent has been revoked. In *Carter v. Dinwiddie County Dep't of Social Servs.*, 1993

Va. App. LEXIS 149, his natural mother placed a child with the Carters shortly after his birth in December of 1988. The Department officially recognized them as foster parents in February of 1989. When the natural mother terminated her parental rights in 1990, the goal of the Carters' foster care plan was changed to adoption. The parties signed an Adoptive Homes Agreement approved by the Board of Public Welfare. Some time later, the child, who had "special needs," became difficult for the Carters to manage. After "several equivocal requests" for help with the child, the parties agreed to place him in a therapeutic foster home. During this placement the child did well. The Department, after discussion with the Carters, decided not to return the child to them, and instead withdrew consent for adoption. Because the Carters did not appeal, the decision became final. The Carters subsequently filed a petition for custody pursuant to Va. Code § 16.1-241(A)(3), which allows petitions from "parties with a legitimate interest" in the custody of a child. The Carters alleged that as former potential adoptive parents they had standing to sue. On appeal, the court of appeals agreed, but found that they had not met their burden of showing that the best interests of the child would be served by changing his custody to them. Ample credible evidence showed that he had caused stress in their household while he had flourished in his new foster placement.

§ 7-23. Social considerations.

A prospective adoptive family's wealth or social position has no bearing upon whether a child may be adopted by them. *Rocka v. Roanoke County Dep't of Public Welfare,* 215 Va. 515, 211 S.E.2d 76 (1975). The proper inquiry is whether it is in the child's best interest. The attachments that develop between child and parent remain of paramount importance.

§ 7-24. Stability of family.

Placement by state agencies or licensed child placement facilities is most often with married couples. This is because it is presumed to be in the child's best interest to have both a father and a mother take part in the child's growth and development. *Adoption of H.,* 69 Misc. 2d 304, 330 N.Y.S.2d 235 (1972). However, Va. Code § 63.1-220.2 specifically allows placement with unmarried as well as married couples.

Should a separation occur between the prospective parents, adoption may not be granted since to do so would jeopardize the child's opportunities for being reared in a two-parent home. This negative factor continues despite a declaration by the prospective parents that they are, and intend to remain, friends, since they could stop being friendly, or divorce and remarry, leaving the child with yet another set of parents. *Watson v. Shepard,* 217 Va. 538, 229 S.E.2d 897 (1976). In *Watson,* custody was retained in the foster mother, who was the child's paternal aunt.

§ 7-25. Race.

Although one state court held, in *Blackburn v. Blackburn,* 168 Ga. App. 66, 308 S.E.2d 193 (1983), that consideration of the race of a child or prospective adoptive parent was permissible in granting a change of custody, *Palmore v. Sidoti,* 466 U.S. 429, 104 S. Ct. 1879, 80 L. Ed. 2d 421 (1984), held that it is not. See also *Roe v. Conn,* 417 F. Supp. 769 (M.D. Ala. 1976).

See generally, Bonnie Kae Grover, *Aren't These Our Children? Vietnamese Amerasian Resettlement and Restitution,* 2 Va. J. Soc. Pol'y & L. 247 (1995).

§ 7-26. Religious preference.

If the natural parents, in voluntarily giving their child up for adoption, indicate a religious preference, compare *Scott v. Family Ministries,* 65 Cal. App. 3d 492, 135 Cal. Rptr. 430 (1977), or if the child is old enough to have particular religious needs, the prospective adoptive parents may be chosen from the desired religious affiliation, if such are available. *In re C.,* 63 Misc. 2d 1019, 314 N.Y.S.2d 255 (1970). Both *Scott* and *In re C.* were decided in states, like Virginia, that have religious matching clauses in their statutes.

However, the state agencies or licensed child care facilities may not otherwise discriminate on the basis of prospective parents' religious preference without violating constitutional prohibitions. *Scott v. Family Ministries,* 65 Cal. App. 3d 492, 135 Cal. Rptr. 430 (1976).

See generally *Religious Matching Statutes and Adoption,* 51 N.Y.U. L. Rev. 262 (1976).

§ 7-27. Age of adoptive parents.

Some cases involve adoption by older parents, whose age more closely resembles that of grandparents. Such adoptions are usually not in the child's best interest since the child has already suffered disruption in life and will need stability through the formative years when the older adoptive parent may die or be in declining health.

In some cases, however, because of an exceptional bond with a particular child, see *In re Haun,* 31 Ohio App. 2d 63, 286 N.E.2d 478 (1972), or if the older parent is related to the child, such adoptions will be in the child's best interest.

§ 7-28. Sexual preference of natural parents.

In some cases, a natural parent who is homosexual wishes to prevent the adoption of the child. In *Doe v. Doe,* 222 Va. 736, 284 S.E.2d 799 (1981), the Virginia Supreme Court indicated that the natural mother's objection to adoption by the child's stepmother could prevent his adoption. This was in a case where the natural mother was not only fit but also to all accounts was an extremely creative and loving parent who maintained an excellent relationship with her son. The court indicated that if custody were in question, or at some later point if the child's well-being were threatened by continued contact through visitation, the mother might have to cease living with her lover. Compare the decision in *Roe v. Roe,* 228 Va. 722, 324 S.E.2d 691 (1985), changing custody from a homosexual father who lived with a male lover since there must of necessity be an adverse impact on the child.

§ 7-29. Presence of siblings.

In some cases, there is a question whether one set of prospective adoptive parents is preferable to another where the child's siblings already reside. In such cases, courts will prefer to keep the siblings together, assuming that both sets of prospective parents are fit. See, e.g., *Watson v. Shepard,* 217 Va. 538, 229 S.E.2d 897 (1976) (custody kept in home of aunt where there was also a cousin with whom child had spent most of her life).

§ 7-30. Consent of child.

Amendments to Va. Code § 63.1-225 provide that consent to adoption is required of a child fourteen years of age or over, unless the court finds that the best interests of the child will be served by not requiring such consent. He or she must also be consulted before parental rights may be terminated if of the age of sufficient discretion. *Deahl v. Winchester Dep't of Social Services,* 224 Va. 664, 299 S.E.2d 863 (1983).

§ 7-31. Adoption of adults.

In some cases, adults over eighteen wish to be adopted in order to change patterns of inheritance, or to cement social relationships. If both parties consent, and no fraud is involved, such adoptions will be approved without the usual home visits by social agencies. Va. Code § 63.1-222. See, e.g., *Armistead v. Hamilton,* 1995 Va. App. LEXIS 318 (no fraud shown by brother of incompetent who adopted an adult before suffering a massive stroke and becoming incompetent).

The entry of a final adoption order that incorporates a name change meets the requirements of Va. Code § 8.01-217, according to Va. Code § 63.1-222, as amended in 1988.

§ 7-32. Removal from prospective adoptive parents.

Should the investigating agency find prospective parents unfit, the child may be removed from their home under Va. Code § 63-1.227. This should not be accomplished without a prior hearing with opportunities for cross-examination and confrontation except in cases of an immediate threat to the child's health and well-being. In such event, a hearing should be scheduled in the very near future to assure due process. *C. v. Superior Court of Sacramento Co.,* 29 Cal. App. 3d 909, 106 Cal. Rptr. 123, 130-31 (1973).

§ 7-33. Finality of adoption.

Once the final decree of adoption has been entered, it will not be subject to attack in any proceedings after six months, Va. Code § 63.1-237, except upon jurisdictional grounds. *Shank v. Dep't of Social Services,* 217 Va. 506, 230 S.E.2d 454 (1976).

Other jurisdictions are finding that adoptive parents may sue agencies that fail to disclose or misrepresent information regarding the adopted children. See, e.g., *Gibbs v. Ernst,* 615 A.2d 851 (Pa. Cmwlth. 1992). In 1995, the legislature amended Va. Code § 63.1-237 so that after six months from the date of the final adoption order, where no appeal has been taken, the order may not be attacked for any reason, including fraud, duress, failure to give required notice to any person, failure of any procedural requirement, or lack of jurisdiction over any person. This amendment should prevent cases like the well-publicized *Schmidt v. DeBoer,* 501 N.W.2d 193 (Mich. App.), *aff'd in part, vacated in part & remanded,* 502 N.W.2d 649 (Mich. 1993), in which birth parents were able to regain custody of a child despite the fact that her adoption had been finalized for some time, because the birth father had not given consent.

An adoption could not be revoked by an adoptee who had been adopted at the age of fourteen without giving her consent. The adoptive father was a necessary party to the proceeding to set aside the adoption. *In re Dwyer,* 18 Va. App. 437, 445 S.E.2d 157 (1994).

§ 7-34. Special needs.

Since 1974, Virginia has provided for special subsidy payments for children with special needs, such as handicapped or mentally retarded children, to be made to parents who are unable financially to care for such a special child. Va. Code § 63.1-238.1 et seq.

§ 7-35. Inheritance rights of adopted child.

The adopted child takes as would a natural child through and by the adoptive parent. Va. Code §§ 63.1-233, 63.1-234 and 64.1-5.1; *McFadden v. McNorton,* 193 Va. 455, 69 S.E.2d 445 (1952). The adopted child is thus an heir at law. *Dickenson v. Buck,* 169 Va. 39, 192 S.E. 748 (1938). He or she may not be able to take as "issue" of an adopted parent's deceased relatives, *Fletcher v. Flanary,* 185 Va. 409, 38 S.E.2d 433 (1946), or as "heir of the body." See *Newsome v. Scott,* 200 Va. 833, 108 S.E.2d 369 (1959) ("die without heirs" did not include an adopted child).

By statute, the adopted child may also inherit from the natural parent, Va. Code § 64.1-5.1(2), if the adoption is by a stepparent.

Virginia does not, however, permit "equitable adoption;" cf. *In re Estate of Cregar,* 30 Ill. App. 3d 798, 333 N.E.2d 540 (1975), and cases cited therein. Thus, if the adoption is by a relative of the natural parent, the child may inherit only one share rather than both the share received as an adopted child and as a natural relative. See generally Johnson, *Inheritance Rights of Children in Virginia,* 12 U. Rich. L. Rev. 275 (1978).

§ 7-36. Access to records.

Upon a showing of good cause before a circuit court where the records are kept, an adult adopted child may have access to records involving the adoption including the identity of the natural parents. In other cases, all information including medical records may be accessed through the adoptive agency by the adoptive parents. Other persons must have a court order to obtain information. Va. Code § 63.1-236.

When an adult adoptee wishes to know identifying information, the commissioner shall direct the agency that made the original home study to attempt to locate the biological family and advise family members of the application. The agency shall report the results of the attempt to locate and advise the biological family to the commissioner, including the relative effects that disclosure of the identifying information may have on the adopted person, the adoptive parents, and the biological family. Upon a showing of good cause, the commissioner shall disclose the identifying information. If the commissioner denies disclosure of identifying information after receiving the report, the adopted person may apply to the circuit court for an order to disclose, which shall be entered only upon a showing of good cause. Va. Code § 63.1-236.

The 1994 legislature provided that biological parents and adult biological siblings may request identifying information from the Commissioner of Social Services if the adoptee is 21 or older. For adoptions occurring after July 1, 1994, if the adoptee is less than 18 years of age, the adoptive parents or other legal custodial may apply for identifying information about the biological family. In both cases, the home study agency allows transmission of medical, psychological, or genetic information if a health care provider indicates that the adult adoptee, either set of parents, or adult biological siblings critically need the information. In parental placement adoptions where consent was executed after July 1, 1994, the entire adoption record is open to adoptive parents, adult adoptees, and the biological parent consenting to the adoption. Va. Code § 63.1-236.

See generally Klibanoff, *Genealogical Information in Adoption: The Adoptee's Quest and the Law,* 11 Fam. L.Q. 185 (1977).

§ 7-37. Visitation by natural relatives.

In most cases, and unless the child is adopted by a stepparent, visitation with the natural parent will only disturb the new relationships formed by adoption. *Katterman v. Di Piazza,* 151 N.J. Super. 209, 376 A.2d 955 (1977). Visitation will therefore not be permitted except with the consent of the adoptive parents. Virginia will apparently follow the tendency of many other states to allow relatives continued contact after a child is adopted by blood relatives. For example, in *In re Adoption of K.B.M.,* 30 Va. Cir. 343 (City of Radford 1993), the circuit court permitted continued visitation by the maternal aunts of an orphan child after he was adopted by his paternal aunt and her husband.

This limitation on visitation would be true for grandparents as well. Grandparents may visit, by statute, even in cases of death of their child or divorce of the grandchild's parents. Va. Code § 20-107.2. However, this right does not extend to the period following an adoption by the step-parent. *Bikos v. Nobliski,* 88 Mich. App. 157, 276 N.W.2d 541 (1979).

§ 7-38. Marriage of adopted children.

Adopted children are subject to the same incest prohibitions as are natural children. Va. Code § 20-38. This is because the incest taboos are partly concerned with the unusual social relationships that might otherwise occur within the family.

On the other hand, adopted children may not marry their natural relatives. Although upon adoption the child becomes the child of the adopting family, the genetic relationship is not changed. Because of the greater tendency for inherited diseases among children of close relatives, marriage between natural relatives, one of whom has been adopted into another family, is prohibited. *State v. H.,* 429 A.2d 1321 (Del. Super. 1981).

CHAPTER 8

Interspousal Torts

§ 8-1. Interspousal immunity and abrogation by statute.

In 1980, the Virginia Supreme Court, in *Counts v. Counts,* 221 Va. 151, 266 S.E.2d 895 (1980), was asked to carve an exception to the doctrine of interspousal immunity. In *Counts,* a wife had hired another man to kill her husband. The attempt failed, although the husband was seriously injured. After the parties were divorced, the husband sued the wife in tort. The supreme court declined to extend the doctrine of *Korman v. Carpenter,* 216 Va. 86, 216 S.E.2d 195 (1975), which had permitted the estate of a wife, who had been murdered by her husband, to sue the committee of the imprisoned spouse. The court reasoned that when there remained a marriage that might be preserved, to allow a tort action might destroy that marriage. 221 Va. at 156, 266 S.E.2d at 898.

In 1981, the Virginia legislature enacted Va. Code § 8.01-220.1, which abolished the doctrine of interspousal immunity for causes of action arising on or after July of 1981. Reasons for abrogating the doctrine are explored at Comment, *The Legislative Abrogation of Interspousal Immunity in Virginia,* 15 U. Rich. L. Rev. 939, 948 (1981). See generally W. Prosser, *Handbook of the Law of Torts* § 122, at 864 (4th ed. 1971).

§ 8-2. What marriages are covered by interspousal immunity.

Interspousal immunity pertains to actions brought after marriage even though the tort occurred before the marriage. *Furey v. Furey,* 193 Va. 727, 71 S.E.2d 191 (1952). The doctrine remains in effect even though the parties are separated and even though they are divorced at the time of suit. *Counts v. Counts,* 221 Va. 151, 266 S.E.2d 895 (1980). See also *Soedler v. Soedler,* 89 Ill. App. 3d 74, 411 N.E.2d 547 (1980). See West Digest, *Husband and Wife* Key No. 205(2). It is also in effect during a voidable marriage, even though the later decree of annulment says the marriage is "void ab initio." *Gordon v. Pollard,* 207 Tenn. 45, 336 S.W.2d 25 (1960). See also *State ex rel. Angvall v. District Court,* 151 Mont. 483, 444 P.2d 370 (1968). See generally Annot., 92 A.L.R.3d 901.

§ 8-3. Exceptions to the doctrine.

The subjects of most tort actions not barred by the statute of limitations in tort would have taken place after the 1981 enactment of Va. Code § 8.01-220.1, abrogating the doctrine. However, for completeness, a few additional words regarding exceptions to the doctrine follow. See, e.g., *Byrd v. Byrd,* 657 F.2d 615 (4th Cir. 1981) (interspousal immunity would not bar federal admiralty negligence action; case brought before the statute).

1. It has not been a defense to tort suits arising from automobile accidents since *Surratt v. Thompson,* 212 Va. 191, 183 S.E.2d 200 (1971), because of ubiquitous and mandatory automobile insurance.

2. Even for suits before 1981, if the death of one spouse was caused by the intentional action of the other, and there were no children or grandchildren surviving, the estate of the deceased spouse may bring an action in tort. *Korman v. Carpenter,* 216 Va. 86, 216 S.E.2d 195 (1975), since there was no marriage to be saved, nor union to be preserved, *id.* at 90, 216 S.E.2d at 198.

3. There may be some other areas where the doctrine does not apply. The first is where the tort did not occur based upon the marriage relationship, but rather upon a coincidental business one, such as that of master and servant, or common carrier and passenger. A Virginia case recognized that when a father owned a bus company, and his child was injured due to the negligence of one of the father's employees, the child could recover in tort. *Worrell v. Worrell,* 174 Va. 11, 26-27, 4 S.E.2d 343, 349-50 (1939). Although many of the ancient bases for the interspousal immunity doctrine [1] are different from the more recent par-

---

1. The idea that husband and wife are of one flesh and therefore unable to sue each other, Keister's Adm'r v. Keister's Ex'r, 123 Va. 157, 177, 96 S.E. 315, 322 (1918) (Burke, J., concurring) (The duties of marriage "forbid the idea that this 'one flesh' may so divide itself that either spouse may sue the other."). *See also* Korman v. Carpenter, 216 Va. at 90, 216 S.E.2d at 197; Surratt v. Thompson, 212 Va. 191, 194, 183 S.E.2d 200, 202 (1971); 1 W. BLACKSTONE, COMMENTARIES *442 (1809).

ent/child immunity,[2] the goal of preserving family harmony would not seem to be affected by either suit. See *Worrell v. Worrell,* 174 Va. 11, 19, 4 S.E.2d 343, 346 (1939); *Counts v. Counts,* 221 Va. at 154, 266 S.E.2d at 896.

4. In places where the doctrine still exists,[3] if an outrageous intentional tort in effect destroyed the family relationship, there would be no immunity defense since the spouse or parent was no longer acting within the marital or familial role. See, e.g., *Lusby v. Lusby,* 283 Md. 334, 352, 390 A.2d 77, 88 (1978) (interspousal immunity; "no domestic tranquility to be preserved"); and *Mahnke v. Moore,* 197 Md. 61, 68, 77 A.2d 923, 926 (1951) (parental immunity; "complete abandonment of the parental relation"); see generally Comment, *Defining the Parent's Duty after Rejection of Parent-Child Immunity: Parental Liability for Emotional Injury to Abandoned Children,* 33 Vand. L. Rev. 775 (1980); Note, *Intrafamilial Tort Immunity in Virginia,* 21 Wm. & Mary L. Rev. 273 (1979). Apparently, according to *Counts,* the Virginia public policy of saving even troubled family relationships if at all possible would preclude such a suit.

§ 8-4. Matters not subject to suit.

In *Merenoff v. Merenoff,* 76 N.J. 535, 388 A.2d 951 (1978), the Supreme Court of New Jersey mentioned that despite the court's abolition of the doctrine of interspousal immunity for that state, some subjects would still not be susceptible of suit.

To paraphrase *Merenoff, id.* at 555, 388 A.2d at 961, suits that still could not be brought might:

(1) involve marital intimacy (but cf. *Kathleen K. v. Robert B.,* 150 Cal. App. 3d 992, 198 Cal. Rptr. 273 (1984), where a suit was brought for intentional fraud in failing to warn the prospective sexual partner that defendant was infected with genital herpes; cf. *Stephen K. v. Roni L.,* 105 Cal. App. 3d 640, 164 Cal. Rptr. 618 (1980); *L. Pamela P. v. Frank S.,* 110 Misc. 2d 978, 443 N.Y.S.2d 343 (1981). As noted in *Smith v. Smith,* 205 Ore. 286, 314, 287 P.2d 572, 584 (1955), "[There is an] area in

---

2. *See* Worrell v. Worrell, supra, 179 Va. at 19, 4 S.E.2d at 346 (idea that the father controlled the family's exchequer).

3. Maryland abolished the immunity in Boblitz v. Boblitz, 296 Md. 242, 462 A.2d 506 (1983).

which the intimacy of the family relationship forbids recovery by the spouses."

(2) Related cases might involve such relatively normal marital exchanges as the "uninvited kiss," *Furey v. Furey,* 193 Va. 727, 733 n.5, 71 S.E.2d 191, 194 n.5 (1952) (quoting from *Wait v. Pierce,* 191 Wis. 202, 209 N.W. 475, 482 (1926) (Eschweiler, J., dissenting), or the nonactionable exchange of harsh words in a domestic quarrel not amounting to a cause of action for divorce on grounds of cruelty:

> In arriving at this conclusion we are mindful that the rights and privileges of husbands and wives with respect to one another are not unaffected by the marriage they have voluntarily undertaken together. Conduct, tortious between two strangers, may not be tortious between spouses because of the mutual concessions implied in the marital relationship.

Lewis v. Lewis, 351 N.E.2d 526, 532 (Mass. 1976) (abrogating interspousal immunity in automobile accident cases).

(3) Some injuries might be based upon simple domestic carelessness, such as a slip and fall due to a newly mopped floor or an unshoveled driveway. Compare *Wright v. Wright,* 213 Va. 177, 191 S.E.2d 223 (1972), where a child was injured by sharp awnings left in the back yard where she played, with *Merenoff v. Merenoff,* 76 N.J. 535, 388 A.2d 951 (1978), which involved injuries through dangerous instrumentalities such as electric hedge trimmers and highly flammable formica cement.

§ 8-5. Special considerations.

Because the parties are married, there has always been a concern that they might fraudulently or collusively bring an action, especially where insurance was involved. This argument was dismissed in *Smith v. Kauffman,* 212 Va. 181, 182, 183 S.E.2d 190, 192 (1971), since judges and juries are accustomed to making similar judgments regarding credibility in many cases. See generally Note, *Litigation Between Husband and Wife,* 79 Harv. L. Rev. 1650, 1659-63 (1966).

CHAPTER 9

Interspousal Contracts

§ 9-1. Historical analysis.

At common law, husband and wife were one, and that one was the husband. The husband held all his wife's property during the marriage, and in return owed her duties of protection and support. *Vigilant Insurance Co. v. Bennett*, 197 Va. 216, 218, 89 S.E.2d 69, 71 (1955) (interspousal tort case). See generally McDowell, *Contracts in the Family*, 45 B.U.L. Rev. 43, 44-45 (1965). The *feme covert*, or woman under coverture, was legally incapable of contracting with anyone. See *Wynn v. Southan's Adm'r & Heirs*, 86 Va. 946, 948-49, 11 S.E. 878 (1890).

The Married Women's Property Acts, Acts of 1876-1877, ch. 329, ended this general disability by providing:

> A married woman may contract and be contracted with and sue and be sued in the same manner and with the same consequences as if she were unmarried, whether the right or liability asserted by or against her accrued heretofore or hereafter.

(Now codified at Va. Code § 55-36).

However, married women were still incapable of contracting with their spouses. This was because of the inherent unity of the marital relationship, *Atwell v. Gordon*, 135 Va. 264, 273-80, 116 S.E. 386, 388-90 (1923), and also because such contracts might either tamper with the marital relationship or lead to its untimely dissolution.

Today, in a series of cases beginning with *Ficklin v. Rixey*, 89 Va. 832, 17 S.E. 325 (1890) (wife could receive land from her husband in exchange for dower rights); see also *Stonebraker v. Hicks*, 94 Va. 618, 27 S.E. 497 (1897) (wife could purchase land from husband); and *De Baun's*

Ex'x v. De Baun, 119 Va. 85, 89 S.E. 239 (1916) (wife could lend money to husband; relationship creditor to debtor), married women are capable of making contracts with their husbands, and vice versa, providing that certain requisites are met. The primary modern concern is the integrity of the marriage relationship.

See generally 9B, Michie's Jurisprudence, *Husband and Wife*, §§ 72-80.

§ 9-2. Validity of interspousal contracts.

Generally speaking, any agreement which does not promote divorce or separation and does not attempt to regulate the essential incidents of the marriage will be valid so long as the usual requisites of contract are met.

In 1986, Virginia became the first state to adopt the Uniform Premarital Agreement Act, 9A U.L.A. 333 (1986 Cum. Supp.), which is now codified at Va. Code § 20-147 et seq. Va. Code § 20-155 gives married persons rights to make similar agreements during marriage, to be effective immediately upon execution.

§ 9-3. Contracts promoting divorce and separation.

The best-known Virginia case dealing with a contract between spouses who were still living together is *Capps v. Capps*, 216 Va. 378, 219 S.E.2d 901 (1975). In *Capps*, the husband agreed to purchase a home jointly with the wife if she would sign the mortgage note and would promise to convey her share to him. In exchange, the husband would deliver a release on the note, should either file a marital action against the other. The wife, who had previously filed a divorce complaint which she had dismissed five days later, signed the agreement. Some time later, the husband filed for and was granted a divorce. The Supreme Court of Virginia upheld the contract since it tended to promote a continuation of the marriage rather than a divorce or separation. *Id.* at 380, 219 S.E.2d at 903. See also *Harlan v. Weatherly*, 183 Va. 49, 54, 31 S.E.2d 263, 265 (1947); *Arrington v. Arrington*, 196 Va. 86, 93, 82 S.E.2d 548, 552 (1954) (separation agreement); 1 J. Bishop on *Marriage, Divorce and Separation* § 1261.

Agreements between husband and wife relating to the adjustment of property rights, even though in contemplation of divorce, are not violative of established public policy unless collusive or made to facilitate a separation or to aid in procuring a divorce. 216 Va. at 380, 219 S.E.2d at 903.

§ 9-4. Contracts attempting to regulate incidents of marriage.

Contracts will not be recognized if they are attempts to change the nature of marriage. Thus, any contract purporting to waive the duty of spousal support during the marriage will be invalid. *In re Marriage of Higgason*, 10 Cal. 3d 476, 516 P.2d 289, 110 Cal. Rptr. 897 (1973) (antenuptial agreement). Likewise, there can be no enforceable contract regarding the performance of the usual marital services, such as entertainment, cooking or laundry. *Matthews v. Matthews*, 2 N.C. App. 143, 146, 162 S.E.2d 697, 698-99 (1968); see generally McDowell, *Contracts in the Family*, 45 B.U.L. Rev. 43, 47-54 (1965). These are performed out of duty or for love and affection. See *Cooper v. Spencer*, 218 Va. 541, 238 S.E.2d 805 (1977) (services performed on egg farm when woman thought she was married). However, if an extraordinary duty is to be performed by a spouse, there may be a contract for consideration. *Department of Human Resources v. Williams*, 130 Ga. App. 149, 202 S.E.2d 504 (1973). See generally *Marriage Contracts for Support and Services: Constitutionality Begins at Home*, 49 N.Y.U. L. Rev. 1161 (1974). However, a Virginia wife was not permitted to recover for "healthcare services necessary" during the last year of her terminally ill husband's life. She tried to recover on an implied contract theory, claiming that the services "were not such as would be required ... as a result of the marital relationship per se" and were "in lieu of provision of same by healthcare professionals." A divided Virginia Supreme Court in *Dade v. Anderson*, 247 Va. 3, 439 S.E.2d 353 (1994), declined to overrule *Alexander v. Kuykendall*, repeating that

> [t]he authorities which allow a recovery on the theory of implied contract seem to us to place the marriage relation on too much of a commercial basis, and to treat the marital relation as any other business association, whereby each expects to obtain material advantage from the marriage. This is not, in our opinion, the true concept of the relation.

Id. at 8, 439 S.E.2d at 356. The dissenting opinions noted that the services involved were beyond normal household duties, and that the public policy against commercialization or disruption of marriage was not furthered when the marriage had terminated through death of a spouse.

As noted in the section regarding antenuptial agreements, contracts purporting to limit the duration of marriage are unenforceable.

Likewise, agreements affecting matters of marital intimacy will not be valid subjects of contract. This would include sexual relations, birth control, and the procreation of children. See generally Comment, *Litigation Between Husband and Wife*, 79 Harv. L. Rev. 1045 (1965). Should the parties disagree about such matters, once they have been married, there may be relief through dissolution of the marriage.

Of course, any contract that would be illegal for another reason, such as an attempt to regulate support of the spouses' children, will not be enforceable.

See generally *Marriage Contracts for Support and Services: Constitutionality Begins at Home*, 49 N.Y.U. L. Rev. 1161 (1974).

§ 9-5. Usual requisites of contract.

Because the parties are husband and wife, they stand in a confidential relationship to one another. McDowell, *Contracts in the Family*, 45 B.U.L. Rev. 43, 59 (1965). Their contracts will be carefully scrutinized to make sure that one party did not have an unfair advantage over the other and that there was mutuality of consideration. *Capps v. Capps*, 216 Va. 378, 381, 219 S.E.2d 901, 903-04 (1975).

Of course there must be agreement between the parties, who must at the time have the mental capacity to contract.

In 1986, Virginia became the first state to adopt the Uniform Premarital Agreement Act, 9A U.L.A. 333 (1986 Cum. Supp.), which is codified at Va. Code §§ 20-147 et seq. Va. Code § 20-155 gives married persons corresponding rights to execute agreements during marriage, and requires the contracts to be in writing and signed by both parties.

See generally Mary Ann Glendon, *The New Family and the New Property* (1981); Lenore Weitzman, *The Marriage Contract* (1981); Marjorie Macguire Schultz, *Contractual Ordering of Marriage: A New Model for State Policy*, 70 Calif. L. Rev. 207 (1982); *Marriage by Contract*, 8 Fam. L.Q. 27 (1974); Judith Younger, *Perspectives on Antenuptial Agreements*, 40 Rutgers L. Rev. 1059 (1988).

CHAPTER 10

Property in the Marital Relationship

§ 10-1. Historical perspective.

The marital rights of spouses in Virginia are the legacy of a common law system in which spouses held property "per tout and not per my," *Vasilion v. Vasilion,* 192 Va. 735, 743, 66 S.E.2d 599 (1951): husband and wife were one, and that one was the husband. When a woman married, the use of all her property belonged to her husband, and she had no control over her property whatsoever. *Edmonds v. Edmonds,* 139 Va. 652, 657, 124 S.E. 415 (1924). Upon his death, she regained the property. The only recompense made to her by the law was the dower right: at the husband's death, she held a life estate in the property, or part of it, if there was issue of the marriage.

Since the time of Jefferson, steps have been taken to ameliorate the inequities inherited from the common law system. The Jeffersonian statute permitted the wife to inherit, if there was no will, on the fourth step: after issue, parents, and siblings of the spouse or their descendants. Spies, *Property Rights of the Surviving Spouse,* 46 Va. L. Rev. 157 (1960). The Married Woman's Property Acts had still greater effect, since they allowed spouses to own their own property while under coverture. *Moreland v. Moreland,* 108 Va. 93, 60 S.E. 730 (1908). See also *Moore v. Glotzbach,* 188 F. Supp. 267, 269 (E.D. Va. 1960). In 1956, spouses were made able to inherit immediately after surviving issue. Va. Code § 64-1. In 1982, the rule was amended by Va. Code § 64-1.1 to allow recovery *before* surviving issue, unless there are surviving issue who are not children of the surviving spouse, who then gets one-third.

The 1990 Legislature abolished the rights of dower and curtesy for property vesting after January 1, 1991. Va. Code § 64.1-19.2. Instead, § 64.1-1 was amended to provide that two-thirds of an intestate decedent's estate shall pass to the intestate's children and to their descendants, and the remaining one-third of such estate shall pass to the intestate's surviving spouse. The surviving share may also claim an elective share of one-third of the testate decedent's augmented estate, if there are children, or one-half, if there are no surviving children. Va. Code § 64.1-16. The definition of "augmented estate" appears in § 64.1-16.1. These statutory shares are barred if the surviving spouse willfully deserts or abandons his or her spouse and the desertion or abandonment continues until the death of the spouse. Va. Code § 64.1-16.3. Finally, the surviving spouse may continue to live in the family residence without payment of rent, taxes, or insurance until that spouse's rights in the principal family residence have been determined and satisfied by an agreement between the parties or a final court decree.

Despite the abolition of dower and curtesy, the Virginia attorney confronts a confusing mosaic of common law and statutory rules, with many exceptions. These are made no less confusing by the equitable distribution law, enacted in 1981, which will be discussed in Chapter 22.

See generally Ann Lacquer Estin, *Love and Obligation: Family Law and the Romance of Economics*, 36 Wm. & Mary L. Rev. 989 (1995); Joan C. Williams, *Married Women and Property*, 1 Va. J. Soc. Pol'y & L. 383 (1994); Glendon, *Marriage and the State: The Withering Away of Marriage*, 62 Va. L. Rev. 663 (1976); Spies, *Property Rights of the Surviving Spouse*, 46 Va. L. Rev. 157 (1960).

§ 10-2. Creation of the tenancy by the entirety.

When real property is conveyed to husband and wife, a deed must specify that a tenancy by the entirety is intended, or a tenancy in common results. Va. Code § 55-20.

For example, a husband and wife owned property as tenants by the entireties. They sold this residence, and the proceeds were used to purchase other real property. When the husband declared bankruptcy, he was unable to claim this second residence exempt as a tenancy by the entirety since the deed did not specify that a tenancy by the entirety was intended, and the proceeds of the sale of the original property lost their character as "proceeds," which could be traced back to the tenancy by the entirety. *In re Manicure,* 29 B.R. 248 (Bankr. 1983).

However, when husband and wife customarily took title as tenants by the entirety, it was reasonable to conclude that the husband acted as the wife's agent when he agreed with a third party that he and the other would jointly bid on property. *Leonard v. Counts,* 221 Va. 582, 272 S.E.2d 190 (1980).

When land was conveyed to two people as tenants by the entirety and they were not married at the time, they held the property as tenants in common even though they were later married. *Vaughan v. McGrew,* 12 Va. Cir. 125 (Chesapeake Co. 1988).

Finally, in *Allen v. Jackson,* 9 Va. Cir. 60 (Nottoway Co. 1987), a woman put a man's name on the deed as co-owner under the false impression that the two had been validly married, and the man died intestate. His personal representative was required to convey back his interest in the property because there was fraud in the procurement of the deed.

§ 10-3. Personalty held by the entireties.

Personalty that is derived from realty held as tenants by the entirety takes on the character of entirety property. For example, a husband and wife owned a home as tenants by the entirety. They sold the home less than twelve months before the husband declared bankruptcy, and the proceeds were held by the wife. The trustee was unable to recover one-half of these proceeds to satisfy the husband's debt since the estate by entireties exists in personalty as well as realty. *Oliver v. Givens, Trustee,* 204 Va. 123, 129 S.E.2d 661 (1963). See also 26 Am. Jur. *Husband and Wife* § 77, pp. 702-03.

Similarly, when a husband owed cabaret taxes, the Internal Revenue Service unsuccessfully sought to collect from rents paid by tenants of husband and wife who held as tenants by the entirety. *Moore v. Glotzbach,* 188 F. Supp. 267 (E.D. Va. 1960).

§ 10-4. Effect on creditors.

When husband and wife own property as tenants by the entirety, the property may not be reached by creditors of either spouse, although it may be available to creditors of both spouses. *Vasilion v. Vasilion,* 192 Va. 735, 742-43, 66 S.E.2d 599 (1951) (citing *Burroughs v. Gorman,* 166 Va.

58, 184 S.E. 174 (1936)). The interest of the wife in entireties property therefore does not pass to the trustee in bankruptcy. *In re Bishop*, 482 F.2d 381, 383 (4th Cir. 1973).

According to the parties' property settlement agreement incorporated into their final divorce decree, Mr. Tribby was to transfer his interest in the jointly owned marital residence to his wife within fifteen days. Although Mrs. Tribby occupied the house following the separation and made payments on the deed of trust, Mr. Tribby never conveyed his interest to her. Instead, he failed to make payments on a loan from the National Bank of Fredericksburg, and the bank obtained a judgment against him. In *Tribby v. Tribby*, 26 Va. Cir. 372 (Spotsylvania Co. 1992), the circuit court found that the property settlement agreement and divorce decree, while binding on the Tribbys, had no effect on third parties. The court reasoned that because the parties held the house as tenants by the entireties, the bank could not reach their home while they were married. After the divorce, however, the bank could extend their judgment lien to Mr. Tribby's interest in the home since the former spouses had become tenants in common. The court noted that Mrs. Tribby could still seek specific performance of the property settlement agreement against Mr. Tribby. She could also obtain damages in an amount equal to the amount of the judgment lien, plus attorney's fees and costs.

§ 10-5. Restriction on conveyances.

When a husband and wife owned property as joint tenants with common law right of survivorship and the husband deserted, the wife conveyed her share to her daughter. The daughter was unable to compel a partition, where the original deed manifestly intended that the portion of the spouse dying should then belong to the cotenant. *Burroughs v. Gorman*, 166 Va. 58, 184 S.E. 174 (1936). This would obviously be true of the spouses as well.

§ 10-6. Division of marital property on divorce.

When spouses who held as tenants by the entirety divorce, their property is converted to a tenancy in common. Va. Code § 20-111.

When the wife then continued to live in the home with the children, while the husband paid alimony and child support, and the wife made insurance and mortgage payments, the wife was able to collect for the sums she had expended, since a cotenant discharging an encumbrance is entitled to a ratable contribution. *Jenkins v. Jenkins,* 211 Va. 797, 180 S.E.2d 516 (1971).

A husband took title to property in his own name that was purchased with the proceeds from the sale of a first home, which was half his wife's. This created a resulting trust in her favor, since no gift by the wife to the husband was shown, even though only an unimproved lot was purchased. *Grubbs v. Grubbs,* 13 Va. Cir. 470 (Henrico Co. 1977).

§ 10-7. Devolution of property upon death.

Where husband and wife were joint owners of a home, and the wife died intestate, leaving her father as her only heir, the husband was unable to seek contribution from her share of the realty for expenses of her last illness, since these were necessaries he had a duty to provide. Nor was he able to recover for funeral expenses since these were his own debt. *Hall v. Stewart,* 135 Va. 384, 116 S.E. 469 (1923).

Money spent by the husband for improvement on the jointly held home was presumed to be a gift for the wife's benefit, even though the couple was estranged. *Norris v. Barbour,* 188 Va. 723, 51 S.E.2d 334 (1949). See also *Eaton v. Davis,* 165 Va. 313, 182 S.E. 229 (1935) (husband not entitled to compensation for improvements, nor wife to accounting for husband's use of home after divorce).

§ 10-8. Defeat of spousal interests.

If a spouse commits a crime in order to inherit the property of the other, he may not profit by the crime, but is rather entitled only to the share held by him otherwise. *Sundin v. Klein,* 221 Va. 232, 269 S.E.2d 787 (1980); Va. Code § 64-1-18 (husband not entitled to whole of property held as tenants by the entirety when he murdered wife; rest of property held in constructive trust). The estate of tenancy by the entireties can be terminated only by the voluntary action of both tenants or the death of one as the result of a cause reasonably contemplated at the time the tenancy is created.

In addition to losing property rights by the commission of crime, a spouse may be barred from enjoying statutory inheritance or dower if she wilfully deserts or abandons her husband, and such desertion continues until his death. Va. Code § 64.1-23; *Brinson v. Metropolitan Life Ins. Co.,* 226 F. Supp. 94 (E.D.N.C. 1963) (not widow for purposes of

Federal Employees' Group Life Insurance Act; parties divorced *a mensa et thoro* on grounds of wife's desertion; wife "married" another).

Similarly, when the husband's physical cruelty forced his wife to leave the marital home, he forfeited his statutory curtesy right to share in her estate upon her death, so that he took nothing since she had not provided for him in her will. *Noland's Executors v. Noland,* 13 Va. Cir. 14 (Fauquier Co. 1987).

Although the husband died intestate during the couple's divorce proceedings in *Sprouse v. Griffin,* 250 Va. 46, 458 S.E.2d 770 (1995), the fund made up of the proceeds from the sale of the marital home became a res over which the divorce court had jurisdiction. The wife could therefore seek a rule on the status of the funds the court held in escrow.

§ 10-9. Dower and curtesy.

The 1990 legislature abolished the rights of dower and curtesy for property vesting after January 1, 1991. Va. Code § 64.1-19.2. Instead, Va. Code § 64.1-1 was amended to provide that two-thirds of an intestate decedent's estate shall pass to the intestate's children and to their descendants, and the remaining one-third of such estate shall pass to the intestate's surviving spouse. The surviving spouse may also claim an elective share of one-third of the testate decedent's augmented estate, if there are children, or one-half, if there are no surviving children. Va. Code § 64.1-16. The definition of "augmented estate" appears in Va. Code § 64.1-16.1. These statutory shares are barred if the surviving spouse willfully deserts or abandons his or her spouse and the desertion or abandonment continues until the death of the spouse. Va. Code § 64.1-16.3. Finally, the surviving spouse may continue to live in the family residence without payment of rent, taxes, or insurance until that spouse's rights in the principal family residence have been determined and satisfied by an agreement between the parties or a final court decree.

Although new dower and curtesy interests are no longer vesting, property conveyed prior to 1991 still retains the incidents of dower and curtesy, so the common law cases are still relevant. For example, when a woman is married, and the husband held property separately, the wife had a dower interest in that property. This meant that upon his death, the surviving wife would have a fee simple estate in the surplus if there were no issue, their descendants who are not children, or their descendants of the surviving spouse, and one-third of the realty, if there were such issue. Va. Code § 64.1-1. There is a life estate in the entire personal property.

Va. Code § 64.1-19. A wife did not obtain a dower interest in the property her husband bought during a bigamous second marriage. Upon his death, his companion acquired his entire estate by right of survivorship, since the couple had purchased the property as "tenants by the entirety." Since the couple was never lawfully married, they took title as joint tenants with right of survivorship. *Funches v. Funches,* 243 Va. 26, 413 S.E.2d 44 (1992).

The husband had similar rights in the wife's separate estate called curtesy, which devolve upon her death. Va. Code § 55-35. Both dower and curtesy were effective only if the spouse has not taken property under a will designed to be in lieu of curtesy (called jointure). Va. Code § 64.1-29.

Where a husband made a postnuptial agreement releasing curtesy and any distributive share in the wife's estate, and the wife released dower, and the wife died intestate with no issue, the husband was not entitled to curtesy since there was no issue but only a foster child, and the postnuptial agreement was valid. *Powell v. Tilson,* 161 Va. 318, 170 S.E. 750 (1933).

Dower rights may be conveyed if property is deeded by husband and wife together, or if the wife conveys her contingent dower rights after the husband disposes of his interest in real estate. Va. Code § 55-40.

Dower rights are cut off by divorce in Virginia. Va. Code §§ 20-107.3 and 20-111 (divorce *a mensa*), even if the divorce is obtained ex parte in another state. *Simons v. Miami Beach First Nat'l Bank,* 381 U.S. 81 (1965).

§ 10-10. Defeating the interest of a spouse.

For some time there has been concern that spouses may, by inter vivos gift or establishment of a trust causa mortis, leave no property for a surviving spouse. See Johnson, *Interspousal Property Rights at Death,* 10 Va. B.A.J. 10 (1984); see also Spies, *Property Rights of the Surviving Spouse,* 46 Va. L. Rev. 157, 164 (1960). The commentators suggest that there should be legislation protecting the public policy in favor of the surviving spouse.

§ 10-11. Separately held property.

Since the Married Woman's Property Acts, both spouses have been able to hold property in their own name.

Women are able to hold property free of curtesy through Va. Code § 55-47, "nothing contained in the previous sections of the chapter shall be construed to prevent the creation of the wife's equitable separate estates." The husband may also hold property free of dower according to *Jacobs v. Meade,* 227 Va. 284, 315 S.E.2d 383 (1984); and Va. Code § 64.1-19.1.

In one case, the husband gave the wife land in Norfolk, upon which an apartment was later built. The couple lived for some years in part of the property, until the wife deserted the husband. She was able to bring a successful ejectment action against the husband, since if the husband has a right to go upon the wife's premises and jointly occupy them with her, it is solely because he has a right of access to *her* because of his marital rights, and not a right of access to her property. *Edmonds v. Edmonds,* 139 Va. 652, 660, 662-63, 124 S.E. 415 (1924). See also *Moreland v. Moreland,* 108 Va. 93, 60 S.E. 730 (1908); *Norris v. Barbour,* 188 Va. 723, 51 S.E.2d 334 (1949). Even though a husband solely owned the marital home, he could not evict his wife when they were in joint possession of the home. In *Singer v. Singer,* 30 Va. Cir. 80 (Fairfax Co. 1993), the court found that "public policy requires a right of access by one spouse to the other during a marriage, and a limited right to go upon, and remain upon the property exists so long as there is a joint occupancy." *Id.* at 82.

§ 10-12. Crimes against property of spouse.

Since it is possible for a spouse to hold property separately, it is also possible for one spouse to commit a crime against the property of the other spouse. See, e.g., *Stewart v. Commonwealth,* 219 Va. 887, 252 S.E.2d 329 (1979) (larceny by estranged husband of wife's station wagon); *Knox v. Commonwealth,* 225 Va. 504, 304 S.E.2d 4 (1983) (burglary of estranged wife's apartment).

CHAPTER 11

Crimes Involving Spouses

§ 11-1. Historical perspective.

At common law, a man was not subject to prosecution for many actions that would have been crimes if the victim had not been his wife. This was because in law the two spouses were one, and he was the one. The system was not reciprocal. Since the use of all property of the wife belonged to the husband during coverture, it was impossible to steal from her. *Stewart v. Commonwealth*, 219 Va. 887, 889, 252 S.E.2d 329, 331 (1979). One ancient commentator, 1 M. Hale, *The History of the Pleas of the Crown* 629 (1736), fostered the doctrine that since by marrying him the wife had given her consent to sexual intercourse, she could not be a victim of nonconsensual intercourse or rape by her husband. Part of the husband's duties as a spouse were to give his wife moderate chastisement and correction, which could involve beating with a stick so long as the punishment inflicted was reasonable. Pollack & Maitland, *A History of the English Law* 436.

Even a "reasonable" chastisement would be criminal behavior today. A number of developments have changed the common law concepts. Since the wife is now able to hold property in her own name, the husband may commit larceny from her. Certainly since the advent of no-fault divorce, it is possible for a wife to maintain a separate domicile with no access given to the husband. During this period of separation, nonconsensual intercourse will be rape. *Weishaupt v. Commonwealth*, 227 Va. 389, 315 S.E.2d 847 (1984). However, the termination of the marriage must be known by the husband. *Kizer v. Commonwealth*, 228 Va. 256, 321 S.E.2d 291 (1984); Va. Code § 18.2-67.2. Although there are no recent cases, the doctrine of corporal punishment of a wife has probably changed as well with her legal equality of status to her husband, so that there will be more prosecutions for spousal abuse or assault that would have gone unnoticed before. At common law, the woman was to obey the husband in all things, so that if she acted under his direction in committing a crime, she was his agent and he the guilty principal. She will now be guilty in her own right unless coerced by threat of physical violence. Indeed, the defense of coercion may be taking a new form that follows the modifications to the doctrine of self-defense occasioned by emerging concepts of long-term inter-spousal abuse. See *State v. Lambert,* 312 S.E.2d 31 (W. Va. 1984).

§ 11-2. Assault and corporal punishment of wives.

For some time it has been possible for a wife to complain of the assault of the husband. See, e.g., *Counts v. Counts,* 221 Va. 151, 266 S.E.2d 895 (1980).

Although at common law a husband could punish his wife, if the blows inflicted were not reasonable, he was subject to punishment for assault. *Bradley v. State,* 1 Miss. (Walker) 156 (1824); Pollack & Maitland, *A History of the English Law* 436. For the Virginia approach to a similar topic, see *Wimbrow v. Wimbrow,* 208 Va. 141, 156 S.E.2d 598 (1967) (husband divorced for constructive desertion when he severely beat his wife for taking money from his wallet and she left the marital home).

As the Virginia Supreme Court noted in *Weishaupt v. Commonwealth,* 227 Va. 389, 315 S.E.2d 847 (1984):

> The trend in the recent cases which have analyzed problems of spousal rape is in accord with the trend in recent Virginia cases touching upon the property rights of women. Both sets of cases point to an increasingly recognized role of the autonomy and independence of women. Both sets of cases suggest a break with the ancient rules that cast women in a subservient posture.

Virginia has enacted a criminal prohibition against spousal abuse. Va. Code § 18.2-57.2. Likewise, a husband or former husband may be convicted of stalking a wife or former wife. *Woolfolk v. Commonwealth,* 18 Va. App. 840, 447 S.E.2d 530 (1994). Va. Code § 18.2-60.3 survived constitutional challenges of vagueness and overbreadth in *Woolfolk.*

Although Virginia does not recognize the so-called battered wife syndrome as a defense to a charge of homicide, the husband's past history of criminal assaults upon the wife would be admissible to prove justifiable self-defense. *Commonwealth v. Hackett,* 32 Va. Cir. 338 (Westmoreland Co. 1994).

§ 11-3. Criminal sexual assault.

Although at common law a woman's consent to her husband's sexual advances could not be retracted, 1 M. Hale, *The History of the Pleas of the Crown* 629 (1736), women today, if living separately from their husbands, have a right to be protected from their society or unwanted intercourse. *Weishaupt v. Commonwealth,* 227 Va. 389, 315 S.E.2d 847 (1984). See also *State v. Smith,* 85 N.J. 193, 202, 426 A.2d 38, 42-43 (1981).

However, the termination of the marriage must be known by the husband; the woman's conduct cannot be equivocal. *Kizer v. Commonwealth,* 228 Va. 256, 321 S.E.2d 291 (1984). In *Kizer,* the husband's conviction was reversed even though on the particular occasion involved, the wife's lack of consent was obvious.

The Virginia no-fault divorce statute, Va. Code § 20-91(9), embodies a legislative endorsement of a woman's unilateral right to withdraw an implied consent to marital sex. The very scheme of the statute contemplates a voluntary withdrawal, by either spouse, from the marital relationship — a de facto termination of the marriage contract. *Weishaupt,* 227 Va. at 403, 315 S.E.2d at 854. The *Weishaupt* court declined, *id.* at 404, 315 S.E.2d at 855, to formulate a rule that would also apply when spouses were living together in a less obvious suspension of the marital relationship; any change must come from Virginia legislature.

The legislature responded to *Weishaupt* by enacting statutes providing for penalties for marital sexual assault as well as special procedures for hearings in such cases. Va. Code §§ 18.2-57.2, 18.2-67.2:1, 19.2-219.1, 19.2-281.2. Marital sexual assault under Va. Code § 18.2-67.2:1 must be reported within 60 days of the offense. The terms of a previous court order prohibiting a husband from having contact with his wife and evidence of previous bad assaults the husband committed against his wife were appropriately admitted into evidence according to *Melville v. Commonwealth,* 1994 Va. App. LEXIS 705 (not designated for publication).

See generally Waterman, *For Better or for Worse: Marital Rape,* 15 Northern Ky. L. Rev. 611 (1988); Comment, *The Marital Relationship Exemption,* 52 N.Y.U. L. Rev. 306 (1977).

§ 11-4. Theft.

When a wife is living separate and apart from her husband, the husband has no right of access to her society and conjugal relations that would allow him to break into her home to commit assault and battery. *Knox v. Commonwealth,* 225 Va. 504, 304 S.E.2d 4 (1983). This is because his "right of consortium is subordinate to the wife's right of exclusive possession." *Id.* at 507, 304 S.E.2d at 6. Neither his right to curtesy nor his traditional marital rights give him any more power or authority over his wife's property than a total stranger would possess. *Id.* (quoting from *Edmonds v. Edmonds,* 139 Va. 652, 124 S.E. 415, 417 (1924)). A husband may also be guilty of larceny of his wife's chattels taken without her permission. *Stewart v. Commonwealth,* 219 Va. 887, 252 S.E.2d 329 (1979).

§ 11-5. Conspiracy.

Because husband and wife were one, it was conceptually and legally impossible at common law for them to join together in a criminal activity requiring two persons, such as conspiracy. See authorities cited in *United States v. Dege,* 364 U.S. 51, 53 (1959). Two of the leading cases collected there, *Dawson v. United States,* 10 F.2d 106 (9th Cir. 1926); and *People v. Miller,* 82 Cal. 107, 22 P. 934 (1889), have since been overruled. *United States v. Dege,* 364 U.S. 51 (1959), *People v. Pierce,* 61 Cal. 2d 879, 40 Cal. Rptr. 845, 395 P.2d 893 (1964). *Dege* noted that the medieval status of women should not obfuscate the Court's view of the conspiracy statute, *id.* at 52, and that imposing the culpability for a couple's criminal enterprise would not lead to unacceptable risks of disharmony between them. The Court rejected the notion that a wife must be presumed to act under the coercive influence of her husband. *Id.* at 53. See also *Commonwealth v. Lawson,* 454 Pa. 23, 309 A.2d 391 (1973) (husband and wife could be convicted of conspiracy to sell illegal drugs).

However, it may still be possible to prevent conviction of a spouse for both conspiracy to commit and commission of one substantive offense when the activity that is the object of the conspiracy in itself requires agreement between two persons, such as in the case of bigamy or adultery. This doctrine is called "Wharton's Rule," and was followed in Virginia in the case of *Stewart v. Commonwealth,* 225 Va. 473, 303 S.E.2d 877 (1983) (no conspiracy to pander where the only alleged coconspirators were prostitutes, and the statute said that pandering required a prostitute). Although *Dege* and *Stewart* involved statutes, their analytical patterns are clearly applicable to common law versions of conspiracy, such as bigamy. Of course, Wharton's Rule does not apply where the conspiracy to commit bigamy, adultery, etc. is joined by a third person. See, e.g., *Gebardi v. United States,* 287 U.S. 112, 122 (1932); *People v. MacMullen,* 134 Cal. App. 81, 24 P.2d 794 (1933) (conspiracy conviction of husband and wife reversed when alleged coconspirators acquitted).

See generally 16 Am. Jur. 2d *Conspiracy* § 12, 41 Am. Jur. 2d *Husband and Wife* § 2.

§ 11-6. Crimes of omission.

Several cases from other states have considered the question of whether a spouse is criminally responsible for failure to provide aid to a dying husband or wife who does not wish such aid. The modern cases, where the decision not to be helped is made while the spouse is capable of making an intelligent choice, hold that the spouse is not so responsible. See, e.g., *Commonwealth v. Konz,* 498 Pa. 639, 450 A.2d 638 (1982); *People v. Robbins,* 83 A.D.2d 271, 443 N.Y.S.2d 1016 (1981).

§ 11-7. Agency or coercion.

At common law, the wife was under the domination of her husband. If he ordered her to commit a crime other than murder or treason, he would be responsible criminally and she would not be guilty since she was merely his instrumentality to commit the crime. *Brown v. Commonwealth,* 135 Va. 480, 115 S.E. 542 (1923); see generally Perkins on *Criminal Law* 909 (2d ed. 1969); 4 Blackstone *Commentaries* *28.

The case of *Wampler v. Norton,* 134 Va. 606, 113 S.E. 733 (1922), modified the rule, so that the presence of the husband of a married woman during her commission of a criminal act no longer excused the wife from responsibility. The modified rule was that the presence of the husband merely raised a prima facie presumption that his wife was acting under his coercion and control. Within a year, the Virginia Supreme Court, in *Brown v. Commonwealth,* 135 Va. 480, 115 S.E. 542 (1923), criticized even this rule on the basis of the change in status of women toward greater independence and capacity. *Id.* at 484, 115 S.E. at 543.

The modern rule is that a wife, like any other adult, is competent to make decisions and therefore capable both of committing and of refusing to commit a crime. She no longer has the defense of her coverture. The nearest related defense is that of compulsion: reasonably acting out of fear of imminent death or grievous bodily injury. See, e.g., *State v. Lambert,* 312 S.E.2d 31 (W. Va. 1984) (wife's conviction for welfare fraud reversed where corroborated evidence showed that she might have acted out of fear of physical abuse by her husband).

See generally Perkins on *Criminal Law* 954 (2d ed. 1969).

CHAPTER 12

Testimony by Spouses

§ 12-1. Introduction.

Although the historical immunity from tort and many criminal actions has largely been abolished in Virginia, attorneys may come across other types of immunities when spouses are involved in lawsuits. These are testimonial immunities and marital privileges.

At common law, the spouse was unable to testify at all, since in law the spouses were one, and there was an inability to give evidence for or against one's self. *Trammel v. United States,* 445 U.S. 40, 44 (1980); *Hoge & Hutchinson v. Turner,* 96 Va. 624, 629, 32 S.E. 291 (1899).

The more modern position has been that the spouse is competent to testify against a spouse without that spouse's permission. This is not a requirement of federal constitutional law, *Trammel v. United States,* 445 U.S. 40 (1980), but is found at Va. Code § 19.2-271.2, which is more protective of individual rights. Each witness is capable of testifying in favor of a spouse at any time, but spouses may testify without the other's permission in criminal actions only where the witness or the child of either the witness or the spouse was a victim, in actions between the spouses, or when the marriage has been dissolved by divorce before trial. The status of the marriage at the time of trial determines the competency. *Stewart v. Commonwealth,* 219 Va. 887, 252 S.E.2d 329 (1979).

In addition to the incompetence to testify, there is also the matter of the marital privilege. If a matter is communicated to the other spouse by virtue of the marital relationship, *Menefee v. Commonwealth,* 189 Va. 900, 912, 55 S.E.2d 9, 15 (1949), it may not be disclosed without permission of the spouse. This is true even though the parties are divorced at time of trial if the privileged communication took place while the spouses were married.

The spousal privilege exists because of the public policy encouraging free communication between husband and wife. See, e.g., *Hawkins v. United States,* 358 U.S. 74, 79 (1958); *Wolfe v. United States,* 291 U.S. 7, 14 (1934):

> That would render susceptible of and expose to public observation and knowledge all confidential conduct, transactions and acts not consisting of spoken or written words, which the continued tranquility, integrity and confidence of their intimate relation demands to be shielded and protected by the inviolate veil of the marital sanctuary.

Menefee v. Commonwealth, 189 Va. 900, 912, 55 S.E.2d 9, 15 (1949).

See generally Friend, *The Law of Evidence in Virginia* §§ 57, 64 (2d ed. 1983); "Spousal Privileges," in Stone & Liebman, ed., *Testimonial Privileges* (1983).

§ 12-2. Need for valid marriage.

The 1996 legislature amended Va. Code Ann. § 19.2-271.2 to revoke the spouse's immunity from adverse testimony. The witness spouse still has the privilege to refuse to testify, in accordance with federal law. The witness spouse may be compelled to testify in cases where the state prosecutes one of the spouses for criminal offense against the other or the child of either, where either is charged with forgery of the other's name or with certain sexual offenses such as child abuse, sodomy, and incest. This changes the common law doctrine. For example, under the former rule, if the parties were not married at the time the crime was committed, but they married before trial, one spouse could not be compelled to give testimony against the other. *Stevens v. Commonwealth,* 207 Va. 371, 150 S.E.2d 229 (1966) (assault by man against woman; marriage after indictment).

In any event, when a marriage was void, the privilege against adverse spousal testimony did not apply. *Leigh v. Commonwealth,* 192 Va. 583, 595, 66 S.E.2d 586 (1951) (woman whose marriage to defendant was void apparently because it was contracted too soon after his divorce was allowed to testify against him at trial for killing her father, even though the wife had believed in good faith that marriage was valid). See also

United States v. Neeley, 475 F.2d 1136 (4th Cir. 1973) (for both immunity and privilege).

Although there are no Virginia cases on the subject, cases from other jurisdictions hold that the immunity does not exist for unmarried co-habitants. See, e.g., *United States v. Neeley,* 475 F.2d 1136 (4th Cir. 1973); *People v. Torre,* 90 Misc. 2d 358, 360, 394 N.Y.S.2d 546, 547 (1977); *People v. Delph,* 94 Cal. App. 3d 411, 156 Cal. Rptr. 422 (1979).

§ 12-3. Action against spouse or child of spouse.

The 1996 legislature amended Va. Code Ann. § 19.2-271.2 to revoke the spouse's immunity from adverse testimony. The witness spouse still has the privilege to refuse to testify, in accordance with federal law. The witness spouse may be compelled to testify in cases where the state prosecutes one of the spouses for criminal offense against the other or the child of either, where either is charged with forgery of the other's name or with certain sexual offenses. Even when the privilege was still in effect, there was an exception for alleged crimes against family members. For example, in *Osborne v. Commonwealth,* 214 Va. 691, 204 S.E.2d 289 (1974), the defendant's wife was permitted to testify against him in his trial for the rape of her daughter. See generally Annot., 93 A.L.R.3d 1018.

The privilege applied, and a husband could prevent his wife from testifying, in a criminal proceeding for assault where the shot fired by the husband was aimed at the wife but hit another. The exception to the statute was limited to the prosecution by one spouse for an offense committed by the other. *Jenkins v. Commonwealth,* 219 Va. 764, 250 S.E.2d 763 (1979). However, it need not be a crime against the person. A spouse could testify adversely when the crime was against the testifying spouse's property. *Brown v. Commonwealth,* 223 Va. 601, 292 S.E.2d 319 (1982). However, a wife could not testify at her estranged husband's arson trial without his consent. *Creech v. Commonwealth,* 242 Va. 385, 410 S.E.2d 650 (1991). Although her furniture was destroyed in the fire at the marital home and she testified that he had threatened to "torch" her property when she told him she was leaving him, he was not charged with nor tried for an offense committed against her. The indictment and trial was for arson of the home, which was owned solely by him.

See generally Comment, *Confidential Communication Privileges under Federal and Virginia Law,* 13 U. Rich. L. Rev. 593 (1979).

§ 12-4. Testimony following separation or divorce.

The privilege did not end when the parties separated. *State v. Freeman,* 302 N.C. 591, 276 S.E.2d 450, 455 n.2 (1981), and cases cited therein. However, once the parties divorced, whether *a vinculo, Menefee v. Commonwealth,* 189 Va. 900, 55 S.E.2d 9 (1949) (confidential communications case, but wife allowed to testify), or *a mensa, Stewart v. Commonwealth,* 219 Va. 887, 252 S.E.2d 329, 333 (1979), the privilege was no longer in effect. In Stewart, a wife was allowed to testify against the husband she had divorced *a mensa* in his trial for stealing her automobile. The Virginia Supreme Court reasoned that "[w]hatever vestige of marital harmony might have remained to be protected by Stewart's exercise of his right to eliminate Mrs. Stewart as a witness had been thoroughly disrupted, if not totally destroyed, by the entry of the *a mensa* decree."

§ 12-5. What constitutes a privileged communication.

In *Menefee v. Commonwealth,* 189 Va. 900, 55 S.E.2d 9 (1949), a wife testified at her husband's murder trial that he had appeared nervous on the night of the crime, and had placed a gun (later found to be the murder weapon) on the mantel, and had "messed around" with the lid of the car trunk. He also asked her to drive him to the vicinity of the crime several times. These actions and gestures were found to be privileged communications. *Id.* at 912, 55 S.E.2d at 15:

> The immunity and ban of the statute applies to and includes all information or knowledge privately imparted and made known by one spouse to the other by virtue of and in consequence of the marital relation through conduct, acts, signs, and spoken or written words.

However, a wife was allowed to testify concerning the beating her husband had given her, for it did not impart knowledge or information. *Osborne v. Commonwealth,* 214 Va. 691, 204 S.E.2d 289, 290 (1974).

§ 12-6. Waiver of the privilege.

The party who could otherwise claim the privilege may waive it by asking the party to testify in favor of him or herself regarding a particular subject matter. *Osborne v. Commonwealth,* 214 Va. 691, 204 S.E.2d 289 (1974) (waiver by defense attorney's questions on cross-examination).

When a defendant at his murder trial adopted the statement made by his wife to a sheriff, he could not claim that her version of the events in question was inadmissible, since his adoption of her words made them his own. His objection to her testimony prevented her from being examined as a witness at trial. *Shiflett v. Commonwealth,* 447 F.2d 50, 58 (4th Cir. 1971), *cert. denied,* 405 U.S. 994 (1972).

The legislature placed upon the commonwealth the burden of first obtaining the consent of the spouse before it will be allowed to call the adverse spousal witness. *Wilson v. Commonwealth,* 157 Va. 962, 968, 162 S.E. 15 (1932).

§ 12-7. Effect of the privilege.

If a spouse witness elects not to testify, or is prevented from testifying by his or her spouse, no comment may be made by opposing counsel regarding the failure to testify. Va. Code § 19-271.2. If such a comment is made a conviction may be reversed. *Jones v. Commonwealth,* 218 Va. 732, 736-37, 240 S.E.2d 526 (1978).

CHAPTER 13

Necessaries

§ 13-1. Introduction.

In common law, the husband was responsible for his wife's support. He was entitled to the use of all her property during coverture as well as her services and consortium. If she was injured, he could sue the tortfeasor for actual damages and also for loss of companionship, sexual attention, and other services. A woman was unable to make contracts while married, but she could purchase goods if her husband did not supply her the necessaries of life: food, clothing, shelter, and medical care. *Hall v. Stewart,* 135 Va. 384, 165 S.E. 469 (1923). In such cases, the third party merchant or professional had a cause of action against the husband. *Richmond Ry. & Elec. Co. v. Bowles,* 92 Va. 738, 24 S.E. 388 (1896). This is the doctrine of necessaries.

Even though the right to recover for loss of consortium was abolished by statute in 1919, the husband was still liable for his wife's necessaries. *Floyd v. Miller,* 190 Va. 303, 307, 57 S.E.2d 114 (1950).

The modern developments of the doctrine of necessaries in Virginia involve its abolition in 1983 in the case of *Schilling v. Bedford County Mem. Hosp.,* 225 Va. 539, 303 S.E.2d 905 (1983), on the basis of unconstitutional gender discrimination, and its reinstatement in 1984 in Va. Code § 55-37, which makes *either* spouse liable for the necessary expenses of the other.

§ 13-2. What is necessary.

Generally speaking, food, clothing, shelter, and medical care must be provided to one's spouse. *Richmond Ry. & Elec. Co. v. Bowles,* 92 Va. 738, 24 S.E. 388 (1896). The degree of luxury required varies with the affluence of the couple. Cf. *Burton v. Commonwealth,* 109 Va. 800, 63 S.E. 464, 466 (1909) (criminal nonsupport). For example, a car may well

121

be a necessary item in today's society, with its reliance upon private transportation. See generally Annot., 56 A.L.R.3d 1335 (for child). One famous case holds that a fur coat was necessary for a wealthy wife. *Louis Berman Co. v. Dahlberg,* 336 Ill. App. 233, 83 N.E.2d 380 (1948) (under a statute permitting recovery for "family expenses," which may be broader than necessaries). However, elective surgery, such as a voluntary abortion, would not be the foundation for such recovery. *Anderson v. Akron Mem. Hosp.,* 68 Ohio Misc. 114, 428 N.E.2d 472 (1981). A recent case holds that the wife was responsible for her husband's legal expenses at trial, although the criminal incident occurred before their marriage. *United States v. O'Neill,* 478 F. Supp. 852 (E.D. Pa. 1979).

§ 13-3. Reimbursement from estate.

Once a necessary service has been provided a spouse, the responsible party cannot successfully sue for reimbursement from either the spouse, the committee appointed for the spouse, *Floyd v. Miller,* 190 Va. 303, 309, 57 S.E.2d 114 (1950), or the estate of the deceased spouse. *Hall v. Stewart,* 135 Va. 384, 389, 116 S.E. 469 (1923).

§ 13-4. Necessity for a valid marriage.

The doctrine depends upon at least the appearance of a valid marriage. If the parties have gone through a ceremony and are living together apparently as husband and wife, third party creditors can recover payment for necessaries even though the marriage turns out to be void. *Abrams v. Trasler,* 244 Ill. App. 533 (1927); *Frank v. Carter,* 219 N.Y. 35, 113 N.E. 549 (1952).

If the parties divorce, the doctrine is no longer in effect. *Hess v. Slutsky,* 224 Ill. App. 419 (1922); *Kleefield v. Funtanellas,* 201 N.Y.S.2d 907 (1960). However, if the parties have separated, there is no longer a family in fact, so a husband will not be liable for his wife's purchases. *Schlesinger v. Keifer,* 30 Ill. App. 253 (1889), *aff'd,* 131 Ill. 104, 22 N.E. 814 (1889). The duty continues where one spouse has abandoned the other without just cause, *Mihalcoe v. Holub,* 130 Va. 425, 429, 107 S.E. 704 (1921), unless the deserting spouse is the one seeking the support.

See generally Annot., 24 A.L.R. 1480; Annot., 11 A.L.R.4th 1160; Annot., 60 A.L.R.2d 7, 41 C.J.S. *Husband and Wife* §§ 307, 309, 355; 41 Am. Jur. *Husband and Wife* § 348; 9B Michie's Jurisprudence *Husband and Wife* § 21.

CHAPTER 14

Use of Maiden Name and Acquisition of Domicile

§ 14-1. Use of maiden name.
§ 14-2. Acquisition of separate domicile.

§ 14-1. Use of maiden name.

A. Introduction. In Virginia, a woman may change her married name to her maiden name while married so long as: (1) no fraud is being perpetrated; (2) her husband consents; and (3) minor children will bear the husband's surname. *In re Strikwerda,* 216 Va. 470, 220 S.E.2d 245 (1975). She might also continue to use her maiden name after she marries. *In re Strikwerda,* 216 Va. 470, 220 S.E.2d at 246 (1975) (citing *Stuart v. Board of Supvrs.,* 295 A.2d 223, 225-27 (Md. 1972)).

B. Limitations on use of maiden name. Flowers v. Cain, 218 Va. 234, 237 S.E.2d 111 (1977), indicated that where the parties were divorced the custodial parent had no right to change their children's names to match her new husband's surname. This decision was based upon the need for the children to maintain the strongest relationship possible with their divorced father. The need for a lack of a disruptive effect on the family is made clear in *In re Strikwerda,* 216 Va. 470, 473, 220 S.E.2d 245, 247 (1975), where the court specifically notes that the husband has consented in each case to the name change and it has been agreed between the spouses that any children born of the marriage will bear the husband's surname.

See generally Annot., 92 A.L.R.3d 1091.

§ 14-2. Acquisition of separate domicile.

At common law the domicile of a married woman was necessarily that of her husband, since the parties were "one flesh" and the wife did not have an independent legal capacity. *Commonwealth v. Rutherfoord,* 160 Va. 524, 530-31, 169 S.E. 909, 915 (1933). This disability was removed in *Commonwealth,* where the wife was held not liable for Virginia taxes although her husband was domiciled in the state and the parties maintained an amicable relationship, since she had retained from before the marriage a separate domicile in New York. This is one of the leading cases in the

United States on this subject. See Restatement of Laws, Conflict of Laws, Second § 21.

This would of necessity be true where the parties had separated pursuant to obtaining a no-fault divorce. *Williamson v. Osenton,* 232 U.S. 619 (1914); cf. *Knox v. Commonwealth,* 225 Va. 504, 506, 304 S.E.2d 4, 6 (1983).

CHAPTER 15

Torts Involving Parent and Child

§ 15-1. Introduction.

At common law, the father held all the property for his children. He owed them support, protection, see *Flippo v. Commonwealth,* 122 Va. 854, 861, 94 S.E. 771, 773 (1918), discipline and education, both secular and religious. In return, the child owed his father his earnings, *Fletcher v. Taylor,* 344 F.2d 93, 95 (4th Cir. 1965); 14A Michie's Jurisprudence *Parent and Child* § 15, obedience, *Cribbins v. Markwood,* 54 Va. (13 Gratt.) 495, 506 (1856) (dicta), respect, and, by statute, care in his old age. This family system was based primarily on the incapacity of children to make decisions, and their inability to defend themselves from enemies in armed combat.

The rules regarding relationships between parent and child, and between the child and the outside world, have been slow to change despite the increasing individual rights of minors. One major area of change in tort law stems from to the universal presence of automobile insurance.

See generally Katz & Schroeder, *Disobeying a Father's Voice: A Comment on Commonwealth v. Brasher,* 57 Mass L.Q. 43 (1971); Zainaldin, *The Emergence of a Modern American Family Law,* 73 Nw. U.L. Rev. 1038 (1979).

§ 15-2. Intrafamilial immunity.

Although parents were not immune from their children's suits at common law, in this country the judicially created doctrine arose in the late 19th century. *Hewlett v. George,* 68 Miss. 703, 9 So. 885 (1891). In

Virginia it was adopted in the case of *Norfolk Southern Railroad v. Gretakis,* 162 Va. 597, 600, 174 S.E. 841, 842 (1934). Together with interspousal immunity, the doctrine has been receding in many states. See, e.g., *Goller v. White,* 20 Wis. 2d 402, 122 N.W.2d 193 (1963); *Gibson v. Gibson,* 3 Cal. 3d 914, 92 Cal. Rptr. 288, 479 P.2d 648 (1971) (and cases cited therein); Restatement (Second) of Torts § 895G; see generally *Defining the Parent's Duty After Rejection of Parent-Child Immunity,* 33 Vand. L. Rev. 775 (1980).

In Virginia, the immunity persists except in cases of automobile accidents, *Smith v. Kauffman,* 212 Va. 181, 186, 183 S.E.2d 190, 194 (1971), or where the relationship of parent and child is purely incidental to the injury: for example, in cases of common carrier, *Worrell v. Worrell,* 174 Va. 11, 26-27, 4 S.E.2d 343, 349-50 (1939), and master and servant, *Norfolk Southern Railroad v. Gretakis,* 162 Va. 597, 600, 174 S.E. 841, 842 (1934).

The immunity stems from the reluctance of courts to disturb family tranquility, their hesitation to second-guess parental decisionmaking and discipline, *Worrell v. Worrell,* 174 Va. 11, 19, 4 S.E.2d 343, 346 (1939), and their concern about collusion. Generally, so long as the parent is acting in the usual parental role with respect to the actions in question, the doctrine obtains. *Wright v. Wright,* 213 Va. 177, 179, 191 S.E.2d 223, 225 (1972); see generally Note, 7 U. Rich. L. Rev. 571 (1973); Note, *Virginia's Intrafamily Immunity Decisions: What Public Policy Giveth, Will the Insurance Policy Taketh Away?,* 22 Cath. U.L. Rev. 167 (1972).

In other jurisdictions, there has been another exception carved for cases in which the action of the parent destroyed the family unit and was so outrageous an intentional tort as to place the parent outside the usual role. See *Mahnke v. Moore,* 197 Md. 61, 77 A.2d 923 (1951); cf. *Korman v. Carpenter,* 216 Va. 86, 216 S.E.2d 195 (1975) (before abolition of interspousal immunity, action maintainable by wife's estate against husband's committee for her murder). This exception is also suggested by the Virginia case of *Brumfield v. Brumfield,* 194 Va. 577, 583, 74 S.E.2d 170, 174 (1953), which mentioned that the result of immunity barring an action despite the parent's grossly negligent driving might be different if an intentional wrong were charged.

There is certainly a reason for a continued refusal to hear tort cases brought by children regarding parent's failure to provide support, see *Yost v. Yost,* 172 Md. 128, 134, 190 A. 753, 756 (1937), or where institutionalized children brought suit for their neglect. Such cases inevitably involve exercises of parental judgment, and if the conduct is extreme, the state provides other relief through nonsupport or neglect and abuse proceedings. *Burnett v. Wahl*, 284 Or. 705, 588 P.2d 1105 (1978); see generally *Defining the Parent's Duty After Rejection of Parent-Child Immunity*, 33 Vand. L. Rev. 775 (1980).

See generally *Intrafamilial Immunity*, 21 Wm. & Mary L. Rev. 273 (1979); and Sandra L. Haley, *The Parental Tort Immunity Doctrine: Is it a Defensible Defense?* 30 U. Rich. L. Rev. 575 (1996).

§ 15-3. Wrongful life and birth.

Until very recently a suit against a doctor for negligently allowing a child to be born would have been unthinkable, since life was always preferable to nonlife, and the joy of being a parent was held to outweigh any of the inconvenience or expenses of an unwanted birth, or the pain and suffering of parenting a handicapped or terminally ill child. *Gleitman v. Cosgrove*, 49 N.J. 22, 227 A.2d 689 (1967). With the advent of effective means of sterilization and voluntary abortion, there have been numerous suits by parents or children against physicians allegedly negligent in failing to give appropriate advice or cautions, or failing to competently perform surgical or diagnostic care. Virginia follows the majority rule, which allows a medical malpractice action for not preventing pregnancy or for failing to terminate an unwanted pregnancy. Damages will be limited to medical expenses, pain and suffering, and lost wages for a reasonable period. Compensation may be for harm directly resulting from a negligently performed abortion, the continuing pregnancy, and the ensuing childbirth, as well as for causally related emotional distress. *Miller v. Johnson*, 231 Va. 177, 343 S.E.2d 301, 305 (1986). However, recompense does not include the costs of rearing a reasonably healthy child to majority, since damages in such cases are not capable of determination with any reasonable certainty. *Id.* at 307.

Cases brought by children complaining that they should never have been born have been unsuccessful in most jurisdictions, excepting California, *Turpin v. Sortini*, 31 Cal. 3d 220, 643 P.2d 954, 182 Cal. Rptr. 337 (1982), and Washington, *Harbeson v. Parke Davis*, 98 Wash. 2d 460, 656 P.2d 483 (1983). However, parents have been able to recover when their offspring would not have been born handicapped, *Procanik v. Cillo*, 97 N.J. 339, 478 A.2d 755 (1984), or seriously ill, *Schroeder v. Perkel*, 87 N.J. 53, 432 A.2d 834 (1981), absent the physician's negligence. See also *Glascock v. Laserna,* 30 Va. Cir. 366 (Spotsylvania Co. 1993).

One Virginia case on the subject, *Burger v. Naccash,* 223 Va. 406, 290 S.E.2d 825 (1982), involved negligence on the part of the supervising physician whose laboratory technician mixed up two patients' blood samples, with the result that the plaintiffs were assured that their expected child would not suffer from the inevitably fatal genetic Tay Sachs' disease. Since they did not have correct information, the parents did not abort the child, who was ultimately born with Tay Sachs'. The court allowed recovery for medical expenses and the pain and suffering the parents suffered watching their daughter become ill and die at less than three years of age. Funeral expenses and a burial marker were held not to be consequences of the doctor's negligence. Of course, neither was the disease itself, or the consequent death. The statute of limitations for a wrongful birth action, where the physical problems were not caused by the defendants, is the two-year period prescribed by Va. Code § 8.01-243(A) for actions for personal injuries, not those specified by § 8.01-243(B), which allows five years for injuries to property, including actions by a parent for "expenses of curing or attempting to cure such infant from the result of personal injury or loss of services." *Glascock v. Laserna,* 247 Va. 108, 111, 439 S.E.2d 380, 382 (1994). The plaintiffs were attempting to recover for medical expenses incurred after defendants negligently failed to inform them of the fetus' abnormalities. Their action was not an action for injury to property, defendants did not cause "personal injury" to the child, and the plaintiffs did not suffer loss of services because of defendants' acts.

Where a sonogram would have shown that the plaintiff's baby had spina bifida and hydrocephalus, viability of the fetus was not a defense to an action when the physician failed to perform the sonogram or advise plaintiff that she could obtain an abortion. *Sawyer v. Childress,* 12 Va. Cir. 184 (City of Norfolk 1988).

See generally Comment, *A Rational Approach to Negligent Infliction of Mental Distress,* 1981 B.Y.U. L. Rev. 208.

§ 15-4. Vicarious parental liability.

At common law parents were liable for the intentional torts of their child only if they knew of the propensity of the child to commit such antisocial acts. See, e.g., *Mitchell v. Wiltfong,* 4 Kan. App. 2d 231, 604 P.2d 79 (1979). The common law rule naturally extends to parents of adult children, as long as the child is not an actual agent or employee of the parent. For example, in *Parlett v. Nelson,* 25 Va. Cir. 257 (City of Winchester 1991), the father was held not legally responsible for the sexual assault made by his twenty-three-year-old son, even though the assault occurred on property the father had recently owned and rented to the victim plaintiff.

Another exception to the rule was for cases in which the parent entrusted the child with a dangerous instrumentality that caused the injury. *Howell v. Hairston,* 261 S.C. 292, 199 S.E.2d 766 (1973) (air rifle). However, parents are not responsible for accidental gun injuries suffered by one of their child's guests when the gun was stored separately from the ammunition and the parents took other reasonable precautions. Hughes v. Brown, 36 Va. Cir. 333 (Stafford Co. 1995).

A final set of cases in which responsibility rested upon the parents was those where the child was directed to do the tortious act, because a role similar to that of master and servant existed. *Blair v. Broadwater,* 121 Va. 301, 309-10, 93 S.E. 632, 634 (1917) (minor daughter given permission to drive father's automobile for her pleasure).

By statute, Virginia has made parents liable for limited damages to private and public property. Va. Code §§ 8.01-43 and 8.01-44. In 1996, the legislature amended Va. Code Ann. § 8.01-43 to raise the limit for vicarious liability of a parent to $2,500.

See generally Shong, *The Legal Responsibility of Parents for Their Children's Delinquency,* 6 Fam. L.Q. 145 (1972); 14A Michie's Jurisprudence *Parent and Child* § 21.

§ 15-5. Kidnapping and false imprisonment in religious deprogramming.

A number of unpopular religious groups have attracted converts among high school and college-aged youths. When their parents attempt to "rescue" their children through the practice known as "deprogramming," or through bringing actions in tort for alienation of the children's affections, *Orlando v. Alamo,* 646 F.2d 1288 (8th Cir. 1981) (no cause of action for alienation of child's affections, and no showing that cult was "intolerable in civilized society" as required for intentional infliction of emotional distress in Arkansas), they have met with little legal success.

Many states have found that the children, particularly if adults, *Schuppin v. Unification Church,* 435 F. Supp. 603 (D. Vt. 1977), were free to make their own decisions regarding religious affiliation, so that the parents had no ability to interfere, despite their natural concern. Similarly, the parents have been unsuccessful in having their children declared incompetent so that a guardian might be appointed. See, e.g., *Cooper v. Molko*, 512 F. Supp. 563 (N.D. Cal. 1981); *Katz v. Superior Court of San Francisco*, 73 Cal. App. 3d 952, 141 Cal. Rptr. 234 (1977).

Some courts have been reluctant to hold the parents liable for an unsuccessful "deprogramming" attempt when the parents believed their child had been coercively persuaded to join the religious group. See, e.g., *Peterson v. Sorlien*, 299 N.W.2d 123 (Minn. 1980), *cert. denied*, 450 U.S. 1031 (1981). However, in *Ward v. Connor*, 657 F.2d 45 (4th Cir.), *cert. denied*, 102 S. Ct. 1253 (1982), the court of appeals reversed dismissal of a conspiracy charge under the private civil rights action statute, § 1985(c), where an adult's parents allegedly kidnapped him, held him captive, and subjected him to deprogramming while on his way from Virginia to New York. The court of appeals found that while the parents were motivated out of concern for his well-being, they also acted out of animosity towards members of the Unification Church. *Id.* at 49. Similarly, persons assisting parents in kidnapping their own minor children are not liable criminally under the federal kidnapping statute, 18 U.S.C. § 1201(a), according to a recent Fourth Circuit Court of Appeals case. *United States v. Boettcher*, 780 F.2d 435 (4th Cir. 1985).

See generally Anthony, *The Fact Pattern Behind the Deprogramming Controversy: An Analysis and an Alternative*, 9 N.Y.U. Rev. L. & Soc. Change 73 (1980); Le Moult, *Deprogramming Members of Religious Sects*, 46 Ford. L. Rev. 599 (1978).

§ 15-6. Corporal punishment.

The first Virginia case involving the measure of punishment that might be inflicted upon a child was *Carpenter v. Commonwealth*, 186 Va. 851, 44 S.E.2d 419 (1947). In that case, a conviction for assault and battery upon a child was affirmed when the man who stood in loco parentis whipped the child over most of her body for stealing candy from his wife. The court stated the Virginia position: "A parent has the right to administer such reasonable and timely punishment as may be necessary to correct faults in his growing children," *id.* at 860, 44 S.E.2d at 423, but "if he exceeds due moderation, he becomes criminally liable." *Id.* at 861, 44 S.E.2d at 423. See also *Bowers v. State*, 283 Md. 115, 389 A.2d 341 (1971).

In 1989, the legislature amended and reenacted Va. Code sections dealing with the reporting of child abuse and neglect as new Code §§ 2.1-380 and 63.1-248.6. The amendments provide that information concerning child abuse may be transmitted to family advocacy representatives of the United States Armed Forces.

In general, the statutes set up telephone contacts for twenty-four hours a day, seven days a week reporting or complaining of alleged incidents of abuse, and provide for necessary protective and rehabilitative services for the child and the child's family.

See generally Rosenberg, *Ingraham v. Wright: The Supreme Court's Whipping Boy*, 78 Colum. L. Rev. 75 (1978); Prele, *Neither Corporal Punishment Cruel Nor Due Process Due: The Supreme Court's Decision in Ingraham v. Wright*, 7 J.L. & Educ. 1 (1978); 14A Michie's Jurisprudence *Parent and Child* § 16; 6 Am. Jur. 2d *Assault and Battery* §§ 57, 58; 67A C.J.S. *Parent and Child* § 12.

§ 15-7. Interference with family relations.

At common law there was no cause of action for alienation of a parent's affection, for the injury depended upon the loss of consortium that applied only to husband and wife. *Hyman v. Moldovan,* 166 Ga. App. 891, 305 S.E.2d 648 (1983) (conspiracy); *Edwards v. Edwards,* 43 N.C. App. 296, 259 S.E.2d 11 (1979); see also Restatement (Second) of Torts § 699. In any event, Virginia has abolished the case of action for alienation of affections. Va. Code § 8.01-220.

However, several cases have allowed recovery in tort for intentional infliction of mental distress, a cause of action recognized in *Womack v. Eldridge,* 215 Va. 338, 210 S.E.2d 145 (1974), for a parent's interference with the other's custodial or even visitation rights. *Raftery v. Scott,* 756 F.2d 335 (4th Cir. 1985); *Lloyd v. Loeffler,* 694 F.2d 489 (7th Cir. 1982); *Wasserman v. Wasserman,* 671 F.2d 832 (4th Cir. 1982) (diversity jurisdiction); *Bennett v. Bennett,* 682 F.2d 1039 (D.C. Cir. 1982); *Kajtazi v. Kajtazi,* 488 F. Supp. 15 (E.D.N.Y. 1978). These actions are most often used when there is no other remedy possible: where one parent has disappeared completely, as in *Lloyd,* or spirited the children out of the country, as in *Kajtazi.*

A Circuit Court in Virginia has allowed a verdict in a tort case where the custodial parent interfered with the other's visitation rights. *Memmer v. Memmer,* Civ. No. L-45503 (Fairfax Co. Cir. Ct. 1982) (unreported case). Such interference is now specifically mentioned as a reason for changing a custody award. Va. Code § 20-108 [amended 1991].

A case for intentional infliction of emotional distress was not made out when a woman misrepresented to the plaintiff that she was pregnant with his child, he developed a bond of love and affection with the child and paid child support, and then plaintiff proved he was not the father and terminated his visitation rights when her husband wished to adopt the child. The reason plaintiff was unable to recover was that there was no proof that the woman's conduct was "intentional or reckless." *Ruth v. Fletcher,* 237 Va. 366, 377 S.E.2d 412 (1989).

§ 15-8. Failure to provide support.

Most often, when a parent fails to provide support, the child does not have a cause of action in tort, even upon reaching majority. When the parties live together as a family, a nonsupport action in juvenile and domestic relations court is appropriate. This may lead to a finding of criminal nonsupport.

For a child to sue directly might have a damaging effect upon the parent's control over the family budget, and upon the harmony of the family itself. See, e.g., *Wright v. Wright,* 213 Va. 177, 191 S.E.2d 223 (1972).

The other possibility is a creditor's action against the parent for the furnishing of necessaries, which operates in the same fashion as the action for necessaries furnished a spouse, discussed at Chapter 13.

CHAPTER 16

Duties of Parent and Child

§ 16-1. Child support.

A. *Introduction.* Children are incapable, at least at an early age, of supporting themselves. From time immemorial, it has been the parents' responsibility, and particularly the father's, to see that the minor child has adequate food, clothing, and shelter. *Buchanan v. Buchanan,* 170 Va. 458, 471, 197 S.E. 426, 432 (1938) (quoting from 1 Minor's *Institutes* 405). In return for support, education and protection, the child's earnings, income from property and services belong to the parent, together with obedience and respect. Katz, Schroeder & Sidman, *Emancipating Our Children — Coming of Legal Age in America,* 7 Fam. L.Q. 211, 212, 214 (1973).

The questions involving child support are basically three: Who is owed support? What kind of support is due? What kind of proceedings are involved in establishing a duty of support or in collecting support? Although some parts of the problem will be treated elsewhere, the following sections are designed to answer these questions.

See generally Margaret F. Brinig, *Finite Horizons: The American Family,* 2 Intl. J. Children's Rts. 293 (1994); Elizabeth S. Scott & Robert E. Scott, *Parents as Fiduciaries,* 81 Va. L. Rev. 2401 (1995); Barbara Bennett Woodhouse, *"Who Owns the Child?" Meyer and Pierce and the Child as Property,* 33 Wm. & Mary L. Rev. 995 (1992); 14A Michie's Jurisprudence *Parent and Child* § 17.

B. *Married parents and natural children.* At common law only the father of a legitimate child had the duty of providing support, since the married woman owned no property of her own, and her wages belonged to her husband. The duty is now, by statute, given to both husband and wife. Va. Code § 20-61. See, e.g., *Featherstone v. Brooks,* 220 Va. 443,

448, 258 S.E.2d 513, 516 (1979) ("Both parents of a child owe that child a duty of support during minority").

This rule holds true even though the marriage between the parents is absolutely void because bigamous. *Brown v. Commonwealth ex rel. Custis,* 218 Va. 40, 48, 235 S.E.2d 325, 330 (1977). See also *Kasey v. Richardson,* 331 F. Supp. 580 (W.D. Va. 1971) (recovery of social security after attempted bigamous common law marriage by parents).

C. *Married parents: artificial insemination.* By statute, a child of a married woman conceived through artificial insemination with her husband's consent is treated as the natural child of the husband. Both parents, therefore, owe the child the duty of support. Va. Code §§ 32.1-257; 64.1-7.1. *S. v. S.,* 105 Wis. 2d 118, 122, 312 N.W.2d 853, 855 (1981); *People v. Sorensen,* 68 Cal. 2d 280, 66 Cal. Rptr. 7, 437 P.2d 495 (1968). Another way of reaching the same result is through estoppel or implied contract. See *L.M.S. v. S.L.S.,* 105 Wis. 2d 118, 121-22, 312 N.W.2d 853, 855 (1981); *Anonymous v. Anonymous,* 41 Misc. 2d 886, 246 N.Y.S.2d 835 (1964).

D. *Unwedded parents, natural children.* The child of unwedded parents was historically the responsibility of the mother, and, secondarily, the state. The father did not become legally responsible until the Supreme Court case of *Gomez v. Perez,* 408 U.S. 920 (1972), which stated that if the parents of legitimate children owed a duty of support, unwedded parents did likewise. This is now confirmed in Va. Code § 20-61.1, which requires support by the father once paternity has been admitted or proven beyond a reasonable doubt. However, a separation agreement that acknowledged that the husband was not the father of his wife's child, born during the marriage, waived her right to enforce express promises made prior to and after the birth to support the child as if it were his own. The agreement allowed the wife to remain in the marital residence for a year and have $6500 to cover the birth expenses and care of the infant. *Mills v. Mills,* 36 Va. Cir. 351 (Fairfax Co. 1995).

A dependent illegitimate child is able to receive compensation under the wrongful death statute, Va. Code § 8-36. *Carroll v. Sneed,* 211 Va. 640, 642, 179 S.E.2d 620, 622 (1971); *Withrow v. Edwards,* 181 Va. 344, 25 S.E.2d 343 (1943). Having established paternity, the illegitimate child must also prove damages — that by the decedent's death he sustained pecuniary loss, and was damaged by the loss of decedent's care, attention, and society or suffered mental anguish. *Carroll v. Sneed,* 211 Va. at 643, 179 S.E.2d at 622 (1971). This is now confirmed in Va. Code § 20-49.1, which requires support by the father once paternity has been admitted or proven by clear and convincing evidence.

E. *De facto parents*. Frequently, a stepparent will assume the role of supporting his new family. The question is whether this role is legally binding, and the answer is that it is, if the stepparent is in other respects acting as a de facto parent, or if some detrimental reliance has taken place. Obviously if there is a contract between the natural parent and the stepparent, it will be binding between them, but if the child's welfare is in question, the court will not hesitate to require the natural parent to support the child. See, e.g., *Huckaby v. Huckaby,* 75 Ill. App. 3d 195, 393 N.E.2d 1256 (1979); *Pappas v. Pappas,* 247 Iowa 638, 75 N.W.2d 264 (1956); cf. *Goodpasture v. Goodpasture,* 7 Va. App. 55, 371 S.E.2d 845 (1988); and *Buchanan v. Buchanan,* 170 Va. 458, 477, 197 S.E. 426, 434 (1938) (contract between natural parents relieving one of support ineffective).

In *T. v. T.,* 216 Va. 867, 224 S.E.2d 148 (1976), a man married a woman he knew was pregnant by another. After the child's birth, the couple lived together for some time, during which the husband supported the child. When the couple separated, the husband was estopped to deny his responsibility for supporting the child, since the woman had given up employment and her plans for relinquishing the child for adoption in reliance upon his promise to support the child as if he were the natural father.

Similarly, when the husband allowed language to be entered in the final degree that acknowledged his responsibility to pay for the infant child born during the parties' marriage, the decree was held res judicata. When the wife sought to collect child support, the husband was barred from introducing genetic evidence showing that he could not have been the child's father. *Rose v. Rose,* 1993 Va. App. LEXIS 375. See also *Stover v. Stover,* 31 Va. Cir. 484 (City of Roanoke 1990).

F. *Adopted children*. Adopted children, by statute, are to be treated in all respects like legitimate children. Va. Code § 63.1-233. They are therefore owed the duty of support by both adoptive parents, but not by their natural parents.

G. *Institutionalized children*. Institutionalized children are still owed the duty of support, unless a court removes that responsibility from their natural parents. Va. Code § 16.1-290.

Likewise, Va. Code § 63.1-251 provides that any payment for a child's welfare under public assistance constitutes a debt on the part of the persons responsible for the child. The homestead exemption in bankruptcy does not apply to debts for child support. Va. Code § 34-5 [amended 1986].

H. *Children in foster placement.* By statute in Virginia, children in foster care must be supported by their natural parents. Va. Code § 16.1-290. Failure to provide support will be one of the indicia in determining whether parental rights should be terminated, or whether children should be returned to their parents. See Va. Code § 16.1-283B(2). This rule is in effect even if the child has been involuntarily removed from the parents through a dependency proceeding. See also Va. Code §§ 16.1-252(F)(3) and 63.1-204.2, which provide for support of a child placed involuntarily in foster care after removal from the parents. Payment is to be made to the local department of social services. The department is to be subrogated to the right of the child to bring a support action for money expended by the department.

I. *Emancipation of minors, in general.* In general, a child is emancipated when there is no longer any need for parental support and control. In many cases, emancipation occurs when some other person or agency, such as a spouse or the armed forces, takes responsibility for the child. In other cases, the minor takes on the responsibilities by becoming financially or otherwise independent from the parents. Finally, emancipation occurs in the majority of cases when the child comes of age, and is deemed by law to be able to make critical decisions independently. Emancipation, except by age, usually requires consent of the parents. These general rules are now codified in Va. Code §§ 8.01-229, 16.1-241, 16.1-309 through 16.1-334, which provide for a uniform procedure governing emancipation of minors over sixteen, and authorize court emancipation if the minor is (1) validly married, (2) in the armed forces, or (3) willingly living apart from his or her parents. In one recent case, the father was able to show that his employed daughter was emancipated, although she continued to live with her mother. *Ware v. Ware,* 10 Va. App. 352, 391 S.E.2d 887 (1990).

Va. Code §§ 8.01-229 and 16.1-334 detail the effects of an emancipation order, which are to free the minor to enter into contracts, execute a will, sue or be sued, and to buy and sell real estate. Va. Code § 16-334. An emancipated minor may marry without parental consent. Va. Code §§ 16.1-334(16) and 20-49.

See generally Katz, Schroeder & Sidman, *Emancipating Our Children — Coming of Legal Age in America,* 7 Fam. L.Q. 211, 217 (1973).

J. *Emancipation by reaching majority.* A husband and wife executed a separation agreement that was incorporated into a final decree of divorce and provided that the husband was to pay child support until the child's education was complete. This amount was later modified upwards, and finally reduced. After the youngest child reached eighteen, the statutory age of majority in Virginia since 1975, the mother sought general relief, alleging arrearages. The Virginia Supreme Court held that although the legal obligation of support terminated the husband's obligation to pay the modified amount under Va. Code § 20-61, the contractual obligation to pay the original amount continued. *Cutshaw v. Cutshaw,* 220 Va. 638, 640-41, 261 S.E.2d 52, 53-4 (1979). See also *Eaton v. Eaton,* 215 Va. 824, 213 S.E.2d 789 (1975) (although parties had an agreement providing for support to age twenty-one, the age of majority changed. They were operating under a court decree modifying the original agreement when the child reached eighteen, so that the court's statutory jurisdiction ceased at the child's reaching majority).

A recent amendment to Va. Code § 20-103 requires that divorcing parents provide support for any child of the marriage under the age of nineteen who is a full-time high school student and who otherwise meets the requirements of dependency.

K. *Emancipation by marriage.* Generally speaking, when a child marries, the parents will no longer be responsible for support, since that duty devolves upon the new spouse. See, e.g., *Bennett v. Bennett,* 179 Va. 239, 243, 18 S.E.2d 911, 913 (1942). However, should the spouse become incapable of supporting the child, the parent would remain liable, not on the grounds of the child's minority but rather under the statute providing for relief for disabled or otherwise necessitous adult children. Va. Code § 20-61; see *Suire v. Miller,* 363 So. 2d 945 (La. App. 1978) (under similar provisions of Napoleonic Code). See also *Stern v. Stern,* 58 Md. App. 280, 473 A.2d 56 (1984).

L. *Emancipation by joining armed forces.* Traditionally, emancipation through enlistment in the armed services constitutes a shifting of responsibility from the parent to the government. See, e.g., *Iroquois Iron Co. v. Industrial Commission,* 294 Ill. 106, 128 N.E. 289 (1920); Va. Code § 8.01-229.

M. *Emancipation by independence.* In the case of *Buxton v. Bishop,* 185 Va. 1, 37 S.E.2d 755 (1946), a minor son supported himself, working away from home, drew his own wages and spent them as he alone desired. His father could not have successfully proceeded against his employer for his wages, and accordingly was not responsible for the hospital expenses occasioned by the son's last illness. See also *Ware v. Ware,* 10 Va. App. 352, 391 S.E.2d 887 (1990) (minor living with mother but employed full-time and able to support herself). A parent who is ready and able to pay support need not do so if a child chooses a different lifestyle against the parent's advice and wishes. *Parker v. Stage,* 43 N.Y.2d 128, 371 N.E.2d 513, 400 N.Y.S.2d 794 (1977).

N. *Support of disabled child or aged parent.* Va. Code § 20-61 provides for misdemeanor punishment for any person deserting or willfully neglecting or refusing to pay support of an adult child or aged parent who is handicapped or otherwise incapacitated when the child or parent is in necessitous circumstances.

Necessitous is a relative term. The son or daughter of sufficient means "must do more than relieve pangs of hunger, provide shelter and furnish only enough clothes to cover the nakedness of the parent." The necessary support should comport with the health, comfort, and welfare of normal individuals according to their standards of living and the means of the child. *Mitchell-Powers Hardware Co. v. Eaton,* 171 Va. 255, 263, 198 S.E. 496, 500 (1938).

The court of appeals has held that the child support guidelines, Va. Code § 20-108.2(B), should be the basis for awards to adult disabled children unless the court gives written reasons for deviation from them. *Miller v. Miller,* 1993 Va. App. LEXIS 646. The support required for adult disabled children will thus normally be higher than that given to needy parents under Va. Code § 20-61. Language requiring support of disabled children past the age of majority has been added to Va. Code Ann. § 16,1-278.15 [amended 1996]. *Jacobs v. Church,* 36 Va. Cir. 277 (Spotsylvania Co. 1995), discusses the reciprocal duty of caring for an aged parent. Mrs. Church took her mother, an Alzheimer's patient, into her home and cared for her during her last two years of life. Mrs. Church reimbursed herself $96 a day for the services she provided. These had to be paid back to her mother's estate because the daughter proved no express contract, and "services performed by a child to an aging parent are presumably rendered in obedience to natural promptings of love and affection, loyalty, and filial duty, rather than upon an expectation of compensation."

O. *Termination of parental rights and responsibilities.* When all parental rights and responsibilities are terminated voluntarily, or by commitment of the child, the duty of parental support ceases. Va. Code § 63.1-56.

P. *Death of obligor parent.* The death of a parent obliged to provide support will terminate the duty to support a child. Thus, there can be no recovery against the estate of a deceased parent, absent a written agreement to the contrary. Va. Code § 20-107.2. This statute supersedes the decision of *Morris v. Henry,* 193 Va. 631, 70 S.E.2d 417 (1952), which found "no express or implied inhibition against the right of a court in a divorce suit to decree that liability for the support of minor children shall survive the death of the parent against whom it is decreed." *Id.* at 639, 70 S.E.2d at 422. There may be a suit against the estate for arrearages, however. On *Morris v. Henry,* see generally Note, 10 Wash. & Lee L. Rev. 226 (1953).

Q. *Contract between parents regarding support.* A contract between parents involving support of a child will not operate to relieve a parent of his duty to support the child. *Goodpasture v. Goodpasture,* 7 Va. App. 55, 371 S.E.2d 845 (1988); *Buchanan v. Buchanan,* 170 Va. 458, 197 S.E. 426 (1938). Likewise, the unwed father in *Lawson v. Murphy,* 36 Va. Cir. 465 (Wise Co. 1995), was unable to enforce a contract according to which he agreed to pay the child's mother $7500 to replace all child support. The mother received AFDC payments and the father had to reimburse the state.

R. *What type of support is due: standard of living.* Although alimony will not increase based upon a change in the obligor parent's income following a divorce, child support is not contingent upon either providing the barest necessities for the child or the continued vitality of the parents' marriage. Therefore, a dramatic increase in a parent's ability to provide support will be reflected in a change of circumstances for child support regardless of when the increase occurs. See, e.g., *Conway v. Conway,* 10 Va. App. 653, 395 S.E.2d 464 (1990); *Cole v. Cole,* 44 Md. App. 435, 409 A.2d 734 (1979).

The fact that the father of two illegitimate children also had two legitimate children to support should not have been ignored by the trial court when applying the guidelines of Va. Code § 20-108.2. Treating the father as though he had only two children was not in the best interests of the legitimate children. *Zubricki v. Motter,* 12 Va. App. 999, 406 S.E.2d 672 (1991).

Orthodontic care, day camp, and music lessons are additional permissible expenses attributable to the increased needs of growing children, and therefore may evidence a need for increased child support payments. *Featherstone v. Brooks,* 220 Va. 443, 447, 258 S.E.2d 513, 515-16 (1979). However, a noncustodial father was not required to pay necessary hospital care for his minor daughter when she gave birth to an illegitimate child when the mother assumed responsibility for the cost of services and signed the hospital admission form. The mother had merely provided the hospital with information concerning hospital insurance carried by the noncustodial father, which did not cover maternity benefits to a child. *Winchester Medical Center v. Giffin,* 9 Va. Cir. 260 (City of Winchester 1987). The court found that any changes in child support provisions would be better served by proceedings for that purpose than by independent actions instituted by ostensible third-party creditors. According to new Va. Code § 20-60.3, all orders directing payment of child support shall state whether there is an order for health care coverage for dependent children. The cost of health care coverage is a guideline factor used in setting support under amended Va. Code § 20-108.1.

S. *College education.* Although generally parents have no duty to supply their children with higher education, courts have upheld orders for college tuition costs as part of divorce decrees. The reasoning is that the children of divorced parents may otherwise be less likely to receive the benefits of higher education than those of married parents. See, e.g., *In re Marriage of Vrban,* 293 N.W.2d 198, 202 (Iowa 1980). This result is typically reached in Virginia through an agreement between the parents. See, e.g., *Cutshaw v. Cutshaw,* 220 Va. 638, 261 S.E.2d 52 (1979).

The Circuit Court of Fairfax County determined in *Ackerson v. Ackerson,* 22 Va. Cir. 215 (1990), that a clause in a property settlement agreement providing that "Husband shall pay all reasonable expenditures for a college education for the minor children" should be construed under the circumstances as including the approximately $21,000 annual tuition at Duke University. The father contended that all he was required to pay was the approximately $10,000 for tuition at a state school. The court found that the school was a reasonable place for the daughter to attend college given the father's income and social circumstances. He is a partner at a Washington, D.C. law firm who attended graduate and law school at Harvard University.

See generally Washburn, *Post-Majority Support: Oh Dad, Poor Dad,* 44 Temple L.Q. 319 (1971).

T. *Domicile or fault of parent or child.* Where the husband is willing to support his children but the wife, without reasonable excuse, refuses to live with him and keeps the children from him, he is not guilty of "willfully neglecting and refusing to support them" within the criminal nonsupport statute. *Butler v. Commonwealth,* 132 Va. 609, 613, 110 S.E. 868, 869 (1922); see also *Mihalcoe v. Holub,* 130 Va. 425, 107 S.E. 704 (1921). This is because the duty to support children is based largely upon his right to their custody and control. *Butler v. Commonwealth,* 132 Va. at 614, 110 S.E. at 869 (1922). He has a right at common law to maintain them in his own home, and he cannot be compelled against his will to do so elsewhere.

However, when one parent has rendered it impossible for his spouse and children to remain in the marital home, "he cannot by his misconduct escape the performance of the duty which the law imposes upon him." *Owens v. Owens,* 96 Va. 191, 195, 31 S.E. 72, 74 (1898). The wife may clearly obtain child support if she is establishing a domicile for the purpose of getting a divorce, Va. Code § 20-97, or if the husband's actions are placing unconstitutional restraints upon her exercise of religion. See *M.I. v. A.I.,* 107 Misc. 2d 663, 435 N.Y.S.2d 928 (1981).

If a child refuses to live with a parent or to obey his reasonable suggestions, abandoning the parent, the parent no longer has a duty to support the child, *Parker v. Stage,* 43 N.Y.2d 128, 371 N.E.2d 513, 400 N.Y.S.2d 794 (1977), even though the child must otherwise be supported by public welfare. However, a family disagreement relative to a child's living in a college dormitory is not sufficient grounds to deny support. *Anthony v. Anthony,* 213 Va. 721, 722, 196 S.E.2d 66, 67 (1973).

U. *Necessaries.* If a father abandons a child or drives him from his home, he is liable to any persons furnishing necessary support. The person furnishing support must prove that there was an unjustified abandonment, that the support furnished was necessary, and that the credit of the father was legally the basis of the advances. *Mihalcoe v. Holub,* 130 Va. 425, 430, 107 S.E. 704, 706 (1921). A defense to an action for necessaries will be that the child was emancipated, so that the parent no longer owed the duty of support. *Buxton v. Bishop,* 185 Va. 1, 37 S.E.2d 755 (1946). Similarly, if the medical expenses that the child incurred were voluntary, as in the case of an elective abortion, the parent will have no duty to pay for them unless authorized by him. *Winchester Medical Center v. Giffin,* 9 Va. Cir. 260 (City of Winchester 1987); *Akron City Hospital v. Anderson,* 68 Ohio Misc. 14, 428 N.E.2d 472 (1981).

V. *Standing to bring cause of action for support.* Actions or suits by a child against a parent will not be encouraged since they tend to disturb familial relationships, and disrupt parental discipline and authority. *Buchanan v. Buchanan,* 170 Va. 458, 472-73, 197 S.E. 426, 432 (1938). Children do not therefore have the power to compel their father to provide them an income out of his estate for their future support and education. Nor do they have a property right in the agreement between their parents regarding their support. *Yarborough v. Yarborough,* 290 U.S. 202 (1933).

However, if a child is in necessitous circumstances, an action in circuit court may be brought by the child through that child's next friend, *McClaugherty v. McClaugherty,* 180 Va. 51, 68-69, 21 S.E.2d 761, 768 (1942), in addition to the usual nonsupport action.

See generally 14A Michie's Jurisprudence *Parent and Child* § 19.

W. *Types of actions available.* The Revised Uniform Reciprocal Enforcement of Support Act (RURESA), Va. Code §§ 20-88.12 to 20-88.31, allows a Virginia parent to enforce a foreign support judgment against a nonresident parent under the doctrine of comity. This is true despite the fact that the foreign decree may be retroactively modified, *Scott v. Sylvester,* 220 Va. 182, 184-85, 257 S.E.2d 774, 775 (1979), and despite the fact that all arrearages did not accrue while the custodial parent was in Virginia. The duty of support is that imposed by the law of the state where the obligor was present during the period for which support is sought. *Id.* at 186, 257 S.E.2d at 776 (citing Childers v. Childers, 9 N.C. App. 220, 224-25, 198 S.E.2d 485, 488 (1973)).

The support decree of a juvenile and domestic relations court under Va. Code §§ 20-61.2 et seq. will not be terminated by a final divorce when the divorce decree is silent as to support. Va. Code § 20-79; *Werner v. Commonwealth,* 212 Va. 623, 625, 186 S.E.2d 76, 78 (1972). See also *Jones v. Richardson,* 320 F. Supp. 929 (W.D. Va. 1970) (ex parte divorce).

X. *Jurisdiction over defendant.* Under the Virginia long-arm statute, Va. Code § 8.01-328.1, an action for child support may be maintained against a nonresident defendant if pursuant to a divorce or separate maintenance action where the matrimonial domicile was in Virginia and the plaintiff spouse resides in Virginia, or when based upon a prior court decree of support pursuant to an absolute or *a mensa* divorce, where in personam jurisdiction was obtained.

In other cases, jurisdiction is obtained pursuant to Va. Code § 8.01-460, which provides that a decree of judgment for support or maintenance of a spouse or child that is payable in future installments shall be a lien upon real estate designated by the court.

Y. *Procedural rules applicable.* A prior finding that a man was the father of a child in a divorce proceeding acts to collaterally estop him from establishing through conclusive blood testing that he was not the biological parent. *Slagle v. Slagle,* 1990 Va. App. LEXIS 212, 398 S.E.2d 346 (1990).

Under amended Va. Code § 20-61.1, fathers between the ages of fourteen and sixteen who are represented by a guardian ad litem may testify and may be required to provide for support and maintenance just as they would be if adult.

When the possible sentence for misdemeanor nonsupport is six months or greater, counsel must be provided indigent parents. *Potts v. Superintendent of Virginia State Penitentiary,* 213 Va. 432, 192 S.E.2d 780 (1972) (rule applied prospectively only).

Forms useful in prosecuting and defending actions for custody and support may be found in L. Bean, *Virginia Law Practice System, Domestic Relations* § 6655 et seq. Forms for *Juvenile and Domestic Relations Actions for Support* appear in § 6905.2 et seq.

§ 16-2. Education.

A. *Introduction.* Until the nineteenth century, most education of minor children took place in the home and was conducted by the parents. See *Wisconsin v. Yoder,* 406 U.S. 205, 226 n.15 (1972). At that time, Virginia, along with all other jurisdictions, established a system of public education. Va. Const. art. VIII, § 3; *Brown v. Board of Education,* 347 U.S. 483, 489 n.4 (1954). Education until a certain age became compulsory. Va. Code § 22.1-254.

Even though parents no longer have direct control over their children's formal education in most cases, teachers have only the privileges ceded to them by the parents. Parents may choose between public, parochial, *Pierce v. Society of Sisters,* 268 U.S. 510 (1925), and private education, and home instruction; for the most part, local school boards control curriculum and library content in the public schools.

B. *Compulsory education.* Va. Code § 22.1-254 provides that every parent of a child between the ages of five and seventeen shall send that child to a public, parochial or private school or have the child specially taught by an approved tutor. The right to a free public education is guaranteed by Va. Const. art. VIII, § 3.

Va. Code § 22.1-3.1, amended in 1991, provides that the principal or the principal's designee shall record the student's official state birth number from a certified copy of the student's birth record before first admission. If there is no birth certificate, the student shall be admitted to public school upon presentation of information sufficient to estimate the age of the child with reasonable certainty.

The statutes, Va. Code § 22.1-256, exempt children who suffer from contagious or infectious disease, who have not yet been immunized under Va. Code § 22.1-271, who live more than specified distances from schools offering no public transportation, whose parents conscientiously object under Va. Code § 22.1-257, or who cannot benefit from school as provided in Va. Code § 22.1-257.

In *Rice v. Commonwealth,* 188 Va. 224, 49 S.E.2d 342 (1948), parents sought exemption from compulsory education statutes because their deeply held religious beliefs included the commandment that parents teach and train their children in the ways of life. They were held not to be exempt from the compulsory education statutes. *Id.* at 234, 49 S.E. at 347. The court also upheld the validity of compulsory education, *id.* at 236, 49 S.E.2d at 348, which it found reasonable.

This holding would apparently be valid despite the intervening United States Supreme Court decision in *Wisconsin v. Yoder,* 406 U.S. 205 (1972), which held that the first amendment, as incorporated through the fourteenth, precluded application of the compulsory education statute for children ages fourteen to sixteen where the children were members of the Amish religion, which had for centuries maintained a position of other-worldliness, at the same time preparing young adults for their role in the Amish religious community by a vocational training. *Grigg v. Commonwealth,* 224 Va. 356, 297 S.E.2d 799 (1982) (home schooling required approval of district superintendent).

Following the lead of Justice Douglas' separate opinion in *Yoder,* when a parent seeks to exempt a sixteen-year-old child on the grounds of religion, the child must also conscientiously object to school attendance. *Downing v. Fairfax County Sch. Bd.,* 28 Va. Cir. 310 (Fairfax Co. 1992). The school board may consider the views of pupils age fourteen or older after interviewing them, and need not base its decision on the training provided by the parents. To qualify for the exemption, the Virginia Supreme Court has held that the objection must not be on the basis of essentially political, sociological, or philosophical views, or a merely personal moral code, but rather must be the product of bona fide religious beliefs. *Johnson v. Prince William County Sch. Bd.,* 241 Va. 383, 404 S.E.2d 209 (1991). In 1995 and 1996, the legislature added and amended

Va. Code Ann. § 22.1-279.3 to require parents to acknowledge receipt of the school board's standards of student conduct. These materials reserve parental rights to disagree with a school's policies or decisions.

C. *Immunization*. Before admission to any Virginia school, a parent must satisfy the requirement of Va. Code § 22.1-271.2 that the child be immunized, unless the student or parent submits an affidavit to the admitting official of the school stating that the administration of immunizations conflicts with the student's religious tenets or practices, or that immunization would be detrimental to the student's specified medical condition. See, e.g., *Davis v. State,* 294 Md. 370, 451 A.2d 107 (1982).

Pupils' sight and hearing shall be tested in the public schools free of expense under Va. Code § 22.1-273.

D. *Curriculum and rights of students*. Parents acting through local boards of education have a great influence on school curriculum. They may not, however, decide which books are to be placed in the school libraries. *Minarcini v. Strongville School District,* 541 F.2d 577 (6th Cir. 1976).

A school may not offer elective classes in transcendental meditation, since this is really a religion and to do so would violate the constitutional prohibition against establishment of religion, *Malnak v. Yogi,* 592 F.2d 197 (3d Cir. 1977), nor require students to participate in coeducational physical education classes when close contact with members of the opposite sex while scantily attired violated the student's deeply held religious beliefs. *Moody v. Cronin,* 484 F. Supp. 270 (C.D. Ill. 1979).

A school may not interfere with a student's first amendment rights so long as the exercise does not interfere with the normal educational process. *Tinker v. Des Moines Independent Community School Board,* 393 U.S. 503 (1969) (arm bands protesting Vietnam War); *Gambino v. Fairfax County School Board,* 564 F.2d 157 (4th Cir. 1977) (student newspaper censorship of article on birth control).

E. *Home instruction*. Education, according to Va. Code § 22.1-254, must be in a public school, a private school, a parochial school or in home instruction given by a qualified tutor or teacher approved by the district superintendent. The question of whether parents without such approval could nevertheless withdraw their children from the public schools and establish their own private school was answered in the negative in *Grigg v. Commonwealth,* 224 Va. 356, 297 S.E.2d 799 (1982). The parents were ordered to provide their children with one of the forms of education listed in the statute.

F. *Controversial subjects in the curriculum.* A variety of cases has addressed the problem of state control over curriculum dealing with controversial topics such as sex education, now required in Virginia public schools by Va. Code §§ 22.1-207.1 et seq. Most cases have held that, so long as excusal privileges are afforded parents, such classes are appropriate subjects for the curriculum and do not violate the parents' first amendment or fourteenth amendment rights nor amount to an establishment of religion. See, e.g., *Citizens for Parental Rights v. San Mateo County Board of Education,* 124 Cal. Rptr. 68 (1975), *appeal dismissed,* 425 U.S. 908 (1976); see also *Medeiros v. Kiyosaki,* 52 Hawaii 436, 478 P.2d 314 (1970). Should the state desire to omit such a topic from study completely, as Michigan did with methods of birth control, that would be permissible as well. *Mercer v. Michigan State Board,* 379 F. Supp. 580 (E.D. Mich. 1974), *aff'd mem.,* 419 U.S. 1081 (1974): "The authorities must choose which portions of the world's knowledge will be included in the curriculum's programs and courses, and what portions will be left for grasping from other sources, such as the family, peers or other institutions." *Id.* at 586.

See generally Hirschoff, *Parents and the Public School Curriculum, Is There a Right to Have One's Child Excused From Objectionable Instruction?,* 50 S. Cal. L. Rev. 871 (1977).

Likewise, a series of cases beginning with *Epperson v. Arkansas,* 393 U.S. 97 (1968), has allowed public schools to teach the theory of evolution. An attempt to require a concurrent instruction in the theory of scientific creationism failed in *McLean v. Arkansas Board of Education,* 529 F. Supp. 1255 (E.D. Ark. 1982), since no basis other than a religious one had been established for the creationist theory. See also *Daniels v. Waters,* 515 F.2d 485 (6th Cir. 1975) (evolution might be taught only at the same time as Biblical creation).

G. *Due process.* Because education is one of the most important functions of the state, *Brown v. Board of Education,* 347 U.S. 483 (1954), and one of the most important assets to an individual, children may not be suspended from public schools without a hearing affording them notice, an opportunity to be heard, and the privilege of confronting witnesses against them, as well as a written statement of reasons for the suspension. *Goss v. Lopez,* 419 U.S. 565 (1975).

The Supreme Court, in the case of *New Jersey v. T.L.O.,* 469 U.S. 325 (1985), held that a search of a student's purse by school officials must be based upon reasonable suspicion that criminal activity is taking place.

In *T.L.O.*, the search of a student's purse was upheld when she had been accused of smoking in the restroom by a teacher.

H. *Discipline.* Public school teachers do have the right, without a prior hearing, to punish students corporally for infraction of rules. *Ingraham v. Wright,* 430 U.S. 651 (1977). The punishment must be reasonable, or tort liability will result. The ability of teachers to use corporal punishment derives from the state's authority to regulate the educational process through compulsory attendance laws.

See generally Piele, *Neither Corporal Punishment Cruel Nor Due Process Due: The U.S. Supreme Court's Decision in Ingraham v. Wright,* 7 J.L. & Educ. 1 (1978); Rosenberg, *Ingraham v. Wright: The Supreme Court's Whipping Boy,* 78 Colum. L. Rev. 75 (1978).

§ 16-3. Religious rights of minors.

A. *Introduction.* Until very recently, the religious preference of a minor was unquestionably that of his parent. A parent had the responsibility for the religious upbringing, and any preference the child might have could only be exercised upon his reaching majority.

The opinion of Justice Douglas, concurring and dissenting in part in *Wisconsin v. Yoder,* 406 U.S. 205, 245 (1972), suggested that the child's wishes regarding exemption from public education should be consulted; that it need not necessarily be the same as the parental desire for separation from non-Amish society.

The other indication that children might now possess rights separate from those of their parents comes from the decisions in the abortion, *Planned Parenthood v. Danforth,* 428 U.S. 52 (1976), and contraception cases, *Carey v. Population Services Int'l,* 431 U.S. 678 (1977), which hold that in these areas involving intimate decisions the parents need not give their consent. This suggests an independent right of religious exercise, if the abortion decision is taken as a relinquishment of a matter of choice to the individual because it is essentially a religious determination.

See generally Hafen, *Children's Liberation and the New Egalitarianism: Some Reservations About Abandoning Youth to Their "Rights,"* 1976 B.Y.U. L. Rev. 605; Minow, *Rights of the Next Generation: A Feminist Approach to Children's Rights,* 9 Harv. Women's L.J. 1 (1986); *Adjudicating What Yoder Left Unresolved: Religious Rights for Minor Children After Danforth and Carey,* 126 U. Pa. L. Rev. 1135 (1978).

§ 16-4. Sexual activities of minors.

A. *Introduction.* In perhaps no area of family law has the change toward individual rights been more apparent than in the cases involving the sexual activities of minors. See, e.g., *Planned Parenthood of Central Missouri v. Danforth,* 428 U.S. 52, 74 (1976). The Supreme Court, in a series of cases that began with the "marital privacy" case of *Griswold v. Connecticut,* 381 U.S. 479 (1965), has held that the personal right of autonomy in matters involving birth control and abortion extends to unmarried minors as well as married adults. State statutes have extended the privacy protection further to include treatment for venereal diseases without parental notification or consent.

B. *Contraception.* In *Griswold v. Connecticut,* 381 U.S. 479 (1965), the Supreme Court declared that the due process clause prevented a statute from prohibiting the use of contraceptive devices to married adults. This new right of privacy was extended to unmarried adults in *Eisenstadt v. Baird,* 405 U.S. 438, 453 (1972), and to minors in *Carey v. Population Services Int'l,* 431 U.S. 678 (1977). The most recent cases have involved parental notification when prescription contraceptives are purchased. Again, the holdings have been that this requirement interferes with the unmarried minor's right to privacy. *Planned Parenthood Federation of America, Inc. v. Schweiker,* 712 F.2d 650 (D.C. Cir. 1983); *New York v. Heckler,* 719 F.2d 1191 (2d Cir. 1983), 10 Fam. L. Rep. (B.N.A.) 1024.

Information regarding contraceptives may be included within secondary school student newspapers without the administration's consent. *Gambino v. Fairfax County School Board,* 564 F.2d 157 (4th Cir. 1977).

C. *Abortion.* A mature unmarried minor possesses the right, with her doctor, to elect whether or not to have an abortion during the first three months of pregnancy. *Bellotti v. Baird,* 443 U.S. 622 (1979). Although parental consent is not necessary, *Planned Parenthood of Central Missouri v. Danforth,* 428 U.S. 52, 72-75 (1976); Va. Code § 54.1-2969D(2), a state statute may require, although Virginia's, cited above, does not, that parents be informed since they might possess important medical information aiding the doctor performing the abortion and to enable the parent to counsel the minor before and after the pregnancy is terminated. *H.L. v. Matheson,* 450 U.S. 398 (1981). As a corollary, information regarding abortions may be published in newspapers circulated within the state, and a Virginia statute prohibiting publications advertising abortion was held unconstitutional in *Bigelow v. Virginia,* 421 U.S. 809 (1975).

A parent may not force her minor child to undergo an abortion for financial reasons against the child's wishes. See, e.g., *In re P.*, 111 Misc. 2d 532, 444 N.Y.S.2d 545 (1981).

After the first trimester, all abortions may be regulated in the interests of maternal health, including, for example, a requirement that a second trimester abortion occur in a hospital. Va. Code § 18.2-73, upheld in *Simopoulos v. Commonwealth*, 221 Va. 1059, 277 S.E.2d 194 (1981), *aff'd*, 462 U.S. 506, 103 S. Ct. 2532 (1983).

D. *Sexually transmitted diseases*. Under Va. Code § 54.1-2969D, minors are to be deemed adults in cases of "medical or health services needed to determine the presence of or to treat venereal disease ...." This means that parental consent or notification is not necessary.

E. *Sterilizations*. According to Va. Code § 54-325.10, a person aged fourteen to eighteen may be sterilized against his or her will only if: (1) the parents request the operation; (2) the child has been served with notice and has been appointed a guardian; (3) the court determines that a reasonable and comprehensible explanation of the procedure, its consequences and alternative methods has been given the child and guardian, spouse if any, and custodial parent; (4) the court has determined by clear and convincing evidence that the child's mental abilities are so impaired that the child is incapable now and will be incapable in the future of making an informed judgment; (5) the child's views have been taken into account; (6) there is a need for contraception, no reasonable alternative to sterilization; and (7) the child is permanently unable to care for and raise a child because of the mental disability.

The statute in effect until 1974 was upheld in *Buck v. Bell*, 274 U.S. 200 (1927). A procedural challenge was unsuccessfully made in *Poe v. Lynchburg Training School & Hospital*, 518 F. Supp. 789 (W.D. Va. 1981). Compare *Wentzel v. Montgomery General Hospital*, 293 Md. 685, 447 A.2d 1244 (1982), *cert. denied*, 459 U.S. 1147 (1983).

§ 16-5. Medical care for children.

A. *Introduction*. One of the duties a parent owes a minor child is the provision of adequate medical care. Failure to provide necessary services and drugs may result in a conviction for child abuse, Va. Code §§ 18.2-314 and 63.1-248.2A(2), or in a finding that the child is neglected and deprived and therefore dependent, see, e.g., *In re Alyne E.*, 113 Misc. 2d 307, 448 N.Y.S.2d 984 (1982) (mental health neglected), warranting state intervention. Va. Code §§ 54-325.2 and 63.1-248.9. However, a noncustodial parent need not pay for necessary medical care in a suit by a third-party creditor when the custodial parent had assumed responsibility on admission for the cost of obstetrical care and hospitalization of the parties' child. *Winchester Medical Center v. Giffin,* 9 Va. Cir. 260 (City of Winchester 1987).

Although there are few Virginia cases involving medical care for minor children, the law from other states is reasonably settled. Although the state will usually not intervene in a parent's considered decision regarding a method of treatment, the state will exercise its parens patriae power in certain circumstances. The easiest of these times to identify are the occasions when the child's very life, or the general well-being of the community, are threatened by parental failure to select an efficacious and accepted course of treatment. The theory in these cases is that the child must be allowed to reach the age when he or she could make the decision for or against treatment independently. *People ex rel. Wallace v. LaBrenz,* 211 Ill. 618, 104 N.E.2d 769 (1952); *Custody of a Minor,* 375 Mass. 733, 379 N.E.2d 1053 (1978); see generally *The Rights of Children: A Trust Model,* 46 Ford. L. Rev. 669 (1978).

On the other extreme are the cases where the corrective treatment is elective, particularly when the treatment itself may carry some measurable risk. In such cases the decision will be made by the parents in consultation with their physician.

In most of the intermediate possibilities, state intervention does not occur, especially when the parents' objections to the usual forms of treatment are based upon their religious beliefs.

Finally, there are cases in which the critical decision is whether treatment should be continued, in the case of critically ill terminal patients, or even offered, in the case of handicapped newborns. Petitions involving medical care for children will be heard in the new family court, once it is funded. The courts will also hear matters involving admission to an inpatient mental health facility, and consent for treatment or other activities normally requiring parental consent including emergency surgical or medical treatment where parental consent cannot be obtained. The court shall also hear petitions filed on behalf of a child, parent, or person standing in the place of the parent to obtain treatment, rehabilitation or other services. Va. Code § 16.1-241(B). Complaints and the processing of petitions to initiate a case shall be the responsibility of the family court intake officer according to § 16.1-260.

B. *Compulsory medical treatment.* In some instances, the state has acted out of its interest in the welfare of the community or its parens patriae interest in each individual, and has compelled forms of medical care.

One familiar example is compulsory vaccination before the child enters school, Va. Code § 22.1-271.1, and eye and hearing tests during elementary school. Va. Code § 22.1-273. Perhaps less obvious are the silver nitrate drops placed in each newborn baby's eyes to treat possible infection, Va. Code §§ 32.1-61 to 32.1-64, phenylketonuria tests, Va. Code § 32.1-65, and vaccinations and quarantines in times of epidemics. Va. Code § 32.1-48.

C. *Life-threatening situations.* Even when the strongest interests of a parent are pitted against the life-saving treatment of his child, these religious freedoms or parental abilities to control family resources will not prevail. Compare *Ginsberg v. New York,* 390 U.S. 629, 639 (1968). The state's interest in assuring that the child reaches maturity will justify a course of court-ordered medical treatment.

Thus, if a child has an illness that requires surgery, a parent must consent or the surgery will be ordered despite a religious tenet prohibiting blood transfusions. This same doctrine has been used to justify a court-ordered transfusion for a woman seven months pregnant, *Raleigh Fitkin-Paul Morgan Memorial Hospital v. Anderson,* 42 N.J. 421, 201 A.2d 537 (1964), and a parent with several small children to care for, *Application of President & Directors of Georgetown College, Inc.,* 331 F.2d 1000 (D.C. Cir. 1964). See generally *Constitutional Limitations on State Intervention in Prenatal Care,* 67 Va. L. Rev. 1051 (1981).

Even if a small child suffers some discomfort, such as stomach cramps, nausea, and pain from injections, a course of treatment for a frequently curable cancer will be followed despite parental objection. *In re Custody of a Minor,* 375 Mass. 733, 379 N.E.2d 1053 (1978).

Regimes of diet and prayer will not suffice if there is an accepted medical treatment that is usually efficacious and a child's life is endangered. *Custody of a Minor,* 375 Mass. 733, 379 N.E.2d 1053 (1978). But so long as a parent follows the advice of a physician who subscribes to a course of treatment accepted by some segment of the medical commentary, even though it is unusual, there will be no state intervention. *In re Hofbauer,* 47 N.Y.2d 648, 419 N.Y.S.2d 936, 393 N.E.2d 1009 (1979).

See generally J. Nelson Thomas, Note, *Prosecuting Religious Parents for Homicide: Compounding a Tragedy,* 1 Va. J. Soc. Pol'y & L. 409 (1994).

If a child's life is threatened, some states have found parental liability for improper prenatal care. See, e.g., *Curlender v. Bio-Science Laboratories,* 106 Cal. App. 3d 811, 829, 165 Cal. Rptr. 477, 488 (1980); N.J. Stat. Ann. § 30:4C-11; see generally Note, *Parental Liability for Prenatal Injury,* 14 Colum. J.L. & Soc. Probs. 47 (1978).

D. *Elective therapy — religious objection.* Where the child's life is not at stake and the parent has a religious objection to his undergoing a particular treatment, a court will not adjudicate neglect and order treatment. If the child is of an age and maturity to have a religious preference to make a decision independently, his opinion will be given great weight, see, e.g., *In re Green,* 448 Pa. 338, 292 A.2d 387 (1972), if not always followed.

When a child's decision does not accord with the parent's — as when a child wishes an abortion but the mother objects on a religious basis, *State v. Smith,* 16 Md. App. 209, 295 A.2d 238 (1972); *J.B. v. Detroit-Macomb Hospital Ass'n,* 9 Fam. L. Rep. (B.N.A.) 2219 (1983), the child's view will prevail if the child is mature, especially when, as in the case of abortion, there are independent constitutional rights of the child at stake.

E. *Elective therapy.* When a parent opposes a particular type of therapy, but not on a religious basis, the parent's wish will usually prevail unless the condition is life-threatening. *In re Hudson,* 13 Wash. 2d 673, 126 P.2d 765 (1942).

A parent may volunteer a child for drug research, but only if there is no appreciable risk to the child. The doctrine of substituted judgment, discussed below, will prevail, as well as the utilitarian policy that important medical information can often not be gleaned absent testing on human subjects.

See generally Glantz et al., *Scientific Research with Children: Legal Incapacity and Proxy Consent,* 11 Fam. L.Q. 253 (1977).

Minors may be voluntarily committed by their parents after a hearing held in the institution with a third party, such as a psychiatrist, acting as an impartial decisionmaker. *Parham v. R.,* 442 U.S. 584 (1979).

The 1991 legislature added Va. Code § 15.1-346.1, which requires that predischarge plans be formulated and explained to the minor admitted to inpatient treatment. Copies shall be sent to the minor's parents or, if the minor is in the custody of the local department of social services, to the department's director or designee. The plan shall, at a minimum, specify the services required by the patient in the community to meet the minor's needs for treatment, housing, nutrition, physical care, and safety; specify any income subsidies for which the minor is eligible, identify all local and state agencies that will be involved in providing treatment and support to the minor, and specify services that would be appropriate for the minor's treatment and support in the community that are currently unavailable.

See generally Richard E. Redding, *Children's Competence to Provide Informed Consent for Mental Health Treatment*, 50 Wash. & Lee L. Rev. 695 (1993).

F. *Life sustaining therapy — risk to other child.* On a few occasions one of two children in a family is ill and in need of an organ that can best be obtained from a healthy sibling. In one well-known case, *Hart v. Brown*, 29 Conn. Supp. 368, 289 A.2d 386 (1972), a kidney removal from a healthy eight-year-old twin was ordered in order to save the life of her ill sister. The court's reasoning was that when the healthy sister reached the age when she could understand a decision of that kind, she would choose to donate her organ — the "doctrine of substituted judgment." See, e.g., *Superintendent of Belchertown State School v. Saikewicz*, 373 Mass. 728, 370 N.E.2d 417 (1977) (discontinuance of treatment for elderly retarded leukemia patient).

In another case, the healthy twin was mentally defective. In *In re Guardianship of Pescinski*, 67 Wis. 2d 4, 226 N.W.2d 180 (1975), the transplant was never ordered because the institutionalized healthy twin could never understand why he would suffer pain in giving up his kidney. But see *Strunk v. Strunk*, 445 S.W.2d 145 (Ky. 1969) (institutionalized brother could be operated on to save healthy sibling dying of kidney disease).

See generally Note, 9 J. Fam. L. 309 (1969-1970).

G. *Decisions to forego therapy.* The landmark case of *In re Quinlan*, 70 N.J. 10, 355 A.2d 647 (1976), brought to the public scrutiny the issue of whether a family should ever be permitted to discontinue extraordinary medical treatment from a child who would not recover from an illness that had already irreversibly terminated conscious mental functions.

More recently, Congressional legislation has addressed the question of whether parents, together with doctors, could decide to forego treatment, extraordinary or routine, of handicapped newborns. The legislation makes the life-terminating omission child abuse under state statutes, except in rare cases when the baby would die in any case in a short time.

See generally Robertson, *Involuntary Euthanasia of Defective Newborns: A Legal Analysis,* 27 Stan. L. Rev. 213 (1975); Bennett, *Allocation of Child Medical Care Decision-Making Authority: A Suggested Interest Analysis,* 62 Va. L. Rev. 285 (1976); Goldstein, *Medical Care for the Child at Risk, On State Supervision of Parental Autonomy,* 86 Yale L.J. 645 (1977).

§ 16-6. Child abuse and neglect and family abuse.

Following the national trend, Virginia has enacted statutes protecting children and adults from the abuse of other family members. Va. Code § 16.1-228 et seq. defines an abused or neglected child as well as a "child in need of supervision" and "family abuse." Recent amendments to the section define a "family or household member" as the person's spouse, former spouse, parents, stepparents, children, stepchildren, siblings, grandparents, in-laws, "any individual who has a child in common with the person," and a cohabitant or recent cohabitant. The spouse, former spouse, co-parent, and cohabitant need not reside in the same home with the abused person.

Jurisdiction for proceedings alleging child neglect or abuse or family abuse lies exclusively in the juvenile and domestic relations district court. Va. Code § 16.1-241.

Guidelines for use by child-protective units that had been enacted by the Commissioner of the Virginia Department of Social Services were upheld in *Jackson v. W.,* 14 Va. App. 391, 419 S.E.2d 385 (1992). Several of the detailed guidelines, particularly those involving "mental abuse," are set forth in the opinion. See also *Doe v. Department of Social Servs.,* 33 Va. Cir. 538 (Prince William Co. 1992) (setting aside finding of mental/emotional abuse). Social workers or other professionals acting in good faith in cases involving abuse enjoy qualified immunity. However, if they violate court orders or act completely outside the proper conduct of family therapy practitioners, they will not be protected from suit. *Tomlin v. McKenzie,* 1996 Va. LEXIS 50.

A single disciplinary blow by a parent to her daughter's face, resulting in two black eyes, constitutes "founded physical abuse" according to *Dart v. Jackson,* 1993 Va. App. LEXIS 161. Neither the mother's due process rights nor Social Services procedures were violated by the hearing officer's refusal to allow that daughter to testify.

However, autoeroticism by the parents that may have been witnessed by the child did not constitute abuse warranting a change of custody when the father showed "an involvement more extensive" than the trial judge had seen "in the great bulk of most of the cases that" he had heard. *Davenport v. Davenport*, 1995 Va. App. LEXIS 75. When the parties were accused of abusing their children, the trial court found that there had been no abuse, and when the Department of Human Development unsuccessfully appealed, the wife was appropriately awarded attorney's fees and costs from the department.

If the local department of social services finds that a complaint of abuse is unfounded, records of the complaint shall be kept for one year in order to provide local departments with information regarding prior investigations. The exception to the rule is when the accused, through a civil suit, proves that the report was made in bad faith or with malicious intent. Va. Code Ann. § 63.1-248.5:1 [amended 1996]. The other important consequence of making a false report of child abuse or neglect is that the complainant shall be subject to criminal action. The first such conviction is a Class 4 misdemeanor; a subsequent conviction is a Class 2 misdemeanor. *Id.* § 5:101 [added 1996].

CHAPTER 17

Separate Maintenance

§ 17-1. Introduction.

Unlike the divorce *a mensa,* the action for separate maintenance is not dependent upon a statutory framework. *White v. White,* 181 Va. 162, 24 S.E.2d 448 (1943). It is a direct descendant of the common law duty of the husband to support his blameless wife, see *Almond v. Almond,* 25 Va. (4 Rand.) 662, 664 (1826), and jurisdiction comes from the inherent equitable power of the chancery court.

Although it is a distinct action from the *a mensa* divorce, and its consequences are different; courts are apt on occasion to confuse separate maintenance with a divorce from bed and board. See, e.g., *Montgomery v. Montgomery,* 183 Va. 96, 101, 31 S.E.2d 284, 286 (1944).

The separate maintenance action is not often used today. Its utility rests with its tax advantage of making payments deductible as alimony by the payor. In addition, the marital relationship continues, with its privileges in case of the obligor spouse's death. *Wilson v. Wilson,* 195 Va. 1060, 81 S.E.2d 605 (1954). There may also be occasions where the cause of action for a fault divorce needed for a divorce *a mensa* could not be made out, but the dependent spouse needs an immediate award of support pending a maturing of a no fault cause of action. See, e.g., *Rowand v. Rowand,* 215 Va. 344, 210 S.E.2d 149 (1974) (husband's ordering "get out" on two occasions was not enough to give wife grounds for divorce *a mensa* on constructive desertion; but since the wife was free from fault, she could be awarded alimony). See also *Alls v. Alls,* 216 Va. 13, 216 S.E.2d 16 (1975). In most of these cases an appropriate separation agreement will not have been agreed to by both parties.

157

§ 17-2. Jurisdiction.

Although jurisdiction does not depend upon statute, as it does in cases of divorce, *White v. White*, 181 Va. 162, 24 S.E.2d 448 (1943), several things must be proven: (1) personal service over the defendant; (2) the existence of a valid marriage, see, e.g., *Purcell v. Purcell*, 14 Va. (4 Hen. & Mun.) 507 (1810); and (3) cause for the living apart. A divorce need not be granted to either party for maintenance to be awarded. See, e.g., *Graham v. Graham*, 210 Va. 608, 172 S.E.2d 724 (1970); *Alls v. Alls*, 216 Va. 13, 216 S.E.2d 16 (1975).

In its 1993 reconvened session, the Virginia legislature established a statewide system of family courts that is yet to be implemented. The new legislation, Chapter 929 of the Virginia Acts of Assembly, provides that the family courts will assume the powers and territorial jurisdiction of the juvenile and domestic relations district courts when it is funded. Va. Code § 16.1-69.8(2). Judges of the juvenile and domestic relations district court shall continue in office as family court judges until the expiration of the term for which appointed or elected, until a vacancy occurs, or until a successor is appointed or elected. Va. Code § 16.1-69.9:01. Like the current juvenile and domestic relations district court judges, family court judges shall be prohibited from engaging in the practice of law. Va. Code § 16.1-12(c). General district court judges, substitute judges, and retired and recalled district court judges may serve on the family court, but only after completing the training program required by the Judicial Council of Virginia. Va. Code §§ 16.1-69.21, 16.1-69.22:1 and 16.1-69.36(8)).

Family court jurisdiction extends to suits for separate maintenance. Va. Code § 16.1-241(T). Venue shall be in the family court in the county or city in which the proceeding is pending. Transfer of venue in suits for separate maintenance shall be governed by §§ 8.01-257 et seq. as these provisions relate to circuit court. The petitioner shall file directly with the clerk of the family court in cases of separate maintenance. Service of process shall continue to be governed by the rules of the Supreme Court or statute. Va. Code § 8.01-285 et seq.; § 8.01-328 et seq., as appropriate. Virginia Code § 16.1-263(F).

In each separate maintenance case, the judge shall consider whether to refer the parties to mediation, and may do so sua sponte or on motion of one of the parties. Upon referral, the parties must attend one evaluation session during which the parties and the mediator assess the case and decide whether to continue with mediation or with adjudication. Further participation in the mediation shall be by consent of all parties, and attorneys for any party may be present during mediation. Va. Code § 16.1-272.1. When the parties are referred to mediation, the court shall set a return date. The parties shall notify the court in writing if the dispute is resolved prior to this return date. The court may, in its discretion, incorporate any mediated agreement into the terms of its final decree. Only if the order is entered incorporating the mediated agreement will the terms of the voluntary settlement agreement affect any outstanding court order. Procedure in cases of separate maintenance shall be governed by provisions of Title 20. Appeals from final orders or judgments of the family court may be taken to the court of appeals as provided in § 17-116.05:5.

Venue does not come under Va. Code § 20-96, but rather under the general venue of suits in equity. *Rochelle v. Rochelle,* 225 Va. 387, 392, 302 S.E.2d 59 (1983). Objections to venue must be made within twenty-one days after service of process by a plea in abatement. It may shift with the abode of children of separated parents. *White v. White,* 181 Va. 162, 24 S.E.2d 448 (1943). See also *Rochelle v. Rochelle,* 225 Va. 387, 393, 302 S.E.2d 59, 62 (1983).

The marriage required for a separate maintenance decree will not be extinguished by a prior ex parte divorce, *Newport v. Newport,* 219 Va. 48, 54-56, 245 S.E.2d 134, 138-39 (1978), but will be by a proceeding in which the dependent spouse generally appeared. *Osborne v. Osborne,* 215 Va. 205, 207 S.E.2d 875 (1974). Following divorce, payments made will be support rather than separate maintenance.

§ 17-3. Proof.

As in a divorce action, witnesses need to be corroborated to make out the essential elements. See, e.g., *Aichner v. Aichner,* 215 Va. 624, 626, 212 S.E.2d 278, 279 (1975).

§ 17-4. Grounds.

Constructive desertion will be grounds for a decree of separate maintenance. For example, permanent alimony was proper where a husband refused to let the wife return to the marital home following her visit to relatives. *Purcell v. Purcell,* 14 Va. (4 Hen. & Mun.) 507 (1810).

However, the presence and undue curiosity of the husband's mother were not excuses for the wife's departure from the marital home and subsequent suit for separate maintenance. *Montgomery v. Montgomery,*

183 Va. 96, 31 S.E.2d 284 (1944). There is no duty for a husband to provide separate maintenance when he has committed no breach of a marital duty, and the wife cannot claim separate maintenance on grounds of her own misconduct. However, had the mother-in-law in *Montgomery* caused the wife to suffer from her cruelty and misconduct, as in the case of a physical beating and an enforced subservience of the wife to the mother-in-law, the husband would have had a duty to protect her and breach of that duty would result in liability for separate maintenance. See *Hutchins v. Hutchins,* 93 Va. 68, 70, 24 S.E. 903, 904 (1896).

Generally, the wife may depart and maintain a separate maintenance action where the husband's mistreatment by ill usage, personal violence, or lack of an adequate and fit home destroy her health or endanger her life by affecting her mind. *Williams v. Williams,* 188 Va. 543, 549-50, 50 S.E.2d 277, 279-80 (1948), citing 42 C.J.S. *Husband and Wife* § 611.

§ 17-5. Defenses.

The dependent spouse, or complainant, cannot recover if he or she departed without lawful excuse, *Almond v. Almond,* 25 Va. (4 Rand.) 662 (1826); see also *Anthony v. Anthony,* 213 Va. 721, 196 S.E.2d 66 (1973), although the justification need not rise to the level of proof needed for a divorce. An inexcusable refusal to engage in sexual intercourse on a permanent basis would bar a separate maintenance award. *Aichner v. Aichner,* 215 Va. 624, 626, 212 S.E.2d 278 (1975).

Where the wife continued to live with the husband after securing a court order that he cease his improper relationship with another woman, she forfeited her right to separate maintenance unless there was a repetition of the offense. *Williams v. Williams,* 188 Va. 543, 551, 50 S.E.2d 277 (1948).

A valid divorce decree will extinguish the duty to pay separate maintenance, but only if there was personal jurisdiction over the dependent spouse. Compare *Ceyte v. Ceyte,* 222 Va. 11, 13, 278 S.E.2d 791, 792 (1981), with *Newport v. Newport,* 219 Va. 48, 54-56, 245 S.E.2d 134, 138-39 (1978).

§ 17-6. Consequences.

Since there has been no divorce, a decree of separation will not sever rights to a share of a deceased spouse's estate, *Wilson v. Wilson,* 195 Va. 1060, 81 S.E.2d 605 (1954) (dower), and so will be greater protection through support for a faultless spouse than alimony, which ceases at the death of the obligor. The court may, however, provide for the custody and support of minor children of the marriage. Va. Code Ann. § 20-107.2 [amended 1996].

However, the separate maintenance decree will not give the court power to award a spouse the use of specific marital property, just as it cannot be awarded in a proceeding for alimony. *Wilson v. Wilson*, 195 Va. 1060, 81 S.E.2d 605 (1954). See also *Almond v. Almond*, 25 Va. (4 Rand.) 662 (1826) (no ability to obtain judgment requiring return of a slave).

An award of separation will cease upon one party's being awarded an absolute divorce. *Hagen v. Hagen*, 205 Va. 791, 139 S.E.2d 821 (1965) (three years' separation as cause of action; statute allowing no-fault divorce enacted after separate maintenance decree). Of course, unless the dependent spouse was seriously at fault, there may be an award of support following divorce. *Lancaster v. Lancaster*, 212 Va. 127, 183 S.E.2d 158 (1971).

The Internal Revenue Code § 71 requires that, for periodic payments to be deductible to the payor and taxable to the payee, they be made under court decree of separation, a divorce, or a property settlement agreement. If the cause of action for divorce has not yet matured, and the parties cannot agree on a property settlement, support payments may still be deductible under an award of separate maintenance.

Property would not be equitably divided at this time under Va. Code § 20-107.3, which requires a dissolution of marriage or divorce.

Separate maintenance will signify a revocation of the wife's implied consent to marital intercourse. See *Weishaupt v. Commonwealth*, 227 Va. 389, 315 S.E.2d 847, 855 (1984).

The amount of the separation allowance lies within the sound judicial discretion of the chancellor, who must take into account the needs of the dependent spouse and the ability of the obligor to pay by virtue of earning capacity and financial resources. *Hinshaw v. Hinshaw*, 201 Va. 668, 670, 112 S.E.2d 902 (1960); *Oliver v. Oliver*, 202 Va. 268, 271-72, 117 S.E.2d 59 (1960).

CHAPTER 18

Property Settlement or Separation Agreements

§ 18-1. Introduction — advantages.

Although formerly any contract between spouses that contemplated a division of property or financial obligations in the event of a separation or divorce was void as against public policy, courts have long recognized that spouses might contract to settle potential disputes concerning the distribution of property upon the death of either.

In the twentieth century, the contract between spouses after they have separated has been seen as a realistic and efficient method of resolving disputes. See, e.g., *Eschner v. Eschner,* 146 Va. 417, 131 S.E. 800 (1926). Especially since the advent of no-fault divorce, private agreements have streamlined the dissolution process so that in the great majority of cases there is no contest either as to the divorce itself or as to the disposing of the incidents of the marriage. See generally Mnookin & Kornhauser, *Bargaining in the Shadow of the Law: The Case of Divorce,* 88 Yale L.J. 950 (1979).

Although they will be regarded with greater scrutiny than the average contract, many of the concerns for the attorney will be the same. The parties, because they are still in a confidential relationship at the time of making, will need roughly equivalent bargaining power. This is most often assured by keeping each party fully informed of the assets and benefits of the other, and by seeing that each is represented by independent counsel. See, e.g., *Friedlander v. Friedlander,* 80 Wash. 2d 293, 494 P.2d 208 (1972). There will also need to be adequate consideration supporting the promises that are made in the contract. *Capps v. Capps,* 216 Va. 378, 219 S.E.2d 901 (1975).

However, once the parties engage attorneys, are dealing at arm's length, and begin the negotiation process, the confidential relationship is severed, for some purposes at least. *Wells v. Wells,* 12 Va. App. 31; 401 S.E.2d 891 (1991). Thus the failure by the wife to disclose a sexual relationship with another man was not fraud in the inducement justifying cancellation of the agreement executed by the parties. *Barnes v. Barnes,* 231 Va. 39, 41, 340 S.E.2d 803 (1986).

Since this is an agreement dealing with the marriage relationship, there are special concerns. These include the requirement that the agreement not "facilitate or promote a divorce or separation." See *Cooley v. Cooley,* 220 Va. 749, 263 S.E.2d 49 (1980). See also *Bailey v. Bailey,* 12 Va. Cir. 67 (City of Norfolk 1987) (property settlement is not void as against public policy when it is prepared before grounds for divorce have ripened). Further, the parties may not divest the court of matters under its jurisdiction, such as those dealing with child custody and support. Va. Code § 20-108; *Wickham v. Wickham,* 215 Va. 694, 213 S.E.2d 750 (1975).

If real property is involved, or if the contract cannot be performed within one year, the statute of frauds will require a writing. Va. Code § 11-2. However, in *Troyer v. Troyer,* 231 Va. 90, 94-95, 341 S.E.2d 182, 184-85 (1986), the Supreme Court upheld an agreement by the husband to convey his interest in the marital home to the wife after their separation where the only "writing" was a deposition in the divorce proceedings. See also *Richardson v. Richardson,* 10 Va. App. 391 (Alexandria, 1990), which approved an oral property settlement agreement read into the court record. However, in *Baskerville v. Baskerville,* 18 Va. Cir. 487 (City of Richmond, 1990), the parties made an oral agreement during depositions. The husband later refused to sign the written agreement, stating that he was mistaken or confused about some of the property. Although Va. Code § 20-109.1 does not require that an agreement be signed, or even that it be in writing, the court disapproved incorporation of the agreement into the final decree to the extent that it involved real property or an understanding that one spouse would pay the debts of another. Therefore, although the agreement remained valid as a contract, the husband could not be placed in contempt for violating its terms since there was doubt about whether he had voluntarily entered into the settlement. The court did not cite *Troyer* in its opinion.

Parol evidence will apparently be allowed to resolve an ambiguity in a property settlement agreement, according to *Kyte v. Kyte,* 18 Va. Cir. 412 (Fairfax Co. 1990), where the ambiguity arose from a single paragraph relating to the question of whether the wife would continue to receive a share of the husband's government pension if she remarried prior to age sixty.

The contractual provisions are usually viewed as a whole, and therefore are not severable. See, e.g., *Buchanan v. Buchanan,* 174 Va. 255, 6 S.E.2d 612 (1939); *Eschner v. Eschner,* 146 Va. 417, 131 S.E. 800 (1926).

The parties may specify which jurisdiction's law is to govern their agreement. Thus, although the agreement was executed in New Jersey, when the intent was that the agreement be governed and construed by the laws of North Carolina, and a paragraph of the agreement reflected this intent, North Carolina law governed. *Knight v. Knight,* 22 Va. Cir. 485 (City of Alexandria 1981) (citing *Tait v. Hain,* 181 Va. 402 (1943)).

The lawyer will also need to consider whether the agreement should be incorporated into the final decree of divorce, so that the court's contempt power can be used in enforcing support clauses. *Durrett v. Durrett,* 204 Va. 59, 129 S.E.2d 50 (1963). Such incorporation will also make it impossible for the court to modify provisions dealing with spousal support, except as provided in the contract itself. Va. Code § 20-109.

The tax advantages of various transactions are also important, and should be considered before a recommendation is made. See §§ 18-11, 18-13, 18-17, 18-31 and 18-35, *infra.*

See generally 27 C.J.S. *Divorce* § 301(1)-(5); Mnookin & Kornhauser, *Bargaining in the Shadow of the Law: The Case of Divorce,* 88 Yale L.J. 950 (1979).

§ 18-2. Capacity of parties to make agreement.

In general, as with any other contract, the parties must be of sufficient age and discretion to make a knowing disposition of their assets and marital rights. See generally 4B Michie's Jurisprudence *Contracts* § 24.

The person seeking to invalidate the agreement because of lack of mental competence must prove that he or she did not understand the nature and character of the agreement and the consequences of executing a legal document. Proof of severe mental depression does not of itself render a person legally incompetent. *Drewry v. Drewry,* 8 Va. App. 460, 383 S.E.2d 12 (1989).

There was no mutual mistake of fact justifying rescission of a property settlement agreement even though the parties referred to Virginia's equitable distribution statute as entitling the wife to 50% of the royalties from the husband's books. *Jennings v. Jennings,* 12 Va. App. 1187, 409 S.E.2d 8 (1991).

§ 18-3. Knowledge of assets — disclosure.

The attorney must take care that each party fully understands the implications of the agreement. This will include a full disclosure of the assets of the other, and a discussion of how much could be expected if the parties chose litigation rather than a property settlement agreement. *Feinberg v. Feinberg,* 96 Misc. 2d 443, 409 N.Y.S.2d 365 (1978).

In *Derby v. Derby,* 8 Va. App. 19, 378 S.E.2d 74 (1989), the court of appeals considered the validity of a settlement agreement executed in a parking lot before the husband's lawyer was available for consultation, in which the parties' real property (the major asset of the marriage) was given completely to the wife. The court found the agreement unconscionable because of the gross disparity of assets each would receive under the agreement, Mr. Derby's emotional weakness, and particularly because the wife had concealed an extramarital relationship and misrepresented her willingness to reconcile.

However, the fact that, at the time the settlement agreement was executed, any or some property was not subject to distribution need not invalidate all or a portion of the agreement. In *Bragan v. Bragan,* 4 Va. App. 516, 358 S.E.2d 757 (1987), the husband and wife executed releases of all existing and future claims as part of a settlement agreement that did not expressly provide for the husband's pension plan. Although the agreement was signed before the equitable distribution statute was enacted, the divorce took place afterward, and the wife sought a monetary award under Va. Code § 20-107.3 based on the value of this plan. The court of appeals held that the release of future claims barred the monetary award. *Id.* at 519. However, there was no unconscionability in *Jennings v. Jennings,* 12 Va. App. 1187, 409 S.E.2d 8 (1991), when the husband, a successful author, suggested an agreement, negotiated its terms, and was not misled by the wife's attorney or the wife. He was afforded and declined an opportunity to obtain his own legal counsel. The agreement was upheld even though it gave the wife a 50% share of the royalties in his books, and even though he "may have possessed some human frailty or compelling personal agenda." 409 S.E.2d at 12. See also *Pillow v. Pillow,* 13 Va. App. 271, 410 S.E.2d 407 (1991), where no unconscionability was found although the husband was not represented by counsel and did not read the agreement thoroughly. The husband retained the car he drove, a boat, personal property, and an interest in the marital home with the right of first refusal should the wife decide to sell the home. In *Thomas v. Thomas,* 36 Va. Cir. 427 (Fairfax Co. 1995), the court found that "all of the benefits available to the Wife" in connection with the Uniformed Services Former Spouses' Protection act means medical and dental care but not the husband's military pension. The wife and her attorney had drafted the property settlement agreement.

§ 18-4. Divorce mediation.

In many civil proceedings, including divorce and separation matters, courts may refer the parties to mediation under Va. Code § 8.01-576.1 et seq. The judge shall consider whether to refer the parties to mediation, and may do so sua sponte or on motion of one of the parties. Upon referral, the parties must attend one evaluation session during which the parties and the mediator assess the case and decide whether to continue with mediation or with adjudication. Further participation in the mediation shall be by consent of all parties, and attorneys for any party may be present during mediation. Va. Code § 16.1-272.1.

When the parties are referred to mediation, the court shall set a return date. The parties shall notify the court in writing if the dispute is resolved prior to the set date. The court may, in its discretion, incorporate any mediated agreement into the terms of its final decree. Only if the order is entered incorporating the mediated agreement will the terms of the voluntary settlement agreement affect any outstanding court order.

The court shall vacate a mediated agreement or an incorporating order if it was procured by fraud or duress or is unconscionable, if disclosure of financial or property information was inadequate, or where evident partiality or misconduct by the mediator prejudiced the rights of a party. Misconduct includes failure of the mediator to inform the parties in writing at the beginning of mediation that:

(1) the mediator does not provide legal advice;

(2) an agreement will affect the legal rights of the parties;

(3) each party may consult with independent legal counsel at any time and is encouraged to do so; and

(4) each party should have any draft agreement reviewed by independent counsel prior to signing the agreement, or should waive this opportunity. Va. Code § 16.1-272.2.

A motion to vacate an order or agreement must be made within two years after the agreement is reached. However, if the motion is based upon fraud, it shall be made within two years after these grounds are discovered or reasonably should have been discovered.

The enactment by every jurisdiction of no-fault grounds of divorce eventually brought about the end of the system that had required extensive input by attorneys. No-fault divorce simplifies trials and places the emphasis upon freeing spouses from unhappy marriages rather than designating blame and defining penalties for breach of family obligations. See, e.g., Jennifer Gerarda Brown & Ian Ayres, *Economic Rationales for Mediation*, 80 Va. L. Rev. 323 (1994); Melli, Erlanger & Chambliss, *The Process of Negotiation: An Exploratory Investigation in the Context of No-Fault Divorce*, 40 Rutgers L. Rev. 1133, 1162 (1988); Pearson, Thoennes, & Vanderkooi, *The Decision to Divorce*, 6 J. Divorce 17, 20

(1982); and Ellen Waldman, *The Role of Legal Norms in Divorce Mediation: An Argument for Inclusion*, 1 Va. J. Soc. Pol'y & L. 87 (1993).

The recent longitudinal study of northern California meditations by Joan M. Kelly shows that on average, mediated disputes (including attorneys' fees) cost about half as much as divorces where only attorneys were involved. Kelly, *Is Mediation Less Expensive? Comparison of Mediated and Adversarial Divorce Costs*, 8 Mediation Q. 15 (1990). The costs of lawyer-mediated divorces are higher than those of their nonlawyer counterparts because lawyers (1) can give legal advice on a broader spectrum of issues, and on more complex issues; (2) will be held to a higher standard of care than their nonlawyer counterparts; (3) will have higher opportunity costs when providing divorce mediation; (4) will have fulfilled more exhaustive educational prerequisites; and (5) are traditionally "reluctan[t] to counter lay competition by cutting fees." Miller, *Lay Divorce Firms and the Unauthorized Practice of Law*, 6 U. Mich. J.L. Ref. 423, 443 (1973).

Some feminist critics suggest that mediation is inappropriate in family law disputes because it reinforces the gender advantages of the husband and removes the judicial check on the process. Woods, *Mediation: A Backlash to Women's Progress on Family Law Issues*, 19 Clearinghouse Rev. 431 (1985). However, the more recent work of Joan Kelly on mediation in California suggests that divorcing wives who used mediation are even more satisfied with their ability to stand up for themselves than are their husbands or divorcing women who used the traditional adversary process. Kelly, *Mediated and Adversarial Divorce: Respondents' Perceptions of Their Processes and Outcomes*, Mediation Q. No. 24 at 71, 78 (Table 1) (1989). Divorce lawyers seem increasingly unnecessary, although in Virginia they do a large proportion of the divorce mediations. See generally Margaret F. Brinig, *Does Mediation Systematically Disadvantage Women?* 2 Wm. & Mary J. Women and the Law 1 (1995).

Alternatives to courtroom battles are generally less expensive than an adjudicated procedure, both in terms of filing fees, costs and attorneys' fees, and particularly in terms of the emotional costs on the parties. For example, Joyce Hauser-Dann found in a recent study of divorced couples that those who had participated in the usual adversary process, even though they did not have a court trial, felt that their involvement with the legal process had made the relationship with their spouse even more difficult than before. This was particularly true of the men who responded to her questionnaire. *Divorce Mediation: A Growing Field?*, 43 Arb. J. 15, 17 (June 1988); and Margaret F. Brinig & Michael V. Alexeev, *Trading at Divorce: Preferences, Legal Rules and Transaction Costs*, 8 Ohio St. J. on Disp. Res. 279 (1993) (analyzing data from Fairfax County and a similar county in Wisconsin).

Particularly where there are children, if the parties can resolve their disputes without resorting to judicial decision making, these non-parties will not have to testify and theoretically will not have to experience their parents' being involved in an expensive and acrimonious procedure. See, e.g., Cochran, *"The Search for Guidance": Reconciling the Primary Caretaker and Joint Custody Preferences,* 20 U. Rich. L. Rev. 1 (1985); Elster, *Solomonic Judgments: Against the Best Interests of the Child,* 54 U. Chi. L. Rev. 1 (1987); Murray, *Improving Parent-Child Relationships Within the Divorced Family: A Call for Legal Reform,* 19 U. Mich. J.L. Ref. 563 (1986).

Further, if the parties have agreed on amounts to be paid in child or spousal support, the obligor spouse will be more likely to carry through on his or her obligations. Noncustodial parents refuse to support their offspring in an alarming number of cases. See D. Chambers, *Making Fathers Pay: The Enforcement of Child Support* (1979); Czapanskiy, *Child Support and Visitation: Rethinking the Connections,* 20 Rutgers L.J. 619 (1989). One reason for this may be that noncustodial parents, primarily fathers, may have little control over how the support money is being spent. See Weiss & Willis, *Children as Collective Goods and Divorce Settlements,* 1 J. Lab. Econ. 268 (1985).

Finally, divorce mediation is designed to focus not only on legal issues, but also on the emotional process of unravelling the marriage. See, e.g., Silberman, *Professional Responsibility Problems of Divorce Mediation,* 16 Fam. L.Q. 107 (1982). Although the stated goal of divorce mediation is not to reconcile the spouses, one of the objectives mentioned by mediators is that of increasing the communication skills of the divorcing couple, who will have to continue in their role as parents regardless of their marital status. In this connection, there is some concern that mediators may have to skillfully intervene to protect power imbalances within the family. See Folger & Bernard, *Divorce Mediation: When Mediators Challenge the Divorcing Parties,* 10 Mediation Q. 5 (1985).

Because the focus is on more than the law, and because the legal issues in most divorces are rather simple, other "helping professionals" can handle most of a divorce mediation, perhaps even to the extent of drafting a memorandum of the parties' understanding. See, e.g., Ethical Considerations and Guidelines of Divorce Mediation, Attachment to a Series of Ethics Opinions of the Virginia State Bar issued April 28, 1983; Family Mediation Rules of the AAA, February 1, 1988, attached to Hauser-Dann, *supra*. Some concerns about the roles that ought to be played by nonlawyers are discussed in *Project, The Unauthorized Practice of Law and Pro Se Divorce: An Empirical Analysis*, 86 Yale L.J. 104 (1976). In meeting the emotional and communications needs of the parties, nonlawyers in fact have more formal training and clinical experience.

Virginia responded to the challenge of nonlawyer mediation by permitting divorce mediation but providing that a lawyer for each spouse must consider any resulting agreement before it is executed. Attachment to a Series of Ethics Opinions of the Virginia State Bar issued April 28, 1983. The mediator, attorney or not, must refrain from attempting to legally represent either party or from giving legal counsel to either or both. In Virginia, any memoranda, work products and other materials, or communications made during a mediation are confidential, and thus are not subject to disclosure in any judicial or administrative proceeding except where all parties agree to waive confidentiality, in an action involving damages arising out of the mediation. Va. Code Ann. § 8.01-581.22 (1990); see generally Comment, *Protecting Confidentiality in Mediation*, 98 Harv. L. Rev. 441 (1984).

Counsel must take care, especially in representing the spouse who has been the dominant or most knowledgeable partner in the marriage, to make sure that the other spouse is adequately represented by counsel. In no event should the attorney undertake to advise the nonrepresented spouse except to urge that he or she obtain counsel. Virginia ethics opinions also forbid the preparation of a waiver of process for the other spouse. Where the wife assured the husband that the attorney she hired would represent both of their interests, and, because of the special relationship of trust between him and his wife, the husband relied on this statement and did not obtain independent legal counsel, the wife's demurrer to his amended complaint attacking the agreement should not have been sustained. *Zdanis v. Deely*, 1995 Va. App. LEXIS 423.

Mr. and Mrs. Bandas executed a separation agreement that provided for binding arbitration of the issues of spousal support and equitable distribution. The final decree of divorce incorporated this agreement, referring specifically to the arbitration provision. The court retained jurisdiction under § 8.01-77 et seq. because of the agreement to arbitrate.

After the divorce, the parties chose the arbitrator, who took evidence over seventeen days and heard argument for an additional seven. During the course of the arbitration, the arbitrator issued five awards concerning spousal and child support, visitation, and property distribution. In *Bandas v. Bandas,* 25 Va. Cir. 492 (City of Richmond 1991), the wife sought to have the court confirm the awards, while the husband argued that they were unconscionable, and that they "gave license to Kay to commit adultery." *Id.* at 496. The Virginia Code sections governing arbitration, §§ 8.01-581.01 — 581.010, require that the party seeking to vacate an arbitrator's award must show arbitrator misconduct by clear proof, and must overcome a presumption that the award is binding. The circuit court found that the record did not reveal anything manifestly unfair or illegal about the arbitrator's determinations. Because there was no plausible view of the law available to defendant that justified him to contest confirmation, causing unnecessary delay and expense to the wife, the court imposed sanctions in the amount of the wife's attorney's fees.

§ 18-5. Consideration.

An agreement between the parties affecting property rights must be supported by mutuality of consideration, binding both parties to perform their promises. This consideration may consist of indemnification on a joint debt. *Capps v. Capps,* 216 Va. 378, 219 S.E.2d 901 (1975). See also *Buchanan v. Buchanan,* 174 Va. 255, 277, 6 S.E.2d 612, 621 (1939). Consideration for a promise may be forbearance by one spouse to bring or prosecute a meritorious suit for divorce against the other. *Upton v. Ames & Webb, Inc.,* 179 Va. 219, 18 S.E.2d 290 (1942). There is also sufficient consideration if one party forgoes a claim for spousal support. *Troyer v. Troyer,* 231 Va. 90, 94, 343 S.E.2d 182 (1986).

§ 18-6. Special requirements — fraud and overreaching.

The agreement must satisfy the approving court as reasonable. *Vellines v. Ely,* 185 Va. 889, 896, 41 S.E.2d 21, 24 (1947). There must not be fraud regarding the purpose of the agreement, *Francois v. Francois,* 599 F.2d 1286 (3d Cir. 1979), or the true nature and extent of financial worth. See, e.g., *Feinberg v. Feinberg,* 96 Misc. 2d 443, 409 N.Y.S.2d 365 (1978).

However, there is no fraud justifying rescission if, after the parties have separated and begun negotiations, one fails to disclose a sexual relationship to the other. *Troyer v. Troyer*, 231 Va. 90, 341 S.E.2d 182 (1986), held that the foregoing would be true even if the parties had not retained counsel at the time of the negotiations. Nor was there reason to declare an agreement invalid in a case where the wife had been receiving psychological counseling for depression and had been hospitalized for this condition. The wife was unable to prove by clear and convincing evidence that she lacked mental capacity to contract or that her husband coerced her into executing the agreement. *Drewry v. Drewry*, 8 Va. App. 460, 383 S.E.2d 12 (1989). The trial court also found no unconscionability since there was no "gross disparity in value exchanged" in the agreement.

A husband could not claim that there had been mutual mistake vitiating an agreement where he participated with counsel in the negotiation and execution of the contract, but did not notice that the agreement contained an error that gave the wife 100% of the net equity in the marital residence. The wife alleged that, although she was surprised when she noticed the apparent change in her husband's position, she thought he had agreed to the change because he "was getting rid of" her. *Ward v. Ward*, 239 Va. 1, 387 S.E.2d 460 (1990). Even though the wife mistakenly believed that the parties' camper would be conveyed along with their North Carolina real estate, she violated their separation agreement by refusing to execute a deed to the property. *Clarke v. Clarke*, 1993 Va. App. LEXIS 113. Since she breached, the wife was liable for her husband's resulting expenses and attorney's fees, but she was not in contempt.

A husband "stunned" his wife by asking her for a divorce. Although the parties continued to live together and to engage in sexual relations, they negotiated a property settlement agreement without the assistance of attorneys. During this time, the husband failed to disclose that he had retained legal counsel, that he had collected a library of "how-to" divorce books and that he was engaged in an extra-marital affair. The husband also met several times with the family's accountant of many years, who prepared a financial statement dramatically understating some of the assets the husband was to retain. Although the wife expressed concern about the accuracy of the property values, the husband and accountant assured her that "that's the way you do it." The court of appeals agreed with the trial court that the agreement was procured by fraud and was unconscionable, and upheld the equitable distribution award giving the wife one-half of the parties' property. *Adams v. Adams*, 1994 Va. App. LEXIS 42. See also *Webb v. Webb*, 16 Va. App. 486, 431 S.E.2d 55 (1993), where an agreement was invalidated because of nondisclosure and overreaching by the attorney husband who prepared the agreement and discouraged his wife from seeking separate legal counsel. The parties negotiated much of the agreement while still living together in the same house and sleeping in the same room, and the husband handled all major financial transactions during the marriage. On the other hand, the unhappy wife was not able to prove she relied on the husband's representations to establish fraud in *Miller v. Miller,* 1994 Va. App. LEXIS 116, nor duress in *Nguyen v. Dang,* 1994 Va. App. LEXIS 138.

However, fraud could be shown where the wife discovered after entry of the decree that part of the real property that was to be conveyed to her according to the separation agreement had been conveyed by the husband to one of his attorneys almost eighteen months before the agreement, and that her signature on that deed had been forged. *Holmes v. Holmes,* 8 Va. App. 457, 382 S.E.2d 27 (1989).

A wife filed a petition requesting vacation of the final decree of divorce, alleging that the husband had made material misrepresentations in a deposition taken before execution of the parties' separation agreement. Although the husband argued that the wife should be held to a standard of knowledge akin to that of a fiduciary relationship, the court of appeals found that such a relationship no longer existed during creation of the agreement, so that she was entitled to rely upon the husband's statements made under oath even though she had suspicions concerning their veracity. *Wells v. Wells,* 12 Va. App. 31, 401 S.E.2d 891 (1991). The court of appeals therefore remanded the case to determine the parties' property and spousal support rights resulting from the invalidity of the settlement agreement. The wife accused her husband of a fraudulent conveyance in *Chattin v. Chattin,* 245 Va. 302, 427 S.E.2d 347 (1993). He moved out of the marital home and began residing with one Barbara Soukup, who was married to another man at the time. He then gave $268,000 to a Delaware corporation in which Soukup was the president and sole stockholder, so that she could purchase property in Henrico County. This property was later sold, and Soukup's corporation used the proceeds to purchase, in its name, a condominium in which Chattin and Soukup were residing at the time of suit. The Virginia Supreme Court agreed with Mrs. Chattin that the conveyance was void as to her, since, before the transfer occurred, she was her husband's creditor under the parties' property settlement agreement. In addition, the court agreed that there was no valuable consideration for the conveyance. Soukup was married at the time the money was given to her, and the transfer was made as an inducement to Soukup to terminate her marriage, which was contrary to public policy.

The court found an agreement unconscionable because of the gross disparity in the assets received through the "over-reaching and oppressive conduct" of the husband at a time when the wife was patently suicidal and operating under impaired judgment. *Scroggins v. Scroggins*, 1996 Va. App. LEXIS 207.

§ 18-7. Facilitating or promoting divorce.

Husband and wife executed an agreement upon separation. After some negotiation about an increased amount of support, the increase was agreed to in exchange for a written promise by the wife that she would not contest the husband's divorce. This was valid since at the time the second agreement was executed there was no dispute that the parties had been separated for one year, so that the husband had valid grounds for an absolute divorce; the general purpose of the contract was to adjust property rights, not to facilitate a divorce, and the agreement was valid. *Cooley v. Cooley*, 220 Va. 749, 263 S.E.2d 49 (1980).

However, where a separation agreement was made solely at the urging of the husband, who wanted to pay his wife not to return to him, it was void as contrary to public policy. *Arrington v. Arrington*, 196 Va. 86, 82 S.E.2d 548 (1954). Likewise, a contract by a wife with a third party that depended upon the continued estrangement of husband and wife and the prosecution of a divorce by the wife was against public policy and void from its inception. *Shelton v. Stewart*, 193 Va. 162, 67 S.E.2d 841 (1951). See also *Upton v. Ames & Webb, Inc.*, 179 Va. 219, 18 S.E.2d 290 (1942).

The public policy rendering agreements facilitating or promoting separation void is the "policy to foster and protect marriage, to encourage the parties to live together, and to prevent separation, marriage being the foundation of the family and of society, without which there would be neither civilization nor progress." *Shelton v. Stewart*, 193 Va. 162, 166, 67 S.E.2d 841, 843 (1951). Therefore, the law will examine a contract between spouses closely and if it appears that it was part of a scheme to effect a separation or obtain a divorce by agreement, where legal grounds therefor did not previously exist, the agreement will be declared a nullity. *Ryan v. Griffin*, 199 Va. 891, 896, 103 S.E.2d 240, 244 (1958).

Although generally speaking a valid separation agreement will preclude a spouse from suing for desertion, if one spouse knows that the other spouse dissents from the separation and he or she nevertheless is determined to continue it, the spouse desiring a reconciliation will not be precluded from obtaining a divorce for desertion. *Butler v. Butler,* 145 Va. 85, 133 S.E. 756 (1926).

§ 18-8. Approval by court.

If the court approves the agreement, but no order for payment of sums in lieu of alimony is made, then the obligation is not alimony but rather a private contractual agreement between the parties. *Shoosmith v. Scott,* 227 Va. 789, 232 S.E.2d 787 (1977). Compare *Durrett v. Durrett,* 204 Va. 59, 62, 63, 129 S.E.2d 50, 53 (1963) (order of payment as alimony).

In order for the court to have power to incorporate the parties' agreement. Va. Code § 20-109 requires the agreement to provide for incorporation. Language directing the court to "approve, ratify and confirm" an agreement is not the same as "incorporation," and the phrase that "it shall be enforceable otherwise" expresses the parties' intention that the agreements not be enforceable through the court's contempt power. *Hoffman v. Hoffman,* 1994 Va. App. LEXIS 137. An "outline" agreement does not have to be incorporated into the final divorce decree. *Brundage v. Brundage,* 1995 Va. App. LEXIS 521.

Where the parties' agreement regarding spousal and child support and mortgage payments, inter alia, was modified by a consent decree before trial, it was proper for the court to enter the agreement filed with it, with modifications as allowed and provided for by the consent decree, as part of the final decree of divorce. *Lindsay v. Lindsay,* 218 Va. 599, 238 S.E.2d 817 (1977).

The circuit court for the City of Fredericksburg has held that when a divorce decree affirms, ratifies, and incorporates the parties' separation agreement, it may also award the dependent spouse a judgment for support arrearages. *Adams v. Adams,* 24 Va. Cir. 380 (City of Fredericksburg 1991).

The agreement will be given full faith and credit if there is a foreign judgment of divorce with personal jurisdiction over both parties, approving and incorporating it. *Wallihan v. Hughes,* 196 Va. 117, 130-31, 82 S.E.2d 553, 561-62 (1954). Full faith and credit need not be given to child custody provisions, or executory child support, which are always subject to modification. Similarly, other states will enforce Virginia property settlement agreements for spousal support since they cannot be modified under Va. Code § 20-109. *Knodel v. Knodel,* 14 Cal. 3d 752, 122 Cal. Rptr. 521, 537 P.2d 353 (1975).

The agreement may be incorporated into the divorce decree either when it has been filed before the final decree of divorce, or when a separate decree is filed after entry of the final divorce decree. Va. Code § 20-109.1.

It was not appropriate to have the former husband sanctioned for appealing a second order of judgment for $45,000 based on an earlier separation agreement providing for child support and conveyance of property, since the appeal was not for improper purposes. *Wetstein v. Wetstein,* 11 Va. App. 331, 369 S.E.2d 96 (1990).

§ 18-9. Effect of court approval.

A. *Termination at remarriage.* Before the addition of Va. Code § 20-109, the obligation to pay under an incorporated agreement did not terminate at the dependent spouse's remarriage unless such termination was provided by its terms, *McLoughlin v. McLoughlin,* 211 Va. 365, 177 S.E.2d 781 (1970), since the court did not have jurisdiction to modify the contractual obligation. The converse is now true: the obligation will now cease upon remarriage unless otherwise provided in the agreement, Va. Code § 20-109.1. For example, in *Miller v. Hawkins,* 14 Va. App. 192, 415 S.E.2d 861 (1992), the parties' agreement provided that the spousal support should terminate when the minor child reached the age of 23 or graduated from college. In the same sentence, the parties agreed that "in the event Wife should pay in full the first lien deed of trust indebtedness owed against the above-described real estate prior to her remarriage," the weekly amount for spousal support should be renegotiated. The wife remarried, and argued that the provisions, read together, were enough to show the parties' intent to continue spousal support notwithstanding her remarriage. Citing cases from other jurisdictions, the court held that in order for the spousal support obligation to survive remarriage of the dependent spouse, the agreement must contain clear and express language evincing the parties' intent that spousal support will continue after remarriage. See also *MacNelly v. MacNelly,* 17 Va. App. 427, 437 S.E.2d 582 (1993), and *Gayler v. Gayler,* 20 Va. App. 83, 455 S.E.2d 278 (1995), where the agreement provided that "the payments shall terminate only upon the Wife's death," but was silent as to the effect of reconciliation. This was not sufficient to avoid the operation of the statutes terminating spousal support. In *Blakey v. Commissioner,* 78 T.C. 963

(1982), the court found that a unitary payment for alimony and child support under *Commissioner v. Lester,* 366 U.S. 299 (1961), still retains alimony characteristics for tax purposes despite the fact that alimony terminates by statute at remarriage.

B. *Termination at death.* Unless husband and wife specify otherwise in the agreement, spousal support will terminate at the death of the payor. Va. Code § 20-107.1. Where husband and wife were separated with no possibility of reconciliation, and agreed that in exchange for all marital rights, save that of prosecuting for divorce, husband would pay wife a sum to discharge a debt secured by her home, his heirs after his death were obligated to continue the payments. *Higgins v. McFarlane,* 196 Va. 889, 86 S.E.2d 168 (1955).

Where husband and wife's agreement was incorporated into a final decree that ordered payments as alimony, she could not recover from the husband's estate at his death. The duty to make alimony payments ceases upon the death of either husband or wife. *Durrett v. Durrett,* 204 Va. 59, 129 S.E.2d 50 (1963). Compare *Moore v. Crutchfield,* 136 Va. 20, 28, 116 S.E. 482, 484 (1923) (in lieu of alimony; no jurisdiction in court to enforce compliance).

C. *Reconciliation.* A separation agreement is not abandoned by a mere conditional, experimental, and temporary living together of the parties, without any intention to abandon the agreement or return to their original situation as husband and wife. For example, in *Higgs v. Higgs,* 12 Va. Cir. 509 (Warren Co. 1983), the husband visited the home where his spouse lived as frequently and regularly as the schedule of the parties would permit. Although the parties had a property settlement agreement, the executory provisions were abrogated and were no longer effective and binding between the parties. See also *Knight v. Knight,* 22 Va. Cir. 485 (City of Alexandria 1981).

Reconciliation of the parties for nearly four years terminated all executory portions of their separation agreement, including a waiver of spousal support. However, there was no abrogation for executed portions of the agreement. *Yeich v. Yeich,* 11 Va. App. 509, 399 S.E.2d 170 (1990). Although the parties resumed their marital relationship for four months after they signed a property settlement agreement, the wife filed for a fault divorce and later was awarded a no-fault divorce incorporating the agreement. The agreement provided: "In the event of a reconciliation and resumption of the marital relationship between the parties, all of the provisions of this Agreement ... shall continue in full force and effect without abatement of any terms." The language of the Agreement demonstrated the parties' intent that it survive any reconciliation. *Jennings v. Jennings,* 12 Va. App. 1187, 409 S.E.2d 8 (1991). See also *Jevcak v. Jevcak,* 1994 Va. App. LEXIS 667 (not designated for publication), and *Smith v. Smith,* 19 Va. App. 155, 449 S.E.2d 506 (1994), where the agreement was enforceable because it was not revoked by a written agreement signed by the parties, as provided in the agreement. Similarly, when the parties agreed in a separation agreement that the husband would convey his rights in the marital residence to the wife, and that she would assume the mortgage, and this was assumed by a deed of assumption, the wife owned the property as feme sole. Although the parties reconciled, the property remained separate and not subject to equitable distribution when they later divorced. At the same time, the wife did not reacquire an interest in the husband's retirement benefits through the reconciliation, since they too had been a subject of the prior agreement. *Garland v. Garland,* 19 Va. Cir. 131 (Spotsylvania Co. 1990).

In *Crenshaw v. Crenshaw,* 12 Va. App. 1129, 408 S.E.2d 556 (1991), the parties executed a property settlement that was approved and confirmed by a 1964 decree for a divorce *a mensa.* After obtaining the divorce *a mensa*, the parties reconciled for 21 years, believing they were married. They never revoked the 1964 decree. In 1974, without the parties' knowledge, the trial court dismissed the suit and removed it from the docket. In 1985, the parties again separated, and in 1986, the husband filed for divorce. The *a mensa* decree remained intact regardless of the intention of the parties, but dismissal of the case under Code § 8.01-335(B) terminated the decree of divorce from bed and board. It was therefore the agreement between the parties, and not the decree, that governed their property rights. The agreement was abrogated by the reconciliation, for when "the parties executed the separation agreement they intended to live separate and apart. When they reestablished a matrimonial home they thereby necessarily intended to void those portions of the agreement that remained executory."

D. *Bankruptcy.* The discharge in bankruptcy of the obligor spouse will not free the bankrupt from his duties to make spousal or child support payments even under a property settlement agreement. 11 U.S.C. § 522(d)(10)(D) allows the spouse to receive support payments. Section 523(a)(5) does not exempt them for the payor. *Douglas v. Douglas,* 17 Va. App. 380, 437 S.E.2d 244 (1993), concerned a divorce decree that required the husband to hold his wife harmless for a joint credit card debt.

Although he paid off the balance, he then incurred a $5,000 additional debt for which the couple remained jointly responsible. He filed for bankruptcy, and failed to list the wife as a creditor or to notify her of the bankruptcy. The court of appeals held that the debt was not discharged in bankruptcy, and the husband was in contempt for failing to comply with the terms of the divorce decree. See also *Tankersley v. Tankersley*, 30 Va. Cir. 273 (Wise Co. 1993); but see *Sexton v. Sexton*, 30 Va. Cir. 271 (Wise Co. 1993) (no contempt since no order to comply with terms of agreement in final decree; wife still had remedy in assumpsit since debt not discharged). However, in *Carter v. Carter*, 18 Va. App. 787, 447 S.E.2d 522 (1994), the husband could discharge his obligation to pay his wife a monetary award to equalize their property distribution. However, by accepting discharge, the husband repudiated the agreement. He therefore gave the wife the right to seek rescission of the agreement. See also *Mosley v. Mosley*, 19 Va. App. 192, 450 S.E.2d 161 (1994) (trial court erred in attempting to hold husband financially responsible for one-half of all marital debts, circumventing the discharge granted him by the federal bankruptcy court). See *In re Calhoun*, 715 F. 2d 1103 (6th Cir. 1983); *Poolman v. Poolman*, 289 F.2d 332 (8th Cir. 1961) (obligation to make payments on deed of trust for family home not dischargeable); see 11 U.S.C.A. § 35. According to the parties' property settlement agreement, incorporated into their final divorce decree, Mr. Tribby was to transfer his interest in the jointly owned marital residence to his wife within fifteen days. Although Mrs. Tribby occupied the house following the separation, and made payments on the deed of trust, Mr. Tribby never conveyed his interest to her. Instead, he failed to make payments on a bank loan to the National Bank of Fredericksburg, which obtained a judgment against him. In *Tribby v. Tribby*, 26 Va. Cir. 372 (Spotsylvania Co. 1992), the circuit court found that the property settlement agreement and divorce decree, while binding on the Tribbys, had no effect on third parties. While they were married, the bank could not reach the home, which the parties owned as tenants by the entireties. After the divorce, however, the bank could extend their judgment lien to Mr. Tribby's interest in the home since the former spouses had become tenants in common.

In their property settlement agreement, Audrey and Alvin Chattin agreed that he would pay her $1,200 per month spousal support for a six and one-half year period; that he would maintain an insurance policy on his life in the amount of $100,000, naming her as irrevocable beneficiary;

and that he would provide health insurance for her. In *Chattin v. Chattin,* 245 Va. 302, 427 S.E.2d 347 (1993), the Virginia Supreme Court determined that the wife was entitled to specific performance of these provisions because she did not have an adequate remedy at law. In order to enforce the contractual provisions for spousal support, she either would have to sue on the contract each time the husband failed to make a payment or would have to wait until a significant arrearage had accumulated before filing suit. If he failed to pay premiums on either insurance policy, it could lapse, thereby requiring her to purchase similar coverage and to bring suit against him each time she paid a renewal premium. If the husband failed to cooperate in providing the necessary information for obtaining life insurance, the wife would be left with no remedy at law whatsoever.

E. *Nonmodifiability.* Va. Code § 20-109 restricts the court's jurisdiction over the modification of alimony. Therefore, where wife and husband had a property settlement agreement incorporated into a divorce decree providing for alimony and child support to be paid to the wife, the court was in error when it ordered an elimination of the duty to pay alimony for a month when the husband was unemployed. *Dienhart v. Dienhart,* 210 Va. 101, 168 S.E.2d 779 (1969).

If the agreement so provides, the amounts payable may be modified based upon such factors as the consumer price index, the age of children, and the income of the spouses. The court may modify a support award in accordance with an agreement between the parties whether filed before or after entry of a final divorce decree. Va. Code § 20-109. See generally Wadlington, *Separation and Settlement Agreements in Virginia: Drafting for Future Modification,* 1976 Va. St. B.A.J. 4. An amendment to a divorce decree could not be entered more than 21 days after the final distribution order. *Bogart v. Bogart,* 21 Va. App. 280, 464 S.E.2d 157 (1995).

F. *Contempt.* Contempt is available once a property settlement agreement is incorporated into the divorce decree and the obligor is directed to pay a specified amount. *McLoughlin v. McLoughlin,* 211 Va. 365, 177 S.E.2d 781 (1970). See also *Adams v. Adams,* 24 Va. Cir. 380 (City of Fredericksburg 1991). It will be available even though, after the decree, the parties agree in writing to a lesser amount. *Capell v. Capell,* 164 Va. 45, 178 S.E. 894 (1935).

However, contempt will not be available as a remedy where the duty to provide some aspect of support under an agreement is not definite, but arises only by implication. *Winn v. Winn,* 218 Va. 8, 235 S.E.2d 307 (1977) (duty to maintain effective health insurance coverage following divorce).

Contempt will be available for any provision reasonably relating to maintenance and care of children that is incorporated into the decree. *Morris v. Morris,* 216 Va. 457, 219 S.E.2d 864 (1975) (custodial parent received residence, etc., and noncustodial parent ordered to keep life insurance policy for the benefit of each child). Whether to find a party in contempt lies within the sound discretion of the trial court. After the wife explained her conduct in *Clarke v. Clarke,* 1993 Va. App. LEXIS 113, the court found that although she had breached the parties' separation agreement, her conduct did not deserve punishment. She had mistakenly thought that a camper would be conveyed to her along with property in North Carolina.

G. *Contractual remedies.* Even though a child has reached majority, the contractual agreement between the parents, if it so provides, will still be in force. The divorce court will not have jurisdiction to enforce the obligation after the child reaches majority. *Cutshaw v. Cutshaw,* 220 Va. 638, 261 S.E.2d 52 (1979).

Garnishment of a federal employee's wages or pension for arrearages of monies due under a support agreement incorporated into a final decree is proper. Although the payments are "alimony" within the federal statute since they are enforceable by contempt, they are not subject to the 25% limitation of the obligor's income since the judgment was not based upon a court order for support but rather upon a violation of a contractual obligation. *Butler v. Butler,* 221 Va. 1035, 277 S.E.2d 180 (1981). However, where yearly additional amounts for child support in a separation agreement were incorporated into a divorce decree, a consent order eliminated not only the effect of the decree but also any contractual obligations under the settlement agreement. The wife therefore had no contractual basis for recovery of the sums allegedly due for additional child support. *Anderson v. Van Landingham,* 236 Va. 85, 372 S.E.2d 137 (1988).

In *Brown v. Brown,* 244 Va. 319, 422 S.E.2d 375 (1992), according to the parties' separation agreement, Winfree Brown was to pay Angela a lump sum of $20,000, while Angela agreed to prepare and execute a deed conveying to him her interest in the family residence. In consideration of the lump sum payment, she also agreed to waive all claims in the husband's employment benefits, including pension plans, or to take property under the law of intestacy. Although the husband made plans to obtain the $20,000, and a check from the employer for nearly $16,000 was found in the glove compartment of his car, Winfree died in September of 1990, before the wife was paid or their divorce finalized. He died intestate, so that if the agreement was enforceable, the couple's two infant children would be his sole heirs at law. The co-administrators of Winfree's estate tendered the wife $20,000 in February, to be delivered to her upon execution of the documents terminating all her interests in the estate and employee benefits. The Virginia Supreme Court, in *Brown v. Brown*, 244 Va. 319, 422 S.E.2d 375 (1992), agreed with the trial court that tender was made within a reasonable time so that the separation agreement was binding upon the wife. Further, the wife's notarized signature of the separation agreement constituted a sufficient spousal consent to a change of beneficiary.

The court of appeals recently upheld provisions of an agreement that required the wife to reimburse the husband for any child support he would be ordered to pay. *Kelley v. Kelley,* 17 Va. App. 93, 435 S.E.2d 421 (1993). Consideration for the provision was the husband's agreement to deed the wife his half interest in the marital home. The court reasoned that the trial court lacked jurisdiction to alter the terms of the agreement or the decree after expiration of the twenty-one-day period provided by Rule 1:1. The dissenting opinion reasoned that the underlying agreement was void as against public policy, and therefore was unaffected by Rule 1:1. The dissent reasoned that the parents could not make an agreement effectively bargaining away the children's right to parental support. See also *Commonwealth ex rel. Sparks,* 1995 Va. App. LEXIS 82. However, provisions of a property settlement agreement could not be specifically enforced by one spouse against the widow of the other. Specific performance is available only where there is privity of contract between plaintiff and defendant. The proper party defendant in such a suit is the executor, the deceased's legal representative. *Fisher v. Bauer,* 246 Va. 490, 436 S.E.2d 602 (1993).

§ 18-10. Who may sue.

Children of parents who executed a property settlement have no ability to enforce it. *Buchanan v. Buchanan,* 170 Va. 458, 197 S.E. 426 (1938). See also *Yarborough v. Yarborough,* 290 U.S. 202 (1933). However, even if the provision for child support has not been incorporated into a final

decree of divorce, the state retains the parents' patriae power to compel
payment for a necessitous child.

§ 18-11. Spousal support — tax consequences.

For agreements entered into before July of 1985, unless an amount was
specifically designated as child support, a sum payable "in lieu of alimony
and for child support," or "for the care, support and maintenance of the
spouse and the minor children" was entirely deductible by the obligor and
taxable as income to the recipient spouse. *Commissioner v. Lester,* 366
U.S. 299 (1961).

If circumstances change so that, for instance, custody reverts to the
obligor spouse, *Carter v. Carter,* 215 Va. 475, 211 S.E.2d 253 (1975),
an allocation between child support and alimony will be made. This will
not be necessary when one spouse seeks an increase in child support,
however. *Wickham v. Wickham,* 215 Va. 694, 213 S.E.2d 750 (1975).

If the agreement provides that the unitary payments will continue
despite the remarriage of the dependent spouse, the amounts received will
still be treated for tax purposes as alimony despite Va. Code § 20-110.
Blakey v. Commissioner, 78 T.C. 963 (1982).

Since the Domestic Relations Tax Reform Act of 1984, payments made
that are contingent upon events relating to the child rather than the spouse
will be treated as child support (not deductible nor taxable) rather than
alimony. Section 422 of Title IV, Subtitle B., P.L. 98-369, amending
I.R.C. § 71(c). Thus, there is currently no advantage to providing for
unitary payments.

Another tax concern is the lump sum payment. Under the former § 71,
the payment was required to be periodic to be classified as alimony. Under
the revised § 71, there is no such requirement. However, § 71(f)(1)
provides that payments in excess of $10,000 will not be treated as alimony
unless made in each of six years, and will not be treated as alimony to the
extent that they decrease by more than $10,000 over the previous taxable
year. Section 71(f)(2). A lump sum would therefore be treated as alimony
so long as paid out somewhat evenly over at least six years following the
separation.

§ 18-12. Termination at death and remarriage.

If the agreement provides that support payments will terminate upon
the dependent spouse's remarriage, the fact that the second marriage is

voidable and annulled will not restore payment under the agreement. *McConkey v. McConkey,* 216 Va. 106, 215 S.E.2d 640 (1975). This is because the obligor spouse has the right to assume the validity of the second marriage and to so reorder his affairs. When the parties specified that the husband's payments of military income or retirement pay should terminate if the wife permanently "cohabited with a male as if to all appearances they were otherwise married," with "permanent" meaning "residence of more than thirty days," the wife's sharing a bedroom with another man for a substantial period of time since 1988 terminated the husband's support obligations under the agreement. *Schweider v. Schweider,* 243 Va. 245, 415 S.E.2d 135 (1992).

If the parties do not clearly and expressly specify that spousal support obligations will survive the dependent spouse's remarriage, Va. Code § 20-109.1 requires that such an obligation will terminate. *Miller v. Hawkins,* 14 Va. App. 192, 415 S.E.2d 861 (1992). See also *MacNelly v. MacNelly,* 17 Va. App. 427, 437 S.E.2d 582 (1993) (spousal support terminated at remarriage when language of property settlement agreement and divorce decree stated that husband should pay $7,000 each month for seven years or until the death of either party, whichever occurred first.)

The trial court should have enforced an indemnification provision of the property settlement agreement that ordered the husband to reimburse the wife for paying his separate debt that had attached as a lien against the marital home. Shortly after the wife filed for divorce, the husband pled guilty to larceny of funds from his employer, and executed a judgment note for $45,000 plus interest secured by a deed of trust on the marital home. Under the parties' agreement, he was to hold her harmless for the debt and reimburse her when she refinanced the home and paid the employer the debt plus interest. This obligation to pay the wife was not in the nature of spousal support and therefore was not extinguished by the remarriage. *Guffey v. Guffey,* 1995 Va. App. LEXIS 819.

§ 18-13. "In exchange for duty of marriage" — asset

Prior to the Tax Reform Act of 1984, in order for periodic payments to qualify as deductible alimony under § 71, they were required to be made in satisfaction of the duty to support, or for release of marital rights such as dower. The Tax Reform Act of 1984 removes this requirement in § 71.

§ 18-14. Modifiability — change in income, custody, etc.

A careful draftsman will consider how to best make the agreement modifiable in the event that various contingencies occur, since unless provided for in the agreement, there will be no modification if the agreement is incorporated into a final decree of divorce. Some possibilities for modification might include a sliding scale based upon the consumer price index, a change in the wages or health of either spouse, completion of a degree program and a change of custody. Another means of providing for contingencies is to say that if a contingency occurs, the agreement will be submitted for arbitration.

However, where yearly additional amounts for child support in a separation agreement were incorporated into a divorce decree, a consent order eliminated not only the effect of the decree but also any contractual obligations under the settlement agreement. *Anderson v. Van Landingham,* 236 Va. 85, 372 S.E.2d 137 (1988).

See generally Wadlington, *Separation and Settlement Agreements in Virginia: Drafting for Future Modification,* 1977 Va. St. B.A.J. 4.

§ 18-15. Provisions for security.

Where the obligor agrees to pay the spouse an annuity, this will be a personal obligation of the obligor. There will not be a lien on the obligor's real estate unless the amount is reduced to judgment and recorded. Va. Code § 8-386. However, if the agreement is affirmed and incorporated into the divorce decree, amounts for spousal support will be considered alimony and constitute a lien upon the obligor's real estate as soon as the decree is recorded on the judgment lien docket. *Durrett v. Durrett,* 204 Va. 59, 129 S.E.2d 50 (1963).

§ 18-16. Medical and life insurance.

Husband and wife may contract that one of them will be required to maintain or pay for medical insurance that covers the other prior to divorce or their children at any time. See, e.g., *Morris v. Morris,* 216 Va. 457, 219 S.E.2d 864 (1975) (life insurance part of general alimony and child support scheme).

In *Chattin v. Chattin,* 245 Va. 302, 427 S.E.2d 347 (1993), the Virginia Supreme Court determined that the wife was entitled to specific performance of a contractual provision that the husband would provide medical insurance. If he failed to pay premiums on the insurance policy, it could lapse, thereby requiring the wife to purchase similar coverage and to bring suit against him each time she paid a renewal premium. Therefore, she did not have an adequate remedy at law. The court of appeals also enforced a contractual medical insurance provision in *Mackie v. Hill,* 16 Va. App. 229, 429 S.E.2d 37 (1993), even though specific language requiring the health insurance for the wife was not included in the divorce decree incorporating the property settlement agreement.

When a husband and wife divorced, the husband agreed to make the children beneficiaries of his life insurance trust, formerly providing for the wife. Thirteen years later, he cancelled all the policies listed in the trust agreement, then totalling $70,000, and obtained other life insurance policies in which he named his second wife as beneficiary. His estate was insolvent, and the children sought to impose a constructive trust upon the proceeds of his life insurance policies. The court of appeals found that the husband breached the contract by canceling his life insurance coverage, and so established a constructive trust on the insurance proceeds, plus interest from the date of the husband's death. *Jones v. Harrison,* 250 Va. 64, 458 S.E.2d 765 (1995).

§ 18-17. Child support, tax of unitary payments, exemptions.

Generally speaking, child support is not taxable to the recipient spouse, nor deductible by the payor spouse. However, under the case of *Commissioner v. Lester,* 366 U.S. 299 (1961), if unitary payments were made to satisfy both spousal and child support obligations, and the exact amount of each was not stated in the agreement or decree, the total amount would be treated as alimony. This position has been removed by the amendments to § 71 found in the Domestic Relations Tax Reform Act of 1984.

If circumstances change so that, for instance, custody reverts to the obligor spouse, *Carter v. Carter,* 215 Va. 475, 211 S.E.2d 253 (1975), an allocation will be made between child support and alimony. This will not be necessary, however, when one spouse merely asks for an increase in child support. *Wickham v. Wickham,* 215 Va. 694, 213 S.E.2d 750 (1975).

The trial judge should not have at the same time incorporated the parties' separation agreement including the obligation to pay for health insurance and college tuition while increasing the agreed-upon amount to match the child support guidelines. *Spagnolo v. Spagnolo,* 20 Va. App. 736, 460 S.E.2d 616 (1995). When the trial judge severed the child support provision as if it were one of a series of separate and independent parts of the agreement, he both violated the parties' express agreement and adopted a remedy exceeding the statutory limitation requiring payments only during the children's minority. When he elected to disregard the agreement and proceed under his authority to make an award for child support, he should not have incorporated the child support provisions of the agreement. As the court noted, he was required to follow the agreement or the statutes, but not both.

§ 18-18. Termination at age of majority of child.

If the parties agree in a contract modified and incorporated into their divorce decree that support of minor children shall be made, and at the time the agreement was written, the law provided that the age of majority was twenty-one, the obligor's duty ceased at the time the child reached eighteen when the state law was changed during the child's minority. *Mack v. Mack,* 217 Va. 534, 229 S.E.2d 895 (1976). Compare *Paul v. Paul,* 214 Va. 651, 203 S.E.2d 123 (1974), where the agreement clearly contemplated that support payments might be made even after the children reached twenty-one.

Two new cases discuss the effect of contractual child support payments extending after the child reaches eighteen. The parties may contract to extend child support beyond the minority of their child. The wife was able to enforce such a contract after the child reached majority in *Gibbs v. Gibbs,* 26 Va. Cir. 27 (Chesterfield Co. 1991). However, a party may not modify an agreement after the child reaches majority to provide for termination of support. The agreement provides that support would continue until age twenty-three or completion of college. *LaReau v. LaReau,* 27 Va. Cir. 133 (Fairfax Co. 1992).

When the parties' property settlement agreement, incorporated into the final decree, required the father to pay child support until the younger child turned eighteen, the support obligation extended until the end of the month and did not end on the child's birthday. *Cory v. Cory,* 1993 Va. App. LEXIS 282.

§ 18-19. College education.

A provision that the husband would endeavor to provide a four-year college education for each child was enforced in *Barnes v. Craig,* 202 Va. 229, 117 S.E.2d 63 (1960). Although such provisions are enforceable, they will not be subject to the contempt power when suit is brought after the child reaches age eighteen. This is because the court's power to enforce the support ends with the child's reaching majority, and any action after that time must be based upon the contract.

The language of the contract will be enforced by the court. Thus, where the contract provided that the "father will participate in the decision making process as to the college to be attended," and he was consulted about college selection by his former wife and son, he was bound to pay support during the son's full-time attendance although he disapproved of the final choice of colleges. *Tiffany v. Tiffany,* 1 Va. App. 11, 15, 332 S.E.2d 796, 799 (1985).

The Circuit Court of Fairfax County determined in *Ackerson v. Ackerson,* 22 Va. Cir. 215 (1990), that a clause in a property settlement agreement providing that "Husband shall pay all reasonable expenditures for a college education for the minor children" should be construed under the circumstances as including the approximately $21,000 annual tuition at Duke University. The father contended that all he was required to pay was the approximately $10,000 for tuition at a state school. The court found that the school was a reasonable place for the daughter to attend college given the father's income and social circumstances. He is a partner at a Washington, D.C. law firm who attended graduate and law school at Harvard University. However, where the terms of the parties' agreement specified that the husband "shall agree on the college of attendance," his obligation to pay was conditioned on his agreement to the college the child attended. *Jones v. Jones,* 19 Va. App. 265, 450 S.E.2d 762 (1994).

On the other hand, a father who promised to pay a pro-rata share of his children's college education if "each of the Parties decide[d] to send any or all of their children to college," would not necessarily have to pay a share of such expenses for his children not yet of college age, although he was responsible for his eldest child's expenses at the University of Virginia. He had no objections to her attending the college, but only to her beginning a year early and before graduating from high school. *Jackson v. Harley,* 1996 Va. App. LEXIS 357.

The trial judge should not have at the same time incorporated the parties' separation agreement including the obligation to pay for health insurance and college tuition while increasing the agreed-upon amount to match the child support guidelines. *Spagnolo v. Spagnolo,* 20 Va. App. 736, 460 S.E.2d 616 (1995). When the father assumed responsibility for paying for the college education, the trial judge might well be justified in approving, ratifying, and incorporating an agreement to pay less than the presumptive guideline amount, so long as written reasons were given for the deviation. *Scott v. Scott,* 12 Va. App. 1245, 1250, 408 S.E.2d 579, 582 (1991).

§ 18-20. Modifiability.

Although under Va. Code § 20-109, an agreed upon amount of payments for spousal support cannot be modified except in accordance with the agreement, the amounts for child support may always be modified, under Va. Code § 20-108. See, e.g., *Morris v. Morris,* 216 Va. 457, 219 S.E.2d 864 (1975); *Parrillo v. Parrillo,* 1 Va. App. 226, 230, 336 S.E.2d 23, 26 (1985). *Parrillo* held that the trial judge erred in concluding that the original agreement had been supplanted by a later court decree involving spousal support. The later decree would only be lawful if it were confined to modification of child support. In 1988, the parties agreed that the $1,687.50 the husband was to pay for child support would be increased beginning January 1, 1990, "by the same percentage that his base salary for the previous year has changed." This agreement was incorporated into their divorce decree. The father later refused to increase the support payments, although the amount payable under the agreement would have been $1,800 per month, claiming that his obligation under the child support guidelines would have been only $1,271.85 per month. In *Jordan v. Jordan,* 23 Va. Cir. 470 (Fairfax Co. 1991), the circuit court held that child support in excess of the guidelines is not in itself a material change in circumstances justifying modification of the child support decree. See also *Scott v. Scott,* 12 Va. App. 1245, 408 S.E.2d 579 (1991). Even if the award is a unitary sum made to effect tax savings under *Commissioner v. Lester,* 366 U.S. 299 (1961), the court may apportion such an award when necessary, *Carter v. Carter,* 215 Va. 475, 211 S.E.2d 253 (1975), such as after the transfer of custody to the obligor spouse. See also *Jarrell v. Jarrell,* 1994 Va. App. LEXIS 672 (not designated for publication). This does not mean that apportionment of a unitary award should be made without a showing of necessity. *Wickham v. Wickham,* 215 Va. 694, 213 S.E.2d 750 (1975). Necessity was not demonstrated when the dependent spouse merely sought an increase in child support.

The provisions for spousal support may be modified in accordance with an agreement filed prior to or following entry of the final decree of divorce, as provided by Va. Code § 20-109.1.

The court will not modify an agreement many years later when to do so would "render the property settlement agreement an absurdity." *Stevenson v. Stevenson,* 22 Va. Cir. 58 (Fairfax Co. 1990). In this case, the wife was receiving 45% of the husband's military pension under the 1980 agreement as alimony, and wished 50% of the pension as a property distribution as well because of the enactment of the Uniform Services Former Spouses Protection Act.

§ 18-21. Attempt to relieve party of duty of support.

A father who is a party to a divorce proceeding "cannot, by contract or otherwise, avoid, or relieve himself from, his primary obligation to maintain a minor child.... After submitting themselves to the jurisdiction of the court, the parents cannot by their agreement deprive it of power to control the custody and maintenance of the child." *Williams v. Woolfolk,* 188 Va. 312, 317, 49 S.E.2d 270, 272 (1948) (quoting from *Emrich v. McNeil,* 75 App. D.C. 307, 126 F.2d 841, 843 (1942)). See also *Buchanan v. Buchanan,* 170 Va. 458, 477, 197 S.E. 426, 434 (1938). See also *Brown v. Brown,* 22 Va. Cir. 263 (Fairfax Co. 1990).

Some jurisdictions that apparently follow this rule have nevertheless held the custodial parent bound by the agreement, so that child support would be forfeited unless the child were actually necessitous. See, e.g., *Pappas v. Pappas,* 247 Iowa 638, 75 N.W.2d 264 (1956). Virginia courts apparently take a stronger position. When the parties agreed that the wife would reimburse the husband for any court-ordered child support payments in exchange for his equity in the marital home, the husband was unable to enforce the covenant because it was against public policy. *Kelley v. Kelley,* 248 Va. 295, 449 S.E.2d 55 (1991). The children's rights to receive support from both parents were substantially abridged, and the court's power to decree support was diminished, violating clearly established law. See also *Commonwealth ex rel. Sparks,* 1995 Va. App. LEXIS 82.

Nor may parents condition receipt of child support upon the custodial mother's permission of visitation with the children or her sharing information about them. *Taxson v. Taxson,* 31 Va. Cir. 348 (Fairfax Co. 1993).

§ 18-22. Large expenditures.

The careful attorney will address the subject of the responsibility for large expenditures in the property settlement agreement, in order to avoid resort to litigation at some future time when the parties might well be distracted. This would include unexpected large medical expenses, payment for orthodontic care, psychiatric services, and private schooling.

§ 18-23. Custody and visitation in general.

Although agreements between parents regarding custody and visitation may be accepted by a court and incorporated into a final decree, they are always subject to a modification based upon a showing of changed circumstances, which so affect the welfare of the child that a change should be made. *Crounse v. Crounse*, 207 Va. 524, 151 S.E.2d 412 (1966). The continuing jurisdiction of the court granting the divorce on the question of custody of minor children cannot be taken away by a contract made between their parents. *Williams v. Woolfolk*, 188 Va. 312, 317, 49 S.E.2d 270, 272 (1948) (citing *Gloth v. Gloth*, 154 Va. 511, 551, 153 S.E. 879, 893 (1930)).

The parents may not agree to condition payment of child support upon the custodial parent's allowing access to the children. *Taxson v. Taxson*, 31 Va. Cir. 348 (Fairfax Co. 1993). The court noted that "the public policy articulated by Virginia law in favor of serving the best interests of the child would be reversed were the provisions in question treated as interdependent." *Id.* at 352.

§ 18-24. Marital debts.

The trial court should have enforced an indemnification provision of the property settlement agreement that ordered the husband to reimburse the wife for paying his separate debt that had attached as a lien against the marital home. Shortly after the wife filed for divorce, the husband pled guilty to larceny of funds from his employer, and executed a judgment note for $45,000 plus interest secured by a deed of trust on the marital home. Under the parties' agreement, he was to hold her harmless for the debt and reimburse her when she refinanced the home and paid the employer the debt plus interest. This obligation to pay the wife was not in the nature of spousal support and therefore was not extinguished by the remarriage. *Guffey v. Guffey*, 1995 Va. App. LEXIS 819.

§ 18-25. Tax exemptions.

Under the former tax law, the custodial spouse generally was entitled to the tax exemption for dependent minor children. However, if the noncustodial spouse provided more than one-half of the child's support, and this exceeded $1,200 per taxable year, under I.R.C. § 152(e)(2)(A), the noncustodial parent would receive the exemption.

The Domestic Relations Tax Reform Act of 1984, Title IV, Subtitle B, P.L. 98-369, § 152 was amended to provide that in all cases where the agreement occurred after July of 1984, the child living with the custodial parent (providing more than one-half the total support) should receive the deduction except when such parent filed a written release of the dependency exemption claim. I.R.C. § 152(e)(2).

§ 18-26. Modifiability by court.

Custody and visitation provisions are always modifiable by the court having jurisdiction over the parties. This modification may occur at the time the agreement is considered for incorporation into the divorce decree, or at any time during the child's minority.

However, modification requires a demonstration of a material change in circumstances. The fact that the agreed-upon amount exceeds the child support guidelines does not in itself constitute such a change. *Jordan v. Jordan,* 23 Va. Cir. 470 (Fairfax Co. 1991). See also *Stevenson v. Stevenson,* 22 Va. Cir. 58 (Fairfax Co. 1990).

§ 18-27. Joint custody.

In many cases the parents may wish to consider an agreement to share custody of minor children. This option has been available in Virginia since the case of *Mullen v. Mullen,* 188 Va. 259, 49 S.E.2d 349 (1948), and may take several forms, all of which allow both parents to have a day-to-day role in child rearing, and simultaneously will permit the child to have a close relationship with both parents. Va. Code § 20-107.2; 20-108.1. Joint custody is most successful in cases where the parties enjoy good relationships with their children, and are able to agree on most issues surrounding their upbringing. If changes of custody are to be frequent, it is helpful if the parties plan to continue living near to each other, so that the children will not have to change schools and youthful companions. Cf.

Lundeen v. Struminger, 209 Va. 548, 165 S.E.2d 285 (1969) (six months' alternating custody not in best interests of children).

§ 18-28. Visitation.

Agreements regarding visitation are appropriate, and will be enforced as part of the custody mechanism by the trial court if the agreement is incorporated into the final decree of divorce. The parties may want to provide for specific hours of visitation, or that visitation will occur on a reasonable notice to the parent having custody. Some couples may wish to include a clause limiting visitation to the times when the noncustodial parent's companions of the opposite sex are not present.

§ 18-29. Keeping in state/area.

The Supreme Court of Virginia has approved an order requiring a child to be kept within the state when the custodial parent wished to move to New York, on grounds that the relationship with the parent making visitation would be weakened by such a move. *Carpenter v. Carpenter,* 220 Va. 299, 257 S.E.2d 845 (1979). See also *Gray v. Gray,* 228 Va. 696, 324 S.E.2d 677 (1985).

Couples may wish to include such a provision in their agreement, which would be enforceable as part of the custody provisions through the contempt power.

§ 18-30. Religious training.

A provision of a divorce decree that children would be reared in the Jewish faith and sent to weekly services and religious instruction was found unconstitutional under Va. Const. § 58 in *Lundeen v. Struminger,* 209 Va. 548, 165 S.E.2d 285 (1969). This was not a case where the parties had a contract that regulated religious upbringing of the children, however.

In *Finnerty v. Finnerty,* 22 Va. Cir. 523 (Frederick Co. 1982), the parties agreed to raise the children as Roman Catholics and to educate them in parochial schools. The agreement was not incorporated into the final decree of divorce, since to ratify and confirm it would violate Art. 1, § 16 of the Constitution of Virginia. The court noted: "If the parties inter se wish to agree that the one having custody will raise the children in a certain faith, the courts, again on grounds of religious freedom, could generally not interfere." *Id.* at 527. Further, the provision that the failure of the custodial parent to raise the children as Catholics would be grounds for termination of custody in such parent "violates the principle that primary consideration will be given to the welfare of the child."

§ 18-31. Property division — general.

In many situations, couples may find it desirable to include provisions pertaining to the division or distribution of marital property. Although these portions of the separation agreement are not enforceable by contempt, a remedy may be sought for breach of contract or specific performance. The parties may by agreement bind themselves to distribute property outside the state of Virginia, and such judgments, if the agreement is incorporated into a final divorce decree, will be given full faith and credit by other states. *Fall v. Eastin,* 215 U.S. 1 (1909).

When the parties agreed in a separation agreement that the husband would convey his rights in the marital residence to the wife, and that she would assume the mortgage, and this was assumed by a deed of assumption, the wife owned the property as feme sole. Although the parties reconciled, the property remained separate and not subject to equitable distribution when they later divorced. At the same time, the wife did not reacquire an interest in the husband's retirement benefits through the reconciliation, since they too had been a subject of the prior agreement. *Garland v. Garland,* 19 Va. Cir. 131 (Spotsylvania Co. 1990). Mr. Tribby agreed to transfer his interest in the jointly owned marital residence to his wife within fifteen days of the signing of the parties' property settlement agreement. Mrs. Tribby occupied the house following the separation, and made payments on the deed of trust. However, Mr. Tribby never conveyed his interest to her. Instead, he failed to make payments on a bank loan to the National Bank of Fredericksburg, which obtained a judgment against him. In *Tribby v. Tribby,* 26 Va. Cir. 372 (Spotsylvania Co. 1992), the circuit court found that the property settlement agreement and divorce decree incorporating it, while binding on the Tribbys, had no effect on third parties. While they were married, the bank could not reach the home that they owned as tenants by the entireties. After the divorce, however, the bank could extend their judgment lien to Mr. Tribby's interest in the home since the former spouses had become tenants in common. The court noted that Mrs. Tribby could still pursue remedies of specific performance against Mr. Tribby for performance of the property settlement agreement. Mrs. Tribby might also be able to win damages in an amount equal to the amount of the judgment lien, plus attorney's fees and costs.

A term allowing the wife a portion of the wife's annuity described as $25,000 per year did not bind the husband to pay her the balance of what the employer actually paid, but was only descriptive. *Morris v. Chatman,* 1995 Va. App. LEXIS 361. The trial court could have awarded a wife a pro rata share of her husband's retirement payment representing the three days in March, 1993, that preceded her remarriage. In the same case, *Gordon v. Whitt,* 1996 Va. App. LEXIS 43, the husband was required to pay the principal as well as the interest due on a home equity credit line when their property settlement agreement provided that he would be liable for the "current indebtedness" on this line of credit.

Newcomb v. Newcomb, 1995 Va. App. LEXIS 596, involved payment of a lump sum due the wife "in lieu of alimony." The parties had a rather complex series of provisions in their agreement involving payment of $100,000 for the wife's interest in the parties' bed and breakfast inn, conveyance of the wife's interest to husband's assignee, and promise of a further payment of 20 percent of the difference between the gross sale price of husband's interest in the property and $250,000 if the inn were sold within fifteen years. Since the assignee had lent $150,000 to husband in consideration of the assignment of wife's share, the "gross sale price" was the stated amount ($470,000) less the $150,000 representing what had been wife's share. After deducting the $250,000 as provided in the agreement, twenty percent of the difference represented $14,000.

Although it may not be possible to have a spouse's professional degree distributed by court order under Va. Code § 20-107.3, obviously provisions may be made through a lump sum payment in a contract between separating spouses.

The agreement should provide that all necessary deeds, etc. will be executed to enable transfer of title as provided in the agreement. See, e.g., *Vellines v. Ely,* 185 Va. 889, 41 S.E.2d 21 (1947) (assignment of insurance proceeds).

§ 18-32. Tax consequences of property distribution.

Under *United States v. Davis,* 370 U.S. 65 (1962), transfers of property in exchange for release of marital rights or obligations were held to be taxable events. This meant that appreciated property transferred was taxed as a capital gain to the transferor. The spouse receiving the property received an adjusted basis as of the time the property was transferred.

Transfers of property incident to divorce within one year after divorce, or within six years if pursuant to a divorce, will not be taxable events. The transferor will not be taxable, and the recipient spouse will have the original adjusted basis. I.R.C. § 1041. If the parties specify that each will be responsible for paying taxes accrued on his or her respective income, there is no need for repayment of any "offset" if it turns out that no tax is owed. *Smith v. Smith,* 15 Va. App. 371, 423 S.E.2d 851 (1992).

§ 18-33. Disclosure of marital property.

As previously noted, the agreement may be found void if the parties did not adequately disclose the extent of their property at the time of its making. See, e.g., *Feinberg v. Feinberg,* 96 Misc. 2d 443, 409 N.Y.S.2d 365 (1978).

§ 18-34. Enforcement provision.

As previously noted, the property distribution portion of a separation agreement cannot be modified except by further contract. Since there is no alimony nor child support involved, the court's contempt power cannot be used for enforcement. The defaulting party will have to be sued in an action on the contract for damages or specific performance. For example, in their property settlement agreement, Audrey and Alvin Chattin agreed that he would pay her $1,200 per month spousal support for a six and one-half year period, that he would maintain an insurance policy on his life in the amount of $100,000, naming her as irrevocable beneficiary, and that he would provide health insurance for her. In *Chattin v. Chattin,* 245 Va. 302, 427 S.E.2d 347 (1993), the Virginia Supreme Court determined that the wife was entitled to specific performance of these provisions because in order to enforce the contractual provisions for spousal support, she either would have to sue on the contract each time the husband failed to make a payment or would have to wait until a significant arrearage had accumulated before filing suit. If the husband failed to pay premiums on either insurance policy, it could lapse, thereby requiring the wife to purchase similar coverage and to bring suit against him each time she paid a renewal premium. If the husband failed to cooperate in providing the necessary information for obtaining life insurance, the wife would be left with no remedy at law whatsoever. Specific performance was therefore appropriate because she did not have an adequate remedy at law.

Whether to find a party in contempt lies within the sound discretion of the trial court. After the wife explained her conduct in *Clarke v. Clarke,* 1993 Va. App. LEXIS 113, the court found that although she had breached the parties' separation agreement, her conduct did not deserve punishment. She had mistakenly thought that a camper would be conveyed to her along with property in North Carolina.

In *Tribby v. Tribby,* 26 Va. Cir. 372 (Spotsylvania Co. 1992), the circuit court upheld a bank's judgment lien against the former marital home. According to the parties' property settlement agreement incorporated into their final divorce decree, Mr. Tribby was to transfer his interest in the jointly owned marital residence to his wife within fifteen days. Although Mrs. Tribby occupied the house following the separation, and made payments on the deed of trust, Mr. Tribby never conveyed his interest to her. Instead, he failed to make payments on a bank loan to the National Bank of Fredericksburg, which obtained a judgment against him. The court noted that Mrs. Tribby could seek specific performance against Mr. Tribby for performance of the property settlement agreement, and might win a judgment against him in an amount equal to the amount of the bank's lien, plus attorney's fees and costs.

According to their separation agreement, Winfree Brown was to pay Angela a lump sum of $20,000, while Angela agreed to prepare and execute a deed conveying to him her interest in the family residence. *Brown v. Brown,* 244 Va. 319, 422 S.E.2d 375 (1992). In consideration of the lump sum payment, she also agreed to waive all claims in the husband's employment benefits, including pension plans. She also agreed to waive her right to take property under the law of intestacy. The husband made plans to obtain the $20,000, and a check from the employer for nearly $16,000 was found in the glove compartment of his car. Winfree died in September of 1990, before his wife was paid or their divorce finalized. He died intestate, so that if the agreement was enforceable, the couple's two infant children would be his sole heirs at law. The co-administrators of Winfree's estate tendered the former wife $20,000 in February, to be delivered to her upon execution of the documents terminating all her interests in the estate and employee benefits. The Virginia Supreme Court agreed with the trial court that tender was made within a reasonable time so that the separation agreement was binding upon the wife and should be enforced as written. See also *Chattin v. Chattin,* 245 Va. 302, 427 S.E.2d 347 (1993), where Audrey and Alvin Chattin agreed that he would pay her $1,200 per month spousal support for a six and one-half year period, that he would maintain an insurance policy on his life in the amount of $100,000, naming her as irrevocable beneficiary, and that he would provide health insurance for her. The Virginia Supreme Court determined that the wife was entitled to specific performance of these provisions because she did not have an adequate remedy at law. In order to enforce the contractual provisions for spousal support, she either would have to sue on the contract each time the husband failed to make a payment or would have to wait until a significant arrearage had accumulated before filing suit. If he failed to pay premiums on either insurance policy, coverage could lapse, thereby requiring her to purchase similar coverage and to bring suit against him each time she paid a renewal premium. If the husband failed to cooperate in providing the necessary information for obtaining life insurance, the wife would be left with no remedy at law whatsoever.

In *Dziarnowski v. Dziarnowski*, 14 Va. App. 758, 418 S.E.2d 724 (1992), the wife failed to provide her former husband with the 1099 forms required by their property settlement by February 15. According to the agreement, she therefore waived her rights to receipt of spousal support. However, the husband made the next month's support payment and continued to insist that she proffer the income documents. He therefore waived the issue of her noncompliance. Similarly, a husband could not sue for breach of the parties' property settlement agreement, incorporated but not merged into their final divorce decree, unless he pleaded that he had upheld his portion of the contract or been excused for failure to perform. *Taxson v. Taxson*, 30 Va. Cir. 134 (Fairfax Co. 1993). He was also unsuccessful in his suit for intentional infliction of emotional distress against the former wife because he failed to adequately allege facts supporting the cause of action.

A North Carolina property settlement agreement that was incorporated by references in the parties' divorce decree was registered and executed in *Sheppard v. Sheppard*, 1996 Va. App. LEXIS 261. The agreement required the husband to make payments on several loans encumbering the wife's residence, to pay her a monthly amount for utilities and an additional amount for spousal support. In another case, the trial court should have enforced an indemnification provision of the property settlement agreement that ordered the husband to reimburse the wife for paying his separate debt that had attached as a lien against the marital home. Shortly after the wife filed for divorce, the husband pled guilty to larceny of funds from his employer, and executed a judgment note for

$45,000 plus interest secured by a deed of trust on the marital home. Under the parties' agreement, he was to hold her harmless for the debt and reimburse her when she refinanced the home and paid the employer the debt plus interest. This obligation to pay the wife was not in the nature of spousal support and therefore was not extinguished by the remarriage. *Guffey v. Guffey*, 1995 Va. App. LEXIS 819.

When a husband and wife divorced, the husband agreed to make the children beneficiaries of his life insurance trust, formerly providing for the wife. Thirteen years later, he cancelled all the policies listed in the trust agreement, then totalling $70,000, and obtained other life insurance policies in which he named his second wife as beneficiary. His estate was insolvent, and the children sought to impose a constructive trust upon the proceeds of his life insurance policies. The court of appeals found that the husband breached the contract by canceling his life insurance coverage, and so established a constructive trust on the insurance proceeds, plus interest from the date of the husband's death. *Jones v. Harrison*, 250 Va. 64, 458 S.E.2d 765 (1995).

§ 18-35. Appraisal and valuation.

It is appropriate before execution of the agreement to have a valuation of the parties' property made by an independent appraiser or accountant. This would be especially important in the case of a small business, a professional practice, or a closely held corporation, or when pension or retirement plans make up a portion of the marital assets. See, e.g., Troyan, *Divorce and the Valuation of a Disability Pension,* 10 Fam. L. Rep. 3043 (1984); Troyan, *Pension Evaluation and Equitable Distribution,* 10 Fam. L. Rep. 3001 (1984).

§ 18-36. Periodic payment.

Although the property may be conveyed in kind, spouses frequently contract to pay in cash over time. Although formerly such payments would not have been treated as alimony for tax purposes, since not in exchange for a marital right or obligation of support, under the Domestic Relations Tax Reform Act of 1984, I.R.C. § 71 provides that for agreements made after July 15, 1984, "alimony" need not be in exchange for a release of the duty to support. However, § 71 provides further that the payment must be made over a period of more than six years to be deductible, and that they not be "front-loaded" if in excess of $10,000 during any calendar year.

§ 18-37. Security.

Under Virginia law, since the divorce court lacked the power to transfer title, it could not affect the obligor's title to property even to guarantee security for making payments under a divorce decree. *Watkins v. Watkins,* 220 Va. 1051, 265 S.E.2d 750 (1980). This would, however, be entirely possible under a property settlement agreement executed by the parties.

CHAPTER 19

Divorce from Bed and Board

§ 19-1. Introduction.

At common law there was no absolute divorce, and the marriage continued until the death of one of the parties. In order to grant aid to cruelly treated, deserted, or abandoned wives, ecclesiastical courts first provided relief through the doctrine of necessaries, allowing third party creditors to recover, and later allowed more direct aid through the divorce from bed and board.

The alternate term *a mensa* divorce comes from the Latin words "divorce *a mensa et thoro*" or, literally, separation from table and pillow. The parties were no longer bound to live together. The first reported

Virginia case to consider a divorce from bed and board is *Bailey v. Bailey,* 62 Va. (21 Gratt.) 43 (1871), a desertion case.

The limited divorce granted the woman a freedom from her consent to her husband's consortium, and allowed her financial relief through the court award of alimony, see, e.g., *Isaacs v. Isaacs,* 115 Va. 562, 79 S.E. 1072 (1913), as replacement for the spousal support to which she would otherwise have been entitled. See, e.g., *Carr v. Carr,* 63 Va. (22 Gratt.) 168, 173 (1872); *Bailey v. Bailey,* 62 Va. (21 Gratt.) 43 (1871).

Although able once more to handle her own property, see, e.g., *Myers v. Myers,* 83 Va. 806, 6 S.E. 630 (1887), *Marshall v. Baynes,* 88 Va. 1040, 1044, 14 S.E. 978, 979 (1892), the divorced wife was not able to marry again, since she was still married ("bound") to her original husband. In order to continue to receive alimony, she had the duty to remain his chaste and virtuous wife. *Courson v. Courson,* 213 Md. 183, 129 A.2d 917 (1957); *G. v. G.,* 67 N.J. Eq. 30, 41, 56 A. 736, 740 (1803). In *Crenshaw v. Crenshaw,* 12 Va. App. 1129, 408 S.E.2d 556 (1991), the parties executed a property settlement that was approved and confirmed by a 1964 decree for divorce *a mensa.* After obtaining the divorce *a mensa,* the parties reconciled for 21 years, believing they were married. They never revoked the 1964 decree. In 1974, without the parties' knowledge, the trial court dismissed the suit and removed it from the docket. In 1985, the parties again separated, and in 1986, the husband filed for divorce. The *a mensa* decree remained intact regardless of the intention of the parties, but dismissal of the case under Code § 8.01-335(B) terminated the decree of divorce from bed and board.

Because the law favored the continuance of marriages, no subsequent remarriage was necessary to terminate the divorce from bed and board, but merely a filing of a joint petition to the court granting the decree of divorce, which stated that there had been a reconciliation and that the parties wished to resume the status of husband and wife. In one case, *Carr v. Carr,* 63 Va. (22 Gratt.) 168 (1872), because the court felt that the parties might still reconcile, the judgment was suspended for six months to allow the wife to return to the husband she had deserted.

See generally 6A Michie's Jurisprudence *Divorce and Alimony* § 4.

§ 19-2. Reasons for modern action.

Although the concept of the divorce from bed and board has changed so that it may now be granted to husbands as well as wives, it is still a viable cause of action in certain circumstances. The limited divorce is still used occasionally despite the existence of absolute divorces.

For religious reasons, some spouses are troubled by the idea of divorce, and are more comfortable with an action that will allow relative freedom, maintenance, and separate property while maintaining the marital status. See Va. Code § 20-118.

The divorce from bed and board may also be quicker to maintain. An *a mensa* divorce, unlike an absolute divorce for causes excluding adultery, may be brought as soon as the grounds appear. See Va. Code § 20-95; 6A Michie's Jurisprudence *Divorce and Alimony* § 19. No waiting period is involved, therefore, and after the expiration of a year the *a mensa* divorce may be converted by either spouse into an absolute divorce. Va. Code § 20-117. The decree for divorce *a mensa* is appealable and a final decree, so that the defendant could not afterwards file an answer, defensive pleadings, and a cross-bill. *Gordon v. Gordon,* 12 Va. Cir. 405 (City of Radford 1953).

§ 19-3. Requisites of proof.

In order to obtain a divorce from bed and board, counsel must establish three elements: (1) a valid marriage, see *Francis v. Francis,* 72 Va. (31 Gratt.) 283 (1879); see generally 6A Michie's Jurisprudence *Divorce and Alimony* § 29; (2) jurisdiction, *Blankenship v. Blankenship,* 125 Va. 595, 100 S.E. 538 (1919), which includes both domicile, *Chandler v. Chandler,* 132 Va. 418, 112 S.E. 856 (1922); *Howe v. Howe,* 179 Va. 111, 118, 18 S.E.2d 294, 297 (1942) (residence or domicile as used in the divorce statutes contemplates intention to live in adoptive home permanently or certainly for an indefinite period) and residence within the state; and (3) grounds.

The acts relied upon for the divorce must be alleged and proved to have occurred prior to the bringing of the suit, not while it is pending. *Beckner v. Beckner,* 204 Va. 580, 132 S.E.2d 715 (1963). A husband failed to overturn a five-year-old divorce from bed and board on grounds of fraud when the court of appeals found that the new evidence amounted at most to evidence of intrinsic fraud that could have been presented to the court in the original proceeding. *Will v. Will,* 1994 Va. App. LEXIS 100. In the original divorce proceeding, husband's counsel cross-examined two psychologists who testified for the wife. On appeal, the husband sought to introduce affidavits from them stating that they had not been fully able to express their opinions that the wife had not been psychologically or physically abused. The trial judge correctly held that this issue regarding the wife's testimony was previously litigated and decided in the divorce proceeding.

The form for a decree of divorce from bed and board is found at Bean, *Domestic Relations Law Practice System* 177.

§ 19-4. Jurisdiction.

Va. Code § 20-97 provides that no suit for limited divorce may be maintained unless one of the parties is domiciled in and is and has been an actual bona fide resident of the state for at least six months preceding the commencement of the suit. If the spouse is a member of the armed forces stationed in Virginia, has lived with the spouse for six months before the separation in the state, and continues to live in the state until suit is filed, Virginia shall be presumed the state of domicile.

Va. Code § 20-104 allows an order for publication to be entered after an affidavit is filed that the defendant is not a Virginia resident or cannot be located within the state. No deposition in such case can be heard until ten days after the making of the publication. The permissible form for such an order is set forth in Va. Code § 20-105.

A change of domicile must be clearly demonstrated. For example, in one case the husband's domicile of origin was in Virginia, and he also resided there for the one year prior to the complaint. The defendant wife was not then a resident of Virginia. The Virginia court had the power to decree a divorce even though the husband did for some years live in the District of Columbia with the wife. *Chandler v. Chandler,* 132 Va. 418, 112 S.E. 856 (1922).

The place where the parties last cohabited means the place where they last dwelled together as husband and wife with some degree of permanency, as opposed to the place where they last had sexual relations. *Colley v. Colley,* 204 Va. 225, 129 S.E.2d 630 (1963).

When the complaining spouse may have resided outside the state for a lengthy time, always with the intent to return to Virginia, more must be shown to indicate a bona fide actual residence. For example, the plaintiff might have left a wife or child in the state while continuing to support them, kept a house or room in the state ready for occupancy, or maintained a permanent mailing address within the state. *Hiles v. Hiles,* 164 Va. 131, 178 S.E. 913 (1935) (no residence shown where husband stationed in China for many years preceding suit).

See generally 6A Michie's Jurisprudence *Divorce and Alimony* § 36.

§ 19-5. Marriage.

In order for there to be a divorce from bed and board, there must first be proof of a valid marriage.

In *Francis v. Francis,* 72 Va. (31 Gratt.) 283 (1879), the wife sought alimony from the husband after his desertion. He claimed that the parties had never married. The court discussed their relationship and found that they had in fact agreed to be married as required by a contemporary statute dealing with marriages between black people, and had held themselves out as married for many years. The wife was therefore entitled to relief.

§ 19-6. Grounds in general.

Va. Code § 20-95 sets forth the grounds for a divorce from bed and board: cruelty, reasonable apprehension of bodily hurt, willful desertion, or abandonment.

§ 19-7. Desertion or abandonment.

Desertion is a breaking off of matrimonial cohabitation, combined with the intent to desert in the mind of the offender. *Bailey v. Bailey,* 62 Va. (21 Gratt.) 43, 48-49 (1871).

The mere unjustified refusal to have sexual relations will not constitute desertion, but withdrawal of the privilege plus such willful breach and neglect of other marital duties as to practically destroy home life in every true sense does afford grounds for divorce. Compare *Chandler v. Chandler,* 132 Va. 418, 112 S.E. 856 (1922) (absolute divorce); with *Goodwyn v. Goodwyn,* 222 Va. 53, 278 S.E.2d 813 (1981).

No desertion was shown where the wife moved the husband's things out of the marital bedroom and they thereafter ceased to have sexual intercourse, since there was no evidence of refusal to engage in sexual relations. The wife's departure to visit relatives on the day the divorce complaint was served was probably desirable to avoid another altercation, and in any event was not desertion. *Johnson v. Johnson,* 213 Va. 204, 191 S.E.2d 206 (1972); see also *Raiford v. Raiford,* 193 Va. 221, 68 S.E.2d 888 (1952) (husband ordered wife to leave after marital quarrel; she later refused to allow him in home although she had no grounds to fear him); compare *Tutwiler v. Tutwiler,* 118 Va. 724, 88 S.E. 86 (1916) (husband ordered or at least acquiesced to wife's leaving house, published notice that she had deserted so that he was not responsible for her debts, and refused to have her back; held desertion by husband).

The refusal by the wife to live with her husband in the home selected by him, without lawful justification, constitutes desertion. *Graves v. Graves,* 193 Va. 659, 70 S.E.2d 339 (1952).

Although the husband did not voice an objection to the wife's departure at that time, the circumstances showed her settled purpose and plan to leave him without just reason. *Miller v. Miller,* 196 Va. 698, 85 S.E.2d 221 (1955). This was desertion on the wife's part.

Desertion was shown where the wife voluntarily and wilfully left the marital home with the intention to permanently break off marital relations with her husband. She had no legal justification for her abandonment nor valid excuse for her failure to live with him. *Stolfi v. Stolfi,* 203 Va. 696, 126 S.E.2d 923 (1962). See also *Haynor v. Haynor,* 112 Va. 123, 127, 70 S.E. 531, 532 (1911); *Good v. Good,* 122 Va. 30, 94 S.E. 176 (1917).

When people understand that they must live together except for a few reasons known to the law, they learn to soften by mutual accommodation to that yoke which they know they cannot shake off. They become good husbands and wives for the necessity of remaining husbands and wives; for necessity is a powerful master in teaching duties which it imposes. *Evans v. Evans,* 1 Hogg. C.R. 35, 161 Eng. Rep. 466 (1790).

When the parties separate by consent, neither can complain of desertion in the other unless there is some desire expressed for reconciliation — some overture made in good faith for a restoration of the conjugal relation. *Latham v. Latham,* 71 Va. (30 Gratt.) 307, 326 (1878). However, Va. Code § 20-102 states that it shall not be necessary to prove an offer of reconciliation to show willful desertion.

Once the fact of desertion is proved, the complainant need not show that such desertion was without legal jurisdiction or excuse, *Graham v. Graham,* 210 Va. 608, 609-10, 172 S.E.2d 724, 725 (1970), since this would require proving that defendant was not entitled to any divorce on other grounds in addition to making out the primary cause of action. The duty of going forward with evidence of justification and excuse rests upon defendant unless such justification appears from plaintiff's case.

A desertion that is complete at the time, and gives no promise of a return within a reasonable time, certainly becomes permanent in the eyes of the law when the offending party refuses without cause to renew the marriage relation at the request in good faith of the other. *Ringgold v. Ringgold,* 128 Va. 485, 104 S.E. 836 (1920).

See generally 6A Michie's Jurisprudence *Divorce and Alimony* § 18.

§ 19-8. Cruelty.

Mental anguish, repeated and unrelenting neglect and humiliation may be visited upon an unoffending spouse in such degree as to amount to cruelty, but it must be so serious that it makes the marriage relationship unendurable or intolerable. Mere coldness and denial of sexual intercourse, where other marital duties are performed, do not constitute cruelty. *Hoback v. Hoback,* 208 Va. 432, 158 S.E.2d 113 (1967). However, a refusal to permit the spouse sexual intercourse coupled with a general withdrawal from matrimonial cohabitation will constitute cruelty, *Ringgold v. Ringgold,* 128 Va. 485, 104 S.E. 836 (1920), where there is an element of danger to the spouse's health.

The wife was authorized a divorce from bed and board where the husband had over many years subjected her to coarse, vile, and abusive language including charges of prostitution and adultery, beaten her many times, failed to afford her proper support and maintenance, and finally deserted and abandoned her without just cause. *Prindes v. Prindes,* 193 Va. 463, 69 S.E.2d 332 (1952). See also *Myers v. Myers,* 83 Va. 806, 6 S.E. 630 (1887).

The wife was allowed an *a mensa* divorce on grounds of cruelty and constructive desertion where she left after the husband's attack. Although she provoked him by taking money from his wallet, the beating she received and that caused her to leave the marital home was out of proportion to this provocation. *Wimbrow v. Wimbrow,* 208 Va. 141, 156 S.E.2d 598 (1967).

Although some acts may be condoned and even forgiven for a time, cruelty is cumulative. Forgiveness will therefore not be a bar to bringing all the former acts out when continued cruelty has rendered the state of affairs intolerable. *Sollie v. Sollie,* 202 Va. 855, 120 S.E.2d 281 (1961). See also *Bennett v. Bennett,* 179 Va. 239, 18 S.E.2d 911 (1942).

See generally 43 Va. L. Rev. 125 (1957); 6A Michie's Jurisprudence *Divorce and Alimony* §§ 14 and 15.

§ 19-9. Pendente lite alimony.

Va. Code § 20-103 provides that the court may order maintenance and support of the spouse and funds enabling the suit; and may restrain a spouse from interfering with the other; may allow custody and support of minor children; may order exclusive use and possession of the family residence and preservation of the spouse's estate; or may require security. There may also be an order restraining the spouse from entering the jointly owned family home for fifteen days from an ex parte order, where there has been a showing of a reasonable apprehension of bodily harm; or for longer after hearing or notice to the other party.

§ 19-10. Attorney's fees.

Even though the wife is a defendant in a divorce action, in many cases it will be proper to award her attorney's fees and costs, where she has no separate estate. Va. Code § 20-103; *Rowlee v. Rowlee,* 211 Va. 689, 179 S.E.2d 461 (1971) (absolute divorce); *Hughes v. Hughes,* 173 Va. 293, 305, 4 S.E.2d 402, 407 (1939).

The amount of fees should be determined not only on the basis of the size of the party's estate, but in greater degree upon the difficulties of the litigation and the demands it makes upon the time, knowledge and skill of counsel. *Twohy v. Twohy,* 130 Va. 557, 565-66, 107 S.E. 642, 645 (1921).

§ 19-11. Conduct of hearing.

Va. Code § 20-106 allows testimony to be heard orally *(ore tenus)* if required by the court; the testimony may be reduced to writing if either party desires it. Such testimony has the same weight as a deposition. No oral evidence may be taken without notice to the adverse party.

The facts must be clearly proved, independently of the admissions of either party in the pleadings or otherwise. *Prindes v. Prindes,* 193 Va. 463, 69 S.E.2d 332 (1952). Corroboration need only be slight where it is apparent that there is no collusion. *Graves v. Graves,* 193 Va. 659, 662, 70 S.E.2d 339, 340 (1952). The court has the duty "to see that the public policy of the State expressed in the statutes is not violated." *Raiford v. Raiford,* 193 Va. at 228, 68 S.E.2d at 893 (1952). The allegations need therefore be proved by full, clear, and adequate evidence. *Westfall v. Westfall,* 196 Va. 97, 102, 82 S.E.2d 487, 490 (1954).

The Chancellor, as in other suits in equity, may refer questions in a divorce from bed and board to a commissioner, who may prepare the cause and place it in a better position to enable the chancellor to decide it expeditiously and correctly. *Raiford v. Raiford,* 193 Va. 221, 224, 68 S.E.2d 888, 891 (1952).

The findings of the trial court, which had the opportunity to hear the witnesses, should be accorded great weight. *Barnard v. Barnard,* 132 Va. 155, 111 S.E. 227 (1922).

§ 19-12. Sexual relations following decree.

Va. Code § 20-117 provides that a divorce from bed and board shall not be a bar to either party's obtaining an absolute divorce unless grounds for such divorce were known to the party applying for the absolute divorce before the *a mensa* decree was entered.

Va. Code § 20-107.1 allows support following divorces for fault, except adultery, and even then when clear and convincing evidence shows that a denial of support would constitute a manifest injustice based upon the respective degrees of fault during the marriage and the relative economic circumstances of the parties.

Even though there were grounds obtained for a divorce from bed and board, since these were not also grounds for absolute divorce, they would not be sufficient to bar the right of the other spouse to an absolute divorce on grounds of adultery if proven. *Haskins v. Haskins,* 188 Va. 525, 50 S.E.2d 437 (1948).

See generally Wadlington, *Sexual Relations After Separation or Divorce: The New Morality and the Old and New Divorce Laws,* 63 Va. L. Rev. 249 (1977).

§ 19-13. Reconciliation — effect.

Va. Code § 20-120 provides that a decree of *a mensa* divorce may be revoked at any time upon the parties' joint application and satisfactory proof of reconciliation.

A mere cohabitation on a spasmodic basis on out of town trips cannot be dignified into the status of a reconciliation demanded by society of a husband and wife living with each other on a permanent basis. Although each of the parties may have unilaterally desired a reconciliation, their individual efforts were abortive and the decree *a mensa* was never revoked. *Roberts v. Pace,* 193 Va. 156, 161, 67 S.E.2d 844, 846 (1951).

§ 19-14. Merger into absolute divorce.

Va. Code § 20-121 provides that after one year from the grounds for the bed and board decree, when the parties have been separated without interruption since the divorce, and no reconciliation is possible, the court may merge the decree into one for absolute divorce upon either party's application. No notice need be given the guilty party to the bed and board decree unless new matters are alleged, but ten days' notice is required to be given to the injured party. The absolute divorce shall not change prior orders for costs, counsel fees, spousal and child support, nor any restraining orders except as provided in the decree.

Merger may also take place after six months from the date of separation, where the divorce will be based upon the six month no-fault ground under amended Va. Code § 20-121.02. This portion of the no-fault ground is only effective where there are no children of the marriage, and where the parties have filed a separation agreement.

The court may itself enter an absolute divorce where desertion or cruelty is stated grounds for the divorce *a mensa* even though the prayer is for a bed and board divorce, under Va. Code § 20-121.02, so long as the statutory period has elapsed and the court is of the opinion that no reconciliation is possible.

There may not be any occupation of the marital bed during the separation period before merger, since in that event the "separation without interruption" is destroyed. Otherwise a man could "in effect make his wife his mere mistress until the final decree." *Anderson v. Anderson,* 196 Va. 26, 82 S.E.2d 562 (1954). This is to be distinguished from the conduct required to effect a reconciliation in order to change property rights, *id.* at 29-30, 82 S.E.2d at 565 (distinguishing the case from *Roberts v. Pace,* 193 Va. 156, 67 S.E.2d 844 (1951)), especially since in *Anderson,* in addition to three admitted acts of intercourse, the husband lived at home with the wife practically every weekend over a period of six months.

The *a mensa* decree will be superseded by the *a vinculo* decree. *Thomas v. Thomas,* 216 Va. 741, 222 S.E.2d 557 (1976). A property settlement agreement incorporated into the *a mensa* decree could not at that time be modified because of Va. Code § 20-109.

For forms see § 6527, *Petition for Merger of Decree from Bed and Board Into Decree from Bond of Matrimony,* Domestic Relations Law Practice System 179.

§ 19-15. Effect of divorce from bed and board on personal marital rights.

Once the parties have separated, particularly if there has been a divorce *a mensa,* certain of the individual rights that are altered during the marital status again have independent significance. For example, when the parties have separated, one spouse no longer has a right of access to and consortium with the other. If the personal freedom and privacy of the spouse is invaded, a criminal cause of action may result. *Knox v. Commonwealth,* 225 Va. 504, 304 S.E.2d 4 (1983) (burglary from entry into estranged wife's apartment to engage in assault). Likewise, any consent to sexual relations by a wife that is normal during a marriage is revoked when the parties separate unequivocally, particularly if pursuant to a judicial decree, as in the divorce from bed and board. *Weishaupt v. Commonwealth,* 227 Va. 389, 315 S.E.2d 847 (1984).

§ 19-16. Change in property rights following divorce from bed and board.

Va. Code § 20-116 provides that a divorce from bed and board operates upon property thereafter acquired and upon personal rights and legal capacities.

Where the parties' agreement following separation was in effect a divorce from bed and board, and the wife thereafter purchased property, the husband had no curtesy interest in the property. *Marshall v. Baynes,* 88 Va. 1040, 1044, 14 S.E. 978, 979 (1892). Where the property in question was acquired by the husband during the marriage, and the decree provided that "the marital rights of each party to the suit in and to any property owned by the other party be and the same are hereby extinguished," the divorce *a mensa* between the parties operated to extinguish the wife's dower rights. *Gum v. Gum,* 122 Va. 32, 94 S.E. 177 (1917).

See generally 6A Michie's Jurisprudence *Divorce and Alimony* § 52.

§ 19-17. Division of property following divorce from bed and board.

Division of the property is not possible under Va. Code § 20-107.3, which requires an absolute divorce or a dissolution of marriage.

There may of course be affirmation, ratification and incorporation of a property settlement or separation agreement under Va. Code § 20-109.1, which would include custody, child support, spousal support "or any other condition or consideration, monetary or nonmonetary."

Property settlement agreements are discussed in Chapter 18, *supra*.

§ 19-18. Alimony following a mensa divorce.

Alimony may be awarded according to the factors set forth in Va. Code § 20-107.1 unless the decree from bed and board is given against the party seeking alimony. Alimony may be made either in periodic payments, in lump sum, or both.

Since the marriage is still in existence, a decree of alimony could theoretically be made at any time following an *a mensa* divorce. Normally, however, if there was personal jurisdiction over the obligor spouse, the right to alimony will at least be reserved in the final decree.

Alimony in general is discussed in Chapter 21, *infra*. Personal jurisdiction must be obtained before an alimony award is made. *Osborne v. Osborne,* 215 Va. 205, 207 S.E.2d 875 (1974); *Bray v. Landergren,* 161 Va. 699, 172 S.E. 252 (1934).

§ 19-19. Custody.

Va. Code § 20-107.2(1) sets forth factors regarding custody and visitation.

Child custody may be awarded following a divorce from bed and board, to either party, based upon the "best interests of the child" standard. *Fussell v. Fussell,* 182 Va. 720, 30 S.E. 555 (1944). Child custody in general is discussed in Chapter 24, *infra*.

§ 19-20. Child support.

Va. Code § 20-107.2(2) sets forth factors for determining child support. Personal jurisdiction must be obtained before such an award is entered. See *Kulko v. Superior Court,* 436 U.S. 84 (1978); *Gramelspacher v. Gramelspacher,* 204 Va. 839, 134 S.E.2d 285 (1964). Child support and its enforcement are discussed in Chapter 23, *infra*.

§ 19-21. Termination of alimony.

The spouse's right to alimony terminates upon the death of the obligor spouse under Va. Code § 20-107.1, unless the decree incorporates a property settlement agreement specifically providing for nontermination upon death. See generally Chapter 21, *infra.*

§ 19-22. Tax aspects.

The careful attorney must be aware of the tax implications of various financial aspects of the limited divorce. Parties may file as married persons filing separately, and alimony may be deducted by the payor and taxable to the payee under 26 U.S.C. § 71.

However, 1984 changes in the tax law limit the attractiveness of the "unitary award," which, according to *Commissioner v. Lester,* 366 U.S. 299 (1961), made a periodic payment for alimony and child support entirely treatable as alimony so long as the portions were not definitely fixed by the decree. The new law will not allow alimony treatment for any portion attributable to child support.

Transfers of property between spouses, even directly following a divorce or pursuant to a divorce, will no longer be taxable events as was required since *United States v. Davis,* 370 U.S. 65 (1962), for decrees rendered after July of 1984. The payment of money treated as alimony no longer need be solely in satisfaction of the support obligation, although the new provisions require payment for at least six years and a structure designed to prevent front-loading if payments are in excess of $10,000 yearly.

§ 19-23. Defenses to action.

Res judicata. If defendant demurred to plaintiff's complaint for an *a mensa* divorce, and the demurrer was sustained, defendant could successfully plead res judicata when plaintiff brought an *a mensa* action for a second time, based upon the same grounds, and merely set forth the facts more specifically. *Griffin v. Griffin,* 183 Va. 443, 32 S.E.2d 700 (1945).

Fraud and duress. Although it was not shown by the facts in *Scott v. Scott,* 142 Va. 31, 128 S.E. 599 (1925), presumably fraud in procuring a divorce will be an affirmative defense causing the decree to be set aside. An absolute divorce was procured through fraud where the plaintiff husband failed to advise the court that his wife was insane and had been placed out of the state through his agreement. The pleadings stated that she was a nonresident, and she was served only by publication. *Taylor v. Taylor,* 159 Va. 338, 165 S.E. 414 (1932).

Condonation. This is a remission by one of the spouses of an offense the other has committed against the marriage, on condition that treatment will be with conjugal kindness thereafter. While the condition remains unbroken there can be no divorce, but a breach of it revives the original offense. *Owens v. Owens,* 96 Va. 191, 31 S.E. 72 (1898) (cruelty). See generally 6A Michie's Jurisprudence *Divorce and Alimony* § 25.

Justifiable desertion. Although one party can demonstrate that the other deserted, if that other can show that the leaving was without fault, even if not constituting separate grounds for divorce, no divorce for desertion will be granted. *Breschel v. Breschel,* 221 Va. 208, 269 S.E.2d 363 (1980) (*a vinculo* divorce); *Graham v. Graham,* 210 Va. 608, 172 S.E.2d 724 (1970) (*a mensa* divorce).

§ 19-24. Effect of subsequent ex parte divorce.

Under Virginia law, a foreign *ex parte* divorce will not cut off a domiciliary spouse's right to alimony under an *a mensa* decree or otherwise. *Newport v. Newport,* 219 Va. 48, 245 S.E.2d 134 (1978); *Isaacs v. Isaacs,* 115 Va. 562, 79 S.E. 1072 (1913) (decided before "divisible divorce" concept of *Vanderbilt v. Vanderbilt,* 354 U.S. 416 (1957)), and *Estin v. Estin,* 334 U.S. 541 (1948); Kentucky *ex parte* absolute divorce could dissolve marital status but not affect property rights under Virginia *a mensa* decree).

However, if there is personal jurisdiction over the dependent spouse in the foreign proceeding, the right to be awarded alimony will end unless there is a reservation of the right to seek alimony in the foreign final decree. *Ceyte v. Ceyte,* 222 Va. 11, 278 S.E.2d 791 (1981); *Osborne v. Osborne,* 215 Va. 205, 207 S.E.2d 875 (1974).

Full faith and credit has always been given a foreign judgment of a divorce based upon comity, where there was notice by publication plus personal service in Virginia, even though the grounds used for the foreign absolute divorce would only have been grounds for an *a mensa* decree in Virginia. *Humphreys v. Strong,* 139 Va. 146, 169-70, 123 S.E. 554, 561 (1924).

§ 19-25. Effect of divorce from bed and board on testimony.

Stewart v. Commonwealth, 219 Va. 887, 252 S.E.2d 329 (1979), states the proposition that the wife will be competent to testify against her husband, and over his objection, following the parties' *a mensa* divorce.

Her legal capacity to testify after the divorce from bed and board was no different from what it would have been if she had obtained a divorce from the bond of matrimony.... Whatever vestige of marital harmony might have remained to be protected by Stewart's exercise of his right to eliminate Mrs. Stewart as a witness against him had been thoroughly disrupted, if not totally destroyed, by the entry of the *a mensa* decree. Hence, the reason for the privilege no longer existed.

Id. at 892, 252 S.E.2d at 333. This limitation on competence has been abandoned by statute. Va. Code § 19.2-271.2. The privilege not to testify now belongs to the spouse witness.

Of course, the competence to testify, which is determined at the time of trial, should be distinguished from the privilege for confidential marital communications. Even though the parties are divorced at trial, the communication is privileged if made while the parties were married. See *Menefee v. Commonwealth,* 189 Va. 900, 55 S.E.2d 9 (1949).

See generally Friend, *Law of Evidence in Virginia* §§ 57 and 64 (2d ed. 1983).

CHAPTER 20

Absolute Divorce

§ 20-1. Introduction.

Until the seventeenth century, it was impossible for a party to remarry unless a first marriage had been terminated by the death of a spouse. However, a divorce *a mensa,* or divorce from bed and board, could be decreed by the ecclesiastical court to protect the wronged wife after proof of her husband's desertion or abuse. In England, after the reign of Henry VIII, an absolute divorce, or divorce *a vinculo* (from the bonds of matrimony), allowing remarriage to another, could be obtained only by a special act of Parliament.

In Virginia, by statute of 1841, absolute divorces were obtainable through a judicial proceeding where the defendant was guilty of adultery. Act of Mar. 18, 1848, [1848-1849] Va. Acts ch. 122, § 2. The causes of action for absolute divorce were gradually augmented, so that they include imprisonment for a felony, cruelty and desertion after a one year period (also causes of action for divorces from bed and board), sodomy and buggery as well as adultery, and finally, since 1960, separation for a statutory period (now one year in most cases). Va. Code § 20-91.

Because divorce is not a common law action, the statutory requisites must all be closely followed. *White v. White,* 181 Va. 162, 24 S.E.2d 448 (1943). This is because courts are given the power to make divorce decrees by statute alone. See, e.g., *Johnson v. Johnson,* 224 Va. 641, 299 S.E.2d 351 (1983) (no power to divide joint checking account between the parties); *McColter v. Carle,* 149 Va. 584, 592-94, 140 S.E. 670, 673-74 (1927).

Another way of looking at the law of divorce is to note that the state has an interest in the marriage relationship, and so may prescribe the conditions under which the parties may sever it. See, e.g., *McFarland v. McFarland,* 179 Va. 418, 19 S.E.2d 77 (1942); *Raiford v. Raiford,* 193 Va. 221, 68 S.E.2d 888 (1952).

The suit is an action in rem, binding upon parties who are privies and also upon strangers. See *Wills v. Spraggins,* 44 Va. (3 Gratt.) 555 (1847) (probate proceeding).

§ 20-2. Elements of proof.

In order for a complainant to prevail in an action for absolute divorce, it is necessary to prove: (1) jurisdiction, achieved through domicile and residence of one of the parties in the state and the existence of a valid marriage; and (2) grounds for divorce under Va. Code § 20-91.

§ 20-3. Jurisdiction.

Jurisdiction to grant divorces is statutory and strictly limited. *Chandler v. Chandler,* 132 Va. 418, 112 S.E. 856 (1922). A new qualification to the requirement of domicile is the 1987 amendment to Va. Code § 20-97, which permits suit for divorce or annulment by a member of the armed forces or the spouse of such person who was stationed in and resided in the Commonwealth for at least six months preceding the action. Being stationed or residing in the Commonwealth includes, but is not limited to, a member of the armed forces being stationed or residing upon a ship with a Virginia home port or at an air, naval, or military base located within the Commonwealth over which the United States enjoys exclusive federal jurisdiction.

In *Eddine v. Eddine,* 12 Va. App. 760, 406 S.E.2d 914 (1991), the husband and wife divorced in 1986. The husband was awarded the marital home as his separate property, and the wife appealed. The court of appeals reversed and remanded the case for further proceedings. At that point, the husband left the United States for Syria, closed his medical practice and stopped making child support payments. He failed to provide either the wife or the trial court with his new address. The wife moved under § 8.01-319(A) to dispense with any further notice to him. Notice of the hearing on her motion was posted on the door of the marital residence. The court entered an order granting the wife's motion, and four months later, in August of 1988, the trial court heard evidence and entered an order awarding her $289,500 as a monetary award and $3,000 in attorney's fees. The husband filed pro se to set aside this order, noting that he had received no notice of the August hearing, and that therefore § 8.01-319 violated his constitutional right to due process. The court of appeals held, one judge dissenting, that due process was not violated because the husband had a duty to advise the clerk of court of his address and any change in it. "To hold otherwise would allow a litigant disappointed in the direction litigation might be taking to thwart the authority of the court by leaving the area without notifying the court of his or her new address."

Further, the 1991 legislature added a new section (3) to the statute, allowing a serviceman stationed in another country or territory who was domiciled in the Commonwealth for the six-month period immediately preceding his being stationed in the state or territory to be deemed domiciled in and a bona fide resident of Virginia for purposes of obtaining an annulment or divorce. For example, Virginia did not have jurisdiction over the marriage of two German citizens who continued to own property in that country and where the wife was on leave of absence from her job there. *Kewisch v. Fliedner-Kewisch,* 1995 Va. App. LEXIS 265.

The suit is brought in the circuit court, which has general equity jurisdiction. Va. Code § 20-96. Jurisdiction is based upon domicile, according to Va. Code § 20-97, for domicile of a party to the marriage relationship results in the presence of the status of marriage within the state. *Williams v. North Carolina,* 317 U.S. 287 (1942); *Howe v. Howe,* 179 Va. 111, 18 S.E.2d 294 (1942). Domicile requires residence in the state with the intent of remaining there for an indefinite period, if not permanently. *Humphreys v. Humphreys,* 139 Va. 146, 123 S.E. 554 (1924).

In its 1993 reconvened session, the Virginia legislature established a statewide system of family courts. The new legislation, Chapter 929 of the Virginia Acts of Assembly, provides that the family courts will be the courts of original jurisdiction in divorce cases beginning January 1, 1996. Va. Code § 16.1-241(S).

After the court is implemented, judges of the current juvenile and domestic relations district court shall continue in office as family court judges until the expiration of the term for which appointed or elected, or until a vacancy occurs or a successor is appointed or elected (§ 16.1-69.9:01). Like the current juvenile and domestic relations district court judges, family court judges shall be prohibited from engaging in the practice of law. Va. Code § 16.1-12(C). General district court judges, substitute judges, and retired and recalled district court judges may serve on the family court, but only after completing the training program required by the Judicial Council of Virginia. Va. Code §§ 16.1-69.21, 16.1-69.22:1 and 16.1-69.36(8).

Venue shall be in the family court in the county or city in which the judgment was rendered or such proceeding is pending. Transfer of venue in suits for divorce will be governed by § 8.01-257 et seq. as these provisions relate to circuit court. Service of process in divorce cases will be governed by the rules of the Supreme Court or statute (§§ 8.01-328 et seq.), as appropriate. Va. Code § 16.1-263(F).

For any issue arising out of the suit for divorce and other child custody, support and visitation cases, the judge shall consider whether to refer the parties to mediation, and may do so sua sponte or on motion of one of the parties. Upon referral, the parties must attend one evaluation session during which they and the mediator assess the case and decide whether to continue with mediation or with adjudication. Further participation in the mediation shall be by consent of all parties, and attorneys for either spouse may be present during mediation. Va. Code § 16.1-272.1. When the parties are referred to mediation, the court shall set a return date. The parties shall notify the court in writing if the dispute is resolved prior to this return date. The court may, in its discretion, incorporate any mediated agreement into the terms of its final decree. Only if the court order incorporates the mediated agreement will the terms of the voluntary settlement agreement affect any outstanding court order.

The court shall vacate a mediated agreement or an incorporating order where the agreement was procured by fraud or duress, where it is unconscionable, where there was inadequate disclosure of financial or property information, or where there was evident partiality or misconduct by the mediator that prejudiced the rights of a party. Misconduct includes failure of the mediator to inform the parties in writing at the beginning of mediation:

(1) that the mediator does not provide legal advice;

(2) that an agreement will affect the legal rights of the parties;

(3) that each party to mediation has the opportunity to consult with independent legal counsel at any time and is encouraged to do so; and

(4) that each party should have any draft agreement reviewed by independent counsel prior to signing the agreement, or should waive this opportunity. Va. Code § 16.1-272.2.

A motion to vacate an order or agreement must be made within two years after the agreement is reached. If the motion is based upon fraud, however, it shall be made within two years after these grounds are discovered or reasonably should have been discovered.

In cases of divorce, annulment and separate maintenance, disposition shall be governed by provisions of Title 20. Appeals from cases of divorce, annulment or separate maintenance shall be to the court of appeals as provided in § 17-116.05:5. Preliminary protective orders shall not normally be suspended during appeals to the court of appeals or subsequent petitions for appeal to the supreme court on writ of error.

Confidentiality of the cases is governed by § 20-124 in the cases involving the status of marriage. Procedures governing fees can be found in new § 14.1-135.1.

The new family court, when funded, will be a "court not of record" similar to the general district court. The description is for classification purposes only, and the method of trials and appeals for the court shall be governed by applicable statutes and rules of court. Va. Code § 16.1-69.5(a). In cases filed before January 1, 1995, the circuit court may transfer enforcement of divorce decrees, including pendente lite orders, to the family court. Once transfer occurs, the circuit court will be divested of any further jurisdiction over the matter. Va. Code § 20-79(c). The family court shall transmit final orders involving the division or transfer of real property between the parties to the circuit court named in the order or decree for docketing on the judgment lien index. Va. Code § 20-107.3.

If a case is filed in an improper venue but no objection or transfer motion is made by the parties, the divorce will be valid under Va. Code §§ 8.01-264 and 8.01-265. If the venue is not a preferred venue, the court, on its own motion and upon notice to all parties, may transfer the suit to the preferred venue so long as such transfer is implemented within sixty days after service upon all parties. Va. Code § 8.01-264(D). See *Ragouzis v. Ragouzis,* 10 Va. App. 312, 391 S.E.2d 607 (1990), where the husband unsuccessfully sought reversal of a divorce decree from Pulaski County to which the case had been transferred by the court in the City of Radford, where the wife thought he was residing and where she had him personally served.

Venue, which is also jurisdictional, *Blankenship v. Blankenship,* 125 Va. 595, 100 S.E. 538 (1919), is in the county in which the defendant resides, Va. Code § 20-98, or where the parties last cohabited. *Colley v. Colley,* 204 Va. 225, 129 S.E.2d 630 (1963), defines "cohabitation" for this purpose as living together as man and wife, rather than as an act of intercourse. See also *Metzer v. Reynolds,* 231 Va. 444, 345 S.E.2d 291 (1986). The husband failed to show that the parties last cohabited in the City of Richmond as alleged in his complaint. He did offer evidence providing that the defendant was a resident of that city, but her residence was not used as a basis for venue in his complaint. The husband was allowed to amend his Bill of Complaint and adopt all prior proceedings, but the court would not grant a divorce on the current pleadings, for there must be no variance between pleadings and proof. *Overby v. Overby,* 24 Va. Cir. 491 (City of Richmond 1970).

Although the spouse need not have been physically present for every day of the statutory period of six months to afford the court jurisdiction, it is essential that during such part of the year as there was actual absence from the state that the spouse maintained in good faith at least a dwelling somewhere in Virginia as a permanent abode. The requirement of actual residence within the state was not changed by the new language of Va. Code § 20-97, which gives jurisdiction to a person in the armed forces or the spouse of such person only when the person "has lived with his or her spouse for a period of six months or more in the Commonwealth," and when this residence continues "until and at the time a suit for divorce or legal separation is commenced." However, if the person is stationed outside the United States, but was domiciled in Virginia for the six months preceding being stationed in the foreign country or territory, he or she will be deemed to have been domiciled in and a bona fide resident of Virginia for purposes of annulment or divorce. Va. Code § 20-97(3) [added 1991].

In *Barbero v. Barbero,* 23 Va. Cir. 301 (Fairfax Co. 1991), the wife lived in Virginia during most of the marriage while the husband was in the Navy. When he retired from the Navy, he went to New York with the hope of beginning a job there. The wife and the parties' child joined the husband in April of 1990, after she quit the job she had in Virginia Beach. They leased a condominium in New York, opened a joint checking account there and began to receive mail at the New York address. They also put their Virginia Beach property on the market. In the summer of 1990, the parties separated. Mr. Barbero remained in New York until July 20, when he returned to Virginia to complete the sale of the marital home. He remained in Virginia thereafter, while Mrs. Barbero continued to reside in New York. The circuit court held that he had not reestablished domicile and residence for six months in Virginia when he filed for divorce in August of 1990.

After separation of husband and wife, the wife may establish her own separate domicile regardless of the circumstances of the separation. Va. Code § 20-97.

When a husband voluntarily nonsuited a divorce action he had brought in Switzerland (after his wife expended considerable sums in defending the Swiss action, and subpoenaed his former live-in paramour to testify), the trial court did not err by refusing to give extraterritorial recognition by way of comity to the Swiss procedural default doctrines. However, the court did err in granting the husband a final divorce and attempting to retain jurisdiction to later adjudicate the equitable distribution issues without having a joint motion of the parties or making a finding of clear necessity due to the complexity of the property issues. The final decree was vacated, and the case remanded for distribution of the property contemporaneous with the adjudication of the divorce. *Clark v. Clark,* 11 Va. App. 286, 398 S.E.2d 82 (1990).

See generally 6A Michie's Jurisprudence *Divorce and Alimony* § 36.

§ 20-4. Marriage.

The use of domicile, or a status adjudication, rather than personal jurisdiction, for dissolution of marriage requires that the status existed in the first place. Thus it will be necessary to prove, usually by introduction of a marriage certificate or testimony of witnesses to a wedding ceremony, that the parties were in fact duly married. Accordingly, a woman could not obtain a declaration of the validity of her marriage necessary before she could proceed with an action for divorce, because the purported husband had been married to another at the time of the ceremony. The marriage was void *ab initio* even though the woman thought that the "husband" was divorced at the time of the ceremony. *Hager v. Hager,* 3 Va. App. 415, 349 S.E.2d 908 (1986).

Where the marriage was performed in Virginia, copies of the certificate furnished by the State Registrar of Vital Statistics are prima facie evidence of the facts set forth therein. Va. Code § 32-353.27.

If the validity of the marriage was determined in a prior proceeding, such as a separation action, even if the proceeding was in another state, the fact will be res judicata in a divorce action between the parties. *Romeo v. Romeo,* 218 Va. 290, 237 S.E.2d 143 (1977).

§ 20-5. Grounds for divorce in general.

Va. Code § 20-91 sets forth grounds for absolute divorce. These include adultery, sodomy and buggery outside the marriage, desertion or cruelty after a waiting period of a year, imprisonment for a felony and sentence to and service of term of imprisonment for a year or more, and living separate and apart for one year (or six months where there are no children and the parties have executed a property settlement agreement).

The no-fault provision, Va. Code § 20-91(9), became effective on July 1, 1960, and was found constitutional in *Hagen v. Hagen,* 205 Va. 791, 139 S.E.2d 821 (1965), despite claims that it was retroactive legislation, since the defendant "had no vested right to prevent her husband from securing a divorce." *Id.* at 796, 139 S.E.2d at 825. The statute was also upheld in *Canavos v. Canavos,* 205 Va. 744, 139 S.E.2d 825 (1965), despite the fact that recrimination is not a bar to the no-fault section. The no-fault ground was a recognition that society was better off calling a legal end to marriages that had ceased to function in fact. The whole concept of no-fault was examined by the General Assembly during the 1996 session, and similar legislation requiring a showing of fault or a lengthy waiting period has been introduced in a number of other states. See, for example Dana Milback, *Blame Game: No-Fault Divorce is Assailed in Michigan, and Debate Heats Up,* Wall Street Journal, January 5, 1996 at A1. Some of the classic debates about no-fault are, e.g., Herbert Jacob, *A Silent Revolution: Routine Policy Making and the Transformation of Divorce Law in the United States* (U. Chicago Press, 1988); Stephen D.

Sugarman & Herma Hill Kay, *Divorce Reform at the Crossroads* (Yale U. Press, 1990); and Martha A. Fineman, *Implementing Equality: Ideology, Contradiction and Social Change. A Study of Rhetoric and Results in the Regulation of the Consequences of Divorce*, 1983 Wis. L. Rev. 789. More recent discussions are Allen Parkman, *No Fault Divorce: What Went Wrong?* (Westview Press); and Margaret F. Brinig, *The Law and Economics of No-Fault Divorce*, 26 Fam. L.Q. 453 (1993).

See generally Comment, 2 U. Rich. L. Notes 278 (1966); 6A Michie's Jurisprudence *Divorce and Alimony* § 23.1.

The court of appeals has indicated that a court may grant a no-fault divorce despite the parties' agreement not to divorce and the husband's objections to divorce on religious grounds. In *Terrell v. Hackett*, 1993 Va. App. LEXIS 487, the husband had not sufficiently raised the issue below, but the court noted that he probably would not have succeeded in any event.

§ 20-6. Adultery.

The crime of adultery, which also constitutes grounds for divorce, occurs when "any person, being married, voluntarily [has] sexual intercourse with any person not his or her spouse." Va. Code § 18.2-365.

Adultery may be proven even though at that time of the intercourse the guilty party is armed with an *a mensa* divorce decree based upon the spouse's cruelty or desertion. The *a mensa* decree authorizes the parties to live apart, but does not finally sever the matrimonial bond, nor the obligations commensurate with it. *Haskins v. Haskins*, 188 Va. 525, 50 S.E.2d 437 (1948). Since this is true, even though the husband deserted the wife before he committed adultery, a divorce could be granted against him based upon the dual grounds, *Robertson v. Robertson*, 215 Va. 425, 211 S.E.2d 41 (1975); *Bennett v. Bennett*, 187 Va. 631, 47 S.E.2d 312 (1948).

The one question that apparently remains is the effect of adultery after the grounds of absolute divorce have already matured, as opposed to during the waiting period before divorce is granted on grounds of separation. *Coe v. Coe*, 225 Va. 616, 303 S.E.2d 923 (1983). Where the alleged adultery by his wife occurred more than 15 years after separation, and where it was the husband's own fault and misconduct that caused the termination of the marriage, his spousal support obligation continued. *Wallace v. Wallace*, 1 Va. App. 183, 336 S.E.2d 27 (1985). This parallels the development in other states. See also *Surbey v. Surbey*, 5 Va. App.

119, 360 S.E.2d 873 (1987) (both parties were at fault in causing separation and neither party was entitled to assert adultery as grounds for divorce because of the doctrine of recrimination). Divorce in such cases can still be obtained on the separate and apart ground. See generally Wadlington, *Sexual Relations Following Separation or Divorce,* 63 Va. L. Rev. 249 (1977).

Proof in an adultery case must be strict, satisfactory and conclusive, *Phipps v. Phipps,* 167 Va. 190, 188 S.E. 168 (1936); *Throckmorton v. Throckmorton,* 86 Va. 768, 11 S.E. 289 (1890), for "as the offense here is an unnatural one and involves the commission of a crime, the proof offered to establish it must be such as would 'lead the guarded discretion of a reasonable and just man to a conclusion of guilt.'" *Holt v. Holt,* 174 Va. 120, 123, 5 S.E.2d 504 (1939). Strongly suspicious circumstances are inadequate, and care and circumspection should accompany consideration of the evidence. *Painter v. Painter,* 215 Va. 418, 211 S.E.2d 37 (1975) (kissing and embracing not sufficient). However, the evidence of this particularly secret type of activity must of necessity be circumstantial in most cases. *Kirby v. Kirby,* 159 Va. 544, 166 S.E. 484 (1932) (husband spent many evenings taking other woman, with whom he engaged in dry cleaning business, out to dinner, going on drives, and staying alone with her in the apartment he rented for her). *Gamer v. Gamer,* 16 Va. App. 335, 429 S.E.2d 618 (1993) (the other woman had moved rugs, furniture, cookbooks, kitchen utensils, and home decorations into the Gamer home; a television and VCR were in the master bedroom; a closet contained her clothes and shoes; and the wife observed her checkbook and other items listing the Gamer address). See also *Davidson v. Davidson,* 1996 Va. App. LEXIS 130, where the wife's investigator observed him visiting a woman's apartment in the morning regularly and the husband knowingly executed an affidavit admitting that he committed adultery with her. Compare *Holt v. Holt,* 174 Va. 120, 5 S.E.2d 504 (1939) (though suspicious and perhaps improper, wife's conduct not sufficient to establish adultery). Testimony of private detectives is given little weight unless corroborated. *Dooley v. Dooley,* 222 Va. 240, 278 S.E.2d 865 (1981); *Martin v. Martin,* 166 Va. 109, 184 S.E. 220 (1936); *Colbert v. Colbert,* 162 Va. 393, 200, 174 S.E. 660 (1934). However, the husband's admission of adultery both to his wife and another, coupled with proof of his living arrangements with the other woman, were sufficient to support a charge of adultery. *Dodge v. Dodge,* 2 Va. App. 238, 343 S.E.2d 363 (1986). See also *Pommerenke v. Pommerenke,* 7 Va. App. 241, 372

S.E.2d 630 (1988) (wife testified that she and one VanWeel had an affair in Holland, and he later visited the Pommerenke's home for an extended period of time. Mrs. Pommerenke and VanWeel were seen in various stages of undress in the home. Husband was allowed to amend his complaint to add his count for adultery that he did not discover until after the parties had separated and filed for divorce on other grounds. Court found that adultery was proved).

In *Iglesias v. Iglesias,* 19 Va. Cir. 263 (Fairfax Co. 1990), the circuit court held that the wife and an alleged correspondent would not be required to answer questions propounded in a deposition that might require confession of the crime of adultery, since the court could not state which questions should be asked in order to avoid a claim of the privilege against self-incrimination. However, a husband who fails to answer allegations of adultery, invoking the privilege against self-incrimination, may not prosecute a cross-bill against the wife on grounds of adultery, nor plead the affirmative defense of recrimination. *Donaldson v. Donaldson,* 27 Va. Cir. 327 (Fairfax Co. 1992).

Two cases reflect the problems inherent in proof of an adultery case. Where a private investigator testified that the wife had been visited in her home until after midnight by the co-respondent, and where the husband's former attorney admitted to falling asleep on the wife's couch and therefore spending the night there, and visiting her on vacation where he stayed in the same motel but in a different room, adultery was not proven. *Dooley v. Dooley,* 222 Va. 240, 278 S.E.2d 865 (1981). In this case, the wife's explanation was that she was allowed to "date," and had done nothing improper. However, when the errant wife spent the entire night in the co-respondent's apartment, and offered no explanation for her conduct, adultery was proven. *Coe v. Coe,* 225 Va. 616, 303 S.E.2d 923 (1983). See also *Fu v. Fu,* 1994 Va. App. LEXIS 314. But see *Seemann v. Seemann,* 233 Va. 290, 355 S.E.2d 884 (1987) (denial of sexual relations; wife's credibility supported by her religious convictions).

See generally 6A Michie's Jurisprudence *Divorce and Alimony* §§ 7-11.

§ 20-7. Desertion.

The fault ground for desertion requires not only a willful separation by one spouse but also an intent carried through the statutory period of one year not to return to the unoffending spouse. *Markley v. Markley,* 145 Va. 596, 134 S.E. 536 (1926). There need not be an offer of reconciliation before a spouse can obtain a divorce based upon the other's desertion. Va. Code § 20-102; see *Colbert v. Colbert,* 162 Va. 393, 174 S.E. 660 (1934) (before statute).

If the deserting spouse was mentally ill during the time of separation, so that there could be neither intent to remain separate nor the desire to return, formerly there could be no cause of action for desertion. *Wright v. Wright,* 125 Va. 526, 99 S.E. 515 (1919) (decided when desertion required three years, and now rendered obsolete by Va. Code § 20-93). In such a case, there could also be a divorce under the no-fault separation ground, Va. Code § 20-91(9), since the insanity of the defendant does not preclude the running of the time required. Compare *Crittenden v. Crittenden,* 210 Va. 76, 168 S.E.2d 115 (1969), decided before amendment of this section.

When husband and wife married, the wife was a Baptist while her husband was Jewish. She converted to Judaism shortly thereafter. After the birth of the couple's son, however, the wife became intensely interested in and a convert to the Jehovah's Witnesses faith. The wife soon filed for separate maintenance while the husband sued for divorce on grounds of desertion and asked for custody of the child. The Circuit Court for the City of Richmond held in *Plotkin v. Plotkin,* 22 Va. Cir. 435 (1975), that the wife's religious persuasion, standing alone, was neither a ground for divorce nor the basis for an award of custody. Her behavior in pursuing the tenets of her new faith did not amount to an act of cruelty justifying the husband's turning her from the marital domicile nor refusing to reconcile unless she abandoned her religion. He was therefore guilty of constructive desertion, which barred his claim for divorce. However, he was successful in obtaining custody because "the zeal with which the defendant [wife] has and will continue to devote herself to the furtherance and advancement of her religious convictions will necessarily relegate the child to a place of secondary importance."

One spouse is not guilty of legal desertion in separating from the other after the institution of a suit for divorce or during its pendency. *Byrd v. Byrd,* 232 Va. 115, 348 S.E.2d 262 (1986) (no desertion although bill of complaint unsuccessful, since wife's suit was not frivolous); *Roberts v. Roberts,* 223 Va. 736, 292 S.E.2d 370 (1982); *Painter v. Painter,* 215 Va. 418, 211 S.E.2d 37 (1975); *Plattner v. Plattner,* 202 Va. 263, 117 S.E.2d 128 (1960).

There need not be a physical leaving of the marital home by the deserting spouse, but in such cases there must be more than an unjustified refusal to engage in sexual relations. There must be a complete abandonment of marital duties "to such an extent as to render the marriage state well nigh intolerable and impossible to be endured." *Chandler v. Chandler,* 132 Va. 418, 430-31, 112 S.E. 856, 861 (1922) (desertion). See also *Jamison v. Jamison,* 3 Va. App. 644, 352 S.E.2d 719 (1987) (willful withdrawal of sexual privileges without just cause or excuse and the willful breach and neglect of other marital duties; desertion). Compare *Goodwyn v. Goodwyn,* 222 Va. 53, 278 S.E.2d 813 (1981) (no desertion).

An allegation, without more, that one spouse left without any reason and could not be found at time of trial will not constitute desertion. There must be evidence of the conduct of the parties prior to separation as well as testimony concerning the period since separation regarding any attempts at reconciliation. Without this, the departure would just as easily be consistent with a mutual separation as with desertion. *Walker v. Walker,* 120 Va. 410, 91 S.E. 180 (1917). See also *DeMott v. DeMott,* 198 Va. 22, 92 S.E.2d 342 (1956) (husband's witnesses only corroborated the fact that wife left the marital home). Compare *Pillow v. Pillow,* 13 Va. App. 271, 410 S.E.2d 407 (1991), where husband left the marital home to move in with another woman with whom he had been having romantic relations for several months, and refused his wife's invitation to move back to the marital home. The trial court correctly granted the wife a divorce on grounds of desertion rather than the no-fault ground; see also *Amos v. Amos,* 16 Va. App. 923, 434 S.E.2d 348 (1993) (credible evidence showing that husband left marital home, contacted a realtor to sell home, wrote utility companies seeking to discontinue service, signed a lease indicating that he and one son would be sole occupants, and moved out his furniture). There would also be no desertion where one party left the other to go into the armed services. *Moltz v. Moltz,* 182 Va. 737, 30 S.E.2d 561 (1944). However, long continued absence without detaining cause is the best proof of intent to desert. See *Dinsmore v. Dinsmore,* 128 Va. 403, 104 S.E. 785 (1920), where the husband indicated that "he did not intend to support or live any longer with his wife." See also *Collier v. Collier,* 2 Va. App. 125, 341 S.E.2d 827 (1986) (physical act of leaving the marital home, coupled with a letter showing the husband's intent to desert without legal justification, were sufficient to support the award of an absolute divorce). There will be no divorce based upon desertion where a mutually consented to separation agreement is in effect. Cf. *Barnes v. Barnes,* 16 Va. App. 98, 428 S.E.2d 294 (1993), (both parties had accepted that the marriage had ended, both intended to separate at some time in future, and the husband acquiesced in the separation); *Bryant v. Bryant*, 1994 Va. App. LEXIS 17. However, *Gerwe v. Gerwe*, 1996 Va. App. LEXIS 21, found that the husband had deserted the wife when he left the home and moved in with another woman, even though the marriage was "dead" since the spouses had had no relations, sexual or otherwise, for many years. But see *Kerr v. Kerr*, 6 Va. App. 620, 371 S.E.2d 30 (1988) (no desertion where wife refused to move with husband when transferred to another city by his employer; leaving marital home is justified when a spouse's conduct creates conditions so intolerable that the other spouse cannot reasonably be expected to remain in the home); *Rigsby v. Rigsby*, 13 Va. Cir. 86 (Spotsylvania Co. 1987) (no desertion because wife free of legal fault for leaving marital home although evidence insufficient to support a finding of cruelty). *Butler v. Butler*, 145 Va. 85, 133 S.E. 756 (1926) (desertion shown where husband in fact wanted reconciliation but wife refused).

The husband generally has the duty of establishing the place of abode for the parties. The wife has a duty to acquiesce in his selection provided that it is not unreasonable, arbitrary or unjust, nor used to provoke a dissolution of the marriage. *Martin v. Martin*, 202 Va. 769, 120 S.E.2d 471 (1961) (desertion found where the wife insisted on moving to Florida); *Graves v. Graves*, 193 Va. 659, 70 S.E.2d 339 (1952) (desertion found where wife insisted upon living with her relatives in overcrowded conditions). This privilege of establishing domicile is of doubtful constitutional validity.

The husband told the wife to "get out" on two occasions after quarrels over financial matters. Without more, this did not constitute sufficient cause for a divorce on grounds of constructive desertion. *Rowand v. Rowand*, 215 Va. 344, 210 S.E.2d 149 (1974). See also *Brawand v. Brawand*, 1 Va. App. 305, 338 S.E.2d 651 (1986) (husband requested during arguments that wife leave the home).

A husband should not have been granted a divorce based upon his wife's desertion when she left the marital home in order to preserve her health. Remission of her condition of multiple sclerosis was threatened by the presence of the husband's son in the home, since he actively sought to get the wife to leave, and by the husband's refusal to obtain household help for the wife. *Breschel v. Breschel*, 221 Va. 208, 269 S.E.2d 363 (1980). She was free from legal fault and therefore could be awarded support. See also *Capps v. Capps*, 216 Va. 382, 219 S.E.2d 898 (1975).

These cases, where the wife was justified in leaving the marital home, should be compared to *D'Auria v. D'Auria,* 1 Va. App. 455, 340 S.E.2d 164 (1986) (wife's physician testified that her physical problems were the result of severe anxiety in contemplation of divorce; court found she was without legal justification for leaving marital home); and *Rexrode v. Rexrode,* 1 Va. App. 385, 339 S.E.2d 544 (1986). See also *Sprott v. Sprott,* 233 Va. 238, 355 S.E.2d 881 (1987); and *Reid v. Reid,* 7 Va. App. 553, 375 S.E.2d 533 (1989), where wife was not justified in removing herself from the marriage where there had been a gradual breakdown in the marriage, *Pillow v. Pillow,* 13 Va. App. 271, 410 S.E.2d 407 (1991); (case decided before Va. Code § 20-107.1 was amended to allow alimony in appropriate cases despite marital fault); *Garland v. Garland,* 19 Va. Cir. 131 (Spotsylvania Co. 1990); *Hairfield v. Hairfield,* 18 Va. Cir. 256 (Chesterfield Co. 1989); and see *Dexter v. Dexter,* 7 Va. App. 36, 371 S.E.2d 816 (1988) (husband failed to prove that wife willfully breached and neglected significant marital duties where he made the decision to voluntarily leave the marital residence as the "gentlemanly thing" to do); *Kerr v. Kerr,* 6 Va. App. 620, 371 S.E.2d 30 (1988) (no desertion where wife refused to move with husband to another city when he came home intoxicated 4 or 5 times a week and frequently and profanely insulted her).

In order for there to be constructive desertion entitling the departing spouse to a divorce, the conduct of the other must amount to grounds for a divorce, usually based upon cruelty. *Ringgold v. Ringgold,* 128 Va. 485, 104 S.E. 836 (1920); *Ford v. Ford,* 200 Va. 674, 107 S.E.2d 397 (1959); *Baytop v. Baytop,* 199 Va. 388, 100 S.E.2d 14 (1957) (husband was unfaithful to wife; refused to make a home for her). Compare *Edwards v. Cuthbert,* 184 Va. 502, 36 S.E.2d 1 (1945) (no constructive desertion where wife unhappy in husband's family's home through no fault of husband). *Zinkhan v. Zinkhan,* 2 Va. App. 200, 342 S.E.2d 658 (1986) (husband established desertion on wife's part; although divorce was granted on one year separation ground, no spousal support could be awarded); *McLaughlin v. McLaughlin,* 2 Va. App. 463, 346 S.E.2d 535 (1986) (no spousal support where wife had previously expressed a desire to end the marriage and left after quarrel; cruelty claims not corroborated). When the husband always provided the wife with food, clothing, and a home, and never struck her or harmed her in any way, she was guilty of desertion in leaving the marital home because she had no legal justification for leaving. The wife argued that she was deprived of her station in the household and financial decisions because the parties' son had been given the sole responsibility of the checking account. *Lee v. Lee,* 13 Va. App. 118, 408 S.E.2d 769 (1991). Her desertion would be taken into account upon remand in determining the amount of spousal support to which she would be entitled. Compare *Johnson v. Johnson,* 1993 Va. App. LEXIS 214, where the husband constructively deserted his wife. The wife testified that the husband continually sexually abused her, using sexual devices that caused her great pain. Her pleas to discontinue the practice were ignored, and she eventually had to undergo psychological counseling. Her sister and a son testified that the devices existed in the marital home, and she introduced a magazine addressed to the husband and offering similar devices for sale.

There should not be desertion if one spouse leaves to preserve the health or safety of a minor child of either spouse. Even an omission or refusal to provide necessary care, or permission for activity that allows a child's life or health to be seriously injured constitutes felony child abuse. Va. Code § 18.2-371.1 [amended 1988]. In cases involving child abuse, spouses are no longer disqualified from testifying. Va. Code § 19.2-271.2; and see *Osborne v. Commonwealth,* 214 Va. 691, 204 S.E.2d 289 (1974), discussed in § 12-3.

The fact that the plaintiff sought a reconciliation after a period of separation that defendant was not at fault in causing did not create desertion on defendant's part. *McDaniel v. McDaniel,* 175 Va. 402, 9 S.E.2d 360 (1940).

§ 20-8. Cruelty.

Although normally the circumstances supporting a divorce for cruelty will involve physical violence or fear of violence, there are some cases in which marital misconduct is so severe that a divorce will be granted where there is no physical cruelty whatsoever. *Ringgold v. Ringgold,* 128 Va. 485, 104 S.E. 836 (1920) (husband continually abused wife by referring to incident in her childhood and, because of his religious fervor, refused to take her back into his home until she was "purged"). In another example, where the wife's alcohol problem caused her to neglect all the household duties and resulted in both public embarrassment of the husband and his continual stomach disorders, a divorce for cruelty was properly granted. *Hoffecker v. Hoffecker,* 200 Va. 119, 104 S.E.2d 771 (1958). See also *Taylor v. Taylor,* 1995 Va. App. LEXIS 51.

Mere coolness and denial of sexual intercourse, where other marital duties are performed, will not constitute cruelty or desertion. *Aichner v. Aichner,* 215 Va. 624, 626, 212 S.E.2d 278, 279 (1975) (wife refused husband sexual intercourse during last year of twenty-five year marriage when, she claimed, husband worked long hours, lacked affection for her, and displayed no warmth towards her). Mere problems between spouses, caused by unruly tempers, lack of patience, and uncongenial natures, do not require a court to grant a fault divorce. The cruelty must render the association intolerable. Although husband and wife in *Davis v. Davis,* 1994 Va. App. LEXIS 146 (not designated for publication), endured what the court characterized "a deplorable marital situation," the conditions did not substantiate either's claim that one spouse could not reasonably be expected to remain in the marriage due to the other's fault. Rather than one party's specific offense, the couple's drinking problems, constant bickering and lack of compassion caused the dissolution of their marriage. *Id.* at *6-7.

Although there may be provocation of acts of physical violence, these cannot be out of proportion to the other spouse's retaliatory conduct. *Graham v. Graham,* 210 Va. 608, 616, 172 S.E.2d 724, 729 (1970); see also *Wimbrow v. Wimbrow,* 208 Va. 141, 156 S.E.2d 598 (1967).

The acts of cruelty are cumulative, augmented by each additional act, although at first they are condoned to a certain point. *Miller v. Miller,* 140 Va. 424, 125 S.E. 220 (1924); see also *Wimbrow v. Wimbrow,* 208 Va. 141, 156 S.E.2d 598 (1967). A single act of violence will not constitute cruelty unless so atrocious as to endanger life, or unless it causes a reasonable apprehension of danger in the future. *DeMott v. DeMott,* 198 Va. 22, 92 S.E.2d 342 (1956) (no cruelty where husband grabbed wife, struck her, and threatened her with butcher knife on one occasion only, when wife stayed with husband for five days thereafter). The act must have occurred before institution of the divorce action. *Beckner v. Beckner,* 204 Va. 580, 132 S.E.2d 715 (1963) (shooting gun and throwing glass bottle during pendency of suit not cruelty).

A single act of cruelty was sufficient recrimination to bar husband from obtaining fault divorce on wife's prior desertion, when the conduct was so severe and atrocious that it endangered her life and caused her to sustain serious and permanent injuries (paralysis from waist down and confinement to a wheelchair as result of husband's shooting her). *Davis v. Davis,* 8 Va. App. 12, 377 S.E.2d 640 (1989).

The charges must be clearly proved by witnesses, stating the facts rather than their opinions. *Prindes v. Prindes,* 193 Va. 463, 69 S.E.2d 332 (1952). See also *Gottlieb v. Gottlieb,* 19 Va. App. 77, 448 S.E.2d 666 (1994). *Tucker v. Tucker,* 1993 Va. App. LEXIS 291.

See generally 6A Michie's Jurisprudence *Divorce and Alimony* §§ 13-16.

§ 20-9. Imprisonment for felony.

This ground for divorce is allowed by Va. Code § 20-91 where a party subsequent to the marriage has been convicted of a felony and sentenced to confinement for more than one year, and has been confined for such felony. Cohabitation cannot have been resumed after knowledge of the confinement. The remaining question is whether parole after serving only a short portion of the sentence will affect the conjugal rights (as will a pardon, according to the statute).

In *Bandas v. Bandas,* 25 Va. Cir. 492 (City of Richmond, 1991), the husband, who had been convicted and sentenced for a felony in 1986, argued that the wife had resumed cohabitation when she visited him several times at the penitentiary. The court found that the parties did not resume cohabitation, for it implies a continuing condition of living together and carrying out of the marital responsibilities. Therefore, the husband was not faultless, and his fault was recrimination against the wife's proven adultery. In *Sealock v. Sealock,* 26 Va. Cir. 379 (Clarke Co. 1971), the wife obtained a divorce based on grounds of separation although the husband had been imprisoned for a parole violation.

§ 20-10. Living separate and apart.

The no-fault ground does not take precedence over other causes of action for divorce. If other proven grounds exist, the court is not obliged to grant a divorce under the separation statute, Va. Code § 20-91(9), to the exclusion of other fault grounds. *Robertson v. Robertson,* 215 Va. 425, 211 S.E.2d 41 (1975).

Amended Va. Code § 20-121.02 allows a cause of action for no-fault divorce to be brought without the filing of an amended bill of complaint, whatever the original grounds for divorce.

Va. Code § 20-91(9) allows a no-fault divorce when the parties have lived separate and apart for a period of one year. However, this period is shortened to a six-month separation if the parties have entered into a written separation agreement and they have no minor children. A recent amendment to this section clarifies the word "children" to include children born of either party or adopted by one or both parties.

Va. Code § 20-121.02 provides that either party to a divorce sought on fault grounds or a divorce from bed and board may move the court for divorce under § 20-91(9) (the separate and apart section) once the statutory period has expired. In cases where there are no children born of either party or adopted by both or either, this would be six months; otherwise it would take one year. The complaint or cross bill need not be amended. The court did not err in granting a divorce on the no-fault ground even though the husband proved his wife's desertion and adultery. *Best v. Best,* 1993 Va. App. LEXIS 471. The conduct will, of course, be taken into account in determining spousal support.

When both parties are sane, there must be an intention to separate to establish the commencement of the statutory period. Thus, when the husband went overseas in connection with his employment, but wrote to an attorney two years later to institute divorce proceedings, the period of separation began at the later time, for "there must be proof of an intention on the part of at least one of the parties to discontinue permanently the marital cohabitation, followed by physical separation" without any cohabitation. *Hooker v. Hooker,* 215 Va. 415, 417, 211 S.E.2d 34, 36 (1975). Otherwise, many extended separations required for other reasons "could ripen into 'instant divorce' without the salutary period of contemplation required by the statute during which the parties have an opportunity for reconciliation." See also 24 Am. Jur. 2d *Divorce and Separation* § 184 at 305. In *Sealock v. Sealock,* 26 Va. Cir. 379 (Clarke Co. 1971), the wife obtained a divorce based on grounds of separation although husband had been imprisoned for a parole violation (decided at time when separation was required to be for two years without cohabitation).

The term "separate and apart" means more than mere physical separation. The separation must be coupled with the intention in the mind of at least one spouse to live separate and apart permanently. This intention must have occurred at the beginning of the one year period. *Hooker v. Hooker, supra.* This does not mean, however, that when the parties initially began living apart, they thought their separation was permanent. In reality, the parties usually separate on a trial or temporary basis at first.

Although apparently some judges have been granting divorces based upon this ground while the parties still reside under the same roof, see

Brightly v. Brightly, C-68816 (Fairfax Co. 1981), appeal denied, 82-0156 (Va. S. Ct. 1982), this seems to fly in the face of the *Hooker* statement that such situations might ripen into "instant divorce." *Doggett v. Doggett,* 5 Va. Cir. 349, 350 (City of Richmond 1986) ("abandonment — desertion — [and thus, living separate and apart] may be as complete under the same shelter as if oceans rolled between"). See generally 20 U. Rich. L. Rev. 811, 823 (1986). But see *Reynolds v. Reynolds,* 9 Va. Cir. 423 (Henrico Co. 1977) (not sufficient to constitute living separate and apart if all marital duties and relations have not ceased); *Yane v. Yane,* 8 Va. Cir. 336 (Henrico Co. 1986) (cohabitation under Va. Code § 20-91(9)(a) means "having dwelled together under the same roof with more or less permanency," so there could be no divorce even though parties slept in different rooms and spent no time together as husband and wife); *Hairfield v. Hairfield,* 18 Va. Cir. 256 (Chesterfield Co. 1989). See also *Brown v. Brown,* 12 Va. Cir. 525 (Warren Co. 1983) (there was cohabitation where parties were staying in same household, wife occasionally prepared meals and husband did chores around the house and occasionally went shopping with wife); *Konefal v. Konefal,* 18 Va. App. 612, 446 S.E.2d 143 (1994); *Higgs v. Higgs,* 12 Va. Cir. 509 (Warren Co. 1983) (cohabitation invalidating executory portions of separation agreement where parties lived together as frequently and regularly as their schedule would permit "in discharge of their mutual conjugal duties"). Cf. *Reel v. Reel,* 12 Va. Cir. 482 (Frederick Co. 1981) (alimony granted although parties still living under same roof; cohabitation "includes the idea of services rendered one to the other, mutual society and companionship, aid and comfort, protection and conjugal affection.... Sexual intercourse is a usual, important, but not necessarily required, element of the concept."). *Emrich v. Emrich,* 9 Va. App. 288, 387 S.E.2d 274 (1989) (The wife was justified in not filing an answer or appearing at deposition when her husband had resumed cohabitation with her and had told her that the divorce suit would be dismissed. The trial court should not have granted a divorce on grounds of living separate and apart without cohabitation and without interruption for more than one year.).

In addition to problems of collusion that are presented by such a situation, there is also absent a tangible sign of when the parties in fact entertained the intent to live separate and apart. A written agreement between them, or a judgment for nonsupport, might satisfy the evidentiary problems and afford the parties the ability to be free from the consortium of the other implied by the statute. See *Knox v. Commonwealth,* 225 Va.

504, 304 S.E.2d 4 (1983). Compare *Weishaupt v. Commonwealth,* 227 Va. 389, 315 S.E.2d 847 (1984) (rape conviction possible after separation for eleven months and consultation regarding divorce proceedings), with *Kizer v. Commonwealth,* 228 Va. 256, 321 S.E.2d 291 (1984) (no rape conviction possible where no clear intention that the marriage was at an end that was communicated to husband).

By statute, support may be awarded to either spouse after the decree for divorce under this section, unless there exists a fault cause of action against such party. Va. Code § 20-91(9).

See generally 6A Michie's Jurisprudence *Divorce and Alimony* § 23.1.

§ 20-11. Defenses to the action.

Condonation, or resumption of cohabitation after learning of conduct constituting grounds for divorce, Va. Code § 20-94, is a matter of specific affirmative defense which must be specially pleaded, and the burden of proof of such defense is upon the defendant. *White v. White,* 121 Va. 244, 92 S.E. 811 (1917). The matter may be raised by the court on its own motion, denying divorce. *Martin v. Martin,* 166 Va. 109, 184 S.E. 220 (1936). A single act of intercourse after knowledge of adultery will suffice. *Tarr v. Tarr,* 184 Va. 443, 35 S.E.2d 401 (1945). However, the voluntary cohabitation need not be for a lengthy period. *Huddle v. Huddle,* 206 Va. 535, 145 S.E.2d 167 (1965) (ten days, husband continued to be suspicious that wife pregnant by another). Repetition of the misconduct revives the original ground of adultery. *McKee v. McKee,* 206 Va. 527, 145 S.E.2d 163 (1965). There must be an intent by the forgiving spouse to resume the marital relationship. For a modern example, see *Brundage v. Brundage,* 1995 Va. App. LEXIS 521, where the court found that substantial evidence demonstrated that the husband knew of wife's ongoing adulterous relationship prior to the parties' reconciliation.

Cohabitation is more than sexual intercourse.

Separate lives is the issue, not separate roofs. To continue to occupy the same marital home after several alleged acts of adultery; to partake of the hospitality, comfort, and satisfaction of enjoying the same shelter, its contents and surroundings; to accept the reputation, privileges, amenities and immunities of wedlock and apparent marital accord; the protection, security and safety of male companionship, or at least such presence, is enough to sustain the presumption of matrimonial cohabitation.

Moran v. Moran, 12 Va. Cir. 340 (City of Roanoke 1988). See also *Konicki v. Konicki,* 32 Va. Cir. 368 (Spotsylvania Co. 1994). Similarly, cohabitation was found in *Emrich v. Emrich,* 9 Va. App. 288, 387 S.E.2d 274 (1989), where the wife failed to answer the complaint or to appear at deposition because the husband had moved back into the marital home for about one month following filing of the divorce complaint, and had told her that the action would be dismissed.

See generally 6A Michie's Jurisprudence *Divorce and Alimony* § 25.

In a desertion case brought against the husband, if he had repented and made any overture to his wife with the intention of ending the separation and if conduct on her part amounting to cruelty had prevented the cohabitation, that would have justified his continuing to live separate from her and *she* would have been guilty of desertion. *Cumming v. Cumming,* 127 Va. 16, 17, 102 S.E. 572 (1920) (dicta). However, an offer of reconciliation that contained no apology or excuse for the plaintiff's actions was not in the spirit of a bona fide offer. *McDaniel v. McDaniel,* 175 Va. 402, 9 S.E.2d 360 (1940).

Cohabitation between spouses during the pendency of the divorce suit is a sufficient reason for the defendant's belief that the plaintiff had abandoned the suit and a justification for not appearing to make a defense. The burden of proving such cohabitation and condonation rests upon the assailant of the decree. *Ware v. Ware,* 203 Va. 189, 193, 194, 123 S.E.2d 357, 360 (1962).

Res judicata will be a defense to all divorces except those based upon separation under Va. Code § 20-91(9). *Robinette v. Robinette,* 253 Va. 347, 149 S.E. 493 (1929); *McDaniel v. McDaniel,* 175 Va. 402, 9 S.E.2d 360 (1940). However, as in all cases of res judicata, the only issues barred will be those actually adjudicated in the first proceeding. For example, a divorce decree entered after publication was not a determination that the former spouse was alive at the time. *Simpson v. Simpson,* 162 Va. 621, 631, 175 S.E. 320, 324 (1934). However, when a complaint was demurred to and the demurrer sustained on the grounds that the allegations were indefinite and ambiguous, and a later complaint was filed based upon the same facts and allegations, the second bill was appropriately dismissed. *Griffin v. Griffin,* 183 Va. 443, 32 S.E.2d 700 (1945).

See generally 6A Michie's Jurisprudence *Divorce and Alimony* § 45.

The insanity of the defendant to a divorce proceeding was enough to invalidate the judgment of divorce (and plaintiff's subsequent remarriage) where plaintiff had not divulged to the trial court that defendant was insane and that he had agreed to her placement in West Virginia, where she was proceeded against by constructive service only. *Taylor v. Taylor,* 159 Va. 338, 165 S.E. 414 (1932). The failure to disclose her insanity amounted to fraud.

The fact that plaintiff has not complied with temporary alimony or child support orders should not result in dismissal of the divorce action. *Davis v. Davis,* 206 Va. 381, 143 S.E.2d 835 (1965). Other remedies, such as the requirement of Va. Code § 20-114 providing for the discretionary ordering of a recognizance, are appropriate in such cases.

Although there may be provocation of acts of physical violence that preclude an action for cruelty, these cannot be out of proportion to the other spouse's retaliatory conduct. *Graham v. Graham,* 210 Va. 608, 616, 172 S.E.2d 724, 729 (1970); see also *Wimbrow v. Wimbrow,* 208 Va. 141, 156 S.E.2d 598 (1967).

Collusion is a defense to a divorce, but the divorce procured through collusion cannot be attacked by either party. *Scott v. Scott,* 142 Va. 31, 39, 128 S.E. 599 (1925). There is no innocent party to be granted relief in such cases, because both are guilty of attempting to commit a fraud upon the court.

The defense of recrimination does not apply to the no-fault ground of separation, Va. Code § 20-91. In other cases, if plaintiff has also been guilty of conduct justifying a divorce, it may be recriminated as a defense and the suit dismissed. *Kirn v. Kirn,* 138 Va. 132, 120 S.E. 850 (1924) (wife guilty of desertion and adultery, husband of cruelty, no divorce to either). See also *Wallace v. Wallace,* 1 Va. App. 183, 336 S.E.2d 27 (1985) (recrimination would prevent husband's obtaining a divorce from wife based upon her adultery when his unjustified conduct had precipitated their separation fifteen years before); *Surbey v. Surbey,* 5 Va. App. 119, 360 S.E.2d 873 (1987) (both parties were at fault in causing separation, and both committed adultery following separation so that recrimination barred either from using adultery as grounds for divorce); See also *Davis v. Davis,* 8 Va. App. 12, 377 S.E.2d 640 (1989) (recrimination barred husband's suit for desertion when he shot and seriously wounded wife following separation).

See 6A Michie's Jurisprudence *Divorce and Alimony* § 26.

In *Hollis v. Hollis,* 16 Va. App. 74, 427 S.E.2d 233 (1993), the court of appeals found that the husband had proved the wife's connivance, or prior consent to his adultery. The wife wrote several handwritten letters that were admitted into evidence, including one hoping that the husband

and the other woman would "rent an apartment and live together for one year as man and wife everyday." When the husband and the other woman first had sexual relations at the Greenbrier Hotel, they received flowers and a card from Mrs. Hollis. The card said, "My very best wishes to you both today, to your new beginning." She therefore was not legally injured because she had consented to the misconduct alleged as grounds for divorce.

See generally C.J.S. *Divorce* §§ 208-212.

Estoppel or unclean hands will also be a defense to suits for divorce. *McNair v. McNair,* 178 Va. 285, 16 S.E.2d 632 (1941) (wife procured bilateral Nevada divorce but later sued husband for divorce in Virginia, stating that Nevada court did not have jurisdiction; wife also estopped by laches).

§ 20-12. Insane person as party to suit.

Even though the original separation took place while the defendant spouse was sane, formerly there could be no divorce on fault grounds requiring a period of separation when during that period the defendant became insane. The reason for this was because the cause of action required an intent to remain separate throughout the statutory period, which intent could not be entertained by the insane spouse. *Wright v. Wright,* 125 Va. 526, 99 S.E. 515 (1919). However, the fact that a defendant to a case of wilful desertion and abandonment became insane after her desertion is no longer a bar to suit. Va. Code § 20-93; *Pollard v. Pollard,* 204 Va. 316, 130 S.E.2d 425 (1963).

Originally the no-fault ground, Va. Code § 20-91(9) also required consciousness by the defendant of the separation. When that spouse was permanently insane, there could be no such knowledge, and the divorce could not be granted. *Crittenden v. Crittenden,* 210 Va. 76, 168 S.E.2d 115 (1969); see 4 U. Rich. L. Rev. 347 (1970). The legislature amended the statute in 1975 to provide that it shall not be a bar to a divorce under the section that either spouse has been adjudged insane before or after the one year period. The rationale for the amendment is set forth in the earlier case of *Gearheart v. Gearheart,* 12 Va. Cir. 447 (Roanoke Co. 1967). The husband was committed to a mental institution in 1941 after he attempted to kill the wife. The parties lived separate and apart for more than 25 years before the wife filed for a no-fault divorce.

When a couple divorces on grounds of insanity, the parties are not necessarily relieved of spousal support obligations. If the institutionalized spouse might be eligible for federal medical assistance services, the court shall first order the institutionalized spouse to make available the maximum income contribution to the other spouse. If the spousal support award exceeds the federally established monthly maintenance needs allowance, the court must find that the increase is necessary because of exceptional circumstances causing financial distress to the other spouse. These circumstances might include threatened loss of basic food, shelter, or medically necessary health care or the financial burden of caring for a disabled child, sibling, or other relative. Effective January, 1994, the maximum spousal resource allowance is $72,660. Va. Code § 20-88.02:1.

The committee of the insane defendant shall be made a party to the case, or the court shall appoint a guardian ad litem to represent the insane defendant. Va. Code § 20-91(9).

The insanity of the defendant to a divorce proceeding was enough to invalidate the judgment of divorce (and plaintiff's subsequent remarriage) where plaintiff had not divulged to the trial court that defendant was insane and that he had agreed to her placement in West Virginia, where she was proceeded against by constructive service only. *Taylor v. Taylor,* 159 Va. 338, 165 S.E. 414 (1932). The failure to disclose her insanity amounted to fraud.

§ 20-13. Alimony pendente lite.

Personal jurisdiction is required in order to enter decrees awarding alimony and child support pending litigation. Pendente lite alimony awards, under Va. Code § 20-103, terminate at the time the final judgment of absolute divorce is rendered, *Osborne v. Osborne,* 215 Va. 205, 207 S.E.2d 875 (1974), but child support may be continued or modified beyond this time. Pendente lite relief is not available on appeal, *Cralle v. Cralle,* 81 Va. 773 (1886), although attorney's fees may be. *Tarr v. Tarr,* 184 Va. 443, 35 S.E.2d 401 (1945).

The guidelines for award of permanent spousal and child support under Va. Code § 20-108.2 are useful for computing the amount of pendente lite awards.

The usual form for pendente lite relief is through notice and motion rather than through a cross-bill. *Davis v. Davis,* 206 Va. 381, 143 S.E.2d 835 (1965). Such payments are tax deductible to the payor and taxable as income to the payee. I.R.C. § 71(a) (3).

Even though a person can support the divorce suit, he or she may still be entitled to sums sufficient for maintenance. The relief grows out of and is of the same nature as the duty of spousal support. *Eddens v. Eddens,* 188 Va. 511, 50 S.E.2d 397 (1948).

A lien upon the real estate of the defendant may be ordered to secure pendente lite allowances. Va. Code § 20-103; *Wilson v. Wilson,* 195 Va. 1060, 81 S.E.2d 605, 613 (1954).

Va. Code § 20-114 provides that the court may require the giving of recognizance, with or without surety, to insure compliance with child support orders, temporary as well as permanent. Contempt is available for violations of pendente lite orders. *McDaniel v. McDaniel,* 175 Va. 402, 9 S.E.2d 360 (1940).

A spouse may be ordered to provide health care coverage for the petitioning spouse, as well as for minor children, at any time pending the suit. Va. Code § 20-103.

§ 20-14. Complaint for divorce.

The pleadings in divorce cases are generally the same as in other equitable proceedings. Va. Code § 20-99.

The jurisdiction of a court to grant a divorce depends upon facts that must be pleaded. The bill of complaint must set forth in detail the specific facts as opposed to legal conclusions giving grounds for relief. *Haynor v. Haynor,* 112 Va. 123, 70 S.E. 531 (1911). Dates, places, and circumstances must be included, *Miller v. Miller,* 92 Va. 196, 23 S.E. 232 (1895), particularly in adultery cases. See generally 6A Michie's Jurisprudence *Divorce and Alimony* § 38.

Pleadings may be amended to state additional grounds for divorce: for example, adultery occurring after the original bill was filed. *Rosenberg v. Rosenberg,* 210 Va. 44, 168 S.E.2d 251 (1969). See Va. Code § 8-119. Amended Va. Code § 20-121.02 allows a party to seek a no-fault divorce under separate and apart grounds without filing an amended bill of complaint, notwithstanding the grounds for divorce originally asserted.

A suit for adultery must be instituted within five years of the act complained of under Va. Code § 20-94.

§ 20-15. Service of divorce complaint.

According to Va. Code § 20-99.2, service in a divorce or annulment case may be made in any manner authorized under Va. Code § 8.01-296. Thus, process may be served by delivering a copy in writing to the party in person, or by substituted service. Service need no longer be made by a sheriff or other law enforcement officer since the 1986 amendment to Va. Code § 8.01-293, but may be made within Virginia by any person eighteen years of age or older who is not a party or otherwise interested in the action. Posting on the door of defendant's last known place of residence will suffice if the defendant has not abandoned the premises. Proof of abandonment lies with the defendant, and the defendant's failure to testify, taken together with circumstantial evidence from which conflicting inferences might be drawn, raised enough questions about abandonment to warrant denial of defendant's motion to quash a divorce complaint. *Wilson v. Wilson,* 9 Va. Cir. 508 (Frederick Co. 1982).

According to Va. Code § 20-99.1:1, a defendant in a divorce or annulment action may accept service by signing the proof of service before any officer authorized to administer oaths. Service may also have the effect of personal service by voluntary and notarized acceptance or waiver. If service is accepted outside the Commonwealth by a nonresident pursuant to § 20-99.1:1, it will have the same effect as an order of publication.

Service may be accepted or waived by a defendant by the filing of an answer by counsel. The acceptance or waiver shall then have the same effect as personal service. Va. Code § 20-99.1. Alternatively, the attorney for either party may prepare a writing to be signed by a party before a notary that, when filed, shows the acceptance of service by the party. Va. Code § 20-99.1. Once the suit has been commenced and an appearance has been made on behalf of defendant by counsel, notices of depositions and other proceedings, but not contempt proceedings, may be served by delivering or mailing a copy to counsel for the opposing party. In such cases, the notices shall bear either acceptance of service or a certificate of counsel.

Counsel for the opposing party includes a pro se party who has entered a general appearance in person or by filing a pleading or endorsing an order of withdrawal of that party's counsel, or who has signed a pleading in the case or who has notified the court clerk or the parties that he or she appears in the case. Va. Code § 20-99(4).

If a defendant cannot be found or served after due diligence, Va. Code § 8.01-316 provides that an order of publication may be entered by the clerk of the court, either stating the last known post office address of the party against whom publication is asked, or declaring that the last address is unknown. The order of publication shall give the abbreviated style of the suit, shall state its object, and require defendants to appear on or before the date stated in the order (no sooner than fifty-one days after entry of the order of publication). The order of publication shall be published once each week for four successive weeks in the newspaper prescribed by the court, or as directed by the clerk, shall be posted at the front door of the courthouse, and shall be mailed to defendant's last known address. Upon completion of the publication, the clerk shall file a certificate in the papers of the case that the requirements have been complied with. Va. Code § 8.01-317. The above Code provisions will be strictly construed and applied. *Robertson v. Stone,* 199 Va. 41, 97 S.E.2d 739 (1957); *Holcomb v. Holcomb,* 122 W. Va. 293, 8 S.E.2d 889 (1940).

When the defendant cannot be found within the state, and the matrimonial domicile was in Virginia, or the separation or facts giving rise to the cause of action for divorce took place within the state, the defendant may be reached personally under the longarm statute. Va. Code § 8.01-328.1(9). Recent amendments to this section allow service to be made by "any law-enforcement officer authorized to service process in the jurisdiction where the nonresident party is located or by any other person authorized to serve process in that jurisdiction in such actions." Depositions may then be taken in accordance with Va. Rule 4:2, but only after the expiration of ten days, as provided in Va. Code § 20-104.

§ 20-16. Answer.

An answer does not serve as evidence for the defendant, Va. Code § 8-123, but only admits or traverses the allegations of the complaint. *Hutcheson v. Savings Bank,* 129 Va. 281, 105 S.E. 677 (1921).

The defendant will be permitted to file a later answer with the court's permission even though the Rules in 2.7 provide for an answer within twenty-one days. This is because Va. Code § 20-99 separates divorce suits from other suits in equity by providing that the cause shall be heard independently of the parties' admissions and that a bill should not be taken for confessed. *Westfall v. Westfall,* 196 Va. 97, 82 S.E.2d 487 (1954).

Once an answer is filed, it confers jurisdiction notwithstanding the fact that the summons was not regularly reserved. *Scott v. Scott,* 142 Va. 31, 128 S.E. 599 (1925).

The defendant may accept service by signing the proof of service before an officer authorized to administer oaths, Va. Code § 20-99.1, or by having counsel prepare a writing to be signed before a notary, or by the filing of an answer by counsel.

Usually a cross-bill is filed separately to obtain affirmative relief. *Simpson v. Simpson,* 162 Va. 621, 175 S.E. 320 (1934) (cross-bill for divorce filed in annulment action). A cross-bill is not needed, however, for obtaining pendente lite relief. *Davis v. Davis,* 206 Va. 381, 143 S.E.2d 835 (1965). A cross-bill may be filed at any time when the defendant would not be in default for failure to file a pleading or thereafter by leave of court. Rule 2:13 of Virginia Equity Rules of Practice and Procedure. This period is twenty-one days after service, subpoena or acceptance of process, or after publication. Va. Equity Rule 2:7. If adultery is alleged in the cross-bill, it must have occurred within five years of the cross-bill, but before the filing of the cross-bill. *Willard v. Willard,* 98 Va. 465, 36 S.E. 518 (1900); *Rosenberg v. Rosenberg,* 210 Va. 44, 168 S.E.2d 251 (1969); Va. Code § 20-94.

Generally speaking, because of the importance of marriage and divorce and the desirability of having hearings on the merits, the courts are inclined to take a very liberal view of pleadings belatedly filed in divorce cases. *Willard v. Willard,* 98 Va. 465, 489, 36 S.E. 518 (1900). See also *Westfall v. Westfall,* 196 Va. 97, 82 S.E.2d 487 (1954). Continuances are also granted with greater liberality because the state has an interest in seeing that everything is done to achieve a just and equitable result. *Gulland v. Gulland,* 62 W. Va. 671, 59 S.E. 612 (1907).

§ 20-17. Injunctive relief pending decree.

Va. Code § 20-103 provides that the court may enjoin a spouse from imposing any restraints on the personal liberty of the other, or for the exclusive use and possession of the marital home during suit or to preserve the estate of either. A spouse may be excluded from the jointly owned or rented family dwelling where the other spouse makes a showing of reasonable apprehension of physical harm.

Brooks v. Brooks, 201 Va. 731, 113 S.E.2d 872 (1960), is an example of such an injunction. The wife was restrained from going to the former husband's home or place of business while the husband was enjoined from going to her home, except, after appeal to the Supreme Court, to pick up or deliver their child for visitation.

In the more recent case of *Vardell v. Vardell,* 225 Va. 361, 302 S.E.2d 41 (1983), the supreme court found that the husband had no case for constructive desertion where the wife obtained first an *ex parte* and then a contested injunction barring him from the marital home or contact with their child. In the divorce action brought by the wife, she was unable to corroborate her charges of cruelty by the husband.

§ 20-18. Discovery.

Depositions may be taken in divorce actions in accordance with Va. Rule 4:5. Proper notice must be given under Va. Code § 20-99(5), Va. Code § 20-104 (after jurisdiction based upon order of publication), and Va. Rule 4:1(D)(5) (providing for methods of service of notice). These rules must be carefully followed. *Mackey v. Mackey,* 203 Va. 526, 125 S.E.2d 194 (1962). Types of discovery, as provided in Va. Rule 4:1(a), include depositions, interrogatories, admission of facts and documents, the subpoena duces tecum, physical and mental examinations, and motions to inspect.

Va. Rule 4:1(B)(5) limits the scope of discovery to "matters which are relevant to the issues in the proceeding." However, given the broad scope of factors required by Va. Code § 20-107.1 (spousal maintenance), Va. Code § 20-107.2 (child custody and support), and Va. Code § 20-107.3 (property distribution), anything is apparently material.

§ 20-19. Commissioners and judges pro tempore.

In some Virginia jurisdictions, as provided by local rule, the divorce action is referred to a commissioner in chancery by the chancellor (court) with a decree of reference directing the commissioner to require and report on the pertinent issues. *Moore v. Moore,* 218 Va. 790, 240 S.E.2d 535 (1978). In such case the procedure is set forth in Equity Rule 2:18. The commissioner is to determine such issues as: (1) whether the court has jurisdiction and venue; (2) whether the marriage ties should be severed; (3) the amount of alimony to be paid to the wronged spouse; and, where applicable, (4) child custody and maintenance. *Raiford v. Raiford,* 193 Va. 221, 68 S.E.2d 888 (1952). More recently, the duties have expanded to include equitable distribution under Va. Code § 20-107.3 as well. The commissioner's work is subject to the absolute review of the chancellor. *Shipman v. Fletcher,* 91 Va. 473, 476, 22 S.E. 458 (1895). In some counties, the work is handled by a judge *pro tempore.*

A nonsuit may be granted unless the action has been submitted to the court for decision. In divorce cases, where both parties have filed pleadings, this requires that both yield the issues to the court for consideration. *Moore v. Moore,* 218 Va. 790, 240 S.E.2d 535 (1978).

The finding of the chancellor after a hearing *ore tenus* will not be disturbed unless plainly wrong or without evidence to support it. *Alls v. Alls,* 216 Va. 13, 216 S.E.2d 16 (1975).

In *Brown v. Brown,* 11 Va. App. 231, 397 S.E.2d 545 (1990), a divorce decree was vacated when the wife's legal counsel contributed money to the commissioner's political campaign. The trial court erred in failing to set aside the commissioner's report, because although the court reviewed the commissioner's report, the review was insufficient to remove the taint caused by the suspicion of improper influence.

The trial judge's expression of "a serious concern" regarding the professional conduct of the father's attorney, standing alone, was not a basis for requiring that he recuse himself. *Buchanan v. Buchanan,* 14 Va. App. 53, 415 S.E.2d 237 (1992). The court noted that such a comment was less problematic than the formation of an opinion on a matter that might come before the judge later. The record reflected no indication that any bias affected the proceedings.

§ 20-20. Conduct of the divorce hearing.

The hearing may also be carried out by a commissioner, who is appointed to assist the chancellor (court), and whose work is subject to court review. The court shall confirm or reject the commissioner's report in whole or in part, according to the view that it entertains of the law and evidence. *Plattner v. Plattner,* 202 Va. 263, 117 S.E.2d 128 (1960).

Where the wife was proceeding pro se, after her counsel had withdrawn, mailing notice to her of the commissioner's hearing was insufficient service, so the final decree of divorce was vacated and the case remanded. *Soliman v. Soliman,* 12 Va. App. 234, 402 S.E.2d 922 (1991). However, after this case was decided, Va. Code § 20-99(5), which allows notices of hearings and other proceedings to be served by delivering or mailing a copy to counsel for opposing party, was amended to read that counsel for the opposing party shall include a pro se party who has entered an appearance by filing a pleading or endorsing an order of withdrawal of that party's counsel.

Evidence may be taken *ore tenus* or by depositions, whichever is determined by the court. Va. Rule 2:17. According to Va. Code § 20-104, evidence in actions where service was obtained by publication cannot be taken until ten days after completion of the order of publication. In such cases, notice of depositions may be given to counsel of record within the state, under Va. Code § 20-99.1(5) and Va. Rule 1:12, except those of adverse witnesses, as provided under Va. Rule 4:2(a)(2).

Va. Code § 20-124 provides that, upon motion of any party, the court may order the record or any agreement of the parties to be sealed and withheld from public inspection. The record and agreement shall thereafter be opened only to the parties, to their respective attorneys, and to such other persons as the judge in his discretion decides have a proper interest in the documents. In order for a spouse to appeal from an adverse judgment, transcripts of all relevant hearings must be made part of the record. *Twardy v. Twardy,* 14 Va. App. 651, 419 S.E.2d 848 (1992). Because no party submitted transcripts from a hearing, the court was unable to determine if the wife presented the issue of estoppel to the trial court.

§ 20-21. Testimony in divorce hearing.

The statutes require that the cause of action be heard independently of the parties' admissions, in pleadings or otherwise. Va. Code § 20-99. The main object of this statute requiring corroboration of divorce testimony is to prevent collusion. *Forbes v. Forbes,* 182 Va. 636, 29 S.E.2d 829 (1944). Where it is apparent that there is no collusion, the corroboration only needs to be slight. *Graves v. Graves,* 193 Va. 659, 70 S.E.2d 339 (1952); *Collier v. Collier,* 2 Va. App. 125, 341 S.E.2d 827 (1986).

The burden of persuasion in desertion cases is that desertion must be shown by a preponderance of the evidence. *Bacon v. Bacon,* 3 Va. App. 484, 351 S.E.2d 37, 40-41 (1986). This is in contrast to the standard of persuasion in adultery cases, which requires that adultery be proved by clear and convincing evidence. *Coe v. Coe,* 225 Va. 616, 622, 303 S.E.2d 923, 927 (1983); *Dooley v. Dooley,* 222 Va. 240, 246, 278 S.E.2d 865, 868 (1981). According to *Bacon,* the reason for the distinction is that the alleged conduct in desertion cases does not deviate from the norm as much as that in adultery cases, where a criminal offense is also being made out. 351 S.E.2d at 40 (citing *Haskins v. Haskins,* 188 Va. 525, 530-31, 50 S.E.2d 437, 439 (1948), and C. Friend, *The Law of Evidence in Virginia* § 86 (2d ed. 1983)).

Letters of the parties may be admitted in evidence in a divorce suit (except where written by collusion) just as in any other case for the purpose of providing or as tending to prove relevant facts. *Bailey v. Bailey,* 62 Va. (21 Gratt.) 43, 51 (1871). See also *Holt v. Holt,* 174 Va. 120, 5 S.E.2d 504 (1939). Admissions of the parties are admissible and are highly credible evidence if corroborated. See, e.g., *Miller v. Miller,* 196 Va. 698, 85 S.E.2d 221 (1955); *Davis v. Davis,* 206 Va. 381, 143 S.E.2d 835 (1965).

The decree of a chancellor that is based upon depositions, while not as strong and conclusive as one based upon oral testimony, is presumed to be correct, and will not be disturbed unless manifestly wrong. *Martin v. Martin,* 202 Va. 769, 120 S.E.2d 471 (1961). Conclusions based upon testimony given *ore tenus* (orally) will not be set aside unless there is clear error. *Barnard v. Barnard,* 132 Va. 155, 111 S.E. 227 (1922). The right to require oral testimony is conferred upon the court, not the parties, to give it the advantage of seeing the witnesses and hearing them testify. *Id.*

The evidence of private investigators should be examined with greatest care and acted upon with great caution. *Dooley v. Dooley,* 222 Va. 240, 278 S.E.2d 865 (1981); *Colbert v. Colbert,* 162 Va. 393, 400, 174 S.E. 660, 662 (1934).

Husband and wife are competent to testify against each other in divorce cases, Va. Code §§ 8-82 and 8-287, but the divorce will not be granted on their uncorroborated testimony. *Black v. Black,* 134 Va. 246, 114 S.E. 592 (1922) (wife never appeared in case; evidence failed to corroborate husband's testimony regarding wife's reprehensible conduct that allegedly caused him to leave marital home). The parties' child may also be a competent witness, *Hepler v. Hepler,* 195 Va. 611, 79 S.E.2d 652 (1954) (custody case; twelve year old child), but should seldom be used in adultery cases. *White v. White,* 121 Va. 244, 92 S.E. 811 (1917).

§ 20-22. Final decree of divorce.

The decree must be appealed within the term of court to enable the court to have any further jurisdiction over the marriage relations, except to compel compliance with provisions of the decree. *Golderos v. Golderos,* 169 Va. 496, 194 S.E. 706 (1938) (alimony not modifiable after end of term of court; Va. Code § 20-109 permitting modification not then in effect).

The invalidation of an antenuptial agreement is not an appealable order because it will not necessarily affect the final disposition of the divorce. *Polumbo v. Polumbo,* 13 Va. App. 306, 411 S.E.2d 229 (1991). See also *Webb v. Webb,* 13 Va. App. 681, 414 S.E.2d 612 (1992).

If the parties' final divorce decree specified that the husband was to make spousal support payments, he could not receive restitution of payments made even when the court ultimately found that the wife had deserted him and therefore was not entitled to spousal support. *Reid v. Reid,* 245 Va. 409, 429 S.E.2d 208 (1993) (reversing 14 Va. App. 505, 419 S.E.2d 398 (1992)).

When a divorce decree is silent as to child support, except for transferring matters of support to the Juvenile and Domestic Relations District Court, the Division of Child Support Enforcement has the administrative authority to issue a support order to establish a debt for public assistance paid on an order for child support. *Powers v. Commonwealth*, 13 Va. App. 309, 411 S.E.2d 230 (1991).

The statement of facts need not be signed by the trial judge for the decree to be valid if this omission is the fault of the judge. *Clary v. Clary*, 15 Va. App. 598, 425 S.E.2d 821 (1993).

When the final decree of divorce did not reflect whether the spousal support payments were to continue from the date of entry of the decree or the execution of the couple's stipulation agreement, but the parties wanted the agreement approved by the trial court and made part of their final divorce decree, the trial court correctly amended the final decree nunc pro tunc. *Garrett v. Forbes-Garrett*, 1995 Va. App. LEXIS 860.

§ 20-23. Counsel fees and costs.

Like alimony, the award by a court of counsel fees and court costs will be enforceable through the use of the contempt power, *Eddens v. Eddens*, 188 Va. 511, 50 S.E.2d 397 (1948), the court reasoning that the fees are necessary to enforce the right to alimony.

In *Klein v. Klein*, 18 Va. Cir. 195 (Fairfax Co. 1989), the husband failed to reimburse the wife for $5000 she had paid in attorney's fees as he had been required by the divorce decree. This was held to be contempt of court.

The award of counsel fees is discretionary with the trial court, Va. Code § 20-103, and will not be disturbed unless there is an abuse of this discretion. *Wilkerson v. Wilkerson*, 214 Va. 395, 200 S.E.2d 581 (1973). Where one party has no separate estate and is the defendant in a divorce action, it is entirely proper for him or her to be allowed a reasonable sum for attorney's fees and costs, provided that the court does not ignore the financial condition of the plaintiff spouse. *Rowlee v. Rowlee*, 211 Va. 689, 179 S.E.2d 461 (1971) (no evidence showing abuse of discretion in failure to award fees to wife). A court may award counsel fees in an appropriate case even when grounds for divorce is not based upon fault. See, e.g., *Bandas v. Bandas*, 32 Va. Cir. 285 (City of Richmond, 1993).

The award of attorneys' fees and costs is personal to the parties. The attorney has no standing to seek relief under this section.

§ 20-24. Resumption of the maiden name.

Virginia Code § 20-121.4 provides that, upon decreeing a divorce and upon motion of the person changing a surname by reason of the marriage, the court shall restore such party's former or maiden name as part of the final decree or a separate order meeting the requirements of Va. Code § 8.01-217. This right would not go so far as to allow the custodial wife the ability to change the children's surnames to that of her new husband. *Flowers v. Cain,* 218 Va. 234, 237 S.E.2d 111 (1977). Whether it would extend to her right to have their names changed to her maiden name is questionable. See, e.g., *Lassiter-Geers v. Reichenbach,* 303 Md. 88, 492 A.2d 303 (1985).

§ 20-25. Effect on dower and curtesy.

The absolute divorce destroys the contingent rights in the property of the other spouse that depend upon the continued existence of the marriage relationship. Va. Code § 20-111. This includes dower and curtesy, even if the divorce is obtained *ex parte. Simons v. Miami Beach First Nat'l Bank,* 381 U.S. 81 (1965). See also *Jones v. Kirby,* 146 Va. 109, 135 S.E.2d 676 (1926). Revocable beneficiary designations are rescinded by final divorces occurring on or after July 1, 1993, so that death benefits shall be paid as though the former spouse predeceased the decedent. Va. Code § 20-111.1.

§ 20-26. Effect on ability to testify.

An absolute (or *a mensa*) divorce will make the former spouses competent to testify in all cases. The marital status at the time of trial determines whether or not the disability to testify is removed. *Menefee v. Commonwealth,* 189 Va. 900, 55 S.E.2d 9 (1949).

However, even though a person may testify against the former wife or husband, if a communication was made during the marriage and was made because of the marital relationship, it will be protected under the privilege for confidential marital communications. *Id.*

See generally Friend, *The Law of Evidence in Virginia* (2d ed. 1983).

§ 20-27. Ability to remarry.

In contrast to the *a mensa* divorce, the absolute divorce gives to each spouse, whether the divorce was awarded for or against that spouse, the ability to remarry. Until 1934, spouses were not allowed to remarry for a period of six months after the final decree to give them time to reconcile before a hasty remarriage made this action impossible and to remove the temptation for married spouses to divorce so that they might marry others. *Simpson v. Simpson,* 162 Va. 621, 633-34, 175 S.E. 320, 325-26 (1934). Since 1975, remarriage has been permissible even for persons divorced because of their adultery. Acts of 1975 c. 644. However, remarriage should not occur if exceptions are noted and a bond is given staying execution of the decree. Va. Code § 20-118. Fraud would certainly be sufficient grounds for vacating a decree. *Taylor v. Taylor,* 159 Va. 338, 165 S.E. 414 (1932). The divorce could be vacated although one party had remarried and had a child born of the second marriage. *Tarr v. Tarr,* 184 Va. 443, 35 S.E.2d 401 (1945) (defendant to divorce thought her conduct had been condoned by cohabitation following service of the complaint, so she failed to appear to make a defense).

§ 20-28. Effect on property held as tenants by the entirety or joint tenancy.

By Va. Code § 20-111, property held as tenants by the entirety is converted to tenancy in common by the absolute divorce. This does not authorize the courts to allocate the property other than evenly between the spouses. *Smith v. Smith,* 200 Va. 77, 104 S.E.2d 17 (1958). Some financial compensation may be necessary if the funds that paid for the property were acquired by one party as a gift, and are therefore separate property under Va. Code § 20-107.3.

Joint property, such as that held in joint bank accounts, may only be changed to a tenancy in common, not distributed under the equitable distribution statute, Va. Code § 20-107.3. *Watkins v. Watkins,* 220 Va. 1051, 265 S.E.2d 750 (1980) (no jurisdiction to impair husband's personal property); *Johnson v. Johnson,* 224 Va. 641, 299 S.E.2d 351 (1983) (joint bank account).

The court of course does have the power to approve and confirm contracts between the parties concerning property division, support and maintenance. Va. Code § 20-109; *Gloth v. Gloth,* 154 Va. 511, 153 S.E. 879 (1930). See generally Chapter 18, *supra.*

§ 20-29. Other financial considerations.

Alimony will be available to a dependent spouse despite the fact that the obligor was awarded the divorce, so long as the decree was based upon the "no-fault" ground of Va. Code § 20-91(9), and the dependent spouse was without fault or misconduct causing the separation. *Mason v. Mason,* 209 Va. 528, 165 S.E.2d 392 (1969). See also *Breschel v. Breschel,* 221 Va. 208, 269 S.E.2d 363 (1980); *Wallace v. Wallace,* 1 Va. App. 183, 336 S.E.2d 27 (1985). Unless alimony is provided for in the decree, or the right to modify it reserved, it cannot afterwards be awarded, since the decree is final. This does not apply to child support or custody, which are always subject to modification in the child's best interest. *Kern v. Lindsey,* 182 Va. 775, 30 S.E.2d 707 (1944).

§ 20-30. Full faith and credit for judgments of final divorce.

Virginia will give full faith and credit to judgments of absolute divorce rendered in other states, *Osborne v. Osborne,* 215 Va. 205, 207 S.E.2d 875 (1974), so long as domicile was validly obtained in the other state. The right to maintain or obtain alimony will not be terminated by an *ex parte,* as opposed to a bilateral, proceeding. *Id.; Ceyte v. Ceyte,* 222 Va. 11, 278 S.E.2d 791 (1981).

The divorce decree may also require that either party provide health care coverage for the children following a final divorce. Va. Code § 20-107.2.

CHAPTER 21

Spousal Support and Maintenance

§ 21-1. Introduction.

The concept of spousal support was originally derived from the duty of the husband to support the wife during marriage. *Harris v. Harris,* 72 Va. (31 Gratt.) 13, 17 (1878). When, through the husband's fault, the parties were forced to live apart, the wife could collect alimony in order to continue to have the material things the husband was obliged to provide her. See *Capell v. Capell,* 164 Va. 45, 178 S.E. 894 (1935); *Purcell v. Purcell,* 14 Va. (4 Hen. & Mun.) 507 (1810). Since there was no absolute divorce, this duty continued until the death of either of the parties. See *Gloth v. Gloth,* 154 Va. 511, 537, 153 S.E. 879, 887 (1930) (case containing history of alimony in Virginia).

In Virginia, courts were empowered by statute to award alimony following divorces from bed and board, and, later, following absolute divorces where no-fault whatsoever existed against the dependent spouse. Law of March 18, 1848, ch. 122, p. 165, § 5; *Latham v. Latham,* 71 Va. (30 Gratt.) 307 (1878). As in the case of divorces, the entire subject, although in many respects equitable, is regulated by statute since this form of relief did not exist at common law. *Watkins v. Watkins,* 220 Va. 1051, 265 S.E.2d 750 (1980); *Bray v. Landergren,* 161 Va. 699, 172 S.E. 252 (1933) (citing cases). The term "support and maintenance" as used in the Virginia Code expresses this change from the original idea of alimony, since support does not necessarily depend upon the continued existence of marriage. See, e.g., Holt, *Support vs. Alimony in Virginia, It's Time to Use the Revised Statutes,* 12 U. Rich. L. Rev. 139, 139-40 (1977).

Alimony was allowed out of the husband's estate, but a specific piece of property could not be assigned the wife as alimony. *Lovegrove v. Lovegrove,* 128 Va. 449, 451, 104 S.E. 804 (1920). See also *Almond v. Almond,* 25 Va. (4 Rand.) 662 (1826).

In recent years, several more of the original concepts have changed. Since in the 1979 Supreme Court case of *Orr v. Orr,* 440 U.S. 268 (1979), support following divorce, if available to wives, must also be available to husbands. *Brooker v. Brooker,* 218 Va. 12, 235 S.E.2d 309 (1977). Additionally, with the growing financial independence of women, support has increasingly been awarded for limited time periods rather than for life or until remarriage, as was the former practice. *Thomas v. Thomas,* 217 Va. 502, 229 S.E.2d 887 (1976), suggested the requirement of evidence showing that the need of the wife or the ability of the husband would change in the immediate future before a two-year limitation was appropriate. Support may be used to compensate spouses for investments made that cannot be divided as marital property, or to allow the dependent spouse the opportunity to obtain an education or to raise a minor child. See Va. Code § 20-107.1(2); see generally Annot., Fineman, *Implementing Equality: Ideology, Contradiction and Social Change,* 1983 Wis. L. Rev. 789; Holt, *Support vs. Alimony in Virginia: It's Time to Use the Revised Statutes,* 12 U. Rich. L. Rev. 139 (1977); Krauskopf, *Recompense for Financing Spouse's Education: Legal Protection for the Marital Investor in Human Capital,* 28 Kan. L. Rev. 379, 411 (1980); O'Kelly, *Entitlements to Spousal Support After Divorce,* 61 N.D.L. Rev. 225 (1985); Weitzman, *The Economics of Divorce: Social and Economic Consequences of Property, Alimony and Child Support Awards,* 28 UCLA L. Rev. 1031, 1229 (1981).

The present support statute, Va. Code § 20-107.1, requires consideration of a number of factors before an award of alimony is made. *Bristow v. Bristow,* 221 Va. 1, 267 S.E.2d 89 (1980); *Brooker v. Brooker,* 218 Va. 12, 235 S.E.2d 309 (1977).

Accrued alimony is not a provable debt in bankruptcy, nor is the obligor relieved from any future payments by a discharge in bankruptcy. *Eaton v. Davis,* 176 Va. 330, 338, 10 S.E.2d 893, 897 (1940).

The award of support should be made on the basis of presently available facts rather than speculation on future needs or incomes. *Jacobs v. Jacobs,* 219 Va. 993, 254 S.E.2d 56 (1979) (an escalator clause violated this policy). See also *Robertson v. Robertson,* 215 Va. 425, 211 S.E.2d 41 (1975).

Although according to Va. Code § 20-108.1, courts are to use all the evidence presented in formulating awards, there is a rebuttable presumption in any proceeding for child support that the amount of the award that would result from the application of the guidelines set forth in the statute is the correct amount of child support to be awarded. To rebut the presumption, the court must make written findings that application of the guidelines would be unjust or inappropriate in a particular case.

The amount ordered by the chancellor will not be disturbed on appeal unless there is a clear abuse of discretion. *Lawrence v. Lawrence,* 212 Va. 44, 48, 181 S.E.2d 640, 643 (1971); 6A Michie's Jurisprudence *Divorce and Alimony* § 66.

Usually alimony is in the form of periodic payments. Va. Code § 20-107.1 also allows payment in the form of a lump sum. In some cases where there are equitable reasons for doing so, payment may be ordered to be both in lump sum and periodic. See *Turner v. Turner,* 213 Va. 42,

189 S.E.2d 361 (1972) (husband ordered to pay $16,000 in lump sum in addition to monthly payments since he had changed locks on marital home and wife owned no furniture).

§ 21-2. When may support be awarded?

There must, of course, be some kind of marriage before the duty to support will attach. See *Purcell v. Purcell,* 14 Va. (4 Hen. & Mun.) 507, 515 (1810).

Following the reasoning of the other support cases involving void marriages, spousal support will apparently not be awarded to a person whose marriage was declared void by reason of insanity. *Somers-Shiflet v. Shiflet,* 29 Va. Cir. 206 (Fairfax Co. 1992). This situation is distinguishable from the case where one party becomes insane after the parties have been validly married, in which case the healthy spouse will be responsible if the other statutory factors are met.

Permanent spousal support may be awarded at the time an absolute or bed and board divorce is granted, if the court decrees that a divorce should be granted to neither party, or following dissolution of marriage. Va. Code § 20-107.1. Although "dissolution of marriage" is not defined in the statutes, it was construed in a child custody case to mean annulment of marriage. *Henderson v. Henderson,* 187 Va. 121, 46 S.E.2d 10 (1948). Dicta in an earlier case, *Bray v. Landergren,* 161 Va. 699, 172 S.E. 252 (1933), suggests that the right to alimony depends upon the existence of at least a voidable marriage. The reasoning of *Bray* was followed in *Mato v. Mato,* 12 Va. Cir. 153 (Spotsylvania Co. 1988), where wife sued husband for divorce for desertion and later adultery, and during deposition the attorneys discovered that the husband was married to someone else. Since the marriage to plaintiff was undoubtedly void as bigamous, no alimony could be awarded. Although *Bray v. Landergren* does not suggest this, in cases of some void marriages there may be an action in tort for damages for fraud and deceit. *Alexander v. Kuykendall,* 192 Va. 8, 63 S.E.2d 746 (1951). Additionally, the right to obtain alimony might "revive" following annulment of a void marriage. Cf. *McConkey v. McConkey,* 216 Va. 106, 215 S.E.2d 640 (1975) (alimony from a first marriage will not begin again following annulment of a voidable second marriage).

There was even less justification for spousal support in *Kleinfield v. Veruki,* 7 Va. App. 183, 372 S.E.2d 407 (1988), where plaintiff spouse had married but never divorced an alien for the sole purpose of allowing him to obtain naturalized citizen status. Her second marriage, to Veruki, was void as bigamous, since the first marriage was voidable (as opposed to void).

At any time during the marriage an action may be brought for criminal nonsupport under Va. Code § 20-61 et seq. These suits should be brought in the juvenile and domestic relations court under Va. Code § 20-67. See *Helfin v. Helfin,* 177 Va. 385, 14 S.E.2d 317 (1941). The court in such cases may order temporary spousal support and may punish violation of such order by contempt. Va. Code § 20-71; *Wright v. Wright,* 164 Va. 245, 178 S.E. 884 (1935). The court may, after providing for support, garnish the wages of the obligor under Va. Code § 20-78.1, or order posting of recognizance under Va. Code § 20-72.1, or have payroll deductions made under Va. Code § 20-79.1. Support orders remain in effect unless removed by the original court, according to Va. Code § 20-74. These orders become inoperative once an order for support is entered by the circuit court in a divorce proceeding. Va. Code § 20-79.

In *Reel v. Reel,* 12 Va. Cir. 482 (Frederick Co. 1981), alimony was correctly granted even though the parties were still living under the same roof, where complainant alleged that she and the defendant were husband and wife and that he ceased supporting her. The court held that the parties were not cohabiting, meaning that they were not rendering services to each other, enjoying mutual society and companionship, aid and comfort, protection and conjugal affection.

Compare *Kerns v. Kerns,* 12 Va. Cir. 260 (Frederick Co. 1988), where the wife sued defendant for an *a mensa* divorce on grounds of constructive desertion, and sought temporary spousal support. In this case, the spouses ceased occupying the same bedroom between four and five months before the hearing, did their own shopping and laundry, and went for as much as a week without seeing each other. The court found that there had not been adequate proof either of fault on the husband's part or of lack of cohabitation, for

[W]hen the marriage bond is forged and the parties so bound commence and continue to reside and have their domestic life under a common roof tree, we view them as being in a state of matrimonial cohabitation ... and one who wishes to establish in a particular instance an exception to this deeply rooted norm bears a considerable burden to prove that the parties are living under the same roof but in a state of separation."

Amendments to Va. Code § 16.1-243 made in 1989 provide that once a divorce proceeding has begun in the circuit court, jurisdiction shall no longer lie in the juvenile and domestic relations district court unless both parties agree to the referral.

Spousal support may be ordered to commence at any time including the date of commencement of the suit. The date as of which support is due is determined by the chancellor, and will not be disturbed unless there has been a clear abuse of discretion. *Lawrence v. Lawrence,* 212 Va. 44, 181 S.E.2d 640 (1971).

Spousal support must be requested in the original pleadings. A mere reference to "such other relief as may be just and equitable" does not give the court a basis for awarding spousal support. *Boyd v. Boyd,* 2 Va. App. 16, 18, 340 S.E.2d 578, 580-81 (1986). Thus there was no jurisdiction to grant a lump sum award of spousal support when there was no explicit reservation of jurisdiction to modify the periodic maintenance contained in the final decree. The wife therefore could not obtain the lump sum award even though the transcript of the hearing indicated that the trial court intended to make a lump sum award at a later time, but inadvertently failed to include the reservation in the final decree. *Dixon v. Pugh,* 244 Va. 539, 423 S.E.2d 169 (1992). However, support may not be awarded in conjunction with a suit to partition property following divorce, *Johnston v. Johnston,* 9 Va. Cir. 450 (Warren Co. 1981), since the issues involved in litigating support are not "germane" to the partition proceeding.

See generally 6A Michie's Jurisprudence *Divorce and Alimony* §§ 60-61.

§ 21-3. Jurisdictional problems in obtaining support.

The award of spousal support creates a personal obligation on the part of the debtor. The adjudication therefore requires personal jurisdiction over the defendant, *Pennoyer v. Neff,* 95 U.S. 714 (1877); *Bray v. Landergren,* 161 Va. 699, 172 S.E. 252 (1933), and not merely personal service outside the state or notice by publication. *Minton v. First Nat'l Exchange Bank,* 206 Va. 589, 145 S.E.2d 139 (1965).

Va. Code § 8-328.1(9) allows long-arm jurisdiction to be maintained when the marital domicile was in the state at the time of separation or when the cause of action for divorce arose or was commenced, and when there is personal service upon the nonresident. However, personal jurisdiction is not obtained when a foreign divorce decree is registered in Virginia pursuant to the uniform acts discussed in § 21-5, and defendant is served in a third state. *Stephens v. Stephens,* 229 Va. 610, 331 S.E.2d 484 (1985). The fact that a settlement agreement including spousal support between the parties was entered into in the Commonwealth will not suffice to give Virginia courts personal jurisdiction for enforcement of a support order. *Morris v. Morris,* 4 Va. App. 539, 359 S.E.2d 104 (1987).

Where there is a valid separation agreement between the parties, jurisdiction by order of publication or by acceptance of service is sufficient to allow the agreement to be affirmed, ratified and incorporated into a final decree. Va. Code § 20-109.1; *Bray v. Landergren,* 161 Va. 699, 172 S.E. 252 (1933), (decided before the Supreme Court's decision of *Shaffer v. Heitner,* 433 U.S. 186 (1977), which restricts such quasi-in-rem jurisdiction to awards from property at issue in the instant proceedings).

Virginia Code § 16.1-243 provides that once a divorce proceeding has begun in the circuit court, jurisdiction shall no longer lie in the juvenile and domestic relations district court unless both parties agree to the referral.

Proof and corroboration of the jurisdictional facts of domicile, residence, and venue were necessary before a husband could obtain a divorce based on his cross-bill to his wife's claim for temporary spousal support. *Passmore v. Passmore,* 12 Va. Cir. 266 (Frederick Co. 1988).

See generally 6A Michie's Jurisprudence *Divorce and Alimony* § 68.

§ 21-4. Support following a foreign ex parte divorce.

The right to support is not extinguished by an *ex parte* decree rendered in another state, although the divorce itself will be given full faith and credit, *Newport v. Newport,* 219 Va. 48, 245 S.E.2d 134 (1978), so long as there was jurisdiction over the subject matter of the suit, obtained by domicile of the party seeking the divorce. *Williams v. North Carolina,* 325 U.S. 226 (1945). The Supreme Court has not yet considered the effect of discrimination against the actions of other states. *Estin v. Estin,* 334 U.S. 541 (1948). The so-called divisible divorce concept changed the former rule in which alimony was extinguished with the severing of the marital bonds by the absolute divorce. See *Wright v. Wright,* 164 Va. 245, 178 S.E. 884 (1935) (husband's Nevada divorce precluded wife from later attacking the jurisdictional basis of the decree or seeking alimony). A domestic *ex parte* decree must reserve the right to collect alimony. See, e.g., *Lenhart v. Burgett,* 1995 Va. App. LEXIS 300, where the husband was served personally in Pennsylvania in the divorce action. The Virginia divorce decree reserved the issues of spousal support and equitable distribution. When the wife brought an action to reinstate the support and distribution matters, the husband appeared personally to contest the case.

If the dependent spouse appears in the foreign proceeding, the ability to later seek support in Virginia is lost, for the right to obtain support is extinguished. *Ceyte v. Ceyte,* 222 Va. 11, 278 S.E.2d 791 (1981); *Osborne v. Osborne,* 215 Va. 205, 207 S.E.2d 875 (1974).

The question remains whether an *ex parte* foreign divorce based upon fault will extinguish the Virginia spouse's support rights. Compare *Ceyte v. Ceyte,* 222 Va. 11, 278 S.E.2d 791 (1981) (personal jurisdiction since wife appeared in foreign proceeding to contest denial of support). The court of appeals held that a Tennessee decree rendered *ex parte* and finding the wife guilty of cruelty did not have to be given full faith and credit for purposes of barring a Virginia spousal support action, since "[a]ny decision or finding by the Tennessee court affecting the personal rights of support and property must be founded on in personam jurisdiction," even though such findings are sufficient to support the divorce award. *Gibson v. Gibson,* 5 Va. App. 426, 434, 364 S.E.2d 518 (1988).

§ 21-5. Revised Uniform Reciprocal Enforcement of Support Act and UIFSA.

The Revised Uniform Reciprocal Enforcement of Support Act (RURESA) or its equivalent has now been enacted in all states and provides a mechanism for obtaining and enforcing interstate support awards. RURESA is available in addition to other actions for child support. Va. Code § 20-88.14. In Virginia, codification of the act is found in Va. Code §§ 20-88.12 to 20-88.31. The act was designed to create an economical and expedient means of enforcing support for dependent Virginia children, *Scott v. Sylvester,* 220 Va. 182, 257 S.E.2d 774 (1979), and is also used for spousal support. *Alig v. Alig,* 220 Va. 80, 255 S.E.2d 494 (1979). The way that the statute works is to provide that the custodial spouse, or a legal custodian, Va. Code § 20-88.20-1, brings an action in the Juvenile and Domestic Relations Court, Va. Code § 20-88.2:2, where the obligee resides (rendering state), Va. Code § 20-88.21, showing that a duty to support exists, either under an existing court order or otherwise. Va. Code § 20-88.22. The court then forwards the petition to the state of the obligor, Va. Code § 20-88.22, called the responding state, which allows that party, in a full hearing, to present any defenses (Va. Code § 20-88.22) and also to demonstrate the extent of the ability to pay. The applicable law is that of the obligor's state at the time for which support is sought. This decision will then be binding upon the obligor. Va. Code § 20-88.15.

Where the obligation is under a foreign support order, the order may be registered in Virginia, Va. Code § 20-88.30:2 et seq., at which point it shall be treated as would be any Virginia support order. Va. Code § 20-88.30:6; *Alig v. Alig,* 220 Va. 80, 255 S.E.2d 494 (1979); *Scott v. Sylvester,* 220 Va. 182, 257 S.E.2d 774 (1979). Past due payments may be collected in Virginia even though accrued when the obligor was outside the state. However, in personam jurisdiction over the defendant is not obtained by registration of a foreign divorce decree pursuant to URESA, when the defendant is served in a third state. *Stephens v. Stephens,* 229 Va. 610, 331 S.E.2d 484 (1985). Enforcement then may be by way of recognizance, contempt, and payment through the court. Va. Code § 20-88.26. Federal legislation designed to aid in the enforcement of child support was enacted in 1984. The federal legislation required changes to various Virginia statutes providing methods of enforcement. The Virginia Dep't of Social Services is now authorized to contract with public or private entities for processing support payments. Va. Code § 20-60.3. A localized system of collection and disbursement of support payments, with local accounting, has been reestablished. At the same time, a system of centralized accounting and enforcement with the Department will be maintained as required by federal law. Va. Code § 20-60.5. A dependent former wife may obtain an award for arrearages under a New Jersey divorce decree, although more than 10 years have elapsed after this foreign support order and eight years have passed since her remarriage. *Bennett v. Department of Social Servs.,* 15 Va. App. 135, 422 S.E.2d 458. The court of appeals noted that a spousal support order adjudicates an ongoing indeterminate support obligation. *Koneczny v. Koneczny,* 1995 Va. App. LEXIS. However, when the husband's liability for sharing the repair costs was not conditioned on her presenting bills or documentation of the total repair costs. The court of appeals noted that a spousal support order adjudicates an ongoing indeterminate support obligation. The responsibility extends for the lifetime of the parties absent a stipulation or contract between them, and is subject only to termination by operation of law on the death of one of the parties or the remarriage of the obligee. The moment that each installment falls due and unpaid, it becomes a vested property right and is immune from modification. Because of the ongoing nature of the order, no time limitation is placed upon the obligee spouse within which to obtain a judgment for accumulated arrearages, and even the doctrine of laches may not defeat the arrearage claim. The court contrasted this situation with a URESA proceeding in which the foreign support order adjudicates a sum certain due and owing, in which Va. Code § 8.01-252 acts as a cutoff provision.

Virginia adopted the Interstate Family Support Act (UIFSA) in Va. Code § 20-88.32 et seq. (1994). The act is similar to the Uniform Reciprocal Support Act in many respects, but does not apply to alimony, as opposed to child support, according to Va. Code § 20-88.32. An award for spousal support only shall be forwarded to the appropriate juvenile and domestic relations or family court, according to amendments to Section 20-88.39. Visitation issues cannot be raised in child support proceedings. Va. Code § 20-88.48.

§ 21-6. Role of fault in precluding support.

Until 1988, Va. Code § 20-107.1 specifically provided that if a cause of action for an absolute fault divorce under Va. Code § 20-91, or a bed and board divorce under Va. Code § 20-95 existed against a spouse, that spouse should not be awarded alimony. See, e.g., *Stolfi v. Stolfi*, 203 Va. 696, 126 S.E.2d 923 (1962). This included fault after the separation but before a cause of action accrues. *Haskins v. Haskins*, 188 Va. 525, 50 S.E.2d 437 (1948) (adultery after *a mensa* decree in favor of wife), see also *Gloth v. Gloth*, 154 Va. 511, 153 S.E. 879 (1930) (even though an *a mensa* divorce decree incorporated a separation agreement between the parties, it could be revoked when the wife subsequently committed adultery; before revision of § 20-109, which will not allow such an agreement to be modified except in accordance with its terms when filed with divorce pleadings). See generally Wadlington, *Sexual Relations After Separation or Divorce*, 63 Va. L. Rev. 249 (1977). The question of whether fault that occurs after the one-year separation period should negate the right to alimony remained, cf. *Coe v. Coe*, 225 Va. 616, 303 S.E.2d 923 (1983), as did the question of whether the dependent spouse's fault after conduct precipitating the marriage's demise on the part of the obligor should also be a bar. See *Wallace v. Wallace*, 46 Md. App. 213, 416 A.2d 1317 (1980). The court of appeals has determined that if the husband's conduct precipitated the parties' separation, and if the adulterous behavior occurred many years later, spousal support for the wife will not be precluded. *Wallace v. Wallace*, 1 Va. App. 183, 336 S.E.2d 27 (1985). See also *Surbey v. Surbey*, 5 Va. App. 119, 360 S.E.2d 873 (1987) (conduct of both parties caused separation, and no divorce could be granted to either on grounds of adultery because of recrimination).

The evolution of the standard for fault required to preclude support culminated in 1988 amendments to Va. Code § 20-107.1. The amendments provide that the court may make a spousal support award notwithstanding the existence of a fault ground for divorce, except in cases of adultery. Even in adultery cases, the court may make an award if it determines from clear and convincing evidence that the denial of support and maintenance would constitute a manifest injustice, based upon the respective degrees of fault during the marriage and the relative economic circumstances of the parties. Fault must, nevertheless, be considered in determining whether to award support, and in deciding the amount to be awarded. See, e.g., *Williams v. Williams,* 14 Va. App. 217, 415 S.E.2d 252 (1992), where the wife was granted spousal support of $200 per month following a no-fault divorce despite the fact that the husband showed that she had become pregnant by another and had obtained a therapeutic abortion during the parties' separation. The trial judge had noted that he had considered factors set forth in § 20-108.1 although he did not elaborate on any specific factor. See also *Barnes v. Barnes,* 16 Va. App. 98, 428 S.E.2d 294 (1993), where both parties had accepted that the marriage had ended, both intended to separate at some time in future, and the husband acquiesced in the separation. Although the husband proved the wife had committed adultery, the court found that it would be manifestly unjust for her not to receive spousal support since the adultery had little, if anything, to do with the deterioration of the marriage and did not prevent a possible reconciliation. See also *Konicki v. Konicki,* 32 Va. Cir. 368 (Spotsylvania Co. 1994) (husband condoned wife's adultery); *Bandas v. Bandas,* 16 Va. App. 427, 430 S.E.2d 706 (1993), where husband divorced on grounds of his imprisonment for a felony had to pay spousal support despite his wife's subsequent adultery and cohabitation; and *Mullins v. Mullins,* 1994 Va. App. LEXIS 655, where parties were separated for fourteen years prior to divorce, and divorce was granted on that ground rather than the husband's adultery. He had lived with another woman for many years and had a child with her. Apparently his fault did not enhance her alimony award.

With the 1988 amendments, the legislature adopted a kind of comparative rectitude standard. See *DeWitt v. DeWitt,* 98 Wis. 2d 44, 296 N.W.2d 761 (1980). That is, like comparative negligence, wrong on the part of an otherwise deserving spouse would reduce, but not eliminate, the ability to receive support. Fault may still be taken into consideration, but usually will not absolutely bar spousal support. The issue of whether a spouse committed fault precluding spousal support may not be raised for the first time on appeal. Therefore, if the payor spouse demurs to a commissioner's finding that a fault ground was not corroborated, he must file an objection at that time to the commissioner's report. *Dukelow v. Dukelow,* 2 Va. App. 21, 24, 341 S.E.2d 208, 209-10 (1986).

The fault ground must be pled, alleged, and proven with corroboration sufficient to have warranted granting a divorce to bar the payee spouse from alimony. *Venable v. Venable,* 2 Va. App. 178, 184, 342 S.E.2d 646, 650 (1986). Compare *Bentz v. Bentz,* 2 Va. App. 486, 345 S.E.2d 773 (1986) (need not be pled nor proven for property distribution).

Even though the husband succeeded in overturning the trial court's finding that there had been no desertion on the wife's part so that she was entitled to spousal support, the husband could not "equitably recoup" the $85,000 he had paid her pursuant to the erroneous decree. He could not recover the money under a theory of restitution, either, because the statutory scheme that allows a divorce court to grant alimony and later to modify that award does not expressly extend to the award of a judgment in favor of the payor spouse for previously paid amounts. Nor might the husband indirectly be reimbursed through a reduction in the monetary award given the wife as property distribution. *Reid v. Reid,* 245 Va. 409, 429 S.E.2d 208 (1993), reversing 14 Va. App. 505, 419 S.E.2d 398 (1992). Similarly, if one spouse is required to pay the other temporary alimony, the court may not order restitution of the amounts paid even though the payor obtains a divorce on fault grounds. *Hurt v. Hurt,* 16 Va. App. 792, 433 S.E.2d 493 (1993).

Since many states have now removed fault completely from consideration in divorce cases, a new body of empirical research discusses the difference between a fault-affected and fault-irrelevant system in terms of the amount received, the effect on marriage, and the effect on the divorce rate. Margaret F. Brinig & Steven M. Crafton, *Marriage and Opportunism,* 23 J. Legal Stud. 869 (1994) (discussing the relationship between fault-based alimony and spousal abuse); Margaret F. Brinig, *Comment on Jana Singer's Alimony and Efficiency,* 82 Geo. L.J. 2461 (1994); Martha Garrison, *How Do Judges Decide Divorce Cases? An Empirical Analysis of Discretionary Decisionmaking,* 74 NC L Rev 403, 407 (1995); Adriaen M. Morse, Jr., *Fault: A Viable Means of Re-Injecting Responsibility in*

Marital Relations, 30 U. Rich. L. Rev. 605 (1996); see generally 6A Michie's Jurisprudence *Divorce and Alimony* § 67.

§ 21-7. The necessity for showing need.

The need of each party must be considered in awarding alimony under Va. Code § 20-107.1(1). This principle is also reflected in Va. Code § 20-107.1(2), which lists the education and training, and ability to receive such, and § 20-107.1(5), which mentions the age and physical and mental condition of each party. For example, a wronged wife could show no need when she had supported herself (and the husband) throughout the marriage while he was in dental school. *Gagliano v. Gagliano,* 215 Va. 447, 211 S.E.2d 62 (1975). Her right to later receive alimony should have been reserved in the decree. See also *Baytop v. Baytop,* 199 Va. 388, 100 S.E.2d 14 (1957) (wife a schoolteacher, and award of alimony disallowed). *Poliquin v. Poliquin,* 12 Va. App. 676, 406 S.E.2d 401 (1991) (wife was psychiatric nurse who was "in no worse financial situation now than she was either before or during the marriage.... Her capabilities to earn have been improved rather than been lessened, except to the extent that the couple had a child which the [wife might raise]." The husband was a vascular surgeon who, during the divorce proceedings, left a position paying $80,000 per year to pursue his own practice. Wife was given a lump sum award of $6,000 payable over twelve months. The trial court should have reserved the right for her to petition the court for periodic spousal support based on changed circumstances. See also *Srinivasan v. Srinivasan,* 10 Va. App. 728, 396 S.E.2d 675 (1990), where the wife was an unemployed former college professor who had been a student during most of the marriage. The court held that the evidence did not support a finding that she had unreasonably refused to accept employment as of the date of divorce and that she was thus entitled to a reasonable time to secure employment, so that the court should at least retain jurisdiction over support, in the event that she should need it in the future. However, the wife is entitled to be maintained at the standard of living to which she was accustomed during marriage and if her income would result in a significantly lower life style, while the husband has the ability to make payments, she may be entitled to an alimony award. *Butler v. Butler,* 217 Va. 195, 227 S.E.2d 688 (1976).

The wife was entitled to spousal support where the parties had significant disparity in earning potential, where she was not at fault, and where the husband did not demonstrate any reason that she should not be entitled to support. *Via v. Via,* 14 Va. App. 868, 419 S.E.2d 431 (1992). See also *Simpson v. Simpson,* 1994 Va. App. LEXIS 123, where the court affirmed an alimony award in a case where the husband earned $70,000 per year and wife $24,600. The court noted that the chancellor must consider the subjective needs of each spouse when examining the statutory factors of need and ability to pay, as well as the "station to which a party may have grown accustomed during marriage." *Id.* at *4. See also *Gelletly v. Gelletly,* 1996 Va. App. LEXIS 39, where the wife was working approximately seventeen and a half hours a week, but was hampered by discomfort from two ruptured discs. *Kasprzak v. Kasprzak,* 1993 Va. App. LEXIS 284; *Rein v. Rein,* 1994 Va. App. LEXIS 699 (wife was nurse who had not worked during the marriage; trial court to consider whether she unreasonably refused to seek employment or whether she needed additional time before she secured employment); *Hauger v. Hauger,* 1995 Va. App. LEXIS 206 (in January of 1990, husband agreed to pay wife sufficient temporary support to enable her to earn masters' degree; at the time of the hearing she still had completed only one-third of thesis research). A husband is not obliged to provide for the wife's expenditures on pet care, charitable contributions, cable television, AAA membership for adult children, and gifts. *Seidenberg v. Seidenberg,* 9 Va. Cir. 83 (Henrico Co. 1987); *Hodges v. Hodges,* 2 Va. App. 508, 347 S.E.2d 134 (1986), where the wife earned $145 weekly, had expended her inheritance during the marriage, and had no separate property of any significance, while the husband had income in excess of $64,000 per year and a net worth of between $167,000 and $189,000. She was appropriately awarded support for "[h]er need for support is clearly established." *Id.,* 347 S.E.2d at 138.

Although formerly the wife's personal estate had no bearing on the husband's obligation to pay alimony, *Ring v. Ring,* 185 Va. 269, 38 S.E.2d 471 (1946), the statute now requires that the financial resources of each be considered. Installment payments to complete property distribution should not have been considered as income to the recipient spouse. *Ray v. Ray,* 4 Va. App. 509, 358 S.E.2d 754 (1987). Both *Ray* and *Zipf v. Zipf,* 8 Va. App. 387, 382 S.E.2d 263 (1989), note that the law does not require the spouse who seeks support to exhaust his or her own estate in order to qualify. But see *McGuire v. McGuire,* 10 Va. App. 248, 391 S.E.2d 344 (1990), holding that it was permissible to consider wife's share of husband's monthly retirement pension as "income of whatever nature" reducing the husband's support obligation.

The wife provided an expert witness concerning her psychological condition and ability to work in *Umbarger v. Umbarger,* 1993 Va. App. LEXIS 132. She had not been employed outside the home for twenty years, and the judge did not impute income to her based on her earning capacity.

All orders for spousal support shall contain a statement as to whether there is already an order requiring provision of coverage, or if the dependent spouse needs such an order, according to Va. Code § 20-60.3(6).

When a couple divorces on grounds of insanity, the parties are not necessarily relieved of spousal support obligations. If the institutionalized spouse might be eligible for federal medical assistance services, the court shall first order the institutionalized spouse to make available the maximum income contribution to the other spouse. If the spousal support award exceeds the federally established monthly maintenance needs allowance, the court must find that the increase is necessary because of exceptional circumstances causing financial distress to the other spouse. These circumstances might include threatened loss of basic food, shelter or medically necessary health care or the financial burden of caring for a disabled child, sibling or other relative. Effective January, 1994, the maximum spousal resource allowance is $72,660. Va. Code § 20-88.02:1.

§ 21-8. Duration of marriage.

The duration of the marriage affects the right to support both directly, under Va. Code § 20-107.1(4), and indirectly, since frequently in marriages of long duration the spouses will have made many contributions to the family's well-being. Va. Code § 20-107.1(6). A rule of thumb might be to limit the period in which alimony was to be received to the number of years' duration of the marriage except in exceptional circumstances. In many current marriages of long standing, the woman will not have sought educational or other training or will have been removed from the job market for such an extended period of time that financial independence is not possible and Va. Code § 20-107.1(2) is relevant. See, e.g., *Reynolds v. Reynolds,* 9 Va. Cir. 423 (Henrico Co. 1977).

§ 21-9. Reservation of right to support in final decree of divorce.

Once a decree for support has been rendered, it remains binding until a contingency occurs for which the decree provides, or until further order of the court. A subsequent contract between the parties will not prevent enforcement under the decree of the amount provided for in the agreement. *Capell v. Capell*, 164 Va. 45, 178 S.E. 894 (1935).

In order to preserve the right to have support, the decree should contain a proper reservation to that effect. *Brinn v. Brinn*, 147 Va. 277, 286, 137 S.E. 503, 505 (1927). If this is not done, the matter will be res judicata, and no support may later be awarded. Thus there was no jurisdiction to grant a lump sum award of spousal support when there was no explicit reservation of jurisdiction to modify the periodic maintenance contained in the final decree. The wife therefore could not obtain the lump sum award even though the transcript of the hearing indicated that the trial court intended to make a lump sum award at a later time, but inadvertently failed to include the reservation in the final decree. *Dixon v. Pugh*, 244 Va. 539, 423 S.E.2d 169 (1992). There was also no adequate reservation in a decree providing only for renegotiation of spousal support. *Sinnott v. Sinnott*, 1993 Va. App. LEXIS 151. See, e.g., *Lauffer v. Lauffer*, 23 Va. Cir. 278 (Fairfax Co. 1991). There may be a reservation of a right to such future periodic support even after a limited lump sum award is made by the divorce court and even though the payee spouse does not request it. *Poliquin v. Poliquin*, 12 Va. App. 676, 406 S.E.2d 401 (1991); *Blank v. Blank*, 10 Va. App. 1, 389 S.E.2d 723 (1990).

§ 21-10. Contributions to the marriage as relevant to support.

Both monetary and nonmonetary contributions to the family's well-being are to be considered under Va. Code § 20-107.1(6). The length of the marriage is relevant under Va. Code § 20-107.1(4), but cannot be the only factor considered in awarding or disallowing alimony. *Bristow v. Bristow*, 221 Va. 1, 267 S.E.2d 89 (1980).

The wife was entitled to spousal support where the parties had significant disparity in earning potential, where she was not at fault, and where the husband did not demonstrate any reason that she should not be entitled to support. *Via v. Via*, 14 Va. App. 868, 419 S.E.2d 431 (1992). Further, she was entitled to attorney's fees because the husband's failure to provide discovery necessitated most of her litigation expenses.

§ 21-11. Ability to pay as relevant to support award.

The earning capacity and financial resources of each party are taken into account in determining alimony. Va. Code § 20-107.1(1). This includes income from pension, profit sharing and retirement plans. It also includes the property possessed by each under Va. Code § 20-107.1(6). For example, an unemployed husband was ordered to pay alimony where there was nothing to prevent him from renting his property or obtaining employment in order to have some visible means of income. *Canavos v. Canavos,* 205 Va. 744, 139 S.E.2d 825 (1965). See also *Hawkins v. Hawkins,* 187 Va. 595, 47 S.E.2d 436 (1948) (defendant able to work full-time but actually worked about three-quarters of the time). The court properly imputed income from a second job held regularly by the obligor, a school teacher, when this summer income was used to establish the standard of living during the marriage. *Cochran v. Cochran,* 14 Va. App. 827, 419 S.E.2d 419 (1992). See also *Gelletly v. Gelletly,* 1996 Va. App. LEXIS 39, where $85,000 income was imputed to the husband when he had "jumped from a place of safety into a dry hole," though he had voluntarily left his former employment for a lower paying job. His payments were reduced, but not eliminated, because "[t]he fact that the new job fell short of his expectations did not relieve him of his pre-existing spousal support obligations."

   Floyd v. Floyd, 17 Va. App. 222, 436 S.E.2d 457 (1993), involved a husband in the construction business who systematically hid assets and income, according to the trial court. During one year, he cashed checks totalling almost $70,000 and received the proceeds in cash, while he claimed no income. The court of appeals affirmed the trial court's estimate of $45,000 in annual income for spousal and child support purposes. See also *Stubblebine v. Stubblebine,* 1996 Va. App. LEXIS 98 (Husband retired from the Army and worked for BDM Corporation, earning $90,000 annually. He resigned from this position, undertaking a variety of independent consulting jobs, and, although not gainfully employed, worked long hours for an organization involved in the study of parapsychology and psychic phenomena.). See also *Reece v. Reece,* 1996 Va. App. LEXIS 323, holding that when a supporting spouse refuses to accept an offer of comparable employment in another geographical location, there is no per se rule holding that the change in income constitutes voluntary unemployment or underemployment.

   An award of 71 percent of the husband's income, leaving him with insufficient funds to pay for basic necessities, was erroneous according to *Justice v. Justice,* 1995 Va. App. LEXIS 212. Nor could a court impute income because the supporting father was one of four contingent beneficiaries of a trust established for his own mother and aunt. *Harrison v. Harrison*, 1996 Va. App. LEXIS 54.

The ability to pay and need must be judged as of the time of the decree or modification. *Thomas v. Thomas,* 217 Va. 502, 229 S.E.2d 887 (1976); *Taylor v. Taylor,* 203 Va. 1, 121 S.E.2d 753 (1961). Therefore, it was erroneous for a court to include a clause escalating the amount of support payments based upon a percentage of increase in the husband's income, *Jacobs v. Jacobs,* 219 Va. 993, 254 S.E.2d 56 (1979), since this would be premised upon an uncertain future circumstance. See also *Robertson v. Robertson,* 215 Va. 425, 211 S.E.2d 41 (1975) (not proper to consider possible future receipt of trust fund).

A prior court order for support and maintenance of a previous spouse and child will clearly reduce the amount that would be available to pay a later one. *Id.* at 429.

§ 21-12. Pendente lite as opposed to permanent support.

Frequently, the first problem confronting an attorney in a divorce suit is the question of temporary spousal support. The Guidelines set forth in Va. Code § 20-108.1 pertain to *pendente lite* (temporary) as well as final support. In addition, the 1991 legislature amended Va. Code § 20-103, providing that for pendente lite spousal support the petitioning spouse may receive health care coverage from the other spouse unless it cannot be obtained.

Pendente lite relief is provided in Va. Code § 20-103, and includes sufficient funds to prosecute the underlying action, if any, plus maintenance. In RURESA actions under Va. Code § 20-88, temporary relief is available under Va. Code § 20-88.1. *Pendente lite* orders pursuant to divorce or annulment are enforceable through contempt proceedings. *Wright v. Wright,* 164 Va. 245, 178 S.E. 884 (1935). The usual form is through notice of motion rather than a cross-bill. *Davis v. Davis,* 206 Va. 381, 143 S.E.2d 835 (1965). If a trial court makes a spousal support order pendente lite and the divorce decree is appealed, the court loses jurisdiction to increase or otherwise modify the award during the appeal. *Decker v. Decker,* 17 Va. App. 562, 440 S.E.2d 411 (1994).

In *Van Heuven v. Van Heuven,* 19 Va. Cir. 542 (Fairfax Co. 1988), the court held that absent fraud or bad faith on the wife's part, it should not vacate retroactively the pendente lite support award to a wife who unsuccessfully challenged a property settlement agreement in which she waived her right to support. The award of a "partial lump sum" alimony constitutes an appealable order, according to *Weizenbaum v. Weizenbaum,* 12 Va. App. 899, 407 S.E.2d 37 (1991). Similarly, the payor spouse could not retrieve money paid as temporary alimony even though he was ultimately awarded a divorce on fault grounds. *Hurt v. Hurt,* 16 Va. App. 792, 433 S.E.2d 493 (1993).

See generally 6A Michie's Jurisprudence *Divorce and Alimony* § 67.

§ 21-13. Standard of living of the marriage as limitation on amount of support.

Under Va. Code § 20-107.1(3), the standard of living the parties established during their marriage shall be taken into consideration. A fair allotment is determined by balancing the needs of the dependent spouse against the ability of the obligor to pay, considering both actual earnings and capacity to earn. *Robertson v. Robertson,* 215 Va. 425, 427, 211 S.E.2d 41, 44 (1975); *Klotz v. Klotz,* 203 Va. 677, 680, 127 S.E.2d 104, 106 (1962). This will require some statement in the record of the computations used to reach the amount awarded. *Robertson, supra.*

The standard of living during the marriage affects both the initial setting of alimony, which should not relegate the dependent spouse to a standard far less than that enjoyed during the marriage, if the obligor can pay, and, in addition, the modification of alimony, since a drastic increase in the obligor spouse's income should not act to enable the dependent spouse to enjoy a higher standard of living than that established during the marriage. *Cole v. Cole,* 44 Md. App. 435, 409 A.2d 734 (1979); *Gagliano v. Gagliano,* 215 Va. 447, 211 S.E.2d 62 (1975). See also *Kasprzak v. Kasprzak,* 1993 Va. App. LEXIS 284; and *Stubblebine v. Stubblebine,* 1996 Va. App. LEXIS 98, where the husband retired from the Army and worked for BDM Corporation, earning $90,000 annually. He resigned from this position, undertaking a variety of independent consulting jobs, and, although not gainfully employed, worked long hours for an organization involved in the study of parapsychology and psychic phenomena. The court found that he was capable of gainful employment, requiring continued support of his former wife. Theoretically, the divorce *a mensa* should not operate to so fix the standard of living since the marriage is continuing at that point. *Gloth v. Gloth,* 154 Va. 511, 153 S.E. 879 (1930).

§ 21-14. Distribution of property as affecting support.

Va. Code § 20-107.1(8) provides that the distribution of property under Va. Code § 20-107.3 will be taken into account. Although property owned by the dependent spouse should be taken into account, this does not require invasion of that estate to relieve the obligations of a former spouse whose actions have brought about the demise of the marriage. *Klotz v. Klotz*, 203 Va. 677, 127 S.E.2d 104 (1962) (wife received marital home, a payment in cash to dissolve the marital business partnership, but had only $90 income per month, with expenses of $400 per month). Nor are installment payments in lieu of support for property owned during marriage income that affects the amount of support. *Ray v. Ray*, 4 Va. App. 509, 358 S.E.2d 754 (1987).

A wife who supported her husband through medical school was entitled to reimbursement alimony in the amount of $75,000 to reflect her monetary contribution to his acquisition of the degree in the form of earnings and inheritance funds expended on his behalf during the period of his education and training, and substantial non-monetary contributions made. The degree itself was held to be the husband's separate property. *Palmer v. Palmer*, 21 Va. Cir. 112 (Fairfax Co. 1990).

Although an antenuptial agreement precludes the divorce court from equitably distributing the parties' property, it will not necessarily prohibit the court from making a spousal support award. *Hankins v. Hankins*, 1993 Va. App. LEXIS 317; *Bracken v. Bracken*, 1993 Va. App. LEXIS 582. As *Bracken* noted, the trial court must make necessary findings under Code § 20-107.3 to determine which assets and debts are marital and separate, the values thereof, and the rights and equities of the parties in the properties and debts.

§ 21-15. Fault leading to breakup of marriage as relevant.

The "catch-all" provision, Va. Code § 20-107.1(9), requires "such other factors ... as are necessary to consider the equities between the parties" to be considered in determining spousal support. Fault amounting to a cause of action will preclude the award of alimony to that spouse under Va. Code § 20-107.1. Fault falling short of such proof might be relevant, as would be the award of support to the spouse in whose favor a fault ground for divorce was entered. *Seidenberg v. Seidenberg*, 9 Va. Cir. 83 (Henrico Co. 1987).

In *Hall v. Hall,* 9 Va. App. 426, 388 S.E.2d 669 (1990), the husband sought a divorce based upon the wife's desertion. Instead of appealing the divorce decree, he obtained a divorce based upon the separate and apart ground, and appealed the later award of spousal support to her based upon her alleged fault in deserting the marriage. The court of appeals held that res judicata barred reconsideration of the alleged misconduct at the spousal support and property distribution hearing, since the issue of fault had been finally and conclusively resolved by the trial court's ruling that the wife was justified in leaving the marital home.

"Although alimony is not to be used as a method of punishment, 'the court will not seek to find how light the burden may possibly be made, but what, under all the circumstances, will be a fair and just allotment.'" *Hawkins v. Hawkins,* 187 Va. 595, 601, 47 S.E.2d 436, 439 (1948) (quoting from *Bailey v. Bailey,* 62 Va. (21 Gratt.) 42, 58 (1871)).

Where the evidence showed that both parties had accepted that the marriage had ended, that both intended to separate at some time in the future, that the husband acquiesced in separation, and the divorce was granted upon the no-fault separation ground, the court found the wife "blameless for the marital breach," and awarded her spousal support. *Lamb v. Lamb,* 33 Va. Cir. 442 (Stafford Co. 1994).

§ 21-16. Ability to obtain support following no-fault divorce.

The existence of fault on the part of the obligor is not necessary to obtain support. In fact, a dependent spouse may obtain support even though the obligor obtains a no-fault divorce against him or her. *Mason v. Mason,* 209 Va. 528, 165 S.E.2d 392 (1969). See also *Brooker v. Brooker,* 218 Va. 12, 235 S.E.2d 309 (1977); *Dukelow v. Dukelow,* 2 Va. App. 21, 25, 341 S.E.2d 208, 210 (1986).

§ 21-17. Lump sum and periodic payments.

Alimony may consist of lump sum or periodic payments, or both, under Va. Code § 20-107.1. The lump sum payment will not be treated as alimony for tax purposes unless paid over more than six years, under I.R.C. § 71. The rule until 1984 was that payment must occur over more than a ten-year period to be deductible by the payor.

The commissioner was in error when he determined that the wife was better served by filing for bankruptcy rather than increasing the amount of periodic spousal support, *Goetz v. Goetz,* 7 Va. App. 50, 371 S.E.2d

567 (1988), and also erred by assuming that the husband could pay a lump sum spousal support award of $15,000 that was premised on the belief that the husband continues to earn a significant amount of unreported cash income from "side jobs."

The obligation to pay lump sum alimony does not end with the wife's remarriage, even though payable in installments, since the obligation was fixed at the time of decree. *Mallery-Sayre v. Mallery*, 6 Va. App. 471, 370 S.E.2d 113 (1988).

It was reversible error for the court to award a lump sum for spousal support without reserving to the recipient the right to petition for further support upon a change of circumstances, where there was no showing that she would be otherwise provided for. *Blank v. Blank*, 10 Va. App. 1, 389 S.E.2d 723 (1990). See also *Weizenbaum v. Weizenbaum*, 12 Va. App. 899, 407 S.E.2d 37 (1991). Thus, in *Poliquin v. Poliquin*, 12 Va. App. 676, 406 S.E.2d 401 (1991), where the wife was a psychiatric nurse who was "in no worse financial situation now than she was either before or during the marriage" and the husband was a vascular surgeon who during the divorce proceedings left a position paying $80,000 per year to pursue his own practice, the wife was properly given a lump sum award of $6,000 payable over twelve months rather than periodic spousal support. However, the trial court should have reserved the right for her to petition the court for periodic spousal support based on changed circumstances.

The reasons for granting lump sum awards include a payor spouse's future unwillingness or potential inability to pay periodic payments, or a payee spouse's immediate need for a lump sum to maintain herself or himself or satisfy debts. *Blank v. Blank*, 10 Va. App. 1, 5, 389 S.E.2d 723, 725 (1990). When no such special needs or circumstances are shown, it is error to grant a lump sum. *Guilfoyle v. Guilfoyle*, 1995 Va. App. LEXIS 24; *Kaufman v. Kaufman*, 12 Va. App. 1200, 409 S.E.2d 1 (1991).

§ 21-18. Tax consequences of support award.

The tax consequences to each party are to be taken into consideration in determining support and maintenance. Va. Code § 20-107.1(9).

Alimony, generally speaking, is deductible by the payor and taxable to the payee spouse. I.R.C. § 71. In order to qualify for this treatment, the payments must be made pursuant to court order or separation agreement and must be periodic: i.e., paid over more than six years, under the 1984 Domestic Relations Tax Reform Act, or ten years under the former § 71.

The Tax Reform Act of 1986, in § 1843(c), amended this provision by eliminating the six-year minimum term rule under § 71(f)(1), and changing the six-year recapture rule of § 71(f)(2) into a new three-year rule. These changes affect any 1985 or 1986 instrument. The new rule further provides that if alimony paid in the second year after divorce or separation exceeds payment in the following year (year three) by more than $15,000, the excess amount is recaptured in the following year (year three) as income to the payor and a credit to the payee. In addition, if the alimony paid in the first year (year one) exceeds the average annual alimony paid in years two and three by more than $15,000, the excess amounts are recaptured. These recapture rules do not apply if payments terminate because of the death of either spouse or the remarriage of the payee, nor do they apply to alimony pendente lite. This law applies to all orders beginning on or after January 1, 1987. I.R.C. § 71(f).

Under the former provisions, to constitute alimony the payments had to be in satisfaction of the spousal duty to support rather than as part of a division of property. The revised provision is not so limited. The other change is that formerly unitary payments of alimony and child support, so long as not divided specifically by the order or contract, were treated as alimony under the rule of *Commissioner v. Lester,* 366 U.S. 299 (1961). Agreements designed to obtain the favorable consequences of such unitary awards were recognized in the case of *Carter v. Carter,* 215 Va. 475, 211 S.E.2d 253 (1975). Payments made after remarriage and not under a separation agreement would not be in pursuance of the obligation of support and therefore would not be alimony. *Brown v. Commissioner of Internal Revenue,* 415 F.2d 310 (4th Cir. 1969). To be treated as alimony, payments must terminate upon the death of the payee spouse. I.R.C. § 71(b)(1). However, the instrument (decree or agreement) need not provide that alimony does not extend beyond the death of the payee.

The circuit court may order that alimony payments be non-taxable to the recipient and non-deductible by the payor under I.R.C § 91. *Hamilton v. Hamilton,* 19 Va. Cir. 241 (City of Alexandria 1990), because, the court reasoned, the Internal Revenue Code appears to allow the parties to agree which of them will bear the tax consequences of alimony payments.

See generally Podell, *The 1986 Tax Reform Act's Impact on Family Law: An Overview,* 13 Fam. L. Rep. 3001 (1986).

§ 21-19. Jurisdiction in support modification cases.

In a divorce case, the court retains jurisdiction to modify its award of spousal support. Va. Code § 20-109; *Thomas v. Thomas,* 217 Va. 502, 229 S.E.2d 887 (1976). The party reopening the matter must give notice to the other. Va. Code § 20-112. Publication will be sufficient. See also *State ex rel. Ravitz v. Fox,* 273 S.E.2d 370 (W. Va. 1980); *Glading v. Furman,* 282 Md. 200, 383 A.2d 398 (1978); 24 Am. Jur. *Divorce & Separation* § 852 (1966).

The parties must continue to make payments under the decree until modified by the court, and cannot elect not to comply because of a change in their circumstances. *Gloth v. Gloth,* 154 Va. 511, 554-55, 153 S.E. 879, 893 (1930).

Alimony decrees of other states are to be given full faith and credit only to the extent that installments are past due and are not subject to modification under the laws of the other state. *Sistare v. Sistare,* 218 U.S. 1 (1910).

A decree that schedules alimony to cease at a certain date may not be modified to extend the time of payments beyond that date without a reservation to that effect in the decree. *Losyk v. Losyk,* 212 Va. 220, 183 S.E.2d 135 (1971).

Cases involving spousal support may be heard in the juvenile and domestic relations court, or in circuit court if a divorce complaint has been filed. After the entry of a divorce decree, the court may transfer matters pertaining to spousal support to the juvenile and domestic relations court. The particular court to which the case is transferred may be in a different location within the state if a party or the court so moves and shows good cause. Va. Code § 20-79, as amended in 1988.

For cases filed before January 1, 1996, the circuit court may transfer enforcement of divorce decrees, including pendente lite orders, to the new family court, when funded. After such a transfer, the circuit court will be divested of any further jurisdiction over the matter. Va. Code § 20-79(c). Virginia adopted the Interstate Family Support Act (UIFSA) in new Va. Code § 20-88.32 et seq. (1994). The act is similar to the Uniform Reciprocal Support Act in many respects. The Act does establish some new concepts. The UIFSA establishes uniform long-arm jurisdiction over nonresidents and provides for discovery and testimony once jurisdiction is obtained. Va. Code §§ 20-88.36, 20-88.59, 20-88.61. The UIFSA may only be used for child support proceedings not alimony under amended Va. Code Ann. § 20-88.32.

The only tribunal that can modify a support order is the one having continuing exclusive jurisdiction except in narrowly defined circumstances. If both parties no longer reside in the issuing state, a tribunal with personal jurisdiction over both or with power given by their agreement may modify. Va. Code §§ 20-88.39, 20-88.40, 20-88.68.

The UIFSA authorizes establishment of parentage in interstate proceedings even when not accompanied by a support proceeding.

§ 21-20. Modification under RURESA.

The uniform act, Va. Code § 20-88, provides for a mechanism for enforcing a support order, but should not normally be used as a mechanism for modification, particularly of an existing court order obtained through in personam jurisdiction. Filing a foreign decree under RURESA will not give the Virginia court in personam jurisdiction, at least where the defendant is not served within the state in the registration action. *Stephens v. Stephens,* 229 Va. 610, 331 S.E.2d 484 (1985).

§ 21-21. Inability to modify if there is property settlement agreement.

Va. Code § 20-109 provides that spousal support may be modified by the court at any time except when a stipulation or contract has been filed by the court. Modifications then may only be made in accordance with the terms of the contract. Recent amendments to Va. Code § 20-109, and the addition of Va. Code § 20-109.1, allow such stipulations or contracts to be filed before or after entry of the final decree. New Va. Code § 20-109.1 permits modification even after the decree in accordance with agreements filed before or after the decree. Support still ceases under the decree at the death of either spouse, Va. Code § 20-110, although it may continue under the agreement if it specifically so provides. Recent amendments to the Internal Revenue Code state that there must be no liability to make payments after death of the payee in order for payments to be considered alimony. I.R.C. § 71(b)(D).

§ 21-22. Substantive standard: change of circumstances.

The court has the inherent right, supplemented by Va. Code § 20-109, to modify an alimony award to meet the changed conditions of the parties and to attain the ends of justice. *Brinn v. Brinn,* 147 Va. 277, 287, 137

S.E. 503, 506 (1927). This is certainly true in cases of divorce *a mensa.* *Gloth v. Gloth*, 154 Va. 511, 535, 153 S.E. 879, 886 (1930). See also *Brown v. Brown*, 22 Va. Cir. 263 (Fairfax Co. 1990). Where the husband agreed to continue payments and was not compelled to do so, he could have ceased making non-obligatory payments at any time, but was required to continue to pay the amount required by the decree. *Buxbaum v. Buxbaum*, 20 Va. App. 181, 455 S.E.2d 752 (1995). See also *Sanford v. Sanford*, 19 Va. App. 241, 450 S.E.2d 185 (1994); and *MacNelly v. MacNelly*, 1995 Va. App. LEXIS 496.

The party seeking to modify alimony must bear the burden of showing there is a change of circumstances by a preponderance of the evidence. *Floyd v. Floyd*, 1 Va. App. 42, 45, 333 S.E.2d 364, 366 (1985) (defendant former husband did not sufficiently show that financial condition of business was deteriorating when there was also testimony that he had made cash withdrawals from company characterized as loans rather than as salary. The increase in expenses he proved may have occurred in large part because of second wife). A sufficient change in circumstances was demonstrated in *Wyatt v. Wyatt*, 19 Va. Cir. 49 (1989), where the wife chose to give up her job earning $20,000 annually, and had moved to North Carolina, and was sharing a condominium with a male friend and earning $320 per week. The Court found that she had shown the ability to earn more money than she was receiving in her current employment, and that her earning capacity exceeded that of her former husband.

Changes in circumstances include various changes in the financial condition of the dependent spouse. For example, one circumstance would be an increase in the needs of the dependent spouse, which might occur because of illness and a consequent increase in medical expenses, or a substantial increase in the cost of living. See, e.g., *Furr v. Furr*, 13 Va. App. 479, 413 S.E.2d 72 (1992) (as a consequence of significantly increased expenses, wife's standard of living declined). Another change would be a decrease in the dependent spouse's ability to provide financial independence. This might occur, again, because of illness or accident, an increase in general unemployment that affects the spouse, or reaching of retirement age. See, e.g., *Richards v. Richards*, 1994 Va. App. LEXIS 376 (not designated for publication) (husband's employment terminated; income dropped from $154,000 to $90,000 per year). The amount owing to a dependent spouse might also decrease. For example, the needs of the spouse might become less over time as, for example, when education or vocational training is completed, or expenses are shared with another.

Similarly, the dependent spouse may have a greater ability to pay upon becoming employed, or inheriting income-producing property. See, e.g., *Ward v. Ward,* 41 Or. App. 447, 599 P.2d 1150 (1979).

Other changes involve the circumstances of the obligor spouse. Ordinarily, remarriage and acquisition of a second family will not constitute grounds for reduction in support. *Morris v. Morris,* 216 Va. 457, 219 S.E.2d 864 (1975) (child support). However, a change in medical or other nonvolitional expenses might be sufficient to warrant a reduction in alimony. The obligor's ability to pay may also decrease if, for example, income is less in a particular year in a professional person's career, or retirement is mandated. The obligor's ability to pay may also increase to the point where a greater amount may be paid to the dependent spouse. See, e.g., *Gammell v. Gammell,* 90 Cal. App. 3d 90, 153 Cal. Rptr. 169 (1979). However, the dependent spouse must carry the burden of demonstrating a change of circumstances. The dependent spouse does not meet this burden merely by alleging an increase in the obligor's income and a decrease in expenses. *McElwrath v. McElwrath,* 1993 Va. App. LEXIS 133. The husband does not necessarily meet his burden of showing changed circumstances when he proves that the wife's income has increased since the original order. No reduction was required when his income had also increased. *Ragland v. Ragland,* 1993 Va. App. LEXIS 195. See also *Norris v. Norris,* 1995 Va. App. LEXIS 237, where a 66-year-old wife had waived any interest in husband's retirement benefits in exchange for $500 in spousal support, the husband could not allege that his retirement was a material change in circumstances. The court may refuse to hear a motion for reduction if the obligor has substantial arrearages in the amount he is to pay the wife for equitable distribution. *Bridgforth v. Bridgforth,* 1995 Va. App. LEXIS 258. This cannot exceed the standard of living established during the marriage, however. See *Cole v. Cole,* 44 Md. App. 435, 409 A.2d 734 (1979).

§ 21-23. Change of custody as affecting support.

If custody is changed from the dependent to the obligor spouse, the amount awarded the dependent spouse may change. For instance, this would be a sufficient change in circumstance to require apportionment of a unified award for spousal and child support, *Carter v. Carter,* 215 Va. 475, 211 S.E.2d 253 (1975), since it was never contemplated by the parties when they entered into their settlement agreement. See, e.g.,

Jarrell v. Jarrell, 1994 Va. App. LEXIS 672; and *Tanger v. Tanger,* 1996 Va. App. LEXIS 297.

§ 21-24. Death of spouse.

The death of the obligor spouse will signal the end of the obligation to pay support. This is because the obligation to support one's spouse ordinarily ceases at death. *Foster v. Foster,* 195 Va. 102, 77 S.E.2d 471 (1953); *Francis v. Francis,* 72 Va. (31 Gratt.) 283 (1879). A contract in lieu of alimony may specifically provide for continued payments, and then would survive the death of the obligor. *Durrett v. Durrett,* 204 Va. 59, 129 S.E.2d 50 (1963). Va. Code § 20-109.1.

The death of the dependent spouse will cause support to cease. However, a contract for property settlement can be enforced by the decedent's estate. *Moore v. Crutchfield,* 136 Va. 20, 116 S.E. 482 (1923).

§ 21-25. Remarriage of dependent spouse.

Remarriage of a dependent spouse causes support and maintenance to cease. Va. Code § 20-110. The only apparent exception to this rule is when an agreement between the parties relating to support allows it to continue after remarriage. Va. Code § 20-110. However, remarriage will not terminate unpaid installments of lump sum alimony, since this obligation becomes fixed at the time of decree. *Mallery-Sayre v. Mallery,* 6 Va. App. 471, 370 S.E.2d 113 (1988).

If the parties do not clearly and expressly specify that spousal support obligations will survive the dependent spouse's remarriage, Va. Code § 20-109.1 requires that such an obligation will terminate. *Penley v. Penley,* 1994 Va. App. LEXIS 417; *Miller v. Hawkins,* 14 Va. App. 192, 415 S.E.2d 861; *MacNelly v. MacNelly,* 17 Va. App. 427, 437 S.E.2d 582 (1993); *Radford v. Radford,* 16 Va. App. 812, 433 S.E.2d 35 (1993). Compare *Gayler v. Gayler,* 20 Va. App. 83, 455 S.E.2d 278 (1995) ("payments ... shall terminate only upon wife's death"). Likewise, "remarriage" that is defined by a property settlement agreement to include "cohabitation, analogous to marriage, with another man" terminated spousal support in *Frey v. Frey,* 14 Va. App. 270, 416 S.E.2d 40 (1992). "Although matters relating to divorce are currently within the jurisdiction of circuits, they may be heard on the equity side, in the absence of a statutory grant cases." *MacNelly v. MacNelly,* 1995 Va. App. LEXIS 496.

If the second marriage is voidable, and it is annulled, the dependent spouse is not entitled to a reinstatement of alimony. This is because the obligor spouse has a right to rely upon the remarriage and to rearrange his or her life and financial affairs, and the dependent spouse in remarrying assumes the risk of misfortune or mistake. The court has not yet expressed itself on the question of whether support would be provided where the second marriage was void. *McConkey v. McConkey,* 216 Va. 106, 215 S.E.2d 640 (1975).

Remarriage, although it signals the end of the duty to pay spousal support, may not signal the end of the tax treatment of payments as alimony. *Ensminger v. Commissioner,* 610 F.2d 189 (4th Cir.), *cert. denied,* 446 U.S. 941 (1979), if payable under a property settlement agreement; *McLoughlin v. McLoughlin,* 211 Va. 365, 177 S.E.2d 781 (1970) (alimony payments due under an incorporated separation agreement will not cease either; case decided before Va. Code § 20-110 required that the extension of the obligation to make payment after remarriage be explicit in contract).

§ 21-26. Cohabitation of dependent spouse.

Although an attempt to include cohabitation with remarriage as an event terminating alimony was defeated in the Virginia legislature in 1981, decisions from other jurisdictions suggest that such an occurrence may provide a basis for altering support. Usually more than sexual activity is required: the couple must actually be living together and have a financial interdependence. See, e.g., *Porter v. Porter,* 137 Vt. 375, 406 A.2d 398 (1979); *Schoenhard v. Schoenhard,* 74 Ill. App. 3d 296, 392 N.E.2d 764 (1979). However, absent a change by the legislature, the court in *deLeeuw v. deLeeuw,* 13 Va. Cir. 148 (City of Norfolk 1988), has held that support would not be terminated upon the wife's living with another man. The parties could have agreed to terminate alimony at some time earlier than remarriage if they had so desired.

In *Frey v. Frey,* 14 Va. App. 270, 416 S.E.2d 40 (1992), the parties provided in their property settlement agreement that the husband's obligation to pay spousal support would terminate upon "her cohabitation, analogous to marriage, with another man." The court of appeals held that the phrase means a status in which a man and woman live together continuously, or with some permanency, mutually assuming duties and obligations normally attendant with a marital relationship. It involves more than living together for a period of time and having sexual relations, but does not require that the other party assume the duty of providing some financial support. See also *Schweider v. Schweider,* 243 Va. 245, 415 S.E.2d 135 (1992) ("R]emarriage" in the parties' agreement was defined to mean "permanent cohabitation with a male as if to all appearances they were otherwise married." "Remarriage" terminating support was found when the wife shared a bedroom with another man for a substantial amount of time from 1988 to 1992); *Dolan v. Dolan,* 1994 Va. App. LEXIS 761 (if legislature intended misconduct or illicit cohabitation to terminate spousal support, it could have provided for termination as it did with remarriage and death).

§ 21-27. Jurisdiction for enforcement proceedings.

Even though the defendant is in military service, the federal statute, 42 U.S.C. § 659(a), allows moneys due from the United States to be subjected to legal process for enforcement of alimony obligations in the same manner as for other private persons. This includes payments ordered under an incorporated separation agreement. *Butler v. Butler,* 221 Va. 1035, 277 S.E.2d 180 (1981).

Notice must be given if a foreign decree is to be enforced so that the defendant has the opportunity to raise defenses such as modification of accrued arrearages. *Griffin v. Griffin,* 327 U.S. 220, 233-34 (1946). This notice may be by constructive service where the defendant is now a nonresident. *Sheffield v. Sheffield,* 207 Va. 288, 148 S.E.2d 771 (1966). However, Virginia does not have personal jurisdiction needed for enforcement, although a property settlement agreement had been filed in case, where the defendant was now a nonresident. *Morris v. Morris,* 4 Va. App. 539, 359 S.E.2d 104 (1987).

Any juvenile and domestic relations district court to which a suit is transferred for enforcement pursuant to Va. Code § 20-79(c) (Uniform Reciprocal Enforcement of Support Act) is authorized to transfer the case to the city or county of the respondent's residence. Va. Code § 16.1-243(b)(5). For cases filed before January 1, 1996, the circuit court may transfer enforcement of divorce decrees, including pendente lite orders, to the new family court, when funded. After such a transfer to the family court, the circuit court will be divested of any further jurisdiction over the matter. Va. Code § 20-79(c).

The court has no power to sequester, for purposes of temporary alimony, property held by husband and wife as tenants by the entireties where the husband is outside the state, since such property could not be made subject to a debt because of the nature of the entireties estate. However, upon partition, the husband's share could be held as security for alimony. *Jenkins v. Jenkins,* 211 Va. 797, 180 S.E.2d 516 (1971).

§ 21-28. Modification of arrearages.

The courts are not given the power to modify amounts already accrued under a decree, see, e.g., *Carter v. Carter,* 215 Va. 475, 211 S.E.2d 253 (1975); *Cralle v. Cralle,* 84 Va. 198, 6 S.E. 12 (1887), since there is a vested property right in such installments, *Eaton v. Davis,* 176 Va. 330, 10 S.E.2d 893 (1940). This means that Virginia alimony arrearages must be given full faith and credit by other state courts. *Sistare v. Sistare,* 218 U.S. 1 (1910). If the parties' final divorce decree specified that the husband was to make spousal support payments, he could not receive restitution of payments made even when it turned out that the wife had deserted him and therefore was not entitled to spousal support. *Reid v. Reid,* 245 Va. 409, 429 S.E.2d 208 (1993) (reversing 14 Va. App. 505, 419 S.E.2d 398 (1992)). The wife was equitably estopped from claiming arrearage when she accepted lower payments for approximately four years when the husband left his law firm. In reliance on her representation that she would "just have to live" with those payments, the husband substantially changed his financial and personal positions. *Wheeler v. Wheeler,* 1994 Va. App. LEXIS 426.

The entry of an order or decree of support for a spouse constitutes a final judgment for any sum or sums in arrears, and shall also include an amount for interest on the arrearage if the payee so requests. Va. Code § 20-78.2. The interest rate shall be the judgment rate of interest, according to the 1987 amendments to that section.

§ 21-29. Enforcement under the Uniform Reciprocal Enforcement of Support Act and UIFSA.

A foreign decree registered in Virginia will be enforceable under the Revised Uniform Reciprocal Enforcement of Support Act. *Scott v. Sylvester,* 220 Va. 182, 257 S.E.2d 774 (1979) (child support). The entire amount owing will be collectible including portions that accrued while the defendant was outside Virginia. *Id.* at 187, 257 S.E.2d at 777. Amounts payable in the future may be treated with full force and effect under the doctrine of comity. *Alig v. Alig,* 220 Va. 80, 255 S.E.2d 494 (1979).

The registration of a foreign decree does not give in personam jurisdiction to Virginia courts where the defendant is served outside the state. *Stephens v. Stephens,* 229 Va. 610, 331 S.E.2d 484 (1985).

A Virginia judgment was enforced in a California order in *Harmon v. Harmon,* 160 Cal. App. 2d 47, 324 P.2d 901, *cert. denied,* 358 U.S. 881 (1958).

Virginia adopted the Interstate Family Support Act (UIFSA) in new Va. Code § 20-88.32 et seq. (1994). The act is similar to the Uniform Reciprocal Support Act in many respects. The Act does establish some new concepts. The UIFSA establishes uniform long-arm jurisdiction over nonresidents and provides for discovery and testimony once jurisdiction is obtained. Va. Code §§ 20-88.36, 20-88.59, 20-88.61. The UIFSA may only be used for spousal and child support proceedings. Visitation issues cannot be raised in child support proceedings. Va. Code § 20-88.48.

The choice of law for interpretation of support orders registered under the UIFSA is that of the state issuing the underlying support orders, except that the longer of different statutes of limitation applies. Continuing exclusive jurisdiction is established, so that only one support order is normally effective at any given time.

The UIFSA provides that a support order may be mailed directly to an obligor's employer, triggering wage withholding without a hearing unless the employee objects. The obligor's state may administratively enforce the order, although all judicial enforcement begins with the registration of the existing order in the responding state.

The only tribunal that can modify a support order is the one having continuing exclusive jurisdiction except in narrowly defined circumstances. If both parties no longer reside in the issuing state, a tribunal with personal jurisdiction over both or with power given by their agreement may modify the order. Va. Code §§ 20-88.39, 20-88.40, 20-88.68.

The UIFSA authorizes establishment of parentage in interstate proceedings even when not accompanied by a support proceeding.

§ 21-30. Full faith and credit for foreign support awards.

A foreign decree for alimony is entitled to full faith and credit under Article IV, § 2 of the Constitution as to past due installments, if the right to the installments is not subject to modification in the state where the decree was rendered. *Sistare v. Sistare,* 218 U.S. 1 (1910). But if modifiable either for past due or future payments, the decree may be recognized nevertheless under principles of comity. *Alig v. Alig,* 220 Va.

80, 255 S.E.2d 494 (1979); *McKeel v. McKeel,* 185 Va. 108, 113, 37 S.E.2d 746, 749 (1946). During the enforcement proceeding, due process requires consideration of questions of modification which could have been presented to the court of the state where the decree was entered. *Griffin v. Griffin,* 327 U.S. 220, 233-34 (1946); *Alig v. Alig,* 220 Va. at 85, 255 S.E.2d at 498.

§ 21-31. Contempt.

A decree for alimony is different from an ordinary judgment or debt.

It is an allowance in the nature of a partition of the husband's property, of which the wife is entitled to a reasonable share for her maintenance. It is an order compelling a husband to support his wife, and this is a public as well as a marital duty — a moral as well as a legal obligation. The liability is not based upon a contract to pay money, but upon the refusal to perform a duty. The imprisonment is not ordered simply to enforce the payment of the money, but to punish for the wilful disobedience of a proper order of a court of competent jurisdiction. *West v. West,* 126 Va. 696, 699, 101 S.E. 876, 877 (1920). Since imprisonment is a severe and harsh remedy, it should not be ordered except where the defendant is contumacious. *Id.* at 700, 101 S.E. at 878. The failure must therefore not stem from an inability to pay. *Branch v. Branch,* 144 Va. 244, 132 S.E. 303 (1926); *Lindsey v. Lindsey,* 158 Va. 647, 164 S.E. 551 (1932).

Contempt is available after a divorce decree providing for spousal support, or an award made independent of a proceeding for divorce. *Helfin v. Helfin,* 177 Va. 385, 14 S.E.2d 317 (1941).

Alimony is to be distinguished from breach of contract between the parties substituting for support, even if confirmed by the divorced couple, so long as the defendant was not ordered by the decree to make alimony payments. *Martin v. Martin,* 205 Va. 181, 135 S.E.2d 815 (1964). Once there is a court order for payment of the agreed upon amount, the decree will be enforceable by contempt. Va. Code § 20-109.1.

The proceeding to enforce spousal support is instituted by a written petition or motion. *Eddens v. Eddens,* 188 Va. 511, 50 S.E.2d 397 (1948). The contempt proceeding is captioned in the names of the parties or in the style of the original suit to be enforced. *Id.,* see also *Davis v. Davis,* 206 Va. 381, 143 S.E.2d 835 (1965) (enforcement of pendente lite order).

If a recognizance is not complied with, or a party is found to be in contempt, he or she may be committed to an institution or work squad for a fixed or indeterminate sentence of not more than twelve months, with the county or city then paying support of five dollars to twenty-five dollars per week to the dependent spouse. Va. Code § 20-115.

The party seeking to have the obligor held in contempt may be entitled to attorney's fees. *McKeel v. McKeel,* 185 Va. 108, 116-17, 37 S.E.2d 746, 750 (1946). See also *Alig v. Alig,* 220 Va. 80, 86, 255 S.E.2d 494, 498 (1979). A defendant may be required to post a bond pending appeal of a contempt finding. *Adams v. El-Amin,* 31 Va. Cir. 451 (City of Richmond 1993).

The defendant in a contempt proceeding for failure to make support payments is entitled to the privilege against self-incrimination. *Gowen v. Wilkerson,* 364 F. Supp. 1043 (W.D. Va. 1973) (harmless error in this case).

See generally 6A Michie's Jurisprudence *Divorce and Alimony* § 74.

§ 21-32. Laches.

Acquiescence of nonpayment, even over an extended period of time, will not prevent a dependent spouse from bringing an action to collect the entire arrearages. *Richardson v. Moore,* 217 Va. 422, 229 S.E.2d 864 (1976) (twenty-six years after husband unilaterally reduced support payments, which reduced amount as accepted by wife). This would especially be true in a case where the dependent spouse at the time was mentally unstable and did not communicate with the obligor for three years. *Alig v. Alig,* 220 Va. 80, 255 S.E.2d 494 (1979). Interest and attorney's fees may be collected on unpaid installments, unless inequitable. *Id.* at 85, 255 S.E.2d at 497. See also *McKeel v. McKeel,* 185 Va. 108, 116, 37 S.E.2d 746, 750-51 (1946).

Husband was ordered by the juvenile and domestic relations court to pay spousal support. He perfected an appeal of this support order to the circuit court. A divorce decree, which was silent as to spousal support, was entered, and the husband stopped making payments. After an unsuccessful URESA proceeding in which the district court found that he was no longer bound to make payments, the wife eventually petitioned the district court requesting a hearing on the issue of husband's failure to make payments. An appeal was taken by the wife to the circuit court, which found that no payments had been made for nearly three years. When the husband appealed, arguing that wife was estopped from proceeding because she had not appealed from the district court URESA decision, the court of appeals held that he did not meet the requirements of estoppel because without legal excuse he had not complied with the lawful support decree. *Martin v. Bales,* 7 Va. App. 141, 371 S.E.2d 823 (1988).

§ 21-33. Other defenses.

The obligor must purge himself of contempt before the writ of execution is issued. Issuance of execution is regarded for this purpose as a new case. *Hall v. Hall,* 192 Va. 721, 66 S.E.2d 595 (1951) (husband had not filed his notice of appeal within time so could not appeal; court noted it would probably have affirmed case anyway on grounds that purging must commence before the court is required to entertain a motion to quash execution).

§ 21-34. Garnishment.

Garnishment for past-due spousal support is authorized by Va. Code § 20-79.1. Orders entered after October 1, 1985, must give notice that arrearages may be withheld from income without amending the order. Va. Code § 20-60.3. Procedures are governed by Va. Code § 8.01-511.

If payment is to be made through the Department of Social Services, as provided since 1985 by Va. Code § 20-60.5, the parties must give the Department thirty days' written notice of changes of address. Further, if the Department does not pay an amount received within thirty days, it must also pay interest on the amount, if the account can be readily identified and the payee is not receiving public assistance.

A receiver may be appointed in the court's discretion to take posses-sion of the property of a nonresident defendant and subject it to the payment of alimony. This would be in the nature of a writ of sequestration or injunction preventing alienation of or interference with the property without the court's consent. *Thornton v. Washington Savings Bank,* 76 Va. 432 (1882); See generally 2 Story's *Equity Jurisprudence* §§ 828-833. But cf. *Watkins v. Watkins,* 220 Va. 1051, 265 S.E.2d 750 (1980), disallowing a lien forbidding sale of the in-state husband's shares of stock in a closely-held family corporation on grounds that this procedure was outside the court's jurisdiction since it affected title to the property. Va. Code § 34-29 limits payroll deduction orders to no more than 50% of the payee's aggregate disposable earnings, which for purposes of Va. Code

§ 20-79.3 include retirement pay from former employers. *Donahue v. Donahue,* 28 Va. Cir. 70 (Fairfax Co. 1992).

A recognizance may be ordered under Va. Code § 20-114.

§ 21-35. Lien against property of obligor spouse.

A decree for alimony is a lien upon the real estate of the obligor. *Isaacs v. Isaacs' Guardian,* 117 Va. 730, 86 S.E. 105 (1915). See, e.g., *Wilson v. Wilson,* 195 Va. 1060, 81 S.E.2d 605 (1954). Once recorded on the judgment lien docket, an execution of *fieri facias* on the decree becomes a statutory lien upon the obligor's intangible property, and when levied upon, an execution lien. *Harper v. Harper,* 159 Va. 210, 165 S.E. 490 (1932). If counsel obtains an order for a lien reduced to a docket judgment on the property, then the judge may require that a surety bond be posted against the sale of the property. Va. Code § 8.01-460.

The usual provision for a lien against the debtor's property within the state is a possible remedy. *Id.* (for sums already owed, and falling due after the decree). The lien should be registered in the city or county where the land is located. *Durrett v. Durrett,* 204 Va. 59, 62, 129 S.E.2d 50, 52 (1963). The court's jurisdiction is bounded by statute. Thus the court has no authority to enjoin a husband from selling his shares of stock in a closely-held family corporation in order to protect the wife or children's right to support. *Watkins v. Watkins,* 220 Va. 1051, 265 S.E.2d 750 (1980).

The order may be referred to the juvenile and domestic relations court for enforcement by the court entering the original order, either if the obligor fails to provide the ordered support or upon the court's own motion. Va. Code § 20-113.

The dependent spouse, as a lien creditor, may have partition of a jointly held estate if the other co-owner is not willing to take the whole property and the property is not susceptible of partition. In such case the property would be sold and the proceeds applied to discharge the lien. Va. Code § 8-690 et seq. See *Jenkins v. Jenkins,* 211 Va. 797, 180 S.E.2d 516 (1971).

§ 21-36. Posting of bond of recognizance.

Va. Code § 20-114 provides that the court in its discretion may require a spouse to give a recognizance bond. See, e.g., *Canavos v. Canavos,* 205 Va. 744, 139 S.E.2d 825 (1965); *Lawrence v. Lawrence,* 212 Va. 44, 181

S.E.2d 640 (1971). This is also provided for in the Uniform Reciprocal Enforcement of Support Act, Va. Code § 20-88.22:1.

CHAPTER 22

Property Distribution

§ 22-1. Overview.

Historically, financial adjustment upon divorce in states following the common law tradition has occurred through alimony, almost always paid by the husband to the wife as the dependent spouse. See generally Vernier & Hurlbut, *The Historical Background of Alimony Law and Its Present Statutory Structure*, 6 Law & Contemp. Probs. 197 (1939). However, the real and personal property acquired during the marriage is not always held by the husband, nor have his efforts been the only ones instrumental in acquiring such property. See, e.g., *Hill v. Hill*, 227 Va. 569, 318 S.E.2d 292 (1984) (wife entitled to one half of shares of corporation because of her contributions during the marriage). The more modern rule, which among other advantages allows both spouses financial independence, allows marital property to be divided in some fashion upon divorce. In general, the equitable distribution of property represents an approach analogous to dissolution of a partnership. See, e.g., *Hinton v. Hinton*, 70 N.C. App. 665, 321 S.E.2d 161, 163 (1984); *Deering v. Deering*, 292 Md. 115, 122, 437 A.2d 883 (1981); see generally Krauskopf, *Theories of Property Division and Spousal Support: Searching for Solutions to the Mystery*, 23 Fam. L.Q. 253 (1989); Krauskopf & Thomas, *Partnership Marriage: The Solution to an Ineffective and Inequitable Law of Support*, 35 Ohio St. L.J. 558 (1974); Sharp, *The Partnership Ideal: The Development of Equitable Distribution in North Carolina*, 65 N.C.L. Rev. 197 (1987).

The value of services performed as a homemaker should be taken into account in determining the share of property accorded to each spouse. See, e.g., Va. Code § 20-107.3; *Gummow v. Gummow*, 356 N.W.2d 426 (Minn. App. 1984). Va. Code § 20-107.3 has been amended so that distribution now includes "all property, real and personal, tangible or intangible." Arguably this could include intangible property such as professional goodwill. *Russell v. Russell*, 11 Va. App. 411, 399 S.E.2d 166 (1990).

The action for property distribution requires that the parties: (1) identify marital property, both real and personal, to be divided between the parties; (2) determine the fair market value of the property so identified; (3) identify the proportionate contribution, financial or through services, each party made to the acquisition of marital property; and (4) determine the manner in which division of the property is to take place. For recent examples of how courts value nonmonetary contributions, see *Aidonis v. Brooks*, 1995 Va. App. LEXIS 471; and *Graham v. Graham*, 1995 Va. App. LEXIS 811. For a case distinguishing between this determination and the considerations required for an award of spousal support, see, e.g., *Stumbo v. Stumbo*, 20 Va. App. 685, 460 S.E.2d 591 (1995).

The Virginia Bar Council has determined that it is ethically improper to represent a client in an equitable distribution case on a contingent fee basis. Op. No. 189, July 1, 1984. The property to be distributed is not a new asset as is a personal injury recovery, and to allow a contingent fee would be to encourage attorneys to concentrate on large monetary awards for the client at the possible expense of devoting time to other important areas of concern, and to minimize any possibility of reconciliation during the period of representation.

Although several states have adopted policies that presume that an equal division is equitable, see, e.g., *White v. White*, 64 N.C. App. 432, 308 S.E.2d 68, 71 (1983), Virginia has not adopted such a presumption of equal distribution, but instead requires consideration of specific factors set out in Va. Code § 20-107.3. *Papuchis v. Papuchis*, 2 Va. App. 130, 132, 341 S.E.2d 829, 830-31 (1986) (citing Report of the Joint Subcommittee Studying Section 20-107 of the Code of Virginia to the Governor and the General Assembly of Virginia, H. Doc. No. 32, at 8 (1982), which expressly rejected any such presumption). See also *Alphin v. Alphin*, 1992 Va. App. LEXIS 296, 424 S.E.2d 572 (1992); *Gaynor v. Hird*, 1995 Va. App. LEXIS 617. However, it is not wrong for the court to make such an award, dividing marital property equally. *Bentz v. Bentz*, 2 Va. App. 486, 345 S.E.2d 773 (1986) (down payment made by mother of husband; all payments made during marriage when each party had substantially the same income). However, once a trial judge makes the determination that the parties have equally contributed to the marriage, reasons must be stated for dividing the property unequally. *Artis v. Artis*, 10 Va. App. 356, 392 S.E.2d 504 (1990).

A division of property, unlike spousal support, should not take into consideration the earning capacity of one spouse and the support needs of the other. *Reid v. Reid*, 7 Va. App. 553, 375 S.E.2d 533 (1989). As the court held in *Brown v. Brown*, 5 Va. App. 238, 246, 361 S.E.2d 364, 368 (1987): "Spousal support involves a legal duty flowing from one spouse to the other by virtue of the marital relationship. By contrast, a monetary award does not flow from any legal duty, but involves an adjustment of the equities, rights and interests of the parties in marital property." See also *Srinivasan v. Srinivasan*, 10 Va. App. 728, 396 S.E.2d 675 (1990).

A pension payment to the wife in advance of the retirement of the husband as part of an equitable distribution, as opposed to alimony, was dischargeable in bankruptcy. *In re Lecak*, 38 B.R. 164 (S.D. Ohio 1984); cf. *In re Calhoun*, 715 F.2d 1103 (6th Cir. 1983) (joint debts dischargeable), superseded by statute, *In re Lewis*, 12 B.C.D. 279, 39 B.R. 842 (1984). Empirical studies of property distribution, the effect of fault, and the effect of litigation, include Eleanor Maccoby and Robert Mnookin, *Dividing the Child* Tables 6.1 and 7.7 (Harvard Univ. Press, 1992) (California litigated and settled divorces); Margaret Brinig & Michael V. Alexeev, *Trading at Divorce: Preferences, Legal Rules and Transaction*

Costs, 8 Ohio St. J. on Disp. Res. 279 (1993) (Wisconsin and Virginia); Martha Garrison, *How Do Judges Decide Divorce Cases? An Empirical Analysis of Discretionary Decisionmaking*, 74 N.C. L. Rev. 403, 407 (1995) (no evidence of financial differences where custody threats were credible); Robert F. Kelly & Greer L. Fox, *Determinants of Alimony Awards: An Empirical Test of Current Theories and a Reflection on Public Policy*, 44 Syracuse L. Rev. 641, 6996-97 & Table 3 (1993) (Michigan); Suzanne Reynolds, *The Relationship of Property Division and Alimony: The Division of Property to Address Need*, 56 Fordham L. Rev. 827, 854-55 (1988) (six states); and Yoram Weiss & Robert Willis, *Transfers among Divorced Couples: Evidence and Interpretation*, 11 J. Labor Econ. 629, 656 & Tab 4 (1993) (a national study).

§ 22-2. Ability to transfer title.

Even with the equitable distribution statute, power does not lie to transfer title from one spouse to the other. Va. Code § 20-107.3C. For example, if property is owned as tenants by the entireties, more than a one-half share cannot be awarded to either spouse. *Ward v. Ward*, 48 Md. App. 307, 426 A.2d 443, appeal after remand, 52 Md. App. 336, 449 A.2d 443 (1982). Nor can a monetary sum be awarded without a prior determination of the value of all marital property. *Id.* (erroneous to award wife $10,000 in substitution of her one half interest when other property was also held by the couple). An important amendment to Va. Code § 20-107.3 that was made during the 1988 legislative session allows the court to order the division or transfer, or both, of jointly owned marital property or any part thereof. Va. Code § 20-107.3(C). This may, according to the statute, be accomplished by (1) ordering the transfer of real or personal property to one of the parties, permitting either party to purchase the interest of the other and directing the allocation of the proceeds, provided that the party purchasing the interest of the other agrees to assume any indebtedness secured by the property, or (2) ordering sale of the property through private or public sale, without the necessity for partition. This is in addition to the court's power to grant a monetary award. The court may itself transfer an interest in property held jointly by the parties, even without a prior order that the parties make such a transfer, followed by a failure to comply. Va. Code § 20-107.3(C).

Case law decided before the enactment of this section recognized that a court may validly order payment of a mortgage pending the divorce and equitable distribution of the marital property, *Taylor v. Taylor*, 5 Va.

App. 436, 440-41, 364 S.E.2d 244 (1988), and may validly order partition when the parties are unable to reach an agreed disposition. *Wagner v. Wagner*, 4 Va. App. 397, 406, 358 S.E.2d 407 (1987). Likewise, it may order satisfaction of an award by transfer of a particular piece of property, but only after exercising sound judicial discretion in light of the particular circumstances. *Payne v. Payne*, 5 Va. App. 359, 367, 363 S.E.2d 428 (1987) (error to satisfy award to wife by transfer of California property that husband had been unable to sell). See also *Fitchett v. Fitchett*, 6 Va. App. 562, 370 S.E.2d 318 (1988) (trial court erred since it made no determination that partition could not be conveniently made before a partition sale was ordered). The trial court had no power to order the husband to convey his interest in the marital residence to the wife, while allowing her to make payments to him over time. *Stroop v. Stroop*, 10 Va. App. 611, 394 S.E.2d 861 (1990).

In *Stainback v. Stainback*, 11 Va. App. 13, 396 S.E.2d 686 (1990), the husband's father began Arlington Enterprises to help the husband toward a career in art. The husband was hired and worked for his father's firm as president and director. His duties included general management of a storage facility, management of various farms, and production of art works. The art works produced by the husband were the property of the firm, and all proceeds from the sale of the art work were deposited into the corporation's accounts. The court of appeals determined that the record supported the trial court's determination that the husband and Arlington Enterprises were alter egos, and therefore, since the paintings came into being because of the labors of the husband, the fruits of that labor were marital property. See also *Jacobs v. Jacobs*, 12 Va. App. 977, 406 S.E.2d 669 (1991), which concerned valuation of the wife's 32% interest in a closely held corporation. Accepting the figure presented by the husband was incorrect when it depended entirely upon what he or the corporation felt the stock was worth. Amendments to Va. Code § 20-107.3 allow for retention of jurisdiction on the motion of either party. However, the right to receive an equitable distribution of property pursuant to a divorce is lost if the party does not reserve such right in the final decree. *Toomey v. Toomey*, 465 S.E.2d 838 (Va. 1996); see also *Lauffer v. Lauffer,* 23 Va. Cir. 278 (Fairfax Co. 1991); *Boyd v. Boyd*, 1996 Va. App. LEXIS 210.

An example of a circumstance in which bifurcation was justified is *Tedesco v. Tedesco*, 1994 Va. App. LEXIS 103. In this case, the husband had cancer and feared that a delay in obtaining the divorce might jeopardize his interests. Further, the property issues were complex.

However, the trial court properly entered a final order of distribution when the husband was incarcerated, since he was present at the equitable distribution hearing and was represented by counsel. *Poppe v. Poppe*, 1995 Va. App. LEXIS 655.

The most common means of avoiding the necessity for transfers of title where there is no separation agreement is by the award of a sum payable by one spouse to the other in satisfaction of property interests. This may be payable in lump sum or over time. The advantage to the recipient spouse is that payment is not contingent upon nonremarriage of the recipient or survival of the obligor, as is alimony. These payments will not be taxable as alimony if made in less than six years. I.R.C. § 71.

§ 22-3. Times distribution is available.

Va. Code § 20-107.3 limits equitable distribution of property to occasions when the court decrees "the dissolution of a marriage, and also upon decreeing a divorce from the bond of matrimony." Because of confusion over whether jurisdiction to hear equitable distribution does continue subsequent to rendering a divorce decree (see *Parra v. Parra*, 1 Va. App. 118, 120, 336 S.E.2d 157, 158 (1985), and *Shaughnessy v. Shaughnessy*, 1 Va. App. 136, 140, 336 S.E.2d 166, 169 (1985)), the Legislature amended Va. Code § 20-107.3(A) to provide that upon motion of both parties, jurisdiction to distribute property may be retained because of the complexities of the parties' property. The section also validates all decrees where such reservations had been made.

Several recent cases have involved situations in which the trial judge failed to find that it was necessary to reserve the issue of equitable distribution because of the complexity of the property. In such cases, the court of appeals has determined, for one reason or another, that jurisdiction was in fact retained. See *Erickson-Dickson v. Erickson-Dickson*, 12 Va. App. 381, 404 S.E. 2d 388 (1991) (husband did not make a timely objection to the trial court's ruling or its failure to make the required findings of fact).

By amendment to Virginia Code § 20-107.3, the court shall determine the value of marital property as of the date of the evidentiary hearing on the evaluation issue. Another date may be used for valuation, upon motion of either party and good cause shown. *Aster v. Gross*, 7 Va. App. 831, 371 S.E.2d 833 (1988) (husband's pension plan should have been valued at date nearest equitable distribution hearing rather than at date nearest filing of complaint).

Where plaintiff sought a divorce and equitable distribution, the equitable distribution proceedings could not be nonsuited once the divorce was granted. *Walker v. Walker*, 19 Va. Cir. 390 (Clarke Co. 1990). The date of valuation of the marital property should be the commissioner's hearing, when evidence was taken, not months later after the filing of the commissioner's report and the filing of exceptions by both parties to that report. *Id.*

Except as authorized by statute, distribution of property is not available. Thus, the wife's dower rights should not have been extinguished in a decree for separate maintenance, as opposed to divorce. *Wilson v. Wilson*, 195 Va. 1060, 81 S.E.2d 605 (1954). In cases of divorce *a mensa*, property acquired during the relationship may be disposed of through a separation agreement between the spouses, see generally Chapter 18, or pursuant to a valid antenuptial agreement. Cf. *Burgess v. Burgess*, 123 Ill. App. 3d 487, 462 N.E.2d 203 (1984).

If there is Virginia property, and if a former Virginia domiciliary obtains a foreign ex parte divorce, the "divisible divorce" doctrine of *Estin v. Estin*, 334 U.S. 541 (1948), should allow a later Virginia distribution proceeding. See *Newport v. Newport*, 219 Va. 48, 245 S.E.2d 134 (1978) (alimony). The difference between an equitable distribution and an alimony proceeding is that the latter requires in personam jurisdiction (so that there could be no alimony decreed in a foreign ex parte divorce). Property distribution may be in rem. In *Lenhart v. Burgett*, 1995 Va. App. LEXIS 300, wife brought an ex parte divorce action against her husband, who lived in Pennsylvania, reserving issues of support and equitable distribution. Later she had him served in Pennsylvania in connection with a spousal support and equitable distribution proceeding, and he appeared personally in Virginia. The court of appeals affirmed the trial court's award of 50 percent of the marital property. See also *Toomey v. Toomey*, 19 Va. App. 756, 454 S.E.2d 735 (1994), where husband brought a Virginia divorce action, serving his wife personally in Oregon. She filed no responsive pleadings, and the divorce decree was entered, making no provision for spousal support, child custody or equitable distribution. The wife was granted leave to file a cross-bill to seek equitable distribution of the husband's military retirement, and this decree was affirmed. *Garrison v. Garrison*, 1994 Va. App. LEXIS 463, gave full faith and credit to an ex parte Texas divorce but allowed the wife to bring a later Virginia action for child custody, child support, spousal support and property distribution.

§ 22-4. Jurisdiction.

So long as marital property is within the state, the court will have in rem jurisdiction to divide it. There must be notice to the other spouse, particularly if out-of-state. This remains true despite the Supreme Court case of *Shaffer v. Heitner*, 433 U.S. 186 (1977), which restricts quasi-in-rem jurisdiction to controversies directly involving the property in the state, since by definition the parties to an equitable distribution proceeding are seeking to determine their interests in marital property. For example, although the husband died intestate during the couple's divorce proceedings, the fund made up of the proceeds from the sale of the marital home became a res over which the divorce court had jurisdiction. The wife could therefore seek a rule on the status of the funds the court held in escrow. *Sprouse v. Griffin*, 250 Va. 46, 458 S.E.2d 770 (1995). When one spouse is incarcerated at the time of the divorce proceedings, appointment of a committee is required under Va. Code § 53.1-223 before property can be distributed. *Mendes v. Mendes*, 1994 Va. App. LEXIS 182.

When property is located outside the state, the court has no jurisdiction to transfer title. *Fall v. Eastin*, 215 U.S. 1 (1909); *Barber v. Barber*, 51 Cal. 2d 244, 331 P.2d 628 (1958); *Kaherl v. Kaherl*, 357 S.W.2d 622 (Tex. Civ. App. 1962). See *Beckwitt v. Beckwitt*, 1993 Va. App. LEXIS 457. However, where there has been personal jurisdiction over the absent spouse, the court may make an order to convey or to pay a sum that may be enforced in Virginia or the spouse's state of residence in another action. *Ivey v. Ivey*, 183 Conn. 490, 439 A.2d 425 (1981); cf. *Fall v. Eastin*, 215 U.S. 1 (1909).

If the property is located outside the state, the law to be applied in deciding whether or not title may be shifted is that of the state where the property is located. *Williams v. Williams*, 390 A.2d 4 (D.C. 1978). See also *Anderson v. Anderson*, 449 A.2d 334 (D.C. 1982).

Husband and wife were married in Georgia and moved to Virginia shortly thereafter. They remained in Virginia for two years, and then were transferred to various other states pursuant to the husband's military orders. They returned to Virginia, purchased a home in Fairfax, and resided there until 1980. From 1980 to 1984 they lived in Ft. Lewis, Washington, and in Turkey on military assignments. While still in Turkey, they separated, and the wife returned to the marital residence in Fairfax. In 1985, the husband returned to Nevada and obtained an ex parte divorce in which the court found that he was a bona fide resident and domiciliary of Nevada at the time of the divorce. The Virginia Court of Appeals determined that this finding was not binding on the Virginia court for purposes of determining whether it could exercise personal jurisdiction under Va. Code § 8.01-328.1(A)(9) for equitable distribution. The husband's course of conduct disclosed that he intended to make Virginia his permanent home: the couple purchased the Virginia residence, which they rented out when away on military assignments; the husband held a Virginia driver's license for fourteen years, including the time of separation; some of his automobiles were registered in Virginia; and in March, 1986, both parties signed a stipulation that they were residents of Virginia for the purposes of a partition suit. The court of appeals in *Mock v. Mock*, 11 Va. App. 616, 400 S.E.2d 543 (1991), found that the Mocks maintained a matrimonial domicile in Virginia at the time of their separation, so that the trial court was correct in asserting personal jurisdiction over the husband, a nonresident, under the long-arm statute. Likewise, the court could not order transfer of property located in Virginia where one of the spouses was domiciled outside of the state and was served only by publication. The court did have jurisdiction to adjudicate the ownership of the property as a proceeding in rem. *Jefferson v. Jefferson*, 27 Va. Cir. 184 (Fairfax Co. 1992).

Personal jurisdiction necessary for distribution of his military pension can be obtained over a serviceman stationed in Virginia through his entry of a general appearance and seeking of various forms of affirmative relief. *Kramer v. Kramer*, 19 Va. Cir. 231 (Fairfax Co. 1990).

Death of either of the spouses would abate a claim for equitable distribution. *Byrne v. Byrne*, 19 Va. Cir. 357 (Chesterfield Co. 1990). This is because the action is purely a personal one, and cannot be filed or maintained separate from divorce proceedings. However, once the court orders a distribution the decree survives the death of a spouse. *Fitzgerald v. Trueworthy*, 476 A.2d 183 (Me. 1984). See also *Byrne v. Byrne*, 19 Va. Cir. 357 (Chesterfield Co. 1990).

The court may have jurisdiction to divide property following divorce without giving notice pursuant to Va. Code § 8.01-319(A) if a spouse departs the country without leaving any forwarding address with the court, counsel or opposing party. *Eddine v. Eddine*, 12 Va. App. 760, 406 S.E.2d 914 (1991). For any issue arising out of suits for divorce, annulment or affirmation of marriage, separate maintenance, or equitable distribution based on foreign decree, the judge shall consider whether to refer the parties to mediation, and may do so sua sponte or on motion of one of the parties. Upon referral, the parties must attend one evaluation session during which they and the mediator assess the case and decide whether to continue with mediation or with adjudication. Further participation in the mediation shall be by consent of all parties, and attorneys for any party may be present during mediation. Va. Code § 16.1-272.1. When the parties are referred to mediation, the court shall set a return date. The parties shall notify the court in writing if the dispute is resolved prior to this date. The court may in its discretion incorporate any mediated agreement into the terms of its final decree. Only if such an order is entered will the terms of the voluntary settlement agreement affect any outstanding court order.

The court shall vacate a mediated agreement or an incorporating order where the agreement was procured by fraud or duress, where it is unconscionable, where there was not adequate disclosure of financial or property information, or where there was evident partiality or misconduct by the mediator that prejudiced the rights of a party. Misconduct includes failure of the mediator to inform the parties in writing at the beginning of mediation:

(1) that the mediator does not provide legal advice;

(2) that an agreement will affect the legal rights of the parties;

(3) that each party to mediation has the opportunity to consult with independent legal counsel at any time and is encouraged to do so; and

(4) that each party should have any draft agreement reviewed by independent counsel prior to signing the agreement, or should waive this opportunity. Va. Code § 16.1-272.2.

A motion to vacate an order or agreement must be made within two years after the agreement is reached, except that if the motion is based upon fraud, it shall be made within two years after these grounds are discovered or reasonably should have been discovered.

§ 22-5. Gifts, bequests, and inheritance.

Gifts by a third party to one spouse, or bequests to or inheritance by a spouse are not marital property according to Va. Code § 20-107.3(1). Compare *Lanier v. Lanier*, 1993 Va. App. LEXIS 246, where husband and wife jointly purchased a home. The husband made the monthly interest payments, and his parents made the five annual $25,000 principal payments directly to the bank. In exchange for each payment, the husband executed a note for $25,000. Later each year, the parents forgave $20,000 of the note and filed a gift tax return for the $20,000. The notes were executed by the husband alone, and the gift tax returns designated him as the only donee. The property became marital property because each initial transaction was a loan from the parents to the husband that acted to relieve the wife of part of her mortgage obligation. Forgiveness of a portion, coming as a gift, could not change the initial character of the transaction.

The acquisition of a farm partnership during the marriage by sale, even though for less than full consideration, will result in its classification as marital property. *Brown v. Brown*, 5 Va. App. 238, 361 S.E.2d 364 (1987). See also *Wagner v. Wagner*, 4 Va. App. 397, 358 S.E.2d 407 (1987) (forgiveness of note to secure debt to father for purchase price did not alter character of property as marital). An acquisition by gift, even as an advancement on inheritance, will not be separate property if it is titled jointly, although consideration as to how and when the property was acquired will be appropriate in determining the amount of, and method for paying, a monetary award. *McClanahan v. McClanahan*, 19 Va. App. 399, 451 S.E.2d 691 (1994) (property was acquired in joint names as a gift from the husband's parents, and the orchard on the property was later sold to purchase other business property, so both became marital property); *Brown v. Brown*, 1996 Va. App. LEXIS 78 (husband's inherited insurance business became marital property when he used the property to form a new Virginia corporation in which he worked during the marriage. The wife worked in the business for some time as well.); *Cousins v. Cousins*, 5 Va. App. 156, 159, 360 S.E.2d 882 (1987). However, if stock is given in the husband's name only, and there is credible evidence that it was intended to be given individually, it remains separate property although the dividends are used for family purposes. *Rein v. Rein*, 1994 Va. App. LEXIS 699; *Stainback v. Stainback*, 11 Va. App. 13, 396 S.E.2d 686 (1990).

§ 22-6. Pensions and retirement plans.

Under Va. Code § 20-107.3, after consideration of the statutory factors, the court may direct payment, in addition to a monetary award, of the marital share of any pension, profit-sharing or deferred compensation plan, or retirement benefits, but only as such benefits are payable. This may be direct assignment to a party from the employer trustee, plan administrator, or other holder of the benefits. Va. Code § 20-107.3(G). The court may order a party to designate a spouse or former spouse as an irrevocable beneficiary during the lifetime of the beneficiary of all or a portion of any survivor benefit or annuity plan, not including a life insurance policy. The court, in its discretion, shall determine as between the parties who shall bear the costs of maintaining the plan. Va. Code § 20-107.3(G)(2).

"Pensions" includes military pensions, *Sawyer v. Sawyer*, 1 Va. App. 75, 78-79, 335 S.E.2d 277, 278 (1985), when military service took place, at least in part, during the marriage. Further, if the statutory factors of Va. Code § 20-107.3 are taken into account, it is not incorrect to make a monetary award, payable in a lump sum or over a period of time, taking into account the present value of some percentage of military or other retirement benefits. *McGinnis v. McGinnis*, 1 Va. App. 272, 277, 338 S.E.2d 159, 161 (1985) (although case had to be remanded since court incorrectly awarded wife a portion of property titled in the husband's name, award of one-third of husband's federal retirement benefits was not incorrect). Va. Code § 20-107.3(G) allows award, as marital property, of deferred compensation plans in addition to pension, profit sharing plans, and retirement benefits. Thus, in *Rigsby v. Rigsby*, 13 Va. Cir. 86 (Spotsylvania Co. 1987), the wife was awarded 25 percent of the husband's military pension as equitable distribution after a twenty-year marriage. Although the parties had been married only six years and the wife had voluntarily agreed to split the remainder of the couple's property evenly, it was error to exclude her from any share in the husband's pension from the government. *Cook v. Cook*, 18 Va. App. 726, 446 S.E.2d 894 (1994) (parties married seven years before separation); *Keyser v. Keyser*, 7 Va. App. 405, 374 S.E.2d 698 (1988). When the parties had executed a valid release of all property claims in a separation agreement, the subsequent enactment of the Uniform Services Former Spouses' Protection Act did not enable them to reopen the divorce proceeding. *Himes v. Himes*, 12 Va. App. 966, 407 S.E.2d 694 (1991). Retroactive application of the Act in this case resulting in the reclassification of the husband's military pension would impair the parties' contractual rights and obligations and disturb those rights that became vested by both the contract and the final divorce decree that incorporated it. See also *Nicholson v. Nicholson*, 21 Va. App. 231, 463 S.E.2d 334 (1995) (The terms of the parties' property settlement agreement were insufficient to support a finding that the wife had expressly waived her share in the husband's retirement annuity under the Foreign Service Act.).

In *Thomas v. Thomas*, 36 Va. Cir. 427 (Fairfax Co. 1995), the court found that "all of the benefits available to the Wife" in connection with the Uniformed Services Former Spouses' Protection act means medical and dental care but not the husband's military pension. "Pensions" also includes deferred compensation in the form of stock options, *Dietz v. Dietz*, 17 Va. App. 203, 436 S.E.2d 463 (1993), and a disability pension if the agreement specifies "benefits and pensions," *McGlathery v. McGlathery*, 1995 Va. App. LEXIS 297. When a wife was awarded her pension as part of a separation agreement that anticipated that it would be $25,000, but upon retirement she actually received only half that amount from her employer, the court of appeals held that the amount included in the separation agreement was merely descriptive and did not constitute a guarantee by the husband. *Morris v. Chatman*, 1995 Va. App. LEXIS 361.

It was permissible for a trial judge to reserve the power to reopen the suit at either party's death, although a pension award could not be charged against decedent's estate prior to the payment of the total award. *Holmes v. Holmes*, 7 Va. App. 472, 375 S.E.2d 387 (1988). After the decree was entered, the trial court could not validly change the order when to do so had the effect of delaying the wife's receipt of a share in the husband's retirement benefits. *Caudle v. Caudle*, 18 Va. App. 795, 447 S.E.2d 247 (1994). On the other hand, the wife could not receive more than 50 percent of the marital share of the husband's pension when the trial court required the husband to pay the cost of extending the wife's allowed benefit for her lifetime. *Gerwe v. Gerwe*, 1996 Va. App. LEXIS 21.

Retirement benefits are funds paid or to be paid upon cessation of employment to the employee by his or her employer as a means of deferred compensation. But once the recipient had deposited them in a bank account, although it was designated a "Retirement Plan," the funds were in the unrestricted control of the recipient, and they lost their character as "pension or retirement benefits" and therefore were not subject to the 50% limitation of the Code. *Robinette v. Robinette*, 10 Va. App. 480, 393 S.E.2d 629 (1990).

ERISA is divisible after five years, *Cody v. Reicher*, 594 F.2d 314 (2d Cir. 1979), and ERISA does not preempt state laws regarding the division of retirement benefits. *Stone v. Stone*, 632 F.2d 740 (9th Cir. 1980); see also *In re Marriage of Lionberger*, 97 Cal. App. 3d 61, 158 Cal. Rptr. 535 (1979).

The division of a police officer's pension rights is a judicial exception to the rule prohibiting alienation of pension benefits. "In the interest of protecting the State's broad public policy of protecting the employee and his family, the law allows family members to be treated differently than third-party creditors." *Barbee v. Barbee*, 23 Va. Cir. 68 (Fairfax Co. 1991). See also *Tenneco, Inc. v. First Va. Bank of Tidewater*, 698 F.2d 688 (E.D. Va. 1983); *Smith v. Mirman*, 749 F.2d 181 (E.D. Va. 1984). The court, in making a Qualified Domestic Relations Order, may direct a retirement system to make payments directly to a plan participant's spouse under 29 U.S.C. § 1001 et seq.

There should be no equitable distribution of a disability settlement, but such payments may be considered as income for spousal support purposes. *Lambert v. Lambert*, 10 Va. App. 623, 395 S.E.2d 207 (1990). It was inappropriate for the court to award interest on the wife's share of her husband's pension benefits, which were not yet due. *Kaufman v. Kaufman*, 12 Va. App. 1200, 409 S.E.2d 1 (1991). However, in *Gamble v. Gamble*, 14 Va. App. 558, 421 S.E.2d 635, the court of appeals found that the trial court was correct in awarding the wife fifty percent of the husband's pension benefits, reduced to twenty percent to offset his interest in the marital home. In *Gamble*, the trial court did not order the transfer of pension property, but merely reduced the share the wife would otherwise have been entitled to receive. See also *Owen v. Owen*, 14 Va. App. 623, 419 S.E.2d 267 (1992) (federal law does not prevent a husband and wife from entering into an agreement to provide a set level of payments, the amount of which is determined by considering both disability and retirement benefits). For another case in which the wife received a portion of her husband's 60 percent disability-rated pension, see *Bullis v. Bullis*, 21 Va. App. 394, 464 S.E.2d 538 (1995) (Arizona community property award enforced in Virginia under Uniform Enforcement of Foreign Judgments Act); and *Gamble v. Gamble*, 14 Va. App. 558, 421 S.E.2d 635 (1992), where the wife was awarded the house while the husband received his entire pension, although distribution would not occur for some years.

Where the husband continued to work at the job he held before divorce, the trial court did not have to "cap" the wife's share of the pension at its present value at the time of divorce. The husband unsuccessfully argued that the amount he would actually receive depended upon his highest five consecutive years of salary, which most likely would occur after the parties' divorce. The only limitation applicable to a pension award, according to Va. Code § 20-107.3, is the limitation that no payment shall exceed fifty percent of the cash benefits actually received. This was the amount the wife was awarded for the marital portion of the pension. *Dietz v. Dietz*, 17 Va. App. 203, 436 S.E.2d 463 (1993). See also *Havird v. Havird*, 1995 Va. App. LEXIS 19; *Herron v. Herron*, 1994 Va. App. LEXIS 208; and *Banagan v. Banagan*, 17 Va. App. 321, 437 S.E.2d 229 (1993) (error to assume spouses would retire from state employment at age 55, because this would deny "to each party a full participation in the statutory marital share of the other's entire pension").

When a husband elected to waive a portion of his military pension in exchange for disability pay, the amount his wife was to receive under their property settlement agreement should not be reduced. In *Owen v. Owen*, 14 Va. App. 623, 419 S.E.2d 267 (1992), the court of appeals held that federal law does not prevent a husband and wife from entering into an agreement to provide a set level of payments, the amount of which is determined by considering disability as well as retirement benefits.

Because an Individual Retirement Account (IRA) is merely a device by which the government gives a present tax advantage as an inducement to save, and does not require the owner to continue employment or attain a given age before withdrawal of the funds, it is not a pension, profit-sharing, or deferred compensation plan within the meaning of Va. Code § 20-107.3(G)(1). The husband's IRA in *Broom v. Broom*, 15 Va. App. 497, 425 S.E.2d 90 (1992), was subject to present equitable distribution because it was created with marital funds.

See generally Hughes, *Profit Sharing and Pension Plans*, 44 Tex. L. Rev. 860 (1966).

§ 22-7. Valuation of Pensions.

It was erroneous for a court, in awarding the wife a 25 percent share of her husband's pension, to discount to present value the current value of the husband's share of the fund, when distribution was to be made only as the husband began receiving payments. A better method would be to calculate the present value of the pension for purposes of evaluating the entire marital estate and the wife's equitable share of the pension, and to allow her a percentage based upon this share upon the husband's retirement. *Zipf v. Zipf*, 8 Va. App. 387, 382 S.E.2d 263 (1989). Compare *Steinberg v. Steinberg*, 11 Va. App. 323, 398 S.E.2d 507 (1990), where husband and wife stipulated to the value of the pension at the time of separation, and neither party indicated whether the stipulated value had been discounted either before or after it had been computed, and pension payments were not being received on the date of the last separation or when the divorce decree was entered. An award of a specified percentage of future pension benefits would have been to postpone the entry of an equitable distribution decree until such time as the pension payments were realized. When the parties' agreement did not specify a date for division of their pensions and IRAs, the date that should be used is the date of the parties' agreement. *Jones v. Jones*, 18 Va. App. 52, 441 S.E.2d 360 (1994). Once the trial court determined that the wife was entitled to a fifty percent marital share of her husband's pension, its current value became irrelevant. What was relevant was the value of the pension when due and owing, so that the parties share equally in any increases or decreases in the pension. *Barnes v. Barnes*, 1995 Va. App. LEXIS 319.

When payments are to be made in the future, the appropriate action is to determine the present value of the pension benefits in determining the total monetary award. However, the value of a retirement plan must be established by the party seeking a share, whether by expert witness or otherwise. *Bowers v. Bowers*, 4 Va. App. 610, 359 S.E.2d 546 (1987). See also *Gamer v. Gamer*, 16 Va. App. 335, 429 S.E.2d 618 (1993), where the wife claimed a portion of Mr. Gamer's military retirement benefits, but did not produce sufficient evidence of the present value of the pension to demonstrate the marital share. The court of appeals held that the trial court did not err when it allowed both parties to retain their respective pensions. Similarly, in *Brundage v. Brundage*, 1995 Va. App. LEXIS 521, the marital share of the husband's pension could not be calculated at the time of divorce, since the husband continued to be employed. The court should have awarded the wife a thirty-five percent portion of the marital share of the pension, to be paid at the time the husband began to receive it. The wife did not present sufficient evidence to enable to the court to segregate proper expenditures from improper ones in *Harvey v. Harvey*, 1995 Va. App. LEXIS 928, where the husband used his pension payments, at least in part, to abide by the *pendente lite* decree's support order.

The award of 40 percent of a husband's disposable military pension meant the amount due him before tax deductions. *Lovell v. Lovell*, 18 Va. Cir. 64 (Fairfax Co. 1988).

§ 22-8. Degrees.

The majority rule is that degrees earned by either spouse are nondivisible. See, e.g., *Graham v. Graham*, 194 Colo. 415, 573 P.2d 100 (1978); *In re Weinstein*, 128 Ill. App. 3d 234, 470 N.E.2d 551 (1984); 11 Fam. L. Rep. (BNA) 1015 (and cases cited therein); *Wright v. Wright*, 469

A.2d 803 (Del. Fam. 1983). Recent cases support the prevailing view that degrees are not marital property. See, e.g., *Hodge v. Hodge*, 513 Pa. 364, 520 A.2d 15 (1986); *Drapek v. Drapek*, 399 Mass. 240, 503 N.E.2d 946 (1987). The most frequently cited exception is *O'Brien v. O'Brien*, 66 N.Y.2d 576, 489 N.E.2d 712, 498 N.Y.S.2d 743 (1985). Goodwill, but not a professional degree, was included as marital property in *Gold v. Gold*, 1 Va. Cir. 390, 396, 397-98 (Roanoke Co. 1983). One alternative solution that gives credit to contributions during the earning of a degree is to award restitution alimony. See *Mahoney v. Mahoney*, 91 N.J. 488, 453 A.2d 527 (1982). Mahoney was followed in the case of *Palmer v. Palmer*, 21 Va. Cir. 112 (Fairfax Co. 1990), which gave the wife reimbursement alimony but held that the husband's medical degree was not marital property.

Useful articles include Krauskopf, *Recompense for Financing Spouse's Education: Legal Protection for the Marital Investor in Human Capital*, 28 Kan. L. Rev. 379, 411 (1980), and Mullinex, *The Valuation of an Educational Degree at Divorce*, 16 Loy. L.A.L. Rev. 227 (1983).

§ 22-9. Professional corporations and goodwill.

Several cases have noted that the goodwill belonging to a small corporation or a professional practice is distributable as marital property. For example, the goodwill included in the value of a doctor's professional practice was marital property, with valuation by the percentage of gross income approach being particularly appropriate since the doctor kept the profit from his practice at an artificially low margin. *Russell v. Russell*, 12 Va. Cir. 326 (Henrico Co. 1988), *aff'd*, 11 Va. App. 411, 399 S.E.2d 166 (1990). See also *Gold v. Gold*, 1 Va. Cir. 390 (Roanoke Co. 1983). When the value of the corporation for which the husband worked increased dramatically during the marriage, the increase in value of its stock, which he held separately, was marital property to the extent that his efforts contributed to the increase. *Decker v. Decker*, 17 Va. App. 12, 435 S.E.2d 407 (1993) (Here, 20 percent, since he was one of five key executives and "first among equals."). See also *Stewart v. Stewart*, 1994 Va. App. LEXIS 88. The value of husband's dental practice should not have been discounted by estimating the capital gains taxes on a hypothetical sale as opposed to the present fair market value of the property. *Arbuckle v. Arbuckle*, 1996 Va. App. LEXIS 322. The parties were to share equally in the marital property; the husband was awarded the value of his practice while the wife received oil company stock.

§ 22-10. Transfers of property to third party.

Should one spouse attempt to transfer what would otherwise be marital property to a third party in order to avoid equitable distribution, the courts will include such property or its value in the marital estate. See, e.g., *Meuhlanthaler v. DeBartolo*, 347 N.W.2d 688 (Iowa 1984); *Abraham v. Abraham*, 203 Neb. 384, 279 N.W.2d 85 (1979). However, the fraud must be proved. *Hofmann v. Hofmann*, 99 Ill. App. 3d 526, 425 N.E.2d 577 (1981) (mortgage foreclosed by relative; fraud not proved); *Ellington v. Ellington*, 8 Va. App. 48, 378 S.E.2d 626, 5 V.L.R. 2100 (1989) (appreciated value of husband's stock in closely held corporation could be marital property). See *Davis v. Davis*, 237 Va. 657, 391 S.E.2d 255 (1990) (fraud when husband conveyed real property to friend after shooting and paralyzing wife. She could be awarded spousal support and the property conveyed was subject to her lien despite a valid antenuptial agreement).

An appreciation in value of separate property is generally the separate property of a spouse. Va. Code § 20-107.3(1)). See, e.g., *In re Marriage of Komnick*, 84 Ill. 2d 89, 417 N.E.2d 1305 (1981); *Painter v. Painter*, 65 N.J. 196, 320 A.2d 484 (1974); *Dillingham v. Dillingham*, 434 S.W.2d 459 (Tex. Civ. App. 1968). But see *Gravenstine v. Gravenstine*, 58 Md. App. 158, 472 A.2d 1001, 1009 (1984), where the parties were able to purchase additional shares of stock because of both parties' contribution.

If the parties agree to divide the proceeds from sale of the marital home, and before the sale one of them remains in the home, the non-possessor is entitled to half the reasonable rental value for the property. *Gaynor v. Hird*, 15 Va. App. 379, 424 S.E.2d 240 (1992); see also *Cole v. Cole*, 27 Va. Cir. 225 (Loudoun Co. 1992).

§ 22-11. Property acquired in part before marriage.

In 1990, the Virginia legislature made significant amendments to Va. Code § 20-107.3, providing that property may be part separate and part marital property. These amendments have the effect of overriding the Virginia Supreme Court's decision in *Smoot v. Smoot*, 233 Va. 435, 357 S.E.2d 728 (1987). According to the amended statute, income received from separate property during the marriage shall be marital property only to the extent due to the personal efforts of either party. Increases in value of separate property during the marriage shall be marital property only to the extent that marital property or the personal efforts of either party have contributed to such increases. Va. Code § 20-107.3(3)(a). However, when marital property and separate property are commingled by contributing one category of property to another, resulting in the loss of the contributed property, the classification of the contributed property shall be transmuted to the category of property receiving the contribution. To the extent that the contributed property is traceable by a preponderance of the evidence and was not a gift, such contributed property shall retain its original classification. Va. Code § 20-107.3(3)(d). When the two classifications of property are commingled into newly acquired property, the commingled property shall be deemed transmuted to marital property. However, to the extent the contributed property is retraceable by a preponderance of evidence and was not a gift, the contributed property shall retain its original classification. Va. Code § 20-107.3(3)(e). *Tschippert v. Tschippert*, 1995 Va. App. LEXIS 514, involved wife's withdrawal of funds in a joint checking account deposited by the husband after the date of separation. These were his separate property, and since traceable, should have retained this classification under Va. Code Ann. § 20-107.3(A)(3)(d). However, the trial judge was not persuaded by husband's tracing evidence concerning Tandem Computer stock and an Oldsmobile.

Where there is no commingling, the property acquired prior to marriage remains separate property. *Atkinson v. Atkinson*, 19 Va. Cir. 340 (1990). The court must determine first the value of the marital portion of the property and then make an equitable distribution of the newly established value of the property. *Gravenstine v. Gravenstine*, 58 Md. App. 158, 472 A.2d 1001, 1007 (1984). Payment of taxes is not a part of the on-going process of payment for property fully purchased prior to the marriage. *Id.* at 171, 472 A.2d at 1007-08. However, the contribution of joint funds to the mortgage may result in its being marital property. *Stallings v. Stallings*, 75 Ill. App. 3d 96, 393 N.E.2d 1065 (1979).

Placing separately acquired assets in a joint bank account before using them to purchase another asset results in the transmutation of the new property into marital property. *Taylor v. Taylor*, 9 Va. App. 341, 387 S.E.2d 797 (1990); *Lassen v. Lassen*, 8 Va. App. 502, 383 S.E.2d 471 (1989).

When funds are acquired prior to marriage but contributions to them are made during the marriage, the party claiming the funds as separate property must overcome the presumption that they are marital property. *Rexrode v. Rexrode*, 1 Va. App. 385, 394, 339 S.E.2d 544, 548-49

(1986). Where a spouse fails to segregate and instead commingles separate property with marital property, the chancellor must classify the commingled property as marital property subject to equitable distribution. *Smoot v. Smoot*, 233 Va. 435, 442, 357 S.E.2d 728, 731 (1987). See also *Price v. Price*, 4 Va. App. 224, 236, 355 S.E.2d 905, 912 (1987) (parties commingled separate and marital property to create a "new" piece of property); *Westbrook v. Westbrook*, 5 Va. App. 446, 364 S.E.2d 523 (1988) (parties agreed that separate property would be marital property); *Rudisill v. Rudisill*, 1995 Va. App. LEXIS 404; and *Walker v. Walker*, 19 Va. Cir. 390 (Clarke Co. 1990) (property purchased prior to marriage, but payments made to purchase price from owner's salary during marriage). In all these cases, however, the original owner's contributions will be considered in determining the final award. Property will be presumed to be marital property unless there is a deed, title, or other clear indication that it is not jointly owned. Va. Code § 20-107.3(A)(2).

It is not error to award one party, whose premarital savings were used to make it, the entire value of a down payment on the property titled in joint names, so long as the court finds that equity dictates such a result upon consideration of all the factors of Va. Code § 20-107.3(E). *Pommerenke v. Pommerenke*, 7 Va. App. 241, 372 S.E.2d 630 (1988). See also *Hauger v. Hauger*, 1995 Va. App. LEXIS 206 (not designated for publication). Further, appreciation of stock acquired prior to marriage by the husband in a closely held corporation may have been marital property, where the wife's affirmative actions may have led in part to the appreciation. *Ellington v. Ellington*, 8 Va. App. 48, 378 S.E.2d 626 (1989). Compensation for improvements (heating, air conditioning, and trim) would be limited to the amount by which the value of the home was enhanced. The husband would also be credited with the mortgage payments made since the wife left the marital home and he assumed the mortgage payments. *Lee v. Lee*, 13 Va. Cir. 239 (Henrico Co. 1988).

The income received from separate property during the marriage is separate property as well if it does not result from the significant personal efforts of either party. The increase in value of separate property during the marriage is separate property unless marital property or the significant and effective personal efforts of either party have contributed to such increases, and then only to the extent of the increases in value attributable to such contributions. Va. Code § 20-107.3(1).

Property that was jointly held at one point during the marriage may become separate property if the parties expressly agree to do so. For example, in *Garland v. Garland*, 19 Va. Cir. 131 (Spotsylvania Co. 1990), husband and wife had separated and the wife received the marital home under their written agreement. They then reconciled, but divorced some years later. The property, still in the wife's name as feme sole, was now her separate property.

In *Amburn v. Amburn*, 13 Va. App. 661, 414 S.E.2d 847 (1992), the husband became a partner in Thomson Instrument Company shortly before the parties' marriage in 1978. He was the president of the company and oversaw its day-to-day operations. In 1979, the wife left her full-time employment to work for the corporation, eventually becoming the full-time office manager. At trial, the parties stipulated that the value of husband's interest in the corporation was $90,000. The court of appeals held that "it is not clear that the trial court abused its discretion by finding that the wife expended labor in the appreciation of the company's value," so that an equal division of the husband's interest was well within the fact finder's discretion. Likewise, in *Barnes v. Barnes*, 16 Va. App. 98, 428 S.E.2d 294 (1993), the husband owned a 40 percent interest in an insurance adjustment business at the time of the marriage. However, he worked to support the family in the adjusting business during the eight-year marriage, while the wife made substantial nonmonetary contributions to the marriage, including entertaining his business associates and accompanying him to business conventions and other business-related functions. The contributions of both parties during the marriage transmuted his interest, which had been separate property, into marital property. It was therefore proper to award the wife 5 percent for her interest in that marital asset.

§ 22-12. Marital debts.

Debts of the parties will also be subject to distribution as a kind of negative marital property. In *Booth v. Booth*, 7 Va. App. 22, 371 S.E.2d 569 (1989), the husband successfully argued that the trial court had erred in failing to consider the wife's "waste" of the marital assets. "Waste" was characterized as the dissipation of marital funds in anticipation of divorce or separation for a purpose unrelated to the marriage and in derogation of the marital relationship at a time when the marriage is in jeopardy. "Waste" would be a negative contribution in the form of squandering and destroying marital resources. The trial court should have included the wasted assets as marital property and should have considered the waste as a factor in determining the monetary award. Similarly, if an encumbrance was created deliberately to reduce the value of the marital property and consequently the amount of the monetary award, the indebtedness must be considered by the trial court but the encumbrance securing that indebtedness does not reduce the value of the marital property for purposes of determining the amount of the monetary award. The trial court in *Trivett v. Trivett*, 7 Va. App. 148, 371 S.E.2d 560, 5 V.L.R. 192 (1988), failed to consider whether the previously unsecured indebtedness was later converted to secured indebtedness on the specific property deliberately to frustrate equitable distribution. There is a presumption if marital funds are spent after separation that they are being dissipated. *Clements v. Clements*, 10 Va. App. 580, 397 S.E.2d 257 (1990).

The court, however, had no authority to require one party to pay specific debts incurred during the marriage at the time of *Day v. Day*, 8 Va. App. 346, 381 S.E.2d 364 (1989). A helpful discussion of these issues appears in McHenry & Sweeny, *Anderson v. Anderson: The Court of Appeals and the Role of Debt*, 11 Fam. L. News 8 (1990). See *Anderson v. Anderson*, 9 Va. App. 446, 389 S.E.2d 175 (1990) (loan of money from father of husband was payable at partition proceeding before distribution of proceeds as marital estate; wife bound by this determination that had been made at equitable distribution proceeding). The court now has authority under 20-107.3 to require one party to pay specific debts incurred during the marriage, *Hayes v. Hayes*, 21 Va. App. 515, 465 S.E.2d 590 (1996), although it did not at the time of the trial of *Gaynor v. Hird*, 1995 Va. App. LEXIS 617, involving some $36,457 of debts in both parties' names and $9,000 in the name of the husband alone.

The trial court should have enforced an indemnification provision of the property settlement agreement that ordered the husband to reimburse the wife for paying his separate debt that had attached as a lien against the marital home. Shortly after the wife filed for divorce, the husband pled guilty to larceny of funds from his employer and executed a judgment note for $45,000 plus interest secured by a deed of trust on the marital home. Under the parties' agreement, he was to hold her harmless for the debt and reimburse her when she refinanced the home and paid the employer the debt plus interest. This obligation to pay the wife was not in the nature of spousal support and therefore was not extinguished by the remarriage. *Guffey v. Guffey*, 1995 Va. App. LEXIS 819. Marital debts and capital gains tax consequences were factors considered in the equitable distribution award affirmed in *Nigh v. Nigh*, 1995 Va App. LEXIS 830.

§ 22-13. Property titled in one spouse's name.

Under the 1988 amendments to Va. Code § 20-107.3, the court has the authority to allot, apportion, or transfer specific property titled jointly. There is no authority, however, to transfer or divide separate property or marital property not jointly owned, absent agreement of the parties. See, e.g., *McGinnis v. McGinnis*, 1 Va. App. 272, 276, 338 S.E.2d 159, 161 (1985); *Taylor v. Taylor*, 5 Va. App. 436, 442-43, 364 S.E.2d 244 (1988) (automobile); *Ellington v. Ellington*, 8 Va. App. 48, 378 S.E.2d 626, 5 V.L.R. 2100 (1989).

For example, it was permissible for the trial court to distribute property in the wife's name, but error to require her to buy out the husband's interest in the marital home over time, since there is no provision in the statute allowing delay in payments to the transferor of monies due for the interest one spouse is required to convey. *Stroop v. Stroop*, 10 Va. App. 611, 394 S.E.2d 861 (1990).

It was a reversible error for a trial court to make a final award requiring husband to pay a sum equal to half the value of the marital property (jewelry) given to the wife when she retained ownership of the items during the marriage. *Kaufman v. Kaufman*, 7 Va. App. 488, 375 S.E.2d 374 (1988).

Wife was held entitled under the parties' property settlement agreement to a fifty percent interest in the husband's royalties from books he wrote or was writing during the marriage in *Jennings v. Jennings*, 12 Va. App. 1187, 409 S.E.2d 8 (1991).

In several recent cases, the court of appeals has dealt with the increasingly common problem of distributing shares in a closely held family corporation. In *Roane v. Roane*, 12 Va. App. 989, 407 S.E.2d 698 (1991), the husband was the sole owner of Dave's Cabinet Shop., Inc., and asserted that the wife made no contribution to the appreciated value of the stock. The husband had, however, obtained a Small Business Administration loan using the wife's signature. The case was remanded for consideration in light of the fact that her nonmonetary contributions were sufficient to meet the test of *Smoot v. Smoot*; she was not foreclosed from asserting that ownership of the stock had been transmuted to marital property, his intent not to give her an interest in the corporation was not controlling, and her efforts contributed to the appreciation in value of the stock. In *Jacobs v. Jacobs*, 12 Va. App. 977, 406 S.E.2d 669 (1991), the parties established International Diversified Products Corporation during the marriage. The corporation was financed from marital funds and funds provided by the husband's father. After a brief separation in 1976, the husband placed fifty percent of his shares of the corporation (32 percent of the outstanding stock) in the wife's name. The issue in the case was how to value the stock. The commissioner found that International Diversified Products had a value of $500,000, so that the wife's share was $175,000. The wife challenged the valuation because Mr. Jacobs and his father together controlled the business. In fact, the court noted, the value of the wife's stock interest depended entirely on what husband or the corporation felt her stock was worth. He had also used a substantial amount of the corporation's assets for his own personal benefit. Upon remand, the circuit court was ordered to take the nonliquid nature of Mrs. Jacob's interest into consideration. See also *Stainback v. Stainback*, 11 Va. App. 13, 396 S.E.2d 686 (1990); *Decker v. Decker*, 17 Va. App. 12, 435 S.E.2d 407 (1993) (one-fifth of increase in value of corporate shares due to efforts of husband, one of five key employees, and therefore marital property); *Hurt v. Hurt*, 16 Va. App. 792, 433 S.E.2d 493 (1993) (earned income received by husband and deposited into personal ledger caused transmutation into marital property); *Reynolds v. Reynolds*, 1994 Va. App. LEXIS 10 (husband's astute management of company transmuted stock that was wife's separate property into marital property); *Bonner v. Bonner*, 1993 Va. App. LEXIS 361 (home originally wife's separate property was transmuted into marital property when the parties used it to procure a home equity loan, most of which paid for improvements on it). Compare *Huger v. Huger*, 16 Va. App. 785, 433 S.E.2d 255 (1993) (value of stock received as gifts from husband's family was not enhanced because of the parties' efforts).

A court may properly consider the parties' premarital contributions, both monetary and nonmonetary, that enhance the value of marital property. Cohabitation that does not have an impact on the marital property values will not justify consideration. *Floyd v. Floyd*, 17 Va. App. 222, 436 S.E.2d 427 (1993). See also *Ingram v. Snarr-Ingram*, 1994 Va. App. LEXIS 437 (husband purchased home in 1978, before couple met. They married in 1983, when the value of the home had increased from $42,000 to $64,500. The husband deeded the house to himself and his wife as tenants by the entirety in 1986. Husband should have been allowed premarital appreciation of property found to be separate property.)

The husband's separate property did not become marital assets when the wife was compensated for her renovation and sales efforts according to the parties' marital agreements. *Cummings v. Cummings*, 1996 Va.

App. LEXIS 72. Similarly, property purchased by the husband and carefully segregated throughout the marriage remained his separate property, though he was responsible to repay $11,000 remaining on loans made to him by the wife. *Baer v. Baer*, 1996 Va. App. LEXIS 73.

§ 22-14. Compensation for personal injuries.

Courts have disagreed as to whether monies paid to compensate one spouse for a personal injury suffered during the marriage is marital property. See, e.g., *Bywater v. Bywater*, 128 Mich. App. 396, 340 N.E.2d 102 (1983) (holding that compensation for pain and suffering was a divisible asset); *Van de Loo v. Van de Loo*, 346 N.W.2d 173 (Minn. 1984) (holding that funds were not divisible as marital property); *Amato v. Amato*, 180 N.J. Super. 210, 434 A.2d 639 (1981) (not divisible; like replacement of separate property).

Two Virginia Circuit Court cases have considered compensation for personal injuries that occurred during the marriage as marital property. *Mabe v. Mabe*, 8 Va. Cir. 339 (Wise Co. 1987) (workers' compensation award to husband for personal injuries suffered after separation was marital property; personal injury award to wife for her pain and suffering due to accident before separation was separate property); *Seidenberg v. Seidenberg*, 9 Va. Cir. 83 (Henrico Co. 1987) (husband shot by spouse of person with whom he was having an affair; marital property unless proved to be separate property, although occurrence, settlement, and payment all occurred after parties had separated). Compare *Lambert v. Lambert*, 10 Va. App. 623, 395 S.E.2d 207 (1990) (disability retirement benefits from employment prior to work were separate property, although the payments might be considered as sources of income for spousal and child support).

A lump sum personal injury settlement that a spouse receives during the course of the marriage for injuries also incurred during the marriage is presumptively marital property subject to equitable distribution at divorce. *Thomas v. Thomas*, 13 Va. App. 92, 408 S.E.2d 596 (1991). The presumption may be rebutted by a showing that the settlement funds consist only of noneconomic damages personal to the injured spouse. See also *Thomas v. Thomas*, 1993 Va. App. LEXIS 408 (trial court erred in treating settlement as separate property, and husband accountable for amount of insurance proceeds existing at time of separation).

§ 22-15. When does time run?

Property acquired before the parties marry, even during a period they are living together, will not be marital property. *Cotter v. Cotter*, 58 Md. App. 529, 473 A.2d 970 (1984); *Wilen v. Wilen*, 61 Md. App. 337, 486 A.2d 775, 780-81 (1985).

Va. Code § 20-107.3 specifies that the period within which acquisition of property will make it marital property expires upon the filing of the complaint for divorce. The question still arises, however, whether property acquired when the parties have been separated for an extended period of time ought to be divisible. Where the marriage relationship is not at an end because of continued contact between the parties, property obtained should be marital property. *Brandenburg v. Brandenburg*, 83 N.J. 198, 416 A.2d 327 (1980) (presumption in state that the marital partnership continued until the divorce complaint was filed); *Wilen v. Wilen*, 61 Md. App. 337, 486 A.2d 775 (Md. App. 1985); cf. *DiGiacomo v. DiGiacomo*, 80 N.J. 155, 402 A.2d 922 (1979) (oral agreement plus division of property sufficient). The situation has been clarified somewhat by the 1986 amendment to Va. Code § 20-107.3(A)(2), which now defines marital property as all property acquired by either spouse during the marriage "and before the last separation of the parties, if at such time or thereafter at least one of the parties intends that the separation be permanent." By amendment to Va. Code § 20-107.3, the court shall determine the value of marital property as of the date of the evidentiary hearing on the evaluation issue, or some other date upon motion of either party and where good cause is shown. See *Aster v. Gross*, 7 Va. App. 831, 371 S.E.2d 833 (1988) (military pension of husband). The value of the property at the time of the equitable distribution proceeding is only res judicata as to its value on that date, rather than at a later partition proceeding. *Anderson v. Anderson*, 9 Va. App. 446, 389 S.E.2d 175 (1990).

In *Taylor v. Taylor*, 23 Va. Cir. 133 (Fairfax Co. 1991), the trial court found in 1988 that 22,000 shares of the Marriott Corporation were separate property of the husband. At this time the stock was valued at $644,000. The court of appeals found that the stock was in fact marital property (9 Va. App. 341, 387 S.E.2d 797 (1990). Upon remand in 1991, the court held that the wife was entitled to receive six and one-half percent of the value of the Marriott stock, or nearly $42,000. The husband claimed that it would be inequitable to require him to pay a monetary award based upon the value the stock had more than two years earlier, since it had declined in value by approximately two-thirds. The court of appeals held that a monetary award including the interest in the Marriott stock must be determined as of December 13, 1990, the date of the final evidentiary hearing. Similarly, if a court remands an equitable distribution award, a second evaluation should establish the value of the property. *Wagner v. Wagner*, 15 Va. App. 120, 421 S.E.2d 218 (1992), *aff'd*, 16 Va. App. 539, 431 S.E.2d 77 (1993).

If the court makes a monetary award where one marital asset is a pension, it need not wait until distribution of the pension before making an offsetting award. Thus in *Gamble v. Gamble*, 14 Va. App. 558, 421 S.E.2d 635 (1992), the wife was awarded the house, while the husband received his entire pension. In *Walls v. Walls*, 1993 Va. App. LEXIS 329, the court of appeals reversed the trial court for finding the two pensions were equal and offsetting. The wife had cashed in her pension, while the husband's continued to accumulate. Based upon values paid in and expected to be paid, the husband's pension was a significant asset.

§ 22-16. Fault as a factor.

In Virginia, fault may be considered in making equitable division of property. Fault was apparently considered in the case of *Bentz v. Bentz*, 2 Va. App. 486, 345 S.E.2d 773 (1986), although the husband was not allowed to amend his complaint to include grounds of adultery. The court was required to consider fault by Va. Code § 20-107.3, and, for this purpose, fault need not be pled nor be sufficient to constitute grounds for divorce. *Id.* at 774. Other Virginia cases holding that fault in breaking up the marriage should be considered include *Westbrook v. Westbrook*, 5 Va. App. 446, 364 S.E.2d 523 (1988) (husband's desertion of wife to resume his relationship with his paramour considered; wife's untruthfulness regarding her sexual relations after separation had no bearing upon the division of property); *Cousins v. Cousins*, 5 Va. App. 156, 360 S.E.2d 882 (1987) (husband's adulterous behavior that contributed to dissolution of marriage properly considered even though divorce granted on no fault grounds); *Seidenberg v. Seidenberg*, 9 Va. Cir. 83 (Henrico Co. 1987) (husband was shot by spouse of woman with whom he was having affair). Cf. *Marion v. Marion*, 11 Va. App. 659, 401 S.E.2d 432 (1991) (no showing that husband spent significant amount of marital assets on vacations with woman with whom he was having an affair). Even though one spouse obtains a fault divorce, if the fault has no economic impact on the value of the marital assets, it will not affect the equitable distribution award. *Donnell v. Donnell*, 40 Va. App. 37, 455 S.E.2d 256 (1995); *Gamer v. Gamer*, 16 Va. App. 335, 429 S.E.2d 618 (1993). See also *Barden v. Barden*, 1995 Va. App. LEXIS 200. However, fault was properly considered when the wife received approximately two-thirds of the marital estate, including the marital home. In *Crump v. Crump*, 1993 Va. App. LEXIS 404, the husband had earned the bulk of the family's income during the 30-year marriage, but had also engaged in a long-term extramarital affair that ultimately broke up the marriage. See also *Lamb v. Lamb*, 33 Va. Cir. 442 (Stafford Co. 1994); *Major v. Major*, 36 Va. Cir. 190 (Pittsylvania Co. 1995)(husband convicted of "several horrible felonies" and divorced for cruelty and imprisonment; wife, who "suffered a disastrous financial setback as a result of his cruel and inhumane treatment," was awarded all the marital property).

In *O'Loughlin v. O'Loughlin*, 20 Va. App. 522, 458 S.E.2d 323 (1995), the husband not only committed adultery but also spent over ten thousand dollars on his paramours, thus affecting the marriage partnership's economic condition. Further, the husband made no nonmonetary contributions to the well-being of the family. The court stated, "Fault is not a 'wild card' that may be employed to justify what otherwise would be an arbitrary or punitive award. When fault is relevant in arriving at an award, the trial judge is required to consider it objectively, and how, if at all, it quantitatively affected the marital estate or well being of the family." See also *D.G.P. v. E.C.P.*, 1995 Va. App. LEXIS 822; *O'Loughlin v. O'Loughlin*, 20 Va. App. 522, 527, 458 S.E.2d 323, 325 (1995). This property distribution rule was established in *Aster v. Gross*, 7 Va. App. 831, 371 S.E.2d 833 (1988).

There is a presumption if marital funds are spent after separation that they are being dissipated. *Clements v. Clements*, 10 Va. App. 580, 397 S.E.2d 257 (1990). Dissipation occurs when one spouse uses marital property for personal benefit and for a purpose unrelated to the marriage at a time when the marriage is undergoing an irreconcilable breakdown. It does not include the use of funds for living expenses while the parties are separated. *Id.*

The husband had no right to introduce evidence of marital fault at the trial court proceeding involving equitable distribution when he did not object to the commissioner's awarding of a no-fault divorce, and no evidence of fault was preserved in the record. *Klein v. Klein*, 11 Va. App. 155, 396 S.E.2d 866 (1990).

§ 22-17. Custody of children.

The party granted custody of the children may need a sizable share of the marital estate in order to provide them a home and perhaps to remain home in order to care for them if they are small.

§ 22-18. Age, income, education and potential.

One of the justifications for an equitable distribution of property is to reward a homemaker spouse for contributions to the marital estate through performance of services that allowed the family unit to accumulate wealth. An award of property may give such a spouse financial independence without the continued dependence and contact resulting from an alimony award. Such contributions are less likely to have occurred in a marriage of short duration. See, e.g., *Duffy v. Duffy*, 94 A.D.2d 711, 462 N.Y.S.2d 240 (1983). The trial court did not err in determining that the primary factor establishing the marital standard of living was the husband's completion of his education before marriage rather than the non-monetary contributions of the wife. An award of 25 percent of the marital property was thus not an abuse of discretion. *Zipf v. Zipf*, 8 Va. App. 387, 382 S.E.2d 263 (1989).

Other equitable considerations such as the health of a party may also be factors. See, e.g., *Campbell v. Campbell*, 554 S.W.2d 10 (Tex. Civ. App. 1977) (husband was 100 percent disabled with severe emphysema and only income Social Security disability; wife was employed and had rental income from separate property).

Where one spouse not only makes the majority of financial contributions towards acquisition of property but also performs most of the normal marital duties, the division of property need not be even. *Stallings v. Stallings*, 75 Ill. App. 3d 96, 393 N.E.2d 1065 (1979).

A nonmarital debt of a party, while not property to be distributed, does impact the economic circumstances of the parties and their ability to meet financial obligations. *Schweizer v. Schweizer*, 301 Md. 626, 484 A.2d 267, 272 (1984). The portion of an acquisition that remains unpaid does not constitute marital property. *Id.*

The fact that a party's financial condition is no worse when the marriage is dissolved than when the party entered the marriage is not a proper basis for denying an award based upon property acquired during the marriage. *Keyser v. Keyser*, 7 Va. App. 405, 374 S.E.2d 698 (1988).

See generally June Carbone and Margaret F. Brinig, *Rethinking Marriage: Feminist Ideology, Economic Change and Divorce Reform*, 65 Tul. L. Rev. 953 (1991).

§ 22-19. Use of expert testimony.

Usually an accountant or actuary will be needed to evaluate pension plans. See, e.g., *Axtell v. Axtell*, 482 A.2d 1261 (Me. 1984); *Bloomer v. Bloomer*, 84 Wis. 2d 124, 267 N.W.2d 235 (1978); *Nisos v. Nisos*, 60 Md. App. 368, 483 A.2d 97 (1984); Troyan, *Pension Evaluation and Equitable Distribution*, 11 Fam. L. Rep. (BNA) 301 (1984). For the interest in a corporation, see, e.g., *Gorman v. Gorman*, 90 Cal. App. 3d 454, 153 Cal. Rptr. 479 (1979). See also *Jacobs v. Jacobs*, 12 Va. App. 977, 406 S.E.2d 669 (1991). Such expert services may be necessary for any property whose fair market value is difficult to ascertain; for example, interests in works of art or in patent or copyright rights. See, e.g., *Donley v. Donley*, 88 Ill. App. 3d 367, 403 N.E.2d 1337 (1980). Frequently, the present value of future payments in distribution of a marital estate must be calculated since the value of the property might increase while the buying power of installments would substantially decrease. See, e.g., *Pankow v. Pankow*, 347 N.W.2d 566 (N.D. 1984). See also *Douty v. Douty*, 1994 Va. App. LEXIS 196 (valuation of car wash business).

An accountant may be necessary for valuation of a small business. For example, the husband in *Bosserman v. Bosserman*, 9 Va. App. 1, 384 S.E.2d 104 (1989), was a 25 percent owner of a closely held family corporation. The bylaws provided for buy-out of stock based upon the "true book value" of the corporation, $28,032 at the time of divorce. The wife's accountant, however, placed the true market value of the farm owned by the corporation at $174,600. The court of appeals followed the majority rule that a buy-out provision does not control the determination of value when the other spouse did not consent or was not otherwise bound by its terms. The reasoning behind this rule is that buy-out provisions do not necessarily reflect the intrinsic worth of the stock to the parties. However, the limitation of alienability created by the restricting agreement necessarily affects the actual marketability of the stock, and thus its value. The valuation accepted by the court of appeals was based upon the corporation's net assets, the farm.

Properly qualified evidence of comparable sales of other real property may be admissible to prove the value of the real property at issue. See, e.g., *In re Marriage of Smith*, 79 Cal. App. 3d 725, 145 Cal. Rptr. 205

(1978). If an equitable distribution award is remanded or the matter is reheard, a second evaluation should establish the value of the property, whether separately or jointly titled. *Wagner v. Wagner*, 15 Va. App. 120, 421 S.E.2d 218 (1992) (second evaluation in 1988 needed when original award was entered in 1984); *Gaynor v. Hird*, 11 Va. App. 588, 400 S.E.2d 788 (1991). The value of the husband's dental practice should not have been discounted by estimating the capital gains taxes on a hypothetical sale as opposed to the present fair market value of the property. *Arbuckle v. Arbuckle*, 1996 Va. App. LEXIS 322. The parties were to share equally in the marital property; the husband was awarded the value of his practice while the wife received oil company stock.

§ 22-20. Tax consequences of distribution.

Since 1984, I.R.C. § 1041 provides that transfers between spouses, or immediately after separation or divorce, are treated as gifts for income tax purposes. This means that they are not taxable, and the spouse receiving the property or interest in property takes the transferor's basis. Installments made by the payor may not be deducted as is alimony. *Slawski v. United States*, 6 Ct. Cl. 433 (1984). In order to receive this tax treatment, the transfer must be before divorce or within one year of divorce, or pursuant to a settlement agreement made in connection with a divorce. The transfers may be treated as alimony even if the decree or agreement does not provide that they will terminate at the death of the payee. I.R.C. § 71(b)(1).

Changes made in the treatment of capital gains affects the 1984 Tax Reform Act's effective elimination of the holding of *United States v. Davis*, 370 U.S. 65 (1962). Capital gains are now taxed as ordinary income for the most part. However, they will now be paid by the transferee rather than by the transferor, as had been true under Davis. I.R.C. § 1202.

The award to the wife of 50 percent of the husband's royalties under a property settlement agreement meant net royalties, since otherwise the husband would be required to bear the entire tax burden. *Jennings v. Jennings*, 12 Va. App. 1187, 409 S.E.2d 8 (1991). If the parties specify that each will be responsible for paying taxes accrued on his or her respective income, there is no need for repayment of any "offset" if it turns out that the parties do not owe any tax. *Smith v. Smith*, 15 Va. App. 371, 423 S.E.2d 851 (1992). Tax liability may be allocated but need not be. *Alphin v. Alphin*, 15 Va. App. 371, 424 S.E.2d 572 (1992).

Calculations of probable taxes must be estimated based on expert opinions. *Mains v. Mains*, 1993 Va. App. LEXIS 362.

§ 22-21. Effect on dower and curtesy, use of marital home, title.

The husband as well as the wife is now able to acquire a sole and separate equitable estate in real property. *Jacobs v. Meade*, 227 Va. 284, 315 S.E.2d 383 (1984).

If the property was held as a married person, even though titled in the name of only one spouse, the other spouse historically had a dower or curtesy interest in the property. For a conveyance in fee simple to a third party, the spouse with the contingent interest must also join in the deed. Contingent property interests such as dower were extinguished by the divorce decree. Va. Code § 20-111.

There is no need for a specific claim in an equitable distribution proceeding, in contrast to a partition suit. Compensation for improvements to the marital home will be limited to the increase in its value plus mortgage payments made after the separation. *Lee v. Lee*, 13 Va. Cir. 239 (Henrico Co. 1988).

§ 22-22. Finality.

A judgment for equitable distribution is a final order, and is not modifiable. See, e.g., *Boschee v. Boschee*, 340 N.W.2d 685 (N.D. 1983). It therefore will be given full faith and credit by other states under U.S. Const. art. IV, § 2. *Varone v. Varone*, 359 F.2d 769 (7th Cir. 1966).

§ 22-23. Res judicata.

Res judicata will be a defense to a second litigation concerning the same parties and property, even though the legal theories used change in each suit. *Whittaker v. Whittaker*, 60 Md. App. 695, 484 A.2d 314 (1984).

§ 22-24. Use of contempt power.

Because the equitable distribution of property is not alimony or child support, the contempt power cannot be used to coerce a spouse into carrying out the court's order since to do otherwise would be to imprison for debt. *McAlear v. McAlear*, 298 Md. 320, 469 A.2d 1256 (1984);

Dvorak v. Dvorak, 329 N.W.2d 868 (N.D. 1983); *In re Fontana*, 24 Cal. App. 3d 1008, 101 Cal. Rptr. 465 (1972). The use of other methods of collection, such as a suit for specific performance, if a contract is involved, see, e.g., N.C. Gen. Stat. § 50-20(g), or appointment of a receiver, see, e.g., *Rosenthal v. Rosenthal*, 240 Cal. App. 2d 927, 50 Cal. Rptr. 385 (1966), may be effective. Although contempt is not an available remedy, an award entered pursuant to § 20-107.3 constitutes a judgment within the meaning of § 8.01-426, so that provisions of § 8.01-382 relating to interest on judgments shall ordinarily apply.

§ 22-25. Attorney's fees.

The Virginia Bar Council has determined that it is ethically improper to represent a client in an equitable distribution case on a contingent fee basis. Op. No. 189, July 1, 1984. The property to be distributed is not an asset as is a personal injury recovery, and to allow a contingent fee would be to encourage attorneys to fix large monetary awards for the client at the possible expense of other areas of disagreement, and to minimize any possibility of reconciliation during the period of representation.

CHAPTER 23

Child Support

§ 23-1. Introduction.

The duty of a parent to support a minor child was considered in general in Chapter 16. The present chapter concerns child support as one of the economic consequences of dissolution or termination of marriage.

Generally speaking, child support can be distinguished from other financial considerations because the relationship of parent and child does not end with the judicial termination of marriage. Although spousal support is fixed by the standard of living enjoyed during the marriage, children are entitled to whatever financial advantages they would have enjoyed had the family remained intact. See, e.g., *Conway v. Conway*, 10 Va. App. 653, 395 S.E.2d 464 (1990). Although a contract between the parties regarding spousal support will, if filed with the pleadings in a divorce action, be nonmodifiable, child support can always be modified by

329

the court in the child's best interest. *Featherstone v. Brooks*, 220 Va. 443, 446, 258 S.E.2d 513, 515 (1979); *Carter v. Carter*, 215 Va. 475, 481, 211 S.E.2d 253, 258 (1975).

Because of problems in the collection of child support from noncustodial parents, a uniform act has been adopted by all states, including Virginia. Va. Code § 20-88.12 et seq. In 1984, Congress passed the Child Support Enforcement Assistance Amendments to the Social Security Act that balance the less favorable tax consequences of child support mandated by the Domestic Relations Tax Reform Act of 1984. The amendments require states, as a condition of receiving federal funds under the Act, to provide for mechanisms for enforcement such as withholding from the obligor's income, imposition of liens against real property, posting of security or bonds if support is overdue, and withholding from state or federal income tax refunds. 42 U.S.C. §§ 658 et seq. They also require the establishment of guidelines for the amount of support, now found in Va. Code § 20-108.1.

Both parents owe a duty of support. *Featherstone v. Brooks*, 220 Va. 443, 448, 258 S.E.2d 513, 516 (1979). In allocating this burden, the court is to consider, inter alia, the "earning capacity, obligations and needs, and financial resources of the parties." Va. Code § 20-107.2.

Clerical mistakes in judgments or other court records may be corrected by a nunc pro tunc order. *Cutshaw v. Cutshaw*, 220 Va. 638, 261 S.E.2d 52 (1979) (failure to prepare order for entry by court); *Dorn v. Dorn*, 222 Va. 288, 279 S.E.2d 393 (1981) (correction of ambiguity as to whether the word "biweekly" inserted by attorney into incorporated stipulation agreement referred to time of payment or frequency of payment. Va. Code § 8.01-428B.

Under Virginia law, a court lacks authority to relieve a delinquent spouse of the obligation to pay accrued installments of child support. The reasoning underlying this rule is that each installment becomes a vested property right the moment it falls due, and therefore is immune from modification. *Taylor v. Taylor*, 14 Va. App. 642, 418 S.E.2d 900 (1992).

Attorney's fees may be awarded to the custodial spouse who is forced to litigate delinquent child support or child custody. *Burke v. Burke*, 25 Va. Cir. 446 (Spotsylvania Co. 1991). Custody orders may be entered even when no divorce is pending. In such cases, orders pendente lite may be directed to any person with a legitimate interest who is a party. The custody and visitation orders in these non-divorce proceedings shall be made in accordance with Va. Code §§ 20-124 et seq. (1994). Pendente lite orders shall have no presumptive effect and shall not determine the ultimate outcome of the case.

When the custodial father gave the mother $1,000 per month so that she could maintain housing and visit the children, and the mother did not use the support for those purposes, the court was justified in obligating the mother to pay him $242.83 a month in child support. The amount she was to pay deviated from the guideline presumptions, but the variation was justified to provide the mother with funds to be used in her attempt to repair the relationship with that child. *Collins v. Alexander*, 1995 Va. App. LEXIS 768.

The trial court's discretion will not be interfered with unless some injustice has been done. *Gramelspacher v. Gramelspacher*, 204 Va. 839, 846, 134 S.E.2d 285, 290 (1964).

See Margaret F. Brinig & F.H. Buckley, *The Market for Deadbeats*, 25 J. Legal Stud. 201 (1996) (discussing why some states might be more successful at collecting child support than others); David L. Chambers, *Fathers, the Welfare System, and the Virtues and Perils Of Child-Support Enforcement* 81 Va. L. Rev. 2575 (1995). See also Krause, *Child Support Reassessed: Limits of Private Responsibility and the Public Interest*, 1989 U. Ill. L. Rev. 367 (1989).

§ 23-2. Who may bring action?

Although child support is for the benefit of the child, in this context it arises from the jurisdiction over the parents' divorce action. In consequence, only a parent may bring an action for enforcement of a child support obligation. *McClaugherty v. McClaugherty*, 180 Va. 51, 21 S.E.2d 761 (1942). See also *Yarborough v. Yarborough*, 290 U.S. 202 (1933) (father satisfied obligation under divorce decree; daughter in another jurisdiction could not sue on own behalf for additional funds including college expenses); *Kelleher v. Kelleher*, 21 Ill. App. 3d 601, 316 N.E.2d 212 (1974) (after custodial wife died, grandmother could not bring action on child's behalf to collect arrearages under divorce decree).

In *Shelton v. Berger*, 12 Va. App. 859, 406 S.E.2d 421 (1991), the court of appeals held that a child, suing through her next friend, was not barred from filing an action against her natural father. Her natural mother had previously been divorced from another man, with the court awarding "custody of the children of the parties" to the mother. The child is not a party to the divorce decree and therefore is not bound by a paternity determination in it unless formally made a party and represented by a guardian ad litem and given the right to litigate. See also *Commonwealth ex rel. Gray v. Johnson*, 7 Va. App. 614, 376 S.E.2d 787 (1989) (divorce decree asserted that there were no children born of the marriage).

However, a separation agreement that acknowledged that the husband was not the father of his wife's child, born during the marriage, waived her right to enforce express promises made prior to and after the birth to support the child as if it were his own. The agreement allowed the wife to remain in the marital residence for a year and gave her $6,500 to cover the birth expenses and care of the infant. *Mills v. Mills*, 36 Va. Cir. 351 (Fairfax Co. 1995).

When Dinkum was identified as the father of Gifford's child, the trial court should have ordered retroactive child support from the date she filed her petition. *Gifford v. Dinkum*, 1996 Va. App. LEXIS 114.

Once the child reaches the age of majority, the nature of the support obligation changes, and such child must bring an action independently of a parent to enforce the statutory obligation to support a necessitous child. *Harmatz v. Harmatz*, 457 A.2d 399 (D.C. 1983) (brain-damaged child; recovery sought by parent under common law duty to support necessitous adult child; parent found not automatically the most suitable guardian).

Arrearages may also be collected at this time by the parent if due under a divorce action.

See generally 6A Michie's Jurisprudence Divorce and Alimony § 57.

§ 23-3. Jurisdiction.

Jurisdiction in child support actions depends wholly upon statute. *Jackson v. Jackson*, 211 Va. 718, 180 S.E.2d 500 (1971) (no jurisdiction to award custodial wife use of marital home as part of alimony and child support provisions); *Buchanan v. Buchanan*, 170 Va. 458, 197 S.E. 426 (1938) (no jurisdiction to award child support as part of habeas corpus proceeding). However, child support may be awarded following annulment of the parent's void marriage under the present Va. Code § 20-107.2, which allows support following "dissolution of marriage." *Henderson v. Henderson*, 187 Va. 121, 46 S.E.2d 10 (1948). The court found in this case that the legislature did not intend to make ineligibility to marry the ground upon which the support of children of the marriage should be denied. Courts may make child support or custody orders and decrees in suits for annulment or separate maintenance. Va. Code Ann. § 20-107.2 [amended 1996].

An agreement between the parents that one will not pay support, or as to a specific amount of payment, will not bind the court. *Featherstone v. Brooks*, 220 Va. 443, 258 S.E.2d 513 (1979). See also *Pilson v. Salvoni*, 65 App. D.C. 55, 79 F.2d 411 (1935); *Weaver v. Garrett*, 13 Md. 283, 282 A.2d 509 (1971).

Once a divorce judgment has been rendered, the court maintains continuing jurisdiction over the matter of child support throughout the child's minority. Because there had been no hearing on the matter nor due process provided to the wife prior to the judge's closing the file, the husband's duty to pay child support was not terminated by the judge's notation that the file was closed, even though thereafter the husband obtained a divorce decree not mentioning support. *Brown v. Brown*, 240 Va. 376, 397 S.E.2d 813 (1990).

A decree for child support is an in personam action. *Gramelspacher v. Gramelspacher*, 204 Va. 839, 842, 134 S.E.2d 285, 288 (1964). The children need not be present or domiciled in the state for the decree to be effective. *Id.* at 843, 134 S.E.2d at 289. Because of the personal nature of the obligation, the requirement of a divorce action that one spouse be domiciled within the forum jurisdiction will not suffice for the financial obligation of child support. It will be necessary in such cases to acquire jurisdiction over the absent spouse either through personal service within Virginia, or through personal jurisdiction effected through the Virginia long-arm statute, Va. Code § 8-328.1. This would allow the action to be maintained in Virginia if the marital domicile had been within the state for six months next preceding the complaint or cause of action, so long as there was service over the absent spouse in the manner prescribed by the foreign state. In other words, service by publication will not suffice. The United States Supreme Court has indicated that the type of transitory contacts such as marriage in the state, presence there for a total of six days, and presence of the wife and children in the state would not constitute the type of "taking advantage of the privileges of doing business in the state" as to give jurisdiction for this personal obligation. *Kulko v. Superior Court of California*, 436 U.S. 84 (1978). Service under the long-arm statute, Va. Code § E8.01-328.1(8) and (9), must be made personally by a person authorized to make such service by § 8.01-320. Posting will not confer in personam jurisdiction in a child support action. *Prillaman v. Prillaman*, 29 Va. Cir. 441 (Warren Co. 1992).

No personal service was given to the husband when a summons was "posted" on his door rather than mailed to him as provided by statute. The default judgment entered against him for support was therefore invalid. *Garrity v. Virginia Dep't of Social Services*, 11 Va. App. 39, 396 S.E.2d 150 (1990).

In its 1993 reconvened session, the Virginia legislature established a statewide system of family courts. The new legislation, Chapter 929 of the Virginia Acts of Assembly, provides that, when implemented, the family courts will assume the powers and territorial jurisdiction of the juvenile and domestic relations district courts when it is funded (Va. Code § 16.1-69.8(2)). Judges of the juvenile and domestic relations district court shall continue in office as family court judges until the expiration of the term for which appointed or elected, or until a vacancy occurs or a successor is appointed or elected (Va. Code § 16.1-69.9:01). Like the current juvenile and domestic relations district court judges, family court judges shall be prohibited from engaging in the practice of law. Va. Code § 16.1-12(c). General district court judges, substitute judges, and retired and recalled district court judges may serve on the family court, but only after completing the training program required by the Judicial Council of Virginia. Va. Code §§ 16.1-69.21, 16.1-69.22:1 and 16.1-69.36(8).

For any issue arising out of suits for divorce, annulment or affirmation of marriage, separate maintenance, and other child custody, support, and visitation cases, the judge shall consider whether to refer the parties to mediation, and may do so sua sponte or on motion of one of the parties. Upon referral, the parties must attend one evaluation session during which they and the mediator assess the case and decide whether to continue with mediation or with adjudication. Further participation in the mediation shall be by consent of all parties, and attorneys for either may be present during mediation. Va. Code § 16.1-272.1. When the parties are referred to mediation, the court shall set a return date. The parties shall notify the court in writing if the dispute is resolved prior to this return date. The court may, in its discretion, incorporate any mediated agreement into the terms of its final decree. Only if such an order is entered will the terms of the voluntary settlement agreement affect any outstanding court order.

For cases filed before January 1, 1995, the circuit court may transfer enforcement of divorce decrees, including pendente lite orders, to the family court, when implemented. After such a transfer, the circuit court is divested of any further jurisdiction over the matter. Va. Code § 20-79(c). However, an appeal from a juvenile domestic relations court, designated an experimental family court when the case was filed, lies in the circuit court rather than the court of appeals. *Rhoades v. Rhoades*, 16 Va. App. 757, 433 S.E.2d 487 (1993).

The wife appealed the family court's order reducing the husband's child support payment, claiming that the family court had no jurisdiction to make the reduction. The circuit court ruled in her favor. The husband in *Kiss v. McDonald*, 1993 Va. App. LEXIS 196, unsuccessfully claimed that he should not be found in arrears for paying only the abated amount. The court of appeals reasoned that the family court's order was ineffective, so the circuit court had no authority to make any changes on past-due installments under Va. Code § 20-108. The circuit court could have made changes had there been a pending petition in a court with jurisdiction. In another appeal from the juvenile court, the father claimed the circuit court lacked jurisdiction to hear the matter because the child Christopher's maternal grandparents had been named his guardians, replacing the mother. The court found that the mother was a proper party to the litigation since when the father filed his petition, she was the custodial parent. *Evans v. Division of Child Support Enforcement*, 1996 Va. App. LEXIS 93.

According to legislation adopted in 1995, foreign orders under the Uniform Interstate Enforcement of Support Act should be registered in the juvenile and domestic relations district court, not the circuit court. Va. Code § 20-88.32.

An alternative way of bringing an action is through the Uniform Reciprocal Enforcement of Support Act, Va. Code §§ 20-88.12 et seq. This allows a petition to be filed in Virginia establishing the duty to support and the need therefor. The state where the absent spouse resides (responding state) allows the spouse to contest the duty to support and the ability to make payments. Once a valid order is obtained, either through a divorce action or through URESA, it will be enforced in Virginia exactly as is a Virginia order. *Scott v. Sylvester*, 220 Va. 182, 185, 257 S.E.2d 774, 776 (1979). URESA is remedial in nature and should be liberally construed so that its purpose of providing support for dependent children is achieved. *Scott v. Sylvester*, 220 Va. at 185, 257 S.E.2d at 776. Thus a foreign order for child support will be given comity and enforced "with the same force and effect as if it had been entered in Virginia." *Id.* (quoting from *Alig v. Alig*, 220 Va. 80, 84, 255 S.E.2d 494, 497 (1979)). Enforcement will proceed in Virginia even though the defendant was only present in the state for a portion of the time during which the arrearage accrued. Va. Code § 20-88.30:6(1); *Scott v. Sylvester*, 220 Va. at 187,

257 S.E.2d at 777. However, Virginia does not obtain in personam jurisdiction over a defendant when the Virginia resident registers a foreign decree under RURESA and serves the defendant in another state. *Stephens v. Stephens*, 229 Va. 610, 331 S.E.2d 484 (1985) (spousal support). This method will be supplanted by the UIFSA, discussed in § 23-20.

The court does not possess the power to relieve an obligor parent of accrued payments of support money. *Cofer v. Cofer*, 205 Va. 834, 838, 140 S.E.2d 663, 666 (1965). This means that arrearages will be final judgments that must be given full faith and credit by other states. Cf. *Griffin v. Griffin*, 327 U.S. 220 (1946).

The wife obtained a pendente lite unitary award for spousal and child support that was to continue until further order of the court, and the husband later obtained a final divorce. The decree reserved custody, support, and property division for later decision. The husband died eight years later, and his estate was subject to a lien for unpaid payments under the temporary support order. *Duke v. Duke*, 239 Va. 501, 391 S.E.2d 77 (1990).

§ 23-4. Proving parentage.

A divorcing spouse need only make payments for the support of his or her own children. Some recent cases have found that a stepparent assumed the responsibility of providing for children of the former spouse, and therefore should be estopped from asserting parenthood as a ground for avoiding such payments after the spouses separate. See, e.g., *In re Marriage of Johnson*, 88 Cal. App. 3d 848, 152 Cal. Rptr. 121 (1979). The duty of support would turn upon whether the spouses had acted in loco parentis during the marriage.

If the parentage of the child is in question, the earlier discussion in Chapters 3 and 16 should be consulted. Where the parents were married at the time of the child's likely conception or birth, the very strong presumption of legitimacy applies. See, e.g., *Landes v. Landes*, 1 N.Y.2d 358, 153 N.Y.S.2d 14, 135 N.E.2d 562 (1956). Whenever parentage of any child is in doubt, the court may require the alleged father, mother, and child to submit to blood grouping tests. The court may order the costs to be borne by the person requesting such tests, unless indigent, and the results of such blood grouping tests shall be admitted in evidence when contained in a written report prepared and sworn to by a duly licensed physician. Blood grouping tests must be ordered during paternity proceedings where child support is in issue under revised Va. Code § 20-49.3.

A child was not barred by res judicata by a previous finding against his mother in a paternity action, since the two were not in privity, or so identified in interest that she represented his legal rights, and the child was not formally named as a party, represented by a guardian ad litem nor given an adequate opportunity to litigate the issue. *Department of Social Services v. Johnson*, 7 Va. App. 614, 376 S.E.2d 787 (1989). See also *Shelton v. Berger*, 12 Va. App. 859, 406 S.E.2d 421 (1991) (child not barred by finding that she was "child of the parties" in divorce action between her natural mother and another man). On the other hand, a prior finding that a man was the father of a child in a divorce proceeding acts to collaterally estop him from establishing through conclusive blood testing that he was not the biological parent. *Slagle v. Slagle*, 11 Va. App. 341, 398 S.E.2d 346 (App. 1990). Similarly, in *Aviles v. Aviles*, 14 Va. App. 360, 416 S.E.2d 716 (1992), the husband filed for divorce, alleging that the child in question was born of the marriage. He testified that he had heard rumors both before and during the divorce proceedings that he might not be the child's father, but did not inform his attorney of this issue. Further, he treated the child as his own and supported the child during the marriage. The Virginia Supreme Court held that the trial court did not err in ruling both that the husband had not proved by clear and convincing evidence that the wife committed fraud on the court and that the evidence did not justify terminating the husband's child support obligation. See also *McFadden v. McFadden*, 1995 Va. App. LEXIS 878; *Dunnaville v. Dunnaville*, 1995 Va. App. LEXIS 222; *Hartman v. Hartman*, 33 Va. Cir. 373 (Fairfax Co. 1994).

However, when the husband had no knowledge prior to the final decree that he was not the father of Natalie, he was not bound, *Batrouny v. Batrouny*, 13 Va. App. 441, 412 S.E.2d 721 (1991), so that the final decree would be corrected to reflect that one child, Ashley, was born to the parties. See also *Schalton v. Schalton*, 31 Va. Cir. 47 (Fairfax Co. 1993). However, a separation agreement that acknowledged that the husband was not the father of his wife's child, born during the marriage, waived her right to enforce express promises made prior to and after the birth to support the child as if it were his own. The agreement allowed the wife to remain in the marital residence for a year and have $6,500 to cover the birth expenses and care of the infant. *Mills v. Mills*, 36 Va. Cir. 351 (Fairfax Co. 1995). Compare *Rose v. Rose*, 1993 Va. App. LEXIS

375 (husband knew he was not the father of the child before entry of the final decree, and agreed to make child support payments anyway); and *Bromley v. Bromley*, 30 Va. Cir. 83 (Fairfax Co. 1993) (after 21 days expired, decree could not be modified to change the statement of child's parentage. However, when another man admitted paternity and DNA testing revealed a 99.3% probability of his parentage, there was a change in circumstances warranting elimination of the husband's duty to pay child support.).

Under amended Va. Code § 20-61.1, fathers between the ages of fourteen and sixteen who are represented by a guardian ad litem may testify and may be required to provide for support and maintenance just as they would be if adult.

§ 23-5. Custody as relieving duty.

A custodial spouse may fulfill the duty of support by providing shelter and day-to-day care for the child. See, e.g., *Suire v. Miller*, 363 So. 2d 945 (La. App. 1978) (adult necessitous child). If the custodial spouse is a person of means, however, the duty will extend to the provision of necessaries or even luxuries for the child. The noncustodial parent should also bear part of the burden to the extent of that spouse's ability.

If the custodial parent has by his or her own volition entered into an agreement to relinquish custody on a permanent basis and has further agreed to the elimination of support payments, and such agreement has been fully performed, the new custodial spouse is entitled to credit under the decree. *Acree v. Acree*, 2 Va. App. 151, 342 S.E.2d 68 (1986). See also *Lipscomb v. Lipscomb*, 18 Va. Cir. 244 (Chesterfield Co. 1989) (relinquishment for two years and three months).

If the custodial parent refuses to abide by a court decree, such as a visitation provision, the court may order payment of child support contingent upon the posting of a bond to guarantee compliance. *Kern v. Lindsey*, 182 Va. 775, 30 S.E.2d 707 (1944). Refusal also may be grounds for a change in custody. Va. Code § 20-108. However, parents may not agree between themselves that one should be relieved of paying support for a minor child. *Kelley v. Kelley*, 248 Va. 295, 449 S.E.2d 55 (1994) (wife agreed to hold husband harmless for child support in exchange for his share of marital home; this did not preclude later action for child support). See also *Commonwealth ex rel. Sparks*, 1995 Va. App. LEXIS 82.

§ 23-6. Shared custody.

Shared custody may relieve a portion of the child support necessary, according to Va. Code § 20-108.2. For an application of this principle, see *Ewing v. Ewing*, 1995 Va. App. LEXIS 192, where a husband argued unsuccessfully that partial days (so long as more than half days) could be counted toward meeting the 110-day requirement of the statute; see also *Steinberg v. Steinberg*, 1996 Va. App. LEXIS 57; *Laverty v. Laverty*, 1995 Va. App. LEXIS 750 (same).

In cases involving split custody, the amount of child support paid shall be the difference between the amounts owed by each parent as a noncustodial parent with the noncustodial parent owing the larger amount paying the difference to the other parent. Split custody shall be limited to those situations where each parent has physical custody of a child or children born of the parents, born of either parent and adopted by the other, or adopted by both parents. For purposes of calculating a child support obligation in such cases, a separate family unit exists for each parent, and the amount of child support is based upon the number of such children that reside with the parent. The parent is considered a noncustodial parent to the children in the other parent's family unit. Va. Code § 20-108.2(G)(2).

§ 23-7. Amount necessary.

Va. Code § 20-108.1 prohibits the courts from utilizing a mathematical formula for computing child support as the sole determinative basis for an award and encourages a complete hearing, stating that any such formula may only be used as a guideline. In 1988, guidelines were added to § 20-108.2. These include a basic support obligation involving gross income subject to reasonable business expenses. To this basic amount is added any extraordinary medical and dental expenses and any child-care costs incurred on behalf of the child or children due to employment. This total child support obligation is to be divided between the parents in the same proportion as their gross incomes bear to their combined gross income. The statute specifically says that the court should consider not only these factors in Va. Code § 20-107.2, which relate to income and expenses, but also listed factors affecting the obligation and ability of each party to provide. Among these factors are actual monetary support for other children, custody arrangements, imputed income to parties voluntarily unemployed or under-employed, debts arising during marriage for child's benefits, debts incurred for production of income, direct payments ordered for health plan coverage, and extraordinary capital gains such as those resulting from the sale of the marital home. The capital gains factor was removed by legislation in 1991. The court must give a rebuttable presumption to the amount given in the guidelines for child support included in that section of the Code. To rebut the presumption, the court must make written findings in the order that the application of the guidelines would be unjust or inappropriate in a particular case as determined by relevant evidence pertaining to the factors set forth in Va. Code § 20-107.2. In determining these amounts, gross income of the obligor shall not include amounts actually paid for spousal support under a preexisting order or written agreement. Va. Code § 108.1(C). The Circuit Court for the City of Charlottesville has held that child support may be increased based upon the percent increase in income when the parties' combined gross income exceeds the statutory guidelines. *May v. May*, 24 Va. Cir. 407 (1991) (husband unemployed but has a net worth in excess of $3,000,000; income increased from $85,000 in 1984 to $154,000 in 1990). This decision is affected by recent additions to § 20-108.2(B), which provide for much lower percentage increases for gross monthly incomes exceeding those in the guideline tables. However, the guidelines may be exceeded if the parties have a written property settlement agreement that specifies the way the amounts will be modified. *Scott v. Scott*, 12 Va. App. 1245, 408 S.E.2d 579 (1991); *Watkinson v. Henley*, 13 Va. App. 151, 409 S.E.2d 470 (1991) (amount agreed to in consent decree exceeded guidelines). See also *Jordan v. Jordan*, 23 Va. Cir. 470 (Fairfax Co. 1991). In *Watkinson*, the court of appeals held that where parents have agreed upon an amount, or agreed upon other provisions, for the support and maintenance of a child, the trial court must consider the provisions of the agreement that relate to the factors in Code §§ 20-107.2 and 20-108.1. Further, if the trial court finds that the presumptive amount is unjust or inappropriate because the provisions in a separation agreement serve the best interest of the child, the court may vary from the guidelines by ordering that support be paid in an amount equal to the benefits provided for in the contract. *Id.* at 159, 409 S.E.2d at 480-81. However, the trial court may not depart from the statutory guidelines because "use of the guidelines would seriously impair [wife's] ability to maintain minimal adequate housing and provide other basic necessities for the child." *Pharo v. Pharo*, 19 Va. App. 236, 450 S.E.2d 183 (1994).

In *Milligan v. Milligan*, 12 Va. App. 982, 407 S.E.2d 702 (1991), the court of appeals held that if the parties' income changes so that the amount awarded is no longer within the statutory guidelines, the material or substantial change of circumstance rule is no longer required as a condition precedent to obtaining a modification of child support.

Amendments to Va. Code § 20-107.2 made in 1991 include the addition of new factors to be considered in assessing the obligation and ability to pay child support. These are the age, physical, and mental condition of the child or children, including extraordinary medical or dental expenses, and child-care expenses; independent financial resources of the child or children; the standard of living for the family established during the marriage; the earning capacity, obligations and needs, and financial resources of each parent; education and training of the parties and the ability and opportunity of the parties to secure such education or training; contributions, monetary and nonmonetary, of each party to the family's well-being; provisions made with regard to the marital property; tax consequences to the parties regarding claims for dependent children and child care; and such other factors including tax consequences to each party, as are necessary to consider the equities for the parents and children. Another consideration is a written agreement between the parties that includes an amount for child support. Va. Code § 20-108.1(B)(16).

The court's authority to award child support under Title 20, Title 16.1, or Title 63.1 shall include the power to order a party to provide health care coverage for dependent children if reasonable under all the circumstances. Va. Code § 20-108.1. Any such costs for health care when actually paid by a parent, to the extent the costs are directly allocable to the child or children, and which are the extra costs of covering the child or children beyond whatever coverage the parent providing the coverage would otherwise have, shall be added to the basic child support obligation. Va. Code § 20-108.2(E). In each child support case the court shall include in its order, among other matters, an order for health care coverage. Va. Code § 20-103(6).

The presumptive amount of child support should be fixed by the guidelines before there is any reduction for other children the parent is supporting. The presumptive amount of support under Va. Code § 20-108.2 must be determined before a court awards the amount of child support contained in the parties' property settlement agreement. *Watson v. Watson*, 17 Va. App. 249, 436 S.E.2d 193 (1993). The trial court need not award child support in the presumptive amount if a deviation is justified by the factors described in Va. Code §§ 20-107.2 and 20-108.1. However, it must first determine the guideline amount and compare this with the provisions of the separation agreement.

Va. Code § 20-108.1(B) requires that in order to rebut the guideline presumption, the court shall make written findings in the order, stating the amount of support that would have been required under the guidelines and the justification of why the order varies from the guidelines. The finding shall be determined by the relevant evidence pertaining to various factors set forth in the statute and the best interests of the child. The new shared custody guidelines justify a modification proceeding when a child support award varies significantly from the earlier guideline amount. *Slonka v. Pennline*, 17 Va. App. 662, 440 S.E.2d 423 (1994). At the proceeding, the court should begin with the new guideline amount and then consider whether the agreed provisions for the child would better serve the interest or "equities" for parents and children. In *Slonka*, for example, the wife argued that she had purchased a new home in reliance on the original agreement. Only actual rather than imputed income is to be used for determining the presumptive amount. Time spent in custody of the other does not directly affect the amount due, because of fixed expenses in caring for the child. *Farley v. Farley*, 12 Va. App. 1, 401 S.E.2d 897(1991).

In order for an increase in the amount of child support to be awarded, the judge must supply written reasons for deviation from the guidelines. *Richardson v. Richardson*, 1991 Va. App. LEXIS 32, 401 S.E.2d 894, 12 Va. App. 18 (1991). See also *Mayers v. Mayers*, 15 Va. App. 587, 425 S.E.2d 808 (1993), (no reasons given, the appeals court was unable to see whether the trial court deducted expenses noncustodial wife incurred during her visits with the children). Similarly, in order to decrease the amount of child support, the trial court must first begin with the presumptive amount of the guidelines, and then state reasons for deviating from that amount. *Alexander v. Alexander*, 12 Va. App. 691, 406 S.E.2d 666 (1991). See also *Hiner v. Hadeed*, 15 Va. App. 575, 425 S.E.2d 811 (1993).

It is erroneous to reduce the child support owed by normal expenses the noncustodial parent incurs in visiting the child, or by the amount the noncustodial parent spends during visitation, unless the custodial spouse's expenses are reduced thereby. *Baumgartner v. Moore*, 14 Va. App. 696, 419 S.E.2d 291 (1992).

The parent has the duty to support the child in accordance with this obligor's fortune and station in life, and not only with the child's needs. This clearly includes education for the children. *Conway v. Conway*, 10 Va. App. 653, 395 S.E.2d 464 (1990). A noncustodial parent may not voluntarily stay home in order to care for the child or children of a second marriage, and therefore avoid a child support obligation. *Horn v. Horn*, 19 Va. Cir. 73 (Henrico Co. 1989).

Even though the child was only two years old, alimony and child support payments of $1,200 monthly were not sufficient where the husband's business earned him $100,000 per year. *Ingram v. Ingram*, 217 Va. 27, 225 S.E.2d 362 (1976).

§ 23-8. Limitation of parental ability to pay.

The amount required for child support is limited by the noncustodial spouse's ability to pay. *Taylor v. Taylor*, 203 Va. 1, 121 S.E.2d 753 (1961); Va. Code § 20-107.2. A voluntary relinquishment of a higher paying position will not change the ability to pay for these purposes. 203 Va. at 5, 121 S.E.2d at 756. But compare *Payne v. Payne*, 5 Va. App. 359, 363 S.E.2d 428 (1987) (no evidence of how much husband could earn in counseling business that had been entered into with wife's support; nor suggestion that he could seek other fields of employment that would yield a higher income).

The ability to pay includes not only the parent's salary, but also the ability to earn and assets generally. *Hawkins v. Hawkins*, 187 Va. 595, 600-01, 47 S.E.2d 436, 439 (1948). See also *Hur v. Department of Social Servs.*, 13 Va. App. 54, 409 S.E.2d 454 (1991) (a parent does not have the unfettered right to remain unproductive under the shelter of college enrollment so as to avoid support obligations); *Hamel v. Hamel*, 1994 Va. App. LEXIS 104, 441 S.E.2d 221 (1994) (trial court should have imputed income to a noncustodial wife who voluntarily quit her job and had no income at the time of the hearing); *Will v. Will*, 1994 Va. App. LEXIS 100 (guideline amount of zero would not be followed when noncustodial father was voluntarily unemployed); *Brody v. Brody*, 16 Va. App. 647, 432 S.E.2d 20 (1993) (income imputed where wife left $54,000 per year job to stay home with children and care for child of second marriage); *O'Brien v. Rose*, 1994 Va. App. LEXIS 97 (income imputed when wife quit teaching position to move with new husband to Thailand, then returned to the United States where she needed to renew her teacher certification); *Auman v. Auman*, 21 Va. App. 275, 464 S.E.2d 154 (1995)

(When a family breaks up, "a party is not free to make career decisions that disregard the needs of his dependents and his potential obligation to them, and 'the risk of his success at his new job [is] upon him and not upon [his child].'"); *Calvert v. Calvert*, 18 Va. App. 781, 447 S.E.2d 875 (1994); *Floyd v. Floyd*, 17 Va. App. 222, 436 S.E.2d 457 (1993) (husband hiding income, so $45,000 yearly income imputed to him). But see *Belke v. Belke*, 1994 Va. App. LEXIS 461 (husband who resigned from the Navy for a job earning two percent less because he was scheduled to go to sea for a fourth submarine tour was not underemployed); *L.C.S. v. S.A.S.*, 19 Va. App. 709, 453 S.E.2d 580 (1995) (no imputed income where husband was legally barred from the practice of law due to the loss of his license). A noncustodial parent may not voluntarily stay home in order to care for the child or children of a second marriage and thereby avoid a child support obligation. *Horn v. Horn*, 19 Va. Cir. 73 (Henrico Co. 1989). However, the fact that a father had two legitimate children must be taken into account in determining the amount of support due to his illegitimate children. *Zubricki v. Motter*, 12 Va. App. 999, 406 S.E.2d 672 (1991). Reduction would not be justified where the noncustodial parent voluntarily contributed to the support of two adult children from a prior marriage. *Lewis v. Lewis*, 1993 Va. App. LEXIS 354.

It is erroneous to reduce the child support owed by the normal expenses the noncustodial parent makes in visiting the child, or by the amount the noncustodial parent spends during visitation, unless the custodial spouse's expenses are reduced thereby. *Baumgartner v. Moore*, 14 Va. App. 696, 419 S.E.2d 291 (1992).

The court may impute income from a second job held regularly by the obligor. In *Cochran v. Cochran*, 14 Va. App. 827, 419 S.E.2d 419 (1992), the obligor was a school teacher, and the summer income was used to establish the standard of living during the marriage.

When a husband received a personal injury settlement embracing his claims for lost earnings and earning capacity, this amount as well as his social security disability benefits should have been included in the computation of his income. The amount that the children independently received from Social Security as dependents of their disabled father should be included in his income as well, but should be credited toward his child support obligation. The court reasoned that the benefits derived from his employment, and offset his incapacity to provide for his children normally. *Colbert v. Whitaker*, 18 Va. App. 202, 442 S.E.2d 429 (1994).

See also *Commonwealth v. Skeens*, 17 Va. App. 154, 442 S.E.2d 432 (1994) (Social Security disability benefits, although constituting an independent entitlement, are in the nature of support made in lieu of a disabled employee's earnings, but the extent to which they should be credited against child support arrearage depends upon the circumstances of each case); but see *Defebo v. Defebo-Carpini*, 1993 Va. App. LEXIS 470 (disability payments made to children should not have been included in either custodial mother's or father's income to determine guideline amount).

Deviation from the guideline amounts was justified when both parties enjoyed substantial incomes, and testimony showed that "these people have taken great pride in giving their children a lot of the better things in life." *Wilson v. Wilson*, 18 Va. App. 193, 196, 442 S.E.2d 694, 696 (1994).

The events leading to husband's conviction and incarceration were entirely voluntary, and he committed destructive acts against the mother knowing of the probable consequences. Therefore, he should be considered "voluntarily unemployed" within the meaning of § 20-108.2(B)(3), and income should be imputed to him for purposes of child support. The amount of the income imputed to him would be based upon his most recent employment at $1,745 per month rather than the job of $32,000 a year he had previously left voluntarily. *Major v. Major*, 36 Va. Cir. 190 (Pittsylvania Co. 1995).

§ 23-9. Age limitation.

Generally speaking, the parent has the legal obligation to support his children only through their minority. Va. Code § 20.61. However, new amendments to Va. Code §§ 16.1-279(F) and 20-107.2 provide that the court may also order that support be paid for any child who is a full-time high school senior, not self-supporting, and living in the home of the parent seeking or receiving child support, until such child reaches the age of nineteen or graduates from high school, whichever first occurs. The jurisdiction of a court to provide for child support pursuant to a divorce is purely statutory. *Jackson v. Jackson*, 211 Va. 718, 719, 180 S.E.2d 500 (1971). After the age of majority is reached, the court's jurisdiction ceases, and the only form of relief is in cases where an agreement extends the liability. See *Eaton v. Eaton*, 215 Va. 824, 213 S.E.2d 789 (1975). However, if the obligor parent moves to another state where the duty may be extended past the child's reaching majority, since the child support obligation is modifiable, the award need not be given full faith and credit and the duty may be extended through college. *Oman v. Oman*, 333 Pa. Super. 356, 482 A.2d 606 (1984) (Virginia agreement).

A written agreement that extends payments past the age of majority will not be enforceable through the divorce court after the child reaches eighteen. In *Cutshaw v. Cutshaw*, 220 Va. 638, 261 S.E.2d 52 (1979), the parties' agreement requiring the father to pay $25 per week for child support until modified by a court or until such time as the last child left home or completed an undergraduate education was incorporated into the divorce decree. The amount was increased in a modification proceeding in 1974, and the same year was reduced again to $35. After the youngest child reached majority the wife sought enforcement of the arrearages. Although the contractual obligation to pay continued, the court lacked the jurisdiction to enforce the support obligation for any amount payable after the child turned eighteen. See also *Hosier v. Hosier*, 221 Va. 827, 273 S.E.2d 564 (1981) (no jurisdiction to award even temporary support for adult son in college). Compare *Fry v. Schwarting*, 4 Va. App. 173, 355 S.E.2d 342 (1987) (agreement incorporated and never modified).

Where the parties' agreement incorporated into the final decree of divorce provided for child support until the children reached age twenty-one or were otherwise emancipated, the obligor husband had a duty to continue making the payments after the children reached eighteen. *Paul v. Paul*, 214 Va. 651, 203 S.E.2d 123 (1974). This is to be contrasted with *Eaton v. Eaton*, 215 Va. 824, 213 S.E.2d 789 (1975), where the parties were operating under a court-ordered modification of the agreement at the time the age of majority was changed.

The court was willing to extend the noncustodial father's child support obligations past the age set by the parties' separation agreement, when the child remained in high school after reaching age 18 due in part to a learning disability. *Arnold v. Royall*, 28 Va. Cir. 205 (City of Richmond 1992). See also *Frey v. Frey*, 33 Va. Cir. 191 (Loudoun Co. 1994) (totally disabled adult child). The duty to pay while the child completes high school or reaches age 19 is now included in Va. Code Ann. §§ 16.1-278.5 and 20-107.2.

§ 23-10. Emancipation.

Emancipation may occur by operation of law when the child reaches the age of majority, see *Eaton v. Eaton*, 215 Va. 824, 213 S.E.2d 789 (1975), or when the parent accepts the child's independence from familial obligations. See, e.g., *Penn et al. v. Whitehead et al.*, 58 Va. (17 Gratt.)

503, 522 (1867). This de facto emancipation usually occurs when the child is married. See *Bennett v. Bennett*, 179 Va. 239, 243, 18 S.E.2d 911, 913 (1942); see also *Corbridge v. Corbridge*, 230 Ind. 201, 102 N.E.2d 764 (1952). In some cases, emancipation will occur when the child moves away from home and begins supporting himself or herself. *Buxton v. Bishop*, 185 Va. 1, 37 S.E.2d 755 (1946). In such cases the child will no longer have the obligation of giving the parent control over earnings, and the parent will have no corresponding duty of support.

Virginia Code § 8.01-229 and §§ 16.1-331 to 16.1-334 define emancipation according to these common law concepts. The statutes allow a minor who has attained the age of sixteen to petition for emancipation to the Juvenile and Domestic Relations Court. The court is to appoint a guardian ad litem for the child, and is authorized to issue an order of emancipation if the minor: (1) is validly married; (2) is on active duty in the armed forces; or (3) willingly lives apart from parents or guardians with their consent and is able to support himself or herself. Va. Code § 16.1-333.

A case decided before this section was enacted found that the minor in question, who was employed full-time but living at home, was emancipated. *Ware v. Ware*, 10 Va. App. 352, 391 S.E.2d 887 (1990).

See generally Katz, *Emancipating Our Children — Coming of Legal Age in America*, 7 Fam. L.Q. 211 (1973).

§ 23-11. Death of parent.

When the spouses were divorced, the husband was ordered to pay child support until further order of the court. The husband conveyed his property to his father despite an injunction restraining him from disposing of it, and died intestate. The father brought suit asking that the real estate conveyed to him be declared free from any encumbrance. The court found that the lien so created was intended to and did by the decree continue after the death of the husband and until the child reached majority. *Morris v. Henry*, 193 Va. 631, 70 S.E.2d 417 (1952):

To deny a court of equity, sitting as a court of divorce, the power to make the estate of a parent liable for the support of infant children, would in some cases make that court helpless to discharge the function of a guardian in the protection of the rights and interests of infant children of divorce....

§ 23-12. Method of payment.

In *Fearon v. Fearon*, 207 Va. 927, 931, 154 S.E.2d 165, 167 (1967), the husband was ordered to pay $400 per month for his wife and the children as part of a divorce decree. He paid money directly to the children, and then sought credit for these amounts in defense of the wife's contempt action. The supreme court found that he must pay the specified amount in accordance with the decree. Likewise, payments made to third parties to provide necessaries for the children could not be credited. *Id.* at 931, 157 S.E.2d at 168 (citing *Bradley v. Fowler*, 30 Wash. 2d 609, 192 P.2d 969 (1948)). The disbursement of the funds paid to provide a home and support for the wife and the children was her privilege and responsibility. 207 Va. at 932, 157 S.E.2d at 168. In *Gagliano v. Gagliano*, 215 Va. 447, 211 S.E.2d 62 (1975), the Virginia Supreme Court, with apparent reluctance, allowed checks made payable to the parties' son to be credited to the father's child support obligation. The court distinguished *Fearon* on the ground that this decree did not specifically require that the payments be made to the custodial mother. In *Lipscomb v. Lipscomb*, 18 Va. Cir. 244 (Chesterfield Co. 1989), the husband stopped making child support payments pursuant to an agreement with the wife under which, at her request, he assumed custody of the children for more than two years. Although he had not sought relief from the court, to award the wife arrearages would be inequitable since it was her desire that he take and support the children, and the father performed his portion of the agreement.

However, should the custodial parent refuse to use the child support for the children's benefit, and instead appropriate it to his or her own use, a constructive trust might be established for the children. *Rosenblatt v. Birnbaum*, 16 N.Y.2d 212, 264 N.Y.S.2d 521, 212 N.E.2d 37 (1965).

Legislation in 1985 and 1986 has changed the method of payment to custodial parents on public assistance, which since October 1, 1985, has been made to conform to federal provisions under the Social Security Act, 42 U.S.C. §§ 651-667. Va. Code § 20-60.5(F) provides that if the custodial parent is receiving public assistance, the Department of Social Services shall be the payee of child support. The custodial parent shall become the payee upon request that support services no longer be provided by the Department.

§ 23-13. Need for schedule.

The need for an itemized statement of expenses as opposed to mere nebulous allegations of where money is spent is demonstrated in the case of *Crosby v. Crosby*, 182 Va. 461, 29 S.E.2d 241 (1944), where the husband was unsuccessful in reducing his large alimony and support obligations despite the fact that his net income had been cut in half. See also *Conway v. Conway*, 10 Va. App. 653, 395 S.E.2d 464 (1990) (mother capable of obtaining increase when she could itemize expenses). A mother seeking an increase in child support was entitled to a discovery of documentation needed to calculate the father's current monthly gross income as well as the parties' combined monthly gross income. The father was therefore not entitled to a protective order even though he admitted that he had the ability to pay. *Harding v. Harding*, 21 Va. Cir. 130 (Fairfax Co. 1990).

§ 23-14. Parent as witness.

Any spousal incompetency to testify remaining after Va. Code § 8.01-398 (1996) does not extend to proceedings between them concerning child support. See, e.g., Va. Code § 20-88.29 (URESA action).

§ 23-15. Tax aspects of child support.

The tax consequences of child support payments upon the parties are among the factors to be considered in determining the amount of child support. Va. Code § 20-107.2.

In general, child support payments are not deductible by the payor nor taxable to the payee as income. The exception to this rule was that if the amount of a sum paid for spousal and child support actually attributable to child support was not expressly stated in the decree or agreement, the entire amount would be taxable as alimony under I.R.C. § 71. *Commissioner v. Lester*, 366 U.S. 299 (1961). However, this exception was abrogated in the Domestic Relations Tax Reform Act of 1984, which treats as child support all amounts dependent upon contingencies associated with the child rather than the spouse receiving support: for example, emancipation or reaching the age of majority.

The other major tax consideration involving child support payments is the dependency exemption. Under the 1984 Tax Reform Act, the custodial parent will normally receive the dependency exemption. The exception to this rule will occur when the decree or agreement says that the other spouse is to receive it, and the noncustodial spouse actually contributes more than half the dependent's support.

The 1986 Tax Reform Act allows unearned income of children under age fourteen to be taxed at the same rate as the custodial parent's income. I.R.C. § 1411; I.R.C. § 1(i), 1986 Tax Reform Act § 1411.

§ 23-16. Modification of support — general.

Child support may be modified when a material change in circumstances and conditions has occurred. In such cases, the burden rests upon the party seeking to alter the decree to establish such a change. *Morris v. Morris*, 216 Va. 457, 219 S.E.2d 864 (1975). The change must be shown by a preponderance of the evidence. *Hammers v. Hammers*, 216 Va. 30, 31, 216 S.E.2d 20, 21 (1975). Because of the requirement of a change in circumstances, a court order establishing an automatic yearly adjustment tied to the percentage increase or decrease in salaries at the payor's Virginia workplace was improper. *Keyser v. Keyser*, 2 Va. App. 459, 461, 345 S.E.2d 12, 14 (1986).

In a modification proceeding, written reasons need to be given for deviation from the guidelines established in Va. Code § 20-108.2. *Richardson v. Richardson*, 12 Va. App. 18, 401 S.E.2d 894 (1991). See also *Maya v. Maya*, 1996 Va. App. LEXIS 8; *Jordan v. Jordan*, 23 Va. Cir. 470 (Fairfax Co. 1991); and *May v. May*, 24 Va. Cir. 407 (City of Charlottesville 1991). In *Milligan v. Milligan*, 12 Va. App. 982, 407 S.E.2d 702 (1991), the court of appeals held that if the parties' income changes so that the amount awarded is no longer within the statutory guidelines, the material or substantial change of circumstance rule is no longer required as a condition precedent to obtaining a modification of child support. See also *Kaplan v. Kaplan*, 1996 Va. App. LEXIS 26 (father's employer ceased its business operations in Virginia; bankruptcy of corporation and financial difficulties that caused the father to renegotiate the arrangement supported the finding that the reduction was involuntary); *Rawlings v. Rawlings*, 20 Va. App. 663, 460 S.E.2d 581 (1995)(father's participation in his trade union's strike did not constitute voluntary underemployment, and thus was grounds for warranting a reduction in child support); *In re Gregory*, 22 Va. Cir. 173 (City of Charlottesville 1990).

If a parent seeks a change in a child support obligation set by a trial court before July 1, 1989, the party need only establish a "significant variance" between the presumptive amount of child support under Code § 20-108.2 and the amount originally awarded. If a modification is ordered, the Code states that the modification will not be retroactive, but will date only from the time that notice of petition has been given to the responding party. *O'Brien v. Rose*, 14 Va. App. 960, 420 S.E.2d 246 (1992). See also *Herbert v. Herbert*, 33 Va. Cir. 155 (Fairfax Co. 1994).

However, the dependent spouse must carry the burden of demonstrating a change of circumstances. The dependent spouse cannot merely allege an increase in the obligor's income and a decrease in expenses. *McElwrath v. McElwrath*, 1993 Va. App. LEXIS 133.

An agreement between the parents cannot prevent the court from modifying a support award. In *Hogge v. Hogge*, 1993 Va. App. LEXIS 121, the trial court first established the guideline amount, and then considered whether the amount agreed upon by the parents would better serve the interests of the parties. The court did not commit error when it settled on the presumptive sum found in the guidelines. However, the trial court could calculate an increase beginning with the formula included in the parties' separation agreement. *Claytor v. Suter*, 1995 Va. App. LEXIS 507. In a modification proceeding, the trial judge is not required to specify in writing why an earlier award of child support should continue to deviate from the guidelines when there has been no material change justifying a modification of the earlier award. *Crabtree v. Crabtree*, 17 Va. App. 81, 435 S.E.2d 883 (1993).

A noncustodial parent may have to reimburse the other parent for extraordinary medical expenses incurred after the original award and before a modification petition has been filed, including amounts for personal expenses the custodial parent incurred during a minor child's illness. *Carter v. Thornhill*, 19 Va. App. 501, 453 S.E.2d 295 (1995). The change from one private school to a more expensive one did not constitute an adequate reason to increase the noncustodial father's child support obligation. *Solomond v. Ball*, 1996 Va. App. LEXIS 330.

A court order incorporating a settlement agreement was amended to reflect the larger payments already being made voluntarily by the noncustodial father. Modifications as each child reached majority should still affect the amount due. The reductions, made according to the plan of the original agreement, should simply be subtracted from the revised as opposed to the original amount. *Schmidt v. Schmidt*, 6 Va. App. 501, 370 S.E.2d 311 (1988).

For example, additional costs of orthodontic care, day camp and music lessons are all expenses attributable to the increased needs of growing children, which, without a substantial change in the custodial spouse's income, warranted a modification of the original decree so that the wife was required for the first time to make support payments. *Id.* See also *Barnes v. Craig*, 202 Va. 229, 117 S.E.2d 63 (1960).

The court may not cancel or modify arrears in support money, but only may change future installments. *Cofer v. Cofer*, 205 Va. 834, 839, 140 S.E.2d 663, 667 (1965). Past-due installments are vested and are immune from change. Nor will laches bar collection of a unitary sum awarded for alimony and child support. The court also found that the requirement that a decree-based modification be based upon a change of circumstances under *Jacobs v. Jacobs*, 219 Va. 993, 254 S.E.2d 56 (1979), should not be applied retroactively. *Barnett v. Barnett*, 24 Va. Cir. 282 (Campbell Co. 1991).

§ 23-17. Change of circumstances.

The father seeking a reduction in his child support obligation must make a full and clear disclosure relating to his ability to pay, and must show that his lack of ability is not voluntary or due to his neglect. *Hammers v. Hammers*, 216 Va. 30, 216 S.E.2d 20 (1975). See also *Ryan v. Kramer*, 21 Va. App. 217, 463 S.E.2d 328 (1995); *Wirth v. Wirth*, 1993 Va. App. LEXIS 131; *Richards v. Richards*, 1994 Va. App. LEXIS 376 (husband involuntarily terminated); and *Barnhill v. Brooks*, 15 Va. App. 696, 427 S.E.2d 209 (1993) (finding that underemployment was voluntary but allowing modification even though obligor was also in arrears in making payments). Another case in which a parent in arrears was allowed to seek modification is *Buland v. Buland*, 25 Va. Cir. 280 (Loudoun Co. 1991). But see *Luciani v. Luciani*, 1995 Va. App. LEXIS 264 (no reduction where father's voluntary misconduct caused him to lose his job); *Smyth v. Smyth*, 1995 Va. App. LEXIS 724 (1995) (father's conviction and incarceration for money laundering were "the direct consequence of his voluntary wrongful act"). The change from a salaried position to one compensated on a commission basis, with less income to the responsible parent than anticipated, constituted a change in circumstances justifying a reduction in child support. *Antonelli v. Antonelli*, 11 Va. App. 89, 396 S.E.2d 698 (1990). Evidence sufficient to reduce a child support obligation was not shown in *Gaunoux v. Gaunoux*, 19 Va. Cir. 22 (Fairfax Co. 1989).

The fact that the husband has remarried and has another family dependent upon him for support is entitled to little, if any consideration. *Id.* at 32, 216 S.E.2d at 21; see also *Morris v. Morris*, 216 Va. 457, 219 S.E.2d 864 (1975); cf. *Treger v. Treger*, 212 Va. 538, 186 S.E.2d 82 (1972) (sufficient change when income decreased from $28,000 to $12,000). However, it was error for a court ordering support for a father's two illegitimate children to ignore the existence of the two children born of his current marriage. *Zubricki v. Motter*, 12 Va. App. 999, 406 S.E.2d 672 (1991). A father's income should be reduced by obligations to his other children. *Hallman v. Hallman*, 25 Va. Cir. 144 (Fairfax Co. 1991). A noncustodial father could also seek a deviation from guideline amounts based upon the birth of his new child. *Evans v. Division of Child Support Enforcement*, 1996 Va. App. LEXIS 93. But see *May v. May*, 31 Va. Cir. 480 (Clarke Co. 1982) (second family, investments, and lower level of unemployment).

Proof of a change in circumstances was not required in order to have support adjusted to conform to the guidelines of Va. Code § 20-108.2, which was enacted following the parties' divorce. *Milligan v. Milligan*, 12 Va. App. 982, 407 S.E.2d 702 (1991). See also *Hiner v. Hadeed*, 15 Va. App. 575, 425 S.E.2d 811 (1993).

If there is a change of custody, child support may be modified even though the original payments were structured for tax purposes as a unitary sum in lieu of child support and alimony. *Carter v. Carter*, 215 Va. 475, 481, 211 S.E.2d 253, 258 (1975) (decided before Domestic Relations Tax Reform Act of 1984 removed the tax advantage to the obligor presented by *Commissioner v. Lester*, 366 U.S. 299 (1961)). In a case where there has been a change of custody, the unitary sum will be apportioned between spousal and child support. See, e.g., *Jarrell v. Jarrell*, 1994 Va. App. LEXIS 672. However, a mere increase in child support engendered by a change in financial circumstances would not require such an apportionment. *Wickham v. Wickham*, 215 Va. 694, 213 S.E.2d 750 (1975). When a husband paid child and spousal support as a lump sum, with no method for determining how it was to be allocated, the husband was required to continue paying until relieved of this responsibility by a court. *Taylor v. Taylor*, 10 Va. App. 681, 394 S.E.2d 864 (1990).

A mother's letter waiving the husband's child support obligation while she and the child were in Louisiana did not relieve the husband of his duty to make the payments, even though he believed that she had to petition the court upon her return to Virginia to reinstate payments. *Goodpasture v. Goodpasture*, 7 Va. App. 55, 371 S.E.2d 845 (1988).

The intentional withholding of visitation of a child from the other parent without just cause may constitute a material change in circumstances justifying a change of custody in the discretion of the court. Va. Code § 20-108. The statute does not provide that withholding of visitation would be a reason for decreasing or terminating child support. As the court reasoned in *Commonwealth v. Hogge*, 16 Va. App. 520, 431 S.E.2d 656 (1993):

> Child support provides for the economic best interest of a dependent child; it is not a weapon with which to punish a parent. Accordingly, we hold that a trial court may not deviate from the presumptive amount of child support because a custodial parent has denied a noncustodial parent visitation with their child.

However, where the parties divorced when the child was three years old, the wife concealed him until he was in college, and she then sought arrearages in child support, no arrearages will be ordered paid. *Hartman v. Hartman*, 33 Va. Cir. 373 (Fairfax Co. 1994).

See generally Czapanskiy, *Child Support and Visitation: Rethinking the Connections*, 20 Rutgers L.J. 619 (1989).

§ 23-18. Jurisdiction for modification.

The court in a divorce action retains continuing jurisdiction to modify the portions of its decree dealing with child support during the minority of the child. Va. Code § 20-108.2. Since personal jurisdiction was already obtained in the divorce action, notice only need be given in the modification proceeding. See, e.g., *Glading v. Furman*, 282 Md. 200, 383 A.2d 398 (1978); *State ex rel. Ravitz v. Fox*, 273 S.E.2d 370 (W. Va. 1980).

Under the Uniform Reciprocal Enforcement of Support Act, Va. Code § 20-88.12 et seq., a valid order of a foreign court must be given comity and recognized as a Virginia decree. *Scott v. Sylvester*, 220 Va. 182, 257 S.E.2d 774 (1979). However, if the foreign court gives no consideration or effect to a prior Virginia decree, and, more importantly, if the foreign proceedings were uncontested, the foreign decree may be modified as to child support provisions without a showing of changed circumstances. *Osborne v. Osborne*, 215 Va. 205, 207 S.E.2d 875 (1974). However, the registration of a foreign order in Virginia, with service upon the obligor outside the state, will not give Virginia in personam jurisdiction. *Stephens v. Stephens*, 229 Va. 610, 331 S.E.2d 484 (1985) (spousal support).

In *Rippy v. Rippy*, 13 Va. Cir. 188 (Caroline Co. 1988), the court held that a father was under continuing obligation to support his child, which could not be satisfied by payments made directly to the child.

A transfer of a child support case to the juvenile and domestic relations court for enforcement purposes does not divest the circuit court of jurisdiction to modify the child support and visitation. *Crabtree v. Crabtree*, 17 Va. App. 81, 435 S.E.2d 883 (1993). The court of appeals would not adopt a construction of the statutes "that would needlessly require issues to be remanded to a court not of record before they can be heard in the circuit court." *Id.* at 886.

§ 23-19. Jurisdiction for enforcement.

Because additional defenses may be involved in a support proceeding, the defendant must be given an opportunity to appear and to contest the judgment. *Sistare v. Sistare*, 218 U.S. 1 (1910). Long-arm jurisdiction may be appropriate. For example, the husband in *Bosserman v. Bosserman*, 9 Va. App. 1, 384 S.E.2d 104 (1989), was a 25 percent owner of a closely-held family corporation. The bylaws provided for buy-out of stock based upon the "true book value" of the corporation, $28,032 at the time of divorce. The wife's accountant, however, placed the true market value of the farm owned by the corporation at $174,600. The court of appeals followed the majority rule that a buy-out provision does not control the determination of value when the other spouse did not consent or was not otherwise bound by its terms. The reasoning behind this rule is that buy-out provisions do not necessarily reflect the intrinsic worth of the stock to the parties. However, the limitation of alienability created by the restricting agreement necessarily affects the actual marketability of the stock, and thus its value. The valuation accepted by the court of appeals was based upon the corporation's net assets, here the farm.

When the divorce court did not have personal jurisdiction over the husband, who was served in another state, it could incorporate the parties' agreement. However, the court did not have power to enter an enforceable support order, so the husband could not be held in contempt for violating the support provisions of the decree. *Price v. Price*, 17 Va. App. 105, 435 S.E.2d 652 (1993). For in personam jurisdiction permitting enforcement, the pleadings must at least allege a connection to Virginia recognized by the long-arm statute. However, the husband could register a foreign state's support order obtained under URESA where his "duty of support" arose from the parties' separation agreement.

§ 23-20. Uniform Reciprocal Enforcement of Support Act and UIFSA.

The Uniform Reciprocal Enforcement of Support Act, Va. Code §§ 20-88.12 et seq., provides that a foreign judgment of support may be registered in Virginia and enforced exactly as though it were a Virginia decree.

For an example of a foreign order under URESA registered for enforcement in Virginia, see *Price v. Price*, 17 Va. App. 105, 435 S.E.2d 652 (1993). In this case, the noncustodial father's duty of support did not arise from the divorce proceeding, which had no in personam jurisdiction, but rather from the parties' separation agreement. See also *Trevino v. Talmage*, 17 Va. App. 514, 438 S.E.2d 489 (1993) (The facts that Virginia established a support obligation before Michigan, that the payor father was a Virginia resident when the Michigan court acted, and that the payee mother should not be permitted to forum shop were considerations that might determine the enforceability of conflicting provisions, but were not sufficient to deny registration of valid final support orders.) Foreign orders should be registered in the juvenile and domestic relations circuit court, according to Va. Code § 20-88.32.

Virginia adopted the Interstate Family Support Act (UIFSA) in new Va. Code §§ 20-88.32 et seq. (1994). The Act is similar to the Uniform Reciprocal Support Act in many respects. The Act does establish some new concepts. The UIFSA establishes uniform long-arm jurisdiction over nonresidents and provides for discovery and testimony once jurisdiction is obtained. Va. Code §§ 20-88.36, 20-88.59, 20-88.61. The UIFSA may only be used for spousal and child support proceedings. Visitation issues cannot be raised in child support proceedings. Va. Code § 20-88.48.

The choice of law for interpretation of support orders registered under the UIFSA is that of the state issuing the underlying support orders, except that the longer of different statutes of limitation applies. Continuing exclusive jurisdiction is established, so that only one support order is normally effective at any given time.

The UIFSA provides that a support order may be mailed directly to an obligor's employer, triggering wage withholding without a hearing unless the employee objects or the parties agree to an alternative payment agreement, or one of the parties demonstrates good cause why there should not be immediate withholding. The employer forwards payments to the department for recording and disbursement to the obligee. The obligor's state may administratively enforce the order, although all judicial enforcement begins with the registration of the existing order in the responding state. See Va. Code § 20-79.2.

The only tribunal that can modify a support order is the one having continuing exclusive jurisdiction except in narrowly defined circumstances. If both parties no longer reside in the issuing state, a tribunal with personal jurisdiction over both or with power given by their agreement may modify. Va. Code §§ 20-88.39, 20-88.40, 20-88.68.

The UIFSA authorizes establishment of parentage in interstate proceedings even when not accompanied by a support proceeding. Registration of foreign child support orders under UIFSA takes place in the juvenile and domestic relations district court. Va. Code §§ 20.88.32 and 20.88.67(A).

§ 23-21. Enforcement of child support.

Recent legislation puts Virginia in conformance with federal statutes. The statutes provide for collection of arrearages through garnishment, and requires that all payors be notified that payroll deductions may be made without amending the order. Va. Code §§ 20-60.3, 20-79.1.

At the birth of a child, the social security number of each parent shall be reported in the manner prescribed and on forms furnished by the state registrar. 42 U.S.C. § 405; Va. Code § 32.1-257.1.

The Department of Social Services may withhold child support payments from banks, savings institutions, other financial institutions, or broker-dealers where the support debtor has an individual or joint account. Va. Code § 63.1-260. Virginia Code § 20-79.3 sets forth the necessary contents for orders for withholding a support debtor's earnings as an employee. At the time of employment, the employer shall ask each new employee whether there is an outstanding child support order. If the answer is yes, then the employer is to begin withholding. Va. Code § 60.2-114.1.

In cases transferred from the courts to the Department of Social Services, the payee shall be deemed to have executed an authorization to seek or enforce a support obligation with the Department's Division of Child Support Enforcement unless the payee specifically indicates that the Division's services are not desired. Va. Code § 20-65.5.

The Department of Social Services is to pay interest at the legal rate on support payments it receives, where the recipient is not on public assistance, if the amount received is not paid out within thirty days of the end of the months in which received, and the accrued interest exceeds five dollars. Va. Code §§ 20-60.5, 20-78.2, 63.1-250.1. Amendments to Va. Code § 16.1-279(F) provide that in any determination of a support obligation, the support obligation as it becomes due and unpaid creates a judgment by operation of law. Such judgment becomes a lien against real estate only when docketed in the county or city where the real estate is located.

The Department of Child Support Enforcement shall have the authority to assess and recover attorneys' fees from the absent responsible parent when the Department has had a proceeding to enforce the child support obligations. It shall also have the authority to assess and recover the actual costs of blood testing against the absent responsible parent, and the actual costs of intercept programs. The fees and costs may be collected using any mechanism provided by Chapter 63. Va. Code § 63.1-274.10.

An attorney representing a husband in a claim against the Division of Child Support Enforcement should not accept or continue representation of the ex-wife, who was petitioning for child support against a man who allegedly fathered her two younger children. The conflict of interest arose because of the substantial relatedness of each client's matter, together with the fact that the paternity issue had not yet been fully resolved. Virginia State Bar Ethics Opinion No. 1279 (September 21, 1989).

An attorney may not advertise that he would represent clients in need of legal advice for the collection of child or spousal support arrearages on a contingent fee basis, unless the advertisement clearly indicated that such an arrangement is only permissible where the child support arrearages have been reduced to judgment. The attorney must still explain to individual clients before accepting employment that the costs and expenses of litigation and the case file remain the client's responsibility. Virginia State Bar Ethics Opinion No. 1229 (April 25, 1989).

Section 20-87 provides that when a chief of police or sheriff becomes satisfied that a person is violating the directions given by a judge for his or her conduct, such officer shall have the authority to arrest such person after issuance of a proper capias or warrant. Another possible remedy is the addition in Va. Code § 20-79.2 of the immediate payroll deduction unless the obligee and obligor agree to an alternative arrangement. Earnings, under § 63.1-250, includes current or future income due from the person's employer, unemployment compensation benefits, workers' compensation benefits, debts owed the responsible person, and any incomes or profits due the responsible person from any source, specifically including gambling, lotteries, prizes, or any other windfall. The procedure for obtaining immediate withholding is set forth in § 63.1-258.1. After issuance of an order under § 20-79, as amended in 1988, the court may upon the motion of any party or on its own motion transfer any matters covered by the decree to any juvenile and domestic relations district court that constitutes a more appropriate forum.

Although a responsible parent need not be present in order for reimbursement to the state of child support payments to be determined, there can be no collection of the money prior to notice and a right to hearing and appeal. *Commonwealth v. Broadnax*, 18 Va. Cir. 276 (City of Richmond, 1989) (due process was provided in this case).

As with spousal support, since a duty is involved, enforcement of child support obligations may be through special remedies, such as contempt, see, e.g., *Boaze v. Commonwealth*, 165 Va. 786, 793, 183 S.E. 263, 266 (1935), and also through the more traditional remedies of garnishment, see, e.g., *In re Marriage of Stutz*, 126 Cal. App. 3d 1038, 179 Cal. Rptr. 312 (1981); see generally attachment of property, Va. Code §§ 20-114 and 8.01-460 (lien if unpaid upon obligor's property). Although a payee may employ other enforcement remedies under URESA or the parties' agreement, contempt is not available unless there was personal jurisdiction in the divorce proceeding. *Price v. Price*, 17 Va. App. 105, 435 S.E.2d 652 (1993).

At the time defendant is found in contempt, there must be an ability to pay, or there will be imprisonment for debt. *Barrett v. Barrett*, 470 Pa. 253, 368 A.2d 616 (1977). However, the inability to pay must be involuntary. See, e.g., *Branch v. Branch*, 144 Va. 244, 132 S.E. 303 (1926) (defendant husband able to work as laborer since healthy and young); *D. v. M.*, 107 Misc. 2d 217, 433 N.Y.S.2d 715 (1980). Where the court may hold a parent guilty of criminal contempt for failure to pay child support, a jury trial is required. *Kessler v. Commonwealth*, 18 Va. App. 14, 441 S.E.2d 223 (1994).

The husband could not prove that the wife made any representations concerning discontinuing spousal support, and therefore establishing his defenses of equitable estoppel or waiver. *West v. West*, 1995 Va. App. LEXIS 582. Contempt may result in commission to a correctional facility, to a work release program, or to perform public service work. Va. Code § 20-115. If a noncustodial parent in arrears fails to post an appeal bond, the circuit court is not required on its own motion to bifurcate the issues and determine whether he intended to separately pursue an appeal from a civil contempt citation. *McCall v. Commonwealth*, 20 Va. App. 348, 457 S.E.2d 389 (1995).

The lien made by a decree, order, or judgment for support and maintenance of a child may be released upon agreement of all obligees, provided they are adults and agree to the release of the specified real property. Va. Code § 8.01-460.

The wife obtained a pendente lite unitary award for spousal and child support that was to continue until further order of the court, and the husband later obtained a final divorce. The decree reserved custody, support, and property division for later decision. The husband died eight years later, and his estate was subject to a lien for unpaid payments under the temporary support order. *Duke v. Duke*, 239 Va. 501, 391 S.E.2d 77 (1990).

Posting of an appeal bond is required in proceedings from the juvenile and domestic relations court, even if the responsible parent is found in civil contempt of court. *Scheer v. Scheer*, 10 Va. App. 338, 392 S.E.2d 201 (1990).

Defenses might be based upon a nonability to pay, see, e.g., *Branch v. Branch*, 144 Va. 244, 132 S.E. 303 (1926) (defendant husband unsuccessful in defense since healthy and able to work as day laborer), or satisfaction of the original order. The failure of the custodial spouse to abide by other portions of the decree will not allow the noncustodial spouse to cease making payments. For example, although the husband argued that since the wife refused him visitation, he was not liable for amounts payable for her support, the court construed the payments required by an incorporated property settlement agreement to be in fact child support rather than alimony. In any event, the parties should comply with the terms of a divorce decree until modified by the court's further order. It was for the court, not the husband, to determine whether the payment of the "household maintenance" item had been forfeited by the alleged breach of the terms of the settlement agreement and the decree by the wife. *Newton v. Newton*, 202 Va. 515, 118 S.E.2d 656 (1961).

Nor could overpayments be set off against any required future payments for child support. *Id.* at 518-19, 118 S.E.2d at 658-59 (citing 17A Am. Jur. Divorce and Separation § 876 at 65). His remedy if the circumstances varied was to apply to the court for a change in the terms of the decree.

§ 23-22. Laches.

Acquiescence of the custodial parent, even though for a very long period of time, will not preclude enforcement by the appropriate court. See *Richardson v. Moore*, 217 Va. 422, 229 S.E.2d 864 (1976) (twenty-five years after husband unilaterally reduced child support payments, the wife was able to enforce the decree). See also *Johnson v. Johnson*, 1 Va. App. 330, 338 S.E.2d 353 (1986) (ten-year delay in seeking support arrearages did not constitute laches because initial decree was lawful).

CHAPTER 24

Child Custody

§ 24-1. Introduction.

In Virginia, "the welfare of the infant is the primary, paramount, and controlling consideration of the court in all controversies between parents over the custody of their minor children." *Mullen v. Mullen*, 188 Va. 259, 269, 49 S.E.2d 349, 354 (1948). See also *Coffee v. Black*, 82 Va. 567, 569 (1866). In fact, "the right of a parent to custody of its minor child is subordinate to the right of a child to a custodial care of a parent." *McCreery v. McCreery*, 218 Va. 352, 237 S.E.2d 167 (1977). This emphasis runs contrary to the perception of many clients that it is the parents' rights that are of concern during custody litigation. The emphasis upon the children, as opposed to the parents, colors many recent substantive and procedural developments in the law of custody. A recently

363

reported circuit court decision outlines the problems the court faces in custody cases:

> A heavy responsibility rests on the court whenever it must make a decision which will sever for one parent or the other the "tender ties of affection," but when this unfortunate necessity arises, neither sentimentality nor sympathy for either parent should alter a course directed to promoting the rights of children to have the more proper award of their custody made. *Shockey v. Shockey*, 30 Va. Cir. 493, 498 (Frederick Co. 1979).

Guardianship is distinguished from custody in *O'Neil v. O'Neil*, 18 Va. App. 674, 446 S.E.2d 475 (1994). According to that case, guardianship of the person and estate of a child entails a broader power to have custody of the ward and the right to take possession of the ward's estate to pay for the ward's maintenance and education. Unlike the legal custodian, the guardian is a fiduciary or guarantor of the child.

This "best interests" standard does not require a showing of unfitness on the part of a parent, although cases certainly refer to unfitness and in fact state that evidence of unfitness must be clear and convincing. See, e.g., *Moore v. Moore*, 212 Va. 153, 156, 183 S.E.2d 172, 174 (1971).

Originally, a father was entitled to the custody of his child when a fit and suitable person, unless custody was voluntarily relinquished. *Coffee v. Black*, 82 Va. 567 (1866) (action against sister-in-law); *Latham v. Latham*, 71 Va. (30 Gratt.) 307 (1878) (husband given custody when no divorce granted to wife). After this, the mother for many years was found to be "the natural custodian of her child of tender years," *Mullen v. Mullen*, 188 Va. 259,270-71, 49 S.E.2d 349, 354 (1948), and thus was given custody if she was fit and all other things were equal. However, Va. Code § 20-107.2 now provides that there is no legal presumption in favor of either parent. See also *Winoe v. Winoe*, 26 Va. Cir. 420 (Henrico Co. 1978). The principle of *Moore v. Moore*, 212 Va. 153, 183 S.E.2d 172 (1971), is that a rebuttable inference exists that when the mother is fit, and other things are equal, she should have custody of a child of tender years. See *Harper v. Harper*, 217 Va. 477, 229 S.E.2d 875 (1976) (custody awarded to mother when both parents were fit and proper persons to have custody). In fact, therefore, although the statute has eliminated any conclusive presumption based upon the gender of the parent and the child's age, a strong preference for the mother exists in many cases where the children are very young, particularly if they are girls. This preference of course may be overcome by evidence showing that all things are not equal and that in fact the child would be better off in the custody of the father.

The parties' contract regarding custody will not prevent the court from exercising its power to alter custody. See, e.g., *Hammers v. Hammers*, 216 Va. 30, 31, 216 S.E.2d 20, 21 (1975) (child support); *Campbell v. Campbell*, 203 Va. 61, 64, 122 S.E.2d 658, 661 (1961). See generally Sharp, *Modification of Agreement-Based Custody Decrees: Unitary or Dual Standard?*, 68 Va. L. Rev. 1263 (1982).

The decision of the trial judge, who has had the opportunity to see the parties and hear witnesses testify, is entitled to great respect, *Brown v. Brown*, 218 Va. 196, 200-01, 237 S.E.2d 89, 92 (1977), and will not be reversed unless there has been an abuse of discretion. A parent may appeal an order entered by a lower court even though counsel has "seen and agreed to" the order, according to *Cox v. Cox*, 16 Va. App. 146, 428 S.E.2d 515 (1993).

The factors involved in custody cases, and definitions of joint and shared custody, appear in Va. Code Ann. § 20-124.1—20-124.3. In any appropriate case, the court may refer the parents to a dispute resolution evaluation session, according to new § 20-124.4.

See generally Robert Cochran, *The Search for Guidance in Determining the Best Interests of the Child at Divorce*, 20 U. Rich. L. Rev. 1 (1985); Martha Fineman, *Dominant Discourse, Professional Language and Legal Change in Child Custody Decisionmaking*, 101 Harv. L. Rev. 727 (1988); Jerry McCant, *The Cultural Contradiction of Fathers as Nonparents*, 21 Fam. L.Q. 127 (1987); Robert Mnookin, *Child Custody Adjudications: Judicial Functions in the Fact of Indeterminacy*, 39 Law & Contemp. Probs. 226 (1975); John Murray, *Improving Parent-Child Relationships Within the Divorced Family: A Call for Legal Reform*, 19 U. Mich. J. Law Reform 563 (1986). See also Stephen B. Bershing, *"Entreat Me Not to Leave Thee": Bottoms v. Bottoms and the Custody Rights of Gay and Lesbian Parents*, 3 Wm. & Mary Bill Rts. J. 289 (1994); Barry M. Parsons, Note, *Bottoms v. Bottoms: Erasing the Presumption Favoring a Natural Parent Over Third Parties — What Makes This Mother Unfit?* 2 Geo. Mason Independent L. Rev. 457 (1994).

§ 24-2. Who may seek custody?

At common law, the mother of an illegitimate child was its natural custodian, and frequently the unwed father was presumed unfit as a matter of law and therefore was given no notice when the mother's rights were terminated before adoption. The United States Supreme Court, in *Stanley v. Illinois*, 405 U.S. 645 (1972), held that such presumptions violated the fourteenth amendment, and that hearings would be required where a substantial relationship existed between parent and child. Later cases suggested that where such a relationship existed, the father could veto an attempted adoption by a stepparent and seek adoption himself, *Caban v. Mohammed*, 441 U.S. 380 (1979), but that an unwed father could not seek to block a stepparent adoption without such a relationship. *Quilloin v. Walcott*, 434 U.S. 246 (1978). See also *Michael H. v. Gerald D.*, 491 U.S. 110 (1989), where the Court held that a married woman's lover was not entitled to a paternity hearing although blood tests showed that in all probability he was the child's father. There have been many Virginia cases dealing with custody disputes other than those between husband and wife pursuant to divorce. In *Commonwealth v. Hayes*, 215 Va. 49, 205 S.E.2d 644 (1974), the Supreme Court of Virginia heard a case considering an unwed father's fitness to take custody when the mother put the child up for adoption. Since the father had never taken any prior interest in the child nor had contact with her, and since his plans for the future were unsatisfactory and speculative, his rights in the child were terminated. The Court found him unfit to have custody. See also *In re Custody of Sloan*, 25 Va. Cir. 227 (Amherst Co. 1991) (father found unfit since he had abandoned children, had disobeyed court orders and exhibited a very unstable lifestyle, including at least two concurrent marriages; custody was awarded to foster parents, and father denied visitation rights).

The right of the natural father of an illegitimate child was also superior to that of the child's maternal grandparents. *Hayes v. Strauss*, 151 Va. 136,141, 144 S.E. 432, 434 (1978). But see *Forbes v. Henry*, 204 Va. 712, 133 S.E.2d 533 (1963), where the maternal grandparents of an illegitimate child were given custody when the natural father was "immoral," since the grandparents were fit and "the welfare of the child is to be regarded more highly than the technical legal rights of the parent." *Id.* at 716, 133 S.E.2d at 536. See also *Patrick v. Byerley*, 228 Va. 691, 325 S.E.2d 99 (1985) (holding that former stepmother ought to be awarded custody since natural mother had abandoned child); and *Bailes v. Sours*, 231 Va. 96, 340 S.E.2d 824 (1986), which held that the presumption favoring a parent over a nonparent was not conclusive, but could be rebutted by clear and convincing evidence of: (1) parental unfitness; (2) a previous divestiture order; (3) voluntary relinquishment; (4) abandonment; or (5) a finding of "special facts and circumstances ... constituting an extraordinary reason for taking a child from its parent, or parents." *Id.* at 100, 340 S.E.2d at 287.

In *Bailes*, the natural mother was a virtual stranger to her son, who had lived with his father and stepmother for eight years before his father's death. The boy considered his stepmother his mother and strongly desired to remain with her. In the opinion of a psychologist who testified, a change of custody would have a significant harmful impact on the child. Custody was left with the stepmother. In contrast to the situation in *Bailes*, when a father was not shown to be unfit, it was not proper to award legal custody to the mother with physical custody to her foster parents. *Terrell v. Hackett*, 1993 Va. App. LEXIS 487.

However, in *Tetrault v. Garber*, 1993 Va. App. LEXIS 430, a stepfather was permitted to adopt an orphan although the child's grandparents also wished to adopt. The child had lived for five years with the stepfather, and considered him his father. In *Nicklaus v. Strong*, 1995 Va. App. LEXIS 737, the man who was identified as the child's father on the birth certificate obtained custody although he was not the biological father. The biological mother had abused the child, the child thought Strong was her father, and Strong and his wife offered a family with "security, stability, constancy, and love." The child's grandmother was awarded custody in a contested dispute with the child's mother in *Bottoms v. Bottoms*, 1995 Va. LEXIS 43, 457 S.E.2d 102. Among other things, the child had spent 70 percent of his time with the grandmother and 30 percent with his mother. Further, the mother "refused to subordinate her own desires and priorities to the child's welfare." She moved frequently, misused welfare funds, and participated in illicit relationships with both men and the woman with whom she presently lived. See also *O'Neil v. O'Neil*, 18 Va. App. 674, 446 S.E.2d 475 (1994) (private petition for transfer of guardianship; action between parents and grandparents).

Where no special facts and circumstances existed, although the child had resided for some time in the home of her maternal great aunt, when the parents were able to resume custody of the child, "there was nothing to justify a finding that the best interest of [the child] would be served" by separating her from her parents and siblings. *Smith v. Pond*, 5 Va. App. 161, 360 S.E.2d 885 (1987).

After the custodial mother died, the maternal grandparents were successful in contesting a change of custody to the father, since the child's best interests were paramount, and the child would be a complete stranger to the father's new wife and her teenage children, with whom the child would have to share a room. *In re Custody of Forrest*, 13 Va. Cir. 424 (City of Roanoke 1970). However, even though the child was in the physical custody of the paternal grandmother, custody was given to a now more adult and remarried mother. *Cunningham v. Crummett*, 13 Va. Cir. 495 (Bath Co. 1980). Further, in *Mason v. Moon*, 9 Va. App. 217, 385 S.E.2d 242 (1989), custody was awarded to the natural mother over the paternal grandmother with whom the custodial father and child had lived since the child's parents separated. The natural mother was favored despite the fact that only thirteen days after the father's death she had married the man who had killed the child's father. See also *Elder v. Evans*, 16 Va. App. 60, 427 S.E.2d 745 (1993), where the natural father sought custody from people with whom mother had placed the child. He was granted custody since despite a number of problems at the beginning, he was now a caring and loving parent, his family life was appropriate, and the child showed an ability to adapt to the family. Likewise, in *Roberts v. Williams*, 1996 Va. App. LEXIS 103, the natural father was able to obtain custody since he had made efforts to gain custody despite placement of the child with the mother's first cousin.

A natural parent may not seek to terminate his own parental rights, even if the custodial parent has actively encouraged the children to be alienated from their father. *Tallent v. Rosenbloom*, 32 Va. Cir. 61 (Fairfax Co. 1993). See also *Walker v. Fagg*, 11 Va. App. 581, 400 S.E.2d 208, 11 Va. App. 581 (1991), where the father was awarded custody over both sets of grandparents despite the fact that he had killed the children's mother and was previously an unfit parent. The award of custody to the father was on the basis that his life "had experienced a complete turnaround," and was tentative, subject to vacation should his change of lifestyle prove not to be permanent. Visitation may be extended to stepparents and former stepparents under Va. Code §§ 16.1-241(A)(6) and 16.1-278.15(B) (juvenile and domestic relations district courts) and § 20-107.2 (circuit courts). For a case before the new provisions in which a stepparent was allowed visitation rights, see *Arnold v. Newberry*, 24 Va. Cir. 431 (Washington Co. 1991).

When, after blood tests, DNA testing excluded Mr. Vaughan as the biological father, he sought continued visitation privileges. The trial court held that the Code does not grant visitation privileges to persons other than "family members." *In re Jones*, 26 Va. Cir. 165 (Amherst Co. 1991).

When a child is adopted after his parents' rights are terminated involuntarily, the natural parent may not seek custody or visitation rights. Nor may a person convicted of sexual assault seek custodial or visitation privileges with a child conceived as the result of the assault. Va. Code §§ 16.1-241 and 20-107.2. Custody orders may be entered even when no divorce is pending. In such cases, there may be orders pendente lite directed to any person with a legitimate interest who is a party. The custody and visitation orders in these non-divorce proceedings shall be made in accordance with §§ 20-124 et seq. Pendente lite orders shall have no presumptive effect and shall not determine the ultimate outcome of the case.

Virginia Code § 20-124.1 allows "persons with a legitimate interest" to seek custody and visitation. This term is to be broadly construed to accommodate the child's best interest, and includes, but is not limited to, grandparents, stepparents, former stepparents, blood relatives, and family members. The term does *not* include persons whose parental rights have been involuntarily terminated when the child has subsequently been legally adopted or parents involved in statutory rape or rape when the child has been conceived of such violations.

§ 24-3. Jurisdiction.

One of the jurisdiction questions in custody cases concerns subject matter jurisdiction. In extreme circumstances, such as when both parents had died in a car accident, custody jurisdiction may attach when the child is present even though both parents are absent. *Falco v. Grills*, 209 Va. 115, 161 S.E.2d 713 (1968). The presence of both parents within the state, or at any rate, personal jurisdiction over them, is necessary for a valid custody decree under *May v. Anderson*, 345 U.S. 528 (1953). This is because a custody decree concerns personal rights (of the parents) at least as important as the property rights that undoubtedly require personal jurisdiction. To the same effect, see *Bailey v. Bailey*, 172 Va. 18, 21, 200 S.E. 622, 623 (1939). Nor will an uncontested foreign decree be given full force and effect. *Osborne v. Osborne*, 215 Va. 205, 207 S.E.2d 875 (1974) (child support).

Personal jurisdiction may be obtained under the long-arm statute, § 8.01-328.1(8) and (9), but only if service is made personally by a person authorized to make such service by Va. Code § 8.01-320.

A court having in personam jurisdiction over both parents may enter a child custody order in the absence of the child. *Gramelspacher v. Gramelspacher*, 204 Va. 839, 134 S.E.2d 285 (1964) (mother and children remained in Indiana, the marital domicile, while defendant husband eventually settled in Virginia, where the action was brought). However, as has been discussed, the Virginia cases indicate that it is the child's right to custody, rather than the parents' that is the heart of custody adjudications. *McCreery v. McCreery*, 218 Va. 352, 237 S.E.2d 167 (1977).

Several cases from other states note that when there is no foreign court asserting jurisdiction, custody may be decided on the basis of the presence of the child and a parent domiciled within the state, since the dispute concerns a family status. See, e.g., *McAtee v. McAtee*, 323 S.E.2d 611(W. Va. 1984) (custody is a status exception under *Shaffer v. Heitner*, 433 U.S. 186 (1977), that may be determined in the absence of personal jurisdiction); *In re Marriage of Myers*, 92 Wash. 2d 113, 594 P.2d 902 (1979); *Perry v. Ponder*, 604 S.W.2d 306 (Tex. Civ. App. 1980). The parent-child relationship would, under this theory, be similar to the marital res necessary for divorce. *Williams v. North Carolina*, 317 U.S. 287 (1942). Support for this argument may also be found in the case of *Falco v. Grills*, discussed above. See generally *Developments in the Law — The Constitution and the Family*, 93 Harv. L. Rev. 1156, 1246 (1980).

Another jurisdictional concern is related to conflict of laws. Even though Virginia courts possess jurisdictional power under at least one of the foregoing rules, and even though there has been personal service or notice, another state may better be able to litigate the custody question. When the child's "home state" is Virginia, even though the parent contesting custody or even the child is outside the state, Virginia will have jurisdiction to decide the custody issue under Va. Code § 20-125, the Uniform Child Custody Jurisdiction Act. This is because the sources of information relative to a determination of the best interests of the child would be located within the state. *Middleton v. Middleton*, 227 Va. 82, 314 S.E.2d 362 (1984).

Where Virginia was the home state of the children at the start of the proceedings, and the father continued to live in the state, and Virginia courts have ruled on visitation motions throughout the intervening period, Virginia had jurisdiction under the UCCJA although the mother and children had lived in California since 1986. *Musser v. Musser*, 1995 Va. App. LEXIS 463. While the children's residence in California might merit a future determination that Virginia is an inconvenient forum, the court did have jurisdiction to rule on the father's rule to show cause for violation of existing visitation orders. See also *Osborne v. Osborne*, 215 Va. 205, 207 S.E.2d 875 (1974) (continuing jurisdiction from pendente lite proceeding).

A parent may not take the child from Virginia once a valid proceeding is pending and begin an action in another state, for to do so violates the UCCJA. Va. Code § 20-129. If the child is taken in violation of a Virginia custody order, the Parental Kidnapping Prevention Act, 28 U.S.C. § 1738A is also violated. Va. Code § 18.2-49.1. Of course, the reciprocal is true for proceedings and court orders in other states. See, e.g., *Middleton v. Middleton*, 227 Va. 82, 314 S.E.2d 362 (1984).

When, on the other hand, the best sources of information lie outside the state, even if they are outside the United States, Virginia will not exercise jurisdiction. *Oehl v. Oehl*, 221 Va. 618, 272 S.E.2d 441 (1980). See also *Barnes v. Barnes*, 1995 Va. App. LEXIS 319. Similarly, it was appropriate to transfer jurisdiction from Virginia to South Carolina under the Uniform Child Custody Jurisdiction Act where there might be adverse publicity in Virginia because of acts of child sexual abuse that allegedly occurred in the state. Transfer was appropriate because the children's home state was South Carolina. Further, the witnesses available to testify about the circumstance, particularly the children and mental health experts, were in South Carolina. *Farley v. Farley*, 9 Va. App. 326, 387 S.E.2d 794 (1990). The court did not abuse its discretion when it transferred jurisdiction over all custody and visitation issues to South Carolina when the legal custodians, the child's paternal grandparents, moved to a retirement community in that state. *Hale v. Hale*, 1994 Va. App. LEXIS 35.

Nor did the grandparents exhibit contemptuous behavior when they failed to obtain court approval prior to relocating, when the noncustodial mother was incarcerated and the child was never comfortable with the infrequent visits with her. See generally Brinig, *Interstate Child Custody Disputes: The Uniform Child Custody Jurisdiction Act in Virginia*, 10 Va. B.A.J. 17 (1984); Comment, 14 U. Rich. L. Rev. 435 (1979).

§ 24-4. Where is the action brought, and when is it appropriate?

For cases filed before January 1, 1996, the circuit court may transfer enforcement of divorce decrees, including pendente lite orders, to the family court, when funded. After such a transfer, the circuit court is divested of any further jurisdiction over the matter. Va. Code § 20-79(c). Final orders involving the division or transfer of real property between the parties to divorce or annulment, or following a foreign divorce, shall, if the decree so directs, be transmitted to the circuit court named in the order or decree for docketing on the judgment lien index. Va. Code § 20-107.3.

Appeals from juvenile and domestic relations court decisions are taken to the circuit court, even when the circuit court later becomes an experimental family court. *Loudoun County Dep't of Social Servs. v. Etzold*, 245 Va. 80, 425 S.E.2d 800 (1993). The requirement that an appealing party post a bond under § 16.1-107 is jurisdictional, so that failure to post such a bond requires dismissal of the appeal. *Shurm v. Shurm*, 27 Va. Cir. 255 (Chesterfield Co. 1992).

Virginia adopted the Interstate Family Support Act (UIFSA) in Va. Code § 20-88.32 et seq. (1994). The Act is similar to the Uniform Reciprocal Support Act in many respects. The Act does establish some new concepts. The UIFSA establishes uniform long-arm jurisdiction over nonresidents and provides for discovery and testimony once jurisdiction is obtained. Va. Code §§ 20-88.36, 20-88.59, 20-88.61. The UIFSA may only be used for child support proceedings. Visitation issues cannot be raised in child support proceedings. Va. Code § 20-88.48.

The UIFSA authorizes establishment of parentage in interstate proceedings even when not accompanied by a support proceeding. Custody orders may be entered even when no divorce is pending. In such cases, there may be orders pendente lite directed to any person with a legitimate interest who is a party. The custody and visitation orders in these non-divorce proceedings shall be made in accordance with § 20-124 et seq. (1994). Pendente lite orders shall have no presumptive effect and shall not determine the ultimate outcome of the case.

Courts may make child support or custody orders and decrees in suits for annulment or separate maintenance. Va. Code Ann. § 20-107.2 [amended 1996]. After the entry of a divorce decree, the court may transfer matters pertaining to child custody to the juvenile and domestic relations court, which may be in a different location within the state if a party or the court so moves, and shows good cause. Va. Code § 20-79. Va. Code § 16.1-243(B)(2) provides that any juvenile and domestic relations district court to which a suit is transferred for enforcement of orders pertaining to custody may transfer the case to a city or county that is the most appropriate of several in which venue lies. The best interests of the child shall determine the most appropriate forum.

According to Va. Code § 20-107.2, an award of custody may be made upon divorce; a declaration that neither party is entitled to divorce,

Latham v. Latham, 71 Va. (30 Gratt.) 307 (1878); or upon dissolution of marriage. "Dissolution of marriage" was interpreted to include annulment of a marriage void as bigamous where the parties had married before the date permitted by the wife's decree in her divorce from her first husband. *Henderson v. Henderson*, 187 Va. 121, 46 S.E.2d 10 (1948). Since the children were legitimated by statute, the father had the same right to their custody, control, and maintenance as if they were the issue of a valid marriage. "The right of a father to have his marriage annulled permits him to be relieved of his obligation as a husband, but does not permit him to rid himself of his obligations as a father." *Id.* at 129, 46 S.E.2d at 14.

§ 24-5. Pendente lite award of custody.

An award of temporary custody may be made under Va. Code § 20-103 when a party has applied for a divorce or annulment.

The usual factors that would be taken into account in determining the child's best interest are the same as those that are required for a permanent custody decision. A decree of temporary custody is not entitled to conclusive weight at a final custody hearing. It was therefore error to refuse to admit any relevant evidence including depositions taken before the temporary hearing. *Armistead v. Armistead*, 228 Va. 352, 322 S.E.2d 836 (1984).

§ 24-6. Attorney for child.

Although an attorney in a divorce proceeding has been hired to represent one of the spouses, in a certain sense the interests of the child must be represented as well, even though these are not necessarily the same. Virginia Informal Ethics Opinion 345 (December 4, 1979) states that an attorney representing one of the spouses at a child custody proceeding should disclose to the court both favorable and unfavorable medical reports pertaining to the client's fitness as a custodial parent, since the child's best interest is paramount.

A guardian ad litem may be appointed for the child in contested custody proceedings. *Verrocchio v. Verrocchio*, 16 Va. App. 314, 429 S.E.2d 82 (1993). Attorneys for children appointed under Va. Code § 16.1-266(D) are not subject to the maximum fee limitations for court-appointed counsel set forth in Va. Code § 16.1-267. *Kaplan v. Kaplan*, 1993 Va. App. LEXIS 420.

See generally *Lawyering for the Child: Principles of Representation in Custody and Visitation Disputes Arising from Divorce*, 87 Yale L.J. 1126 (1978).

§ 24-7. Psychiatric reports.

Any reports must be subject to cross-examination and rebuttal. See, e.g., *Collins v. Collins*, 283 S.C. 526, 324 S.E.2d 82 (1984).

Some commentators conclude that psychiatric and psychological experts have little to contribute to a best interests determination and that they interfere with the judicial function. See, e.g., Robert Cochran, *The Search for Guidance in Determining the Best Interests of the Child at Divorce*, 20 U. Rich. L. Rev. 1 (1985); Martha Fineman, *Dominant Discourse, Professional Language and Legal Change in Child Custody Decision-making*, 101 Harv. L. Rev. 727 (1988); Ohpaku, *Psychology: Impediment or Aid in Child Custody Cases?*, 29 Rutgers L. Rev. 1117 (1976). On the other hand, others suggest that judges may not be well-equipped to handle the developmental issues posed by custody cases. See, e.g., Watson, *The Children of Armageddon: Problems of Custody Following Divorce*, 21 Syracuse L. Rev. 55 (1969-1970); Batt, *Child Custody Disputes — A Developmental-Psychological Approach to Proof and Decisionmaking*, 12 Willamette L.J. 491 (1976). The classic work in the field is J. Goldstein, A. Freud & A. Solnit's *Beyond the Best Interests of the Child* (1973).

§ 24-8. School reports; siblings and friends.

In representing a parent seeking custody, the attorney must show that the client's home would be "best" for the child. This is done by examining the physical situation, but also the affection each parent has for the child, the school environment, siblings or playmates in the neighborhood, child care for young children, and the plans for religious upbringing. This is sometimes done through a series of photographs or through depositions from the persons who will be providing services.

A mother whose concern for her job and her employer were stronger than her concern for the children, while the father was willing to place the welfare of the children above all else, and was a "very nurturing parent," was denied custody after testimony by a babysitter, a psychiatrist, and some neighbors. *McCreery v. McCreery*, 218 Va. 352, 237 S.E.2d 167 (1977). See also *Peple v. Peple*, 5 Va. App. 414, 423, 364 S.E.2d 232 (1988) (father had become an "exceptionally attentive parent, actively involved in the physical, mental, and religious guidance of the child," and the mother, "while a loving and fit parent, was more occupied by her employment and not able to provide the same quality of care").

Similarly, a father was awarded custody on the basis of changed circumstances when the mother seemed overly concerned with the child's medical problems. He had retired and could devote his full energies to rearing his daughter, while there was also evidence that the mother had interfered with visitation. *Grubb v. Grubb*, 1994 Va. App. LEXIS 92. Where a father was imprisoned for sexually abusing children, including his own son, and was ordered not to have any contact with the son during his minority, there was "good cause" for limiting dissemination of the child's medical, psychiatric, and school records. *L.C.S. v. S.A.S.*, 19 Va. App. 709, 453 S.E.2d 580 (1995).

> The court's desire to award custody to the parent with the "best" situation does not necessarily mean the most expensive home, or the one with the prettiest furnishings, or the one with the greatest number of "creature comforts." For we are firmly of the view that a house is not a home, that a home is more than bricks and mortar. "Best" to us is the home that will provide the children the greatest opportunity to fulfill their potential as individuals and as members of society. *Keel v. Keel*, 225 Va. 606, 613, 303 S.E.2d 917, 922 (1983).

Where the two parents' homes in a custody dispute were similar, and both parents were employed full-time so that they could spend the same amount of time with the boy, the choice to award custody to the father was made on the basis of companionship of other children in the neighborhood and the affectionate interest of the child's relatives who lived in the area and who were alienated from the mother. *White v. White*, 215 Va. 765, 213 S.E.2d 766 (1975).

The fact that four siblings were already in the custody of the natural parents was an important consideration in the case of *Smith v. Pond*, 5 Va. App. 161, 360 S.E.2d 885 (1987), where the court wrote that "the trial judge is not required to disregard the fact that familial bonds may be a significant factor in a child's life," so that there was nothing that "would justify a finding that the best interest of [the child] would be served by separating her from her siblings."

§ 24-9. Stability of situation.

Once the child has been in a custodial situation for an extended period of time, courts will be reluctant to change the arrangement. See *Bailes v. Sours*, 231 Va. 96, 340 S.E.2d 824 (1986) (though both mother and stepmother were fit, child had been with stepmother for so long that for him, she was his mother. *Id.* at 100-01, 340 S.E.2d at 827). Likewise, where the noncustodial mother made no effort to obtain custody until the children had been living with their father for nearly three years, nor had she seen them until testifying in the custody case, to require a change of custody "would be a painful disruption" to the children's lives. *Hall v. Hall*, 210 Va. 668, 672, 173 S.E.2d 865, 868 (1970). See also *Patrick v. Byerley*, 228 Va. 691, 325 S.E.2d 99 (1985) (former stepmother who had cared for child for five years awarded custody when to do otherwise would "be highly disruptive to Chris and not in his best interest").

When the aunt and uncle of the child in question, who had previously been awarded custody by the Juvenile and Domestic Relations Court after a voluntary relinquishment by the mother, sought to adopt the child, they were not permitted to do so because they were separated. Nor would custody be returned to the natural mother because her life was still unstable and the child was fast friends with her cousin who was nearly the same age. *Watson v. Shepard*, 217 Va. 538, 229 S.E.2d 897 (1976). Cf. *Lundeen v. Struminger*, 209 Va. 548, 165 S.E.2d 285 (1969) (two children not separated in modification of alternating custody award since not in their best interests). The natural father's lifestyle, attitude, behavior, instability, living circumstances, personal habits, and emotional status made him unfit in *In re Custody of Sloan*, 25 Va. Cir. 227 (Amherst Co. 1991), so that foster parents who had assumed the child's care at the mother's request were entitled to custody. However, in *Terrell v. Hackett*, 1993 Va. App. LEXIS 487, the trial court was in error to grant custody to the mother's foster parents when the father was fit and wanted custody. This was despite testimony from the child's social worker that she was comfortable living with the foster parents and uncomfortable seeing her father.

§ 24-10. Fault.

Historically the party not at fault was usually awarded custody. *Owens v. Owens*, 96 Va. 191, 196, 31 S.E. 72, 74 (1898). However, the custody of minor children has never been given to one parent to punish the other.

Rowlee v. Rowlee, 211 Va. 689, 690, 179 S.E.2d 461, 462 (1971) (citing cases). The rule favoring the "innocent" spouse most often obtains where the fault itself has a deleterious effect on the child. For example, where the mother continued an adulterous relationship during the time she was separated, and one of the children developed a hyperactive condition and was obviously disturbed about the other man sleeping with his mother, custody was transferred to the father, since the relationship had an adverse impact on the children. *Brown v. Brown*, 218 Va. 196, 237 S.E.2d 89 (1977). See also *Keel v. Keel*, 225 Va. 606, 303 S.E.2d 917 (1983) (relationship of custodial mother with married man relevant in change of custody); *Miller v. Miller*, 22 Va. Cir. 470 (Henrico Co. 1981).

However, in several cases, the mother was awarded custody despite the existence of adultery, since the child had not been exposed to the immoral relationship. *Brinkley v. Brinkley*, 1 Va. App. 222, 336 S.E.2d 901 (1985) (no showing of improper conduct in the presence of the child); *Venable v. Venable*, 2 Va. App. 178, 342 S.E.2d 646 (1986) (although trial court attempted to restrict children's contact with mother's lover until such time as he and the mother might marry; father had also committed adultery). See also *Sutherland v. Sutherland*, 14 Va. App. 42, 414 S.E.2d 617 (1992) (wife awarded custody although she began live-in, adulterous relationship with man she intends to marry when he obtains his divorce, and children are often present in the house when the adultery occurs); and *Ford v. Ford*, 14 Va. App. 551, 419 S.E.2d 415 (1992) (father and companion not only went to great lengths to shield daughter from their adultery, they were also open with her about their ultimate intentions with regard to one another, telling her that they intended to marry); *Lewis v. Lewis*, 1993 Va. App. LEXIS 632 (custody awarded to mother where both parents guilty of adultery but planning to marry respective companions, child well-established in school and preferred to live with mother).

The adverse impact of extramarital sexual conduct is also related to the parent's fitness as a custodian. The Virginia Supreme Court recently reversed a custody award made by a circuit court to a homosexual father with a live-in male companion. Finding that the case was controlled by *Brown*, the court noted that the harm to the child could be presumed since the homosexual acts were illegal and the child would also suffer from ostracism by his peers and the larger community. The father's unfitness was manifested by his willingness to impose this burden upon her in exchange for his own gratification. *Roe v. Roe*, 228 Va. 722, 324 S.E.2d 691 (1985). Cf. *Doe v. Doe*, 222 Va. 736, 284 S.E.2d 799 (1981), where the Supreme Court refused to terminate all the parental rights of a lesbian mother who was otherwise very fit. In *Doe* the issue was visitation, which could take place when the lover was not present. In the day-to-day living situation posed by *Roe*, the child would of necessity be exposed to the homosexual lifestyle of the father.

In the nationally publicized case of *Bottoms v. Bottoms*, 1995 Va. LEXIS 43, 457 S.E.2d 102, a maternal grandmother was awarded custody of her daughter's child. The court wrote that "living daily under conditions stemming from active lesbianism practiced in the home may impose a burden upon a child"because of the condemnation of others "which will inevitably afflict the child's relationships." *Id.* at *18. See Stephen B. Bershing, *"Entreat Me Not to Leave Thee": Bottoms v. Bottoms and the Custody Rights of Gay and Lesbian Parents*, 3 Wm. & Mary Bill Rts. J. 289 (1994); Barry M. Parsons, Note, *Bottoms v. Bottoms: Erasing the Presumption Favoring a Natural Parent Over Third Parties — What Makes This Mother Unfit?* 2 Geo. Mason Independent L. Rev. 457 (1994).

The fact that a parent was involved in family abuse, as discussed *supra* § 7-15, will be a factor in determining child custody under Va. Code § 20-124.3. See, e.g., *L.C.S. v. S.A.S.*, 19 Va. App. 709, 453 S.E.2d 580 (1995). However, a spouse should not file a malicious or knowingly unfounded report of child abuse or neglect, for he or she may then be subject to criminal action. The first such conviction is a Class 4 misdemeanor; a subsequent conviction is a Class 2 misdemeanor. *Id.* Va. Code § 5:101 [added 1996]. Further, a court has found that a custodial mother's persistent questioning of her three children concerning her allegations of the father's sexual abuse was a negative change in the mother's circumstances, amounting to emotional abuse of the children, and clearly not in their best interests. The mother was denied all visitation until a plan for supervised visitation could be approved. *Juarez v. Juarez*, 1996 Va. App. LEXIS 108. See generally Katharine A. Salmon, Note, *Child Custody Modification Based on a Parent's Non-Marital Cohabitation: Protecting the Best Interests of the Child in Virginia*, 27 U. Rich. L. Rev. 915 (1993).

§ 24-11. Religion and morality.

The concept of morality is closely related to that of fault, although the presence of grounds for divorce will require a higher degree of proof. The morality of a would-be custodial parent is important for:

The moral climate in which children are to be raised is an important consideration for the court in determining custody, and adultery is a reflection of a mother's moral values. An illicit relationship to which minor children are exposed cannot be condoned. Such a relationship must necessarily be given the most careful consideration in a custody proceeding.

Brown v. Brown, 218 Va. 196, 199, 237 S.E.2d 89, 91 (1977). For example, custody of two teenaged boys was awarded to the mother, a Jehovah's Witness, whose religion did not interfere with her duties as a parent and who was a fit and suitable person, in *Crute v. Crute*, 12 Va. Cir. 190 (Henrico Co. 1988). The father had been involved in psychotherapy for seven years and had been treated for depression, and had never taken an active role in the boys' activities. In *Plotkin v. Plotkin*, 22 Va. Cir. 435 (City of Richmond 1975), the wife converted to the Jehovah's Witnesses faith during the marriage. The husband was successful in obtaining custody because "the zeal with which the defendant [wife] has and will continue to devote herself to the furtherance and advancement of her religious convictions will necessarily relegate the child to a place of secondary importance." See also *Petersen v. Petersen*, 13 Va. Cir. 216 (City of Norfolk 1988), where the mother had "dated" while still married and worked in a bar, while the father of the nine-year-old boy was stable, mature, and hardworking, and had "immediately accepted the pleasures and responsibilities of fatherhood." See generally Walter Wadlington, *Sexual Relations After Separation or Divorce: The New Morality and the Old and New Divorce Laws*, 63 Va. L. Rev. 249 (1977).

§ 24-12. Joint custody.

Virginia was one of the first states to endorse the practice of joint custody.

The advisability of dividing or alternating the custody of the child has been seriously considered. While there are certain disadvantages in such division, ere are also important advantages and benefits. It gives the child the experience of two separate homes. The child is entitled to the love, advice and training of both her father and her mother. Frequent associations, contact, and friendly relations with both of her parents will protect her future welfare if one of her parents should die.

It gives recognition to the rights of parents who have performed obligations as parents.

Mullen v. Mullen, 188 Va. 259, 272-73, 49 S.E.2d 349, 355 (1948) (mother awarded custody during school year; father in summer). Cf. *Andrews v. Geyer*, 200 Va. 107, 104 S.E.2d 747 (1958) (substantial visitation by mother continued); *Parrish v. Parrish*, 116 Va. 476, 82 S.E. 119 (1914) (boy's custody awarded to father, but because of his delicate health and tender years he was to live with mother in Virginia during school year).

The concept of joint custody, as defined below, was explicitly recognized in Va. Code § 20-107.2. The first type of joint custody is joint legal custody, where both parents retain joint responsibility for the care and control of the child and joint authority to make decisions concerning the child, even though the child's primary residence may be with only one parent. The second is joint physical custody, where both parents share physical and custodial care of the child. The section now provides in part that:

In awarding the custody of the child or children, the court may give consideration to joint custody or to sole custody, but shall give primary consideration to the welfare of the child or children, and, as between the parents, there shall be no presumption or inference of law in favor of either.

Split custody is also discussed in Va. Code § 20-108.1. Split custody is limited to those situations where each parent has physical custody of a child or children born of the parents, born of either parent and adopted by the other, or adopted by both parents. Although it has certain benefits for the child, joint custody is not always appropriate. One of the problems stems from frequent moving of the child between the two parents. For example, in *Brooks v. Brooks*, 201 Va. 731, 113 S.E.2d 872 (1960), the court disapproved of an arrangement giving the wife custody but allowing the father visitation from Friday afternoon to Monday morning, since the frequent shifting of custody between the parents for short periods would be detrimental to his welfare, and would result in his having no real home and no permanent environment and associations. Instead, the arrangement was changed to allow visitation for the month of July and each weekend. See also *Lundeen v. Struminger*, 209 Va. 548, 165 S.E.2d 285 (1969) (modifying alternate six months' arrangement so that children would be with one parent during the school year).

Joint custody with unsupervised visitation should not have been continued when the father violated court orders that he not feed the son with a baby bottle, that the son be in charge of his own body for bathing and cleaning purposes, and that the son sleep in his own bed. *Wilson v. Wilson*, 12 Va. App. 1251, 408 S.E.2d 576 (1991). Custody was awarded to the mother and the case was remanded for establishment of visitation subject to appropriate safeguards. Joint custody requires cooperation, open communication and mutual respect between the parents. Therefore, it should not be awarded where there is conflict and enmity between the parents and they are unable to communicate effectively with one another. *Gonella v. Gonella*, 1994 Va. App. LEXIS 183. Compare *Pope v. Pope*, 1994 Va. App. LEXIS 52, where the court of appeals affirmed an order for joint custody. In *Pope*, both parents enjoyed good relationships with the child and played an equal role in her upbringing. Sole custody is defined in Va. Code § 20-124.1 as a court award to one person of primary responsibility for making decisions affecting the child. This parent retains responsibility for the child's care and control. Shared custody, which triggers allocation of child support responsibilities, is described in Va. Code § 20-108.2. See, e.g., *Ewing v. Ewing*, 1995 Va. App. LEXIS 192; *Laverty v. Laverty*, 1995 Va. App. LEXIS 750 (1995); *Hiner v. Hadeed*, 31 Va. Cir. 193 (City of Richmond 1993).

§ 24-13. Evidence in custody hearings.

The wishes of the minor concerning which parent the minor would prefer to be the custodian will be considered if the child is of the age of discretion. See Va. Code § 20-107.2. In each such case, the court looks to the capacity, information, intelligence, and judgment of the child to determine competency. The wishes of the minor should be given great weight, although they will not be conclusive. *Hall v. Hall*, 210 Va. 668, 672, 173 S.E.2d 865, 868 (1970) (citing cases). Testimony in these cases is usually taken in camera. For example, the wishes of an intelligent, sensitive, eight-year-old were the primary reason custody was transferred from the father to the mother, who had remarried. *Turner v. Turner*, 3 Va. App. 31, 348 S.E.2d 21 (1986). One of the factors a court shall consider in granting custody is the "reasonable preference of the child, if the court deems the child to be of reasonable intelligence, understanding and experience to express such a preference." Va. Code § 20-124.3. See, e.g., *Schalow v. Schalow*, 1993 Va. App. LEXIS 212 (opinions of eight- and ten-year-old children considered); *Sargent v. Sargent*, 20 Va. App. 694, 460 S.E.2d 596 (1995) (nine-year-old child was not of sufficient age to decide with whom he should live, while other factors favored the mother's retaining custody). However, the chancellor did not err in refusing over the mother's objection to receive testimony from the couple's children where expert testimony suggested that requiring them to testify would be detrimental to their welfare. Instead, the commissioner correctly proceeded to receive the children's testimony in an informal proceeding in camera without counsel or the parties present. *Haase v. Haase*, 20 Va. App. 671, 460 S.E.2d 585 (1995).

§ 24-14. Agreements between parties to mediation.

In recent years, an agreement frequently is reached by the spouses after mediation pursuant to Va. St. Bar Ethics Opinion of April 28, 1983, and attachment. Since the mediator does not represent either spouse, and the parties are concerned with their own interests, although they may couch their arguments in terms of what is best for the children, the question arises whether there is any representative of the children's interests. In litigated custody cases, the judge will decide which parent will be "best" for the child. In mediation, the parties themselves reach an agreement, which merely requires approval by the court. See, e.g., John Murray, *Improving Parent-Child Relationships Within the Divorced Family: A Call for Legal Reform*, 19 U. Mich. J. Law Reform 563 (1986). On the other hand, parties to mediation will have increased communications skills and will presumably be able to better cooperate on custody and visitation arrangements. See generally Pearson and Thoennes, *Mediation of Divorce: The Benefits Outweigh the Costs*, 4 Fam. Advocate 26 (1984).

Court-directed mediation has been sanctioned by Va. Code § 16.1-274, which provides that when the court services unit is directed to provide mediation services in matters involving a child's custody, visitation, or support, the court shall assess a fee against the petitioner, the respondent, or both, in accordance with regulations and fee schedules established by the State Board of Social Services. Similarly, when requested by another court services unit or by a similar entity in another state to conduct an investigation or to provide mediation services or supervised visitation, the local department or the court services unit performing the service may require payment of fees prior to conducting the investigation or providing mediation services or supervised visitation. For any issue arising out of suits for divorce, annulment or affirmation of marriage, separate maintenance or equitable distribution based on foreign decree, termination of residual parental rights, and other child custody, support, and visitation cases, the judge shall consider whether to refer the parties to mediation, and may do so sua sponte or on motion of one of the parties. Upon referral, the parties must attend one evaluation session during which they and the mediator assess the case and decide whether to continue with mediation or with adjudication. Further participation in the mediation shall be by consent of all parties, and attorneys for any party may be present during mediation. Va. Code § 16.1-272.1; Va. Code § 20-124.4.

When the parties are referred to mediation, the court shall set a return date. The parties shall notify the court in writing if the dispute is resolved prior to this date. The court may in its discretion incorporate any mediated agreement into the terms of its final decree disposing of a case. Only if such an order is entered will the terms of the voluntary settlement agreement affect any outstanding court order. The court shall vacate a mediated agreement or an incorporating order where the agreement was procured by fraud or duress, where it is unconscionable, where there was not adequate disclosure of financial or property information, or where there was evident partiality or misconduct by the mediator that prejudiced the rights of a party.

Misconduct includes failure of the mediator to inform the parties in writing at the beginning of mediation that (1) the mediator does not provide legal advice; (2) an agreement will affect the legal rights of the parties; (3) each party to mediation has the opportunity to consult with independent legal counsel at any time and is encouraged to do so; and (4) each party should have any draft agreement reviewed by independent counsel prior to signing the agreement, or should waive this opportunity. Va. Code § 16.1-272.2. A motion to vacate an order or agreement must be made within two years after the agreement is reached, except that if the motion is based upon fraud, it shall be made within two years after these grounds are discovered or reasonably should have been discovered.

§ 24-15. Removal of child from state.

The court may require that the custodial parent keep the child within the state, see, e.g., *Carpenter v. Carpenter*, 220 Va. 299, 257 S.E.2d 845 (Va. 1979), unless the child's best interest would be served elsewhere. In *Carpenter*, a custodial mother sought to move from the Tidewater area to

New York, where she felt employment opportunities might be better and she would live near her mother. Noting that any job prospects were speculative at the time of the decision, the court refused to approve the move, stating that the cultural and social advantages of the Tidewater area were not less than those found in New York, and that visitation by the father would be more difficult. However, when removal to Arizona was found to be in the children's best interest, the trial court was in error in denying the mother's request to move with them out of Virginia. *Gray v. Gray*, 228 Va. 696, 324 S.E.2d 677, 678 (1985). See also *Simmons v. Simmons*, 1 Va. App. 358, 339 S.E.2d 198 (1986). The rule allowing removal only when in the child's best interest apparently does not extend to movement within the state, perhaps because the problems of full faith and credit then do not apply. Failure to return a child to the state in violation of a court order may result in loss of custody. The custodial parent would not then be a fit and proper person to have custody. *Rowlee v. Rowlee*, 211 Va. 689, 179 S.E.2d 461 (1971). See also Va. Code § 20-108.1, explicitly mentioning that intentional denial of visitation may constitute a change in circumstances justifying modification of custody. Another consequence may be restraint on visitation. For example, a father's visitation privileges could only be exercised within Dickenson County, Virginia, where the trial court found that he would not return the children to the county if permitted to take them therefrom. *Branham v. Raines*, 209 Va. 702, 167 S.E.2d 355 (1969). Virginia Code § 18.2-49.1 makes parental abduction a class six felony and therefore subject to the provisions of the federal Parental Kidnapping Prevention Act, 28 U.S.C. § 1738A. The Virginia statute proscribes any person from knowingly, wrongfully, and intentionally withholding a child from the child's custodial parent in a clear and significant violation of a court order respecting the custody or visitation of such child, so long as such child is withheld outside the Commonwealth.

In *Wilson v. Wilson*, 12 Va. App. 1251, 408 S.E.2d 576 (1991), the trial court erred in ordering that the father should become the primary physical custodian of the son should the wife ever move from her current residence of Nashville, Tennessee. The court of appeals found that a "predetermined automatic reversal of primary custody, based on an undetermined move in the future, is clearly an abuse of discretion." While a move from Nashville to another location at some time in the future might prove to be in the son's best interest, this could not be determined until the move was contemplated and all the circumstances associated with it known. See also *Laing v. Walker*, 1995 Va. App. LEXIS 592, where the mother proposed a move to Egypt. Although she canceled her plans to move, the trial court entered a final decree awarding the father sole legal and physical custody of the children, subject to her visitation rights; and *DeCapri v. DeCapri*, 1996 Va. App. LEXIS 36 (mother's move to Cleveland to attend community college resulted in a change from joint to sole custody in the father; father had a very close relationship with his daughter and maintained an active role in her care, education, and development). The fact that the custodial mother was transferred overseas pursuant to her military assignment did not constitute a change in circumstances where there was testimony that her duties at the base would most likely require only regular daytime work hours and the base had all standard facilities, including a new child care center. *Lee v. Lee*, 1994 Va. App. LEXIS 206. See also *Mortimer v. Mortimer*, 1995 Va. App. LEXIS 930 (mother retained custody although moved to California without giving notice to husband, who had joint legal custody); *Boyles v. Boyles*, 1996 Va. App. LEXIS 318 (mother permitted to move from Virginia Beach to Charlottesville, where she had siblings and family support; father continued to contact and harass her despite prior court orders requiring no contact, and made derogatory comments to the children about her).

Under new Va. Code § 20-124.5, a court shall require in all custody and visitation orders that a custodial parent give 30 days' notice to the court and the other party of an intent to relocate or any intended change of address. This is not necessary in cases where the court finds that there is good cause for omitting such an order. See generally Comment, *Residence Restrictions on Custodial Parents*, 12 Rutgers L.J. 341 (1980).

§ 24-16. Visitation.

The visitation rights of a noncustodial parent are subordinate to the welfare of the infant. *Oehl v. Oehl*, 221 Va. 618, 272 S.E.2d 441 (1980) (citing *Branham v. Raines*, 209 Va. 702, 167 S.E.2d 355 (1969)). Many of the decided cases involve issues of parental morality. Where there was no harm shown to the son of a lesbian mother by her unconventional lifestyle, and in all other respects she was shown to be a fit parent, her parental rights could not be terminated, and visitation privileges were continued. There might be a future time when it would become necessary to sever her relationship with the woman with whom she lived. *Doe v. Doe*, 222 Va. 736, 284 S.E.2d 799 (1981). In *Roe v. Roe*, 228 Va. 722, 324 S.E.2d 691 (1985), custody of the girl child was changed from the homosexual father who lived with another man to the mother, and visitation by the father was restricted to places outside the home and times when his homosexual lover was not present. Cf. *Brown v. Brown*, 218 Va. 196, 237 S.E.2d 89 (1977) (heterosexual lover not to be present while wife visited with children).

Even though the mother was living in Arizona in a house occupied by two males, psychiatrists testified that the children would be adversely affected if they were prohibited from visiting her in Arizona in her home. In addition, the children wished to visit with her at her Arizona residence. Therefore, it was improper for the trial judge to decree that visitation between the mother and her children was to take place only in Virginia. *Robinson v. Robinson*, 5 Va. App. 222, 361 S.E.2d 356 (1987). However, it was permissible to order that the noncustodial wife have no overnight guests of the opposite sex during the child's visitation. *Carrico v. Blevins*, 12 Va. App. 47, 402 S.E.2d 235 (1991). The wife lived with a man to whom she was not married and his two daughters. The husband testified that sometimes after the child visited with his mother he was difficult and did not mind well, and that on one occasion he returned home upset that the wife's male companion had walked into the bathroom while he was naked. The husband had strong religious and moral views against the child being in the home with the mother and her boyfriend, which should have been considered in imposing visitation restraints.

Joint custody with unsupervised visitation should not have been continued when the father violated court orders that he not feed the son with a baby bottle, that the son be in charge of his own body for bathing and cleaning purposes, and that the son sleep in his own bed. *Wilson v. Wilson*, 12 Va. App. 1251, 408 S.E.2d 576 (1991). Custody was awarded to the mother and the case was remanded for establishment of visitation subject to appropriate safeguards. See also *Hale v. Hale*, 1994 Va. App. LEXIS 35 (supervised visitation appropriate); *Smith v. McPeak*, 1993 Va. App. LEXIS 241 (contact restricted to letters screened by guardian ad litem).

Recent legislation allows grandparents, stepparents, former stepparents and other relatives to seek visitation through the juvenile and domestic relations courts, who are to determine custody and visitation according to the best interests of the child, Va. Code §§ 16.1-241(A)(6) and 16.1-278.15(B), as well as under Va. Code § 20-107.2. Before enactment of these amendments, a stepparent who had lived with a child for seven years was able to obtain visitation over the objection of the natural father of the child, who then had custody. *Arnold v. Newberry*, 24 Va. Cir. 431 (Washington Co. 1991).

Some cases involve other restrictions the custodial parent has wished to place on the other. The custodial parent may not force the noncustodial parent to dispose of recreational vehicles the custodial parent does not approve of, so long as they are not dangerous or do not affect the child's welfare. *Eichelberger v. Eichelberger*, 2 Va. App. 409, 345 S.E.2d 10 (1986). Nor may the custodial parent force the children to attend religious services during the time spent with the noncustodial parent. *Carrico v. Blevins*, 12 Va. App. 47, 402 S.E.2d 235 (1991). The trial court had the authority to require the custodial mother's husband to refrain from making derogatory comments about the noncustodial father in the presence of the children. *Forrest v. Ruhlin*, 1995 Va. App. LEXIS 579. By statute, grandparents have standing to seek visitation after the death or divorce of the parents, even after the child is adopted by a stepparent. Va. Code § 16.1-241 (juvenile and domestic relations court jurisdiction); § 20-107.2 (divorce).

§ 24-17. Powers in joint custody.

In the divorce decree, husband and wife were awarded alternate custody of their two children. Later, each moved for sole custody. The arrangement was modified so that the mother was awarded custody during the school year, so that the situation would be less disruptive to the child. Moreover, a portion of the decree requiring that the children be reared in the Jewish faith and that they attend religious school each week violated the free exercise clause of the Virginia Constitution. *Lundeen v. Struminger*, 209 Va. 548, 165 S.E.2d 285 (1969).

§ 24-18. Name change.

Even though a mother has sole custody of the children and remarries, she cannot have the children's surname changed to that of her new husband. This is because the father's rights were not terminated, and, more important still, the already strained bond between the noncustodial parent and child should not be further weakened. Unless the child is being adopted, the effect of a change of name would be to deprive the child of the one father known to him or her. *Flowers v. Cain*, 218 Va. 234, 237 S.E.2d 111 (1977). However, when the mother and the father never married, and the child from birth bore his mother's surname, the mother could change the name to that of her new husband despite the natural father's opposition. *In re Change of Name of O.*, 27 Va. Cir. 260 (Loudoun Co. 1992). Although the father was a loving parent who had made substantial commitments to the child's well-being, the strong bond between parent and child had never before been in any way dependent upon his use of the surname.

§ 24-19. Modification.

The standard in a modification proceeding is also the welfare, or "best interests," of the child. The cases require a "change in circumstances," which may be due to a change in either parents' condition or simply a change in the child's needs or situation. Although stability in the custodial relationship is important, it is simply another factor to be considered in determining the best interests of the child. There is no requirement that the current environment actually be harmful to the child. *Keel v. Keel*, 225 Va. 606, 607, 303 S.E.2d 917, 920 (1983). See also *Turner v. Turner*, 3 Va. App. 31, 348 S.E.2d 21 (1986); *Peple v. Peple*, 5 Va. App. 414, 364 S.E.2d 232 (1988).

The intentional withholding of visitation of a child from the other parent without just cause may constitute a material change of circumstances justifying a change of custody in the discretion of the court. Va. Code § 20-108. The inquiry, then, is twofold: (1) has there been a change in circumstances; and (2) would a change in custody be in the child's best interests? *Id.* at 611-12, 303 S.E.2d at 921; *Collins v. Collins*, 183 Va. 408, 32 S.E.2d 657 (1945).

A noncustodial parent does not establish a prima facie case for a change in custody based solely on an affidavit. *Ohlen v. Shively*, 16 Va. App. 419, 430 S.E.2d 559 (1993). By accepting an affidavit as the only substantive evidence required to establish father's prima facie case, the trial judge improperly shifted to the custodial mother the burden of proving the absence of a change in circumstances. However, the parent seeking a change in custody need not prove by clear and convincing evidence that a change was in the child's best interests. *Newland v. Neal*, 1996 Va. App. LEXIS 105. The preponderance of the evidence standard is appropriate for a change in custody motion. A noncustodial father, as a defense in a civil contempt proceeding for failure to pay spousal support, contested the validity of a consent order granting his wife custody on grounds that she testified falsely about the children and their relationship with their parents. In *Peet v. Peet*, 16 Va. App. 623, 429 S.E.2d 487

(1993), the court of appeals held that this was an allegation of intrinsic fraud. Fraud must be addressed either during cross-examination and impeachment, or in a separate proceeding directly attacking the decree. See also *Ohlen (Shively) v. Shively*, 16 Va. App. 419, 430 S.E.2d 559 (1993) (error to change custody on father's deposition alone).

The trial court appropriately ordered a change of custody from mother to father in *Schalow v. Schalow*, 1993 Va. App. LEXIS 212. The mother frequently interfered with the father's court-ordered visitation, while her boyfriend, who had been ordered by the trial court to stay away from her home, engaged the father in a fight in the presence of at least one child. Finally, the parties' children preferred to live with their father. See also *Flinchum v. Flinchum*, 1993 Va. App. LEXIS 207, where the children were frequently absent or late arriving at school, and lacked stability and security while in their mother's custody. Further, the mother attempted to interfere with the love and affection between the children and their father and intentionally impeded his visitation with them.

§ 24-20. Jurisdiction in modification proceedings.

Some cases allow modification of custody awards when the children and one parent are within the state even though there is no in personam jurisdiction over the absent parent. See, e.g., *Ben-Levi v. Ben-Levi*, 87 N.J. 308, 434 A.2d 63, dismissed for want of jurisdiction, # 80-1894, 8 Fam. L. Rep. (BNA) 2016 (1981). The Uniform Child Custody Jurisdiction Act requires that the child's "home state" retain jurisdiction unless at some time another state assumes it. Va. Code § 20-126. A husband and wife separated in Texas, where they had been living. The father took the children to Virginia, while the mother remained in Texas. In 1976, the Arlington County, Virginia, Juvenile and Domestic Relations Court awarded the father custody and ordered the mother to pay child support. The mother was to visit with the child only in Arlington. Later the father threatened the mother that she would never see the children again if she disobeyed his wishes. When she took them to Texas for a visit, she unsuccessfully petitioned the Texas court for custody. She then returned the children to the father and procured a Texas divorce. While the custody matter was under appeal, the father took the children overseas where he had been stationed by the military. The mother then tried unsuccessfully for three years to obtain visitation. She finally petitioned Arlington County Circuit Court for a change in custody based on his noncompliance with the visitation order. After she was granted custody, the father appealed, alleging lack of jurisdiction. In *Lutes v. Alexander*, 14 Va. App. 1075, 421 S.E.2d 857 (1992), the court of appeals affirmed the change of custody, finding that the Virginia courts had continuing jurisdiction over the matter. The mother, through her attorney, had attempted to serve the father "in every conceivable manner." The service was unsuccessful only because Major Lutes refused to accept it. To allow the father to defeat jurisdiction by refusing to accept service is "tantamount to granting anyone the right to avoid the valid jurisdiction of our courts based on a personal whim."

§ 24-21. Enforcement of custody decrees.

If a parent fails to abide by court orders relating to custody, several remedies are available. The most obvious, of course, is contempt. If the parent fails to afford visitation to the noncustodial parent, custody may be changed since such conduct shows that the custodial parent is not fit. The intentional withholding of visitation of a child from the other parent without just cause may constitute a material change of circumstances justifying a change of custody in the discretion of the court. Va. Code § 20-108. See, e.g., *Rowlee v. Rowlee*, 211 Va. 689, 179 S.E.2d 461 (1971).

The aggrieved parent may bring charges under Va. Code § 18.2-49.1, which makes parental abduction from the state a felony. The Parental Kidnapping Prevention Act, 28 U.S.C. § 1738A, is only available where the crime is a felony in Virginia: where the child is removed from the Commonwealth. A parent, or one assisting a parent, is immune from prosecution under the federal kidnapping statute (as opposed to the Parental Kidnapping statute). *United States v. Boettcher*, 780 F.2d 435 (4th Cir. 1985). Recent legislation provides that the first time that a parent knowingly, willfully, and wrongfully engages in conduct constituting a clear and significant violation of a custody or visitation order, he or she is guilty of a Class 4 misdemeanor. A second conviction within a year constitutes a Class 3 misdemeanor, while a third within 24 months is a Class 2 misdemeanor. These cases are in the jurisdiction of the juvenile and domestic relations court, regardless of the court issuing the original custody or visitation order. Va. Code § 18.2-49.1.

One other possibility for relief lies in a tort action for intentional infliction of emotional distress. See *Womack v. Eldridge*, 215 Va. 338, 210 S.E.2d 145 (1974). The specific torts might be interference with familial relationships or kidnapping. See, e.g., *Kajtazi v. Kajtazi*, 488 F.

Supp. 15 (E.D.N.Y. 1978); *Bennett v. Bennett*, 682 F.2d 1039 (D.C. Cir. 1982); *Bartanus v. Lis*, 332 Pa. Super. 48, 480 A.2d 1178 (1984). The action might be brought either in federal court, *Lloyd v. Loeffler*, 694 F.2d 489 (7th Cir. 1982),where the child has been taken outside the state, or in Virginia. The Fourth Circuit, using the lines of reasoning in both *Lloyd v. Loeffler* and *Kajtazi* (although neither was cited), has found both that recovery would lie for intentional infliction of emotional distress despite Virginia's abolition of the alienation of affections action and that such a proceeding could be brought in federal court despite the "domestic relations exception" to federal jurisdiction. *Raftery v. Scott*, 756 F.2d 335 (4th Cir. 1985).

§ 24-22. Enforcement of foreign custody judgments.

A child custody order is never final. Therefore res judicata would not apply, and the decision would not be entitled to full faith and credit absent the Parental Kidnapping Prevention Act, which provides that full faith and credit must be given to other states' valid custody orders. 28 U.S.C. § 1738A. Because courts were quick to find "changed circumstances" immediately after entry of a foreign decree if one of their domiciliaries was involved, see, e.g., *Webb v. Webb*, 451 U.S. 493 (1981); *Borys v. Borys*, 76 N.J. 103, 386 A.2d 366 (1978), Congress enacted the Parental Kidnapping Prevention Act, 48 U.S.C. § 1738A, which mandates full faith and credit for a valid foreign order. In order to enjoin a foreign proceeding under this action in federal court, there must be two judgments in conflict. In *Middleton v. Middleton*, 227 Va. 82, 314 S.E.2d 362 (1984), the Virginia Supreme Court noted that the U.C.C.J.A. must be followed, absent emergency allowing cases involving foreign custody awards to be decided in Virginia only when Virginia was the child's "home state," i.e., the state where the child resided for the six months preceding the action or where removal from Virginia occurred in defiance of a court order. This result is mandated because of the need for the forum court to have the most substantial connection with information concerning the child. Clearly, no full faith and credit need be given a foreign custody decision where there was no personal jurisdiction over the absent spouse. *May v. Anderson*, 345 U.S. 528 (1953). More recently, courts have questioned whether this jurisdiction might be acquired by the long-arm statute, Va. Code § 8.01-328.1(9), plus personal service in the foreign state, see, e.g.,

Taylor v. Taylor, 332 Pa. Super. 62, 480 A.2d 1188 (1984) (citing cases), or through the domicile of one parent plus the presence of the other in the state as a family status to be adjudicated. See, e.g., *McAtee v. McAtee*, 323 S.E.2d 611 (W. Va. 1984).

APPENDIX

Forms

Form 1. Bill of complaint for divorce.
Form 2. Affidavit for service by publication.
Form 3. Order of publication.
Form 4. Answer.
Form 5. Cross-bill of complaint.
Form 6. Answer to cross-bill.
Form 7. Request for production of documents.
Form 8. Notice of taking discovery depositions.
Form 9. Notice of motion for decree of reference.
Form 10. Motion for decree of reference.
Form 11. Decree of reference.
Form 12. Notice of pendente lite hearing.
Form 13. Pendente lite decree.
Form 14. Notice of entry of final decree.
Form 15. Decree of divorce.
Form 16. Final decree for divorce (no answer).
Form 17. Petition for custody and support.
Form 18. Decree for custody and support.
Form 19. Petition for rule to show cause.
Form 20. Affidavit for rule to show cause.
Form 21. Rule to show cause.
Form 22. Income and expense summary.
Form 23. Assets and liabilities disclosure statement.
Form 24. Premarital agreement.
Form 25. Separation agreement.
Form 26. Petition for adoption.
Form 27. Consent to adoption.
Form 28. Order of reference for adoption.
Form 29. Interlocutory order of adoption.
Form 30. Final order of adoption.

Form 1. Bill of complaint for divorce.

NOTE: Because most law offices have word processing equipment, these forms have been designed to make the production of the complaint, and various other documents, a matter of selecting from alternative paragraphs. Here those paragraphs that might appear in a bill of complaint for divorce are set forth, with a cover sheet that can be copied so that the complaint may be customized easily. Each complaint for divorce must allege (1) marriage, (2) domicile, (3) grounds, and (4) relief sought. It should be reemphasized that the matters set forth in the complaint are those which must be proved at the divorce hearing. Within each of these four categories, variations are possible. Optional paragraphs are indicated by bracketed numbers. Applicable Virginia Code sections (as of the date of publication) appear in parenthesis.

The bill of complaint for annulment will be similar, except that the grounds for annulment (paragraph 31 et seq. for divorce) should be drawn from Va. Code §§ 20-38.1, 20-45 (void marriages) or 20-89.1 (voidable marriages). Several of the paragraphs may also be used in the filing of cross-bills for divorce or for answers.

Alternative Paragraphs for Bill of Complaint for Divorce

Marriage 10	Domicile 20	Grounds 30	Relief 40
	(Code § 20-97)	(Code § 20-91)	(Code §§ 20-107.1 to 20-109.1)
11 Ceremonial marriage	21 Domicile and residence in Virginia	31 No fault separation (6 months)	41 Divorce
OR			[42] Separation Agreement
	OR	*OR*	
12 Common law marriage in another state	22 Military and stationed in state	32 No fault separation (12 months)	[43] Custody of children
[13] Minor children			[44] Spousal Support
	OR	*OR*	[45] Child Support
[14] Separation Agreement	23 Military, domiciled in Virginia, now stationed abroad	33 Adultery	[46] Property Distribution
[15] No military service		*OR*	
		34 Cruelty	[47] Resumption of maiden or former name
	24 Plaintiff and defendant last cohabited at [address] in [city or county], Virginia	*OR*	[48] Fees and costs
		35 Desertion	
		OR	[49] Other relief
		36 Imprisonment	

VIRGINIA:

IN THE CIRCUIT COURT FOR THE COUNTY (CITY) OF [NAME]

[Name of plaintiff]	)	
	)	
v.	)	In Chancery No. _____
	)	
[Name of defendant]	)	

BILL OF COMPLAINT

The plaintiff respectfully represents as follows:

11 Plaintiff and defendant were married on [date] in [locality].

12 On or about [date, plaintiff and defendant, being then domiciliaries of the state of [name], which recognizes common law marriage, entered into a present agreement to be husband and wife on or about [date]. They cohabited as husband and wife and held themselves out to the community as husband and wife.

13 [Number] children were born of this marriage (have been adopted by the parties), namely: [name, date of birth, and age of each child].

14 Since the separation, the parties, while each was represented by counsel of his or her own choosing, entered into a separation agreement dated [date] concerning [custody, support, child support, property division, and other matters relating to the marriage.] A copy of this agreement is attached as Exhibit A.

15 Plaintiff and defendant are over the age of 18 years, and neither of them is in the military service of the United States.

21 Plaintiff and defendant (plaintiff is) (defendant is) are domiciled in and have been bona fide residents of the State of Virginia for more than six months next preceding the commencement of this suit.

22 Plaintiff (defendant) is in the military service of the United States. For the six months next preceding the complaint, plaintiff (defendant) was stationed at [name of base], [name of city or county], Virginia. Plaintiff (defendant) continues to live in this state.

23 Plaintiff is in the military service of the United States. Plaintiff is now stationed outside the United States in [locality in foreign country or territory]. For the six months before being stationed in [country], plaintiff was domiciled in and a bona fide resident of Virginia.

24 Plaintiff and defendant last cohabited at [address] in [city or county], Virginia.

31 The plaintiff and defendant have lived separate and apart, without any cohabitation and without interruption for a period exceeding six months. Plaintiff (defendant) had the intention to remain permanently separated from defendant (plaintiff) since [date]. There are no minor children of the marriage, and plaintiff

and defendant have entered into a separation agreement dated [date], a copy of which is attached as Exhibit A.

32 The plaintiff and defendant have lived separate and apart, without any cohabitation, and without interruption, for a period exceeding twelve months. Plaintiff (defendant) had the intention to remain permanently separated from defendant (plaintiff) since [date].

33 On or about [date], and on various other occasions, defendant committed adultery (sodomy or buggery) with [name or names].

34 On or about [date], defendant committed the following acts of cruelty toward the plaintiff (caused plaintiff reasonable apprehension of bodily hurt), namely [state actions].

35 On or about [date], defendant willfully deserted and abandoned plaintiff, without just cause or excuse, and the parties have lived separate and apart since that date.

36 On [date], defendant was sentenced to [name of prison] for a term of [state term] for the crime of [state felony]. Defendant began service of this sentence on [date of incarceration for felony]. Plaintiff and defendant have not resumed cohabitation since plaintiff has known of this confinement.

41 WHEREFORE, plaintiff prays that she/he be awarded a divorce from the bond of matrimony from defendant.

42 that the agreement dated [date] between the parties be affirmed and ratified by this Court and incorporated as a part of any decree entered herein, pursuant to § 20-109.1, Code of Virginia.

43 that the plaintiff (and defendant) be awarded joint legal custody and that plaintiff (defendant) be awarded primary physical custody) of the minor children born of this marriage. (or that the best interests of the minor children of the parties require that plaintiff (defendant) be awarded responsibility for their care and custody).

44 Defendant is gainfully employed as [job] at [place of employment]. Plaintiff is not gainfully employed. (or Plaintiff is gainfully employed as [job] at [place of employment]). The earning capacity, obligations, and financial training of each, require that the defendant be ordered to pay for the maintenance and support of the plaintiff pursuant to Virginia Code § 20-107.1.

45 Defendant is gainfully employed as [job] at [place of employment]. Plaintiff is not gainfully employed. (or Plaintiff is gainfully employed as [job] at [place of employment]). The earning capacity, obligations, and financial training of each require that the defendant be ordered to pay for the maintenance, education, and support of the minor children of the marriage, pursuant to Virginia Code § 20-107.2.

46 Pursuant to § 20-107.3, Code of Virginia, plaintiff moves that the court determine legal title as between the parties and the ownership and value of all real and personal property of the parties, and that the court classify such property into separate and marital property categories, and order the division or transfer of

jointly owned marital property (order that plaintiff be granted a monetary award based upon the rights and equities in such property).

47 that plaintiff (defendant) be allowed to resume her maiden (his former) name.

48 that plaintiff be awarded attorneys' fees and court costs expended in this suit.

49 and for such other and further relief as may be just and equitable.

[Signed by plaintiff]

[Name and address of plaintiff's counsel]

Form 2. Affidavit for service by publication.

VIRGINIA:

IN THE CIRCUIT COURT FOR THE COUNTY (CITY) OF [NAME]

[Name of plaintiff]	)	
	)	
v.	)	In Chancery No. _____
	)	
[Name of defendant]	)	

AFFIDAVIT FOR SERVICE BY PUBLICATION

Comes now [name], plaintiff herein, and being first duly sworn, upon oath deposes and states that [name], defendant in the above cause, is not a resident of the State of Virginia (defendant's residence cannot be found after diligent search), his last known post office address or place of abode being, to the best of plaintiffs knowledge, information and belief, [address], and further states upon oath that to the best of her knowledge, information and belief that said defendant is not a member of the Armed Forces of the United States, nor has he been such within the past thirty (30) days, nor is he a member of the United States Public Health Service.

[Signed by plaintiff]

Subscribed and sworn to before me this [date].

[Signed by notary public]

My commission expires:

Form 3. Order of publication.

VIRGINIA:

IN THE CIRCUIT COURT FOR THE COUNTY (CITY) OF [NAME]

[Name of plaintiff]   )
)
v.   )   In Chancery No. _____
)
[Name of defendant]   )

ORDER OF PUBLICATION

The object of this suit is for the plaintiff to obtain a divorce from the defendant on the ground that [specify grounds].

An affidavit having been filed that the defendant is a nonresident of the State of Virginia (defendant's whereabouts cannot be ascertained after diligent search), the Clerk enters this order of publication this [date].

UPON CONSIDERATION WHEREOF, it is ordered that the defendant appear here within ten (10) days after due publication of this order of publication and do what is necessary to protect his interest in this suit.

[Signed by clerk or deputy clerk]

[Name and address of plaintiff's counsel]

Form 4. Answer.

VIRGINIA:

IN THE CIRCUIT COURT FOR THE COUNTY (CITY) OF [NAME]

[Name of plaintiff]	)	
	)	
v.	)	In Chancery No. _____
	)	
[Name of defendant]	)	

ANSWER

Defendant answers the bill of complaint filed against him (her) and states as follows:

1. He admits the allegations contained in paragraphs [number] through [number] of the bill of complaint.

2. He denies the allegations contained in paragraphs [number] through [number] of the bill of complaint.

[3.] Defendant asserts that plaintiff and defendant have resumed cohabitation, and that therefore plaintiff has no cause of action for divorce.

[4.] Even if plaintiff proves that defendant was involved in certain of the conduct alleged in his (her) complaint, by continuing to live as husband and wife with defendants after the date such conduct allegedly occurred, plaintiff has condoned any such conduct by the defendant.

[5.] Defendant was required to leave the marital residence because the conduct of plaintiff threatened defendant's health and well-being.

WHEREFORE, defendant prays that his interests in this matter be protected.

[Signed by defendant]

[Name and address of defendant's counsel]

CERTIFICATE OF SERVICE

This is to certify that a copy hereof was mailed, first class postage prepaid, to [name and address of plaintiff's counsel], as counsel for Plaintiff, on [date].

[Signed by defendant's counsel]

Form 5. Cross-bill of complaint.

VIRGINIA:

IN THE CIRCUIT COURT FOR THE COUNTY (CITY) OF [NAME]

[Name of plaintiff]	)	
	)	
v.	)	In Chancery No. _____
	)	
[Name of defendant]	)	

CROSS-BILL OF COMPLAINT

Comes now the defendant, and for his (her) Cross-Bill of Complaint to the Bill of Complaint filed against him (her), states as follows:

1. He (she) incorporates by reference the allegations contained in paragraphs [number] through [number] of the bill of complaint.

2. On or about [date], the plaintiff [set out grounds for divorce, from Form 1, paragraphs 31-36, and supporting allegations].

3. Defendant alleges he (she) was always a good and faithful husband (wife) to plaintiff and gave her (him) no just cause for her (his) actions.

WHEREFORE, defendant prays that he (she) be granted a divorce from the bond of matrimony from plaintiff on the grounds of [specify grounds]; [*add as applicable* prayers for relief, as found in Form 1, paragraphs 41-49].

[Signed by defendant]

[Name and address of defendant's counsel]

Form 6. Answer to cross-bill.

VIRGINIA:

IN THE CIRCUIT COURT FOR THE COUNTY (CITY) OF [NAME]

[Name of plaintiff]	)	
	)	
v.	)	In Chancery No. _____
	)	
[Name of defendant]	)	

ANSWER TO CROSS-BILL OF COMPLAINT

Comes now plaintiff, by counsel, and for her (his) answer to the cross-bill of complaint filed against her (him), states as follows:

1. She (he) admits the allegations contained in paragraphs [number] and [number] of the cross-bill of complaint.

2. She (he) denies the allegations of paragraphs [number] and [number] of the cross-bill of complaint.

[3.] She (he) affirmatively defends against the divorce sought by plaintiff as follows [insert applicable affirmative defenses as in Form 5, paragraphs 3-5].

WHEREFORE, plaintiff moves that the prayers of her bill of complaint be granted.

[Signed by plaintiff's counsel]

[Name and address of plaintiff's counsel]

CERTIFICATE OF SERVICE

This is to certify that a copy hereof was mailed, first class postage prepaid, to [name and address of defendant's counsel], as counsel for Defendant, on [date].

[Signed by plaintiff's counsel]

Form 7. Request for production of documents.

VIRGINIA:

IN THE CIRCUIT COURT FOR THE COUNTY (CITY) OF [NAME]

[Name of plaintiff]	)	
	)	
v.	)	In Chancery No. _____
	)	
[Name of defendant]	)	

REQUEST FOR PRODUCTION OF DOCUMENTS

TO: [Name of defendant]
          c/o [Name and address of defendant's counsel]

Plaintiff, by counsel, pursuant to Rule 4:9 of the Rules of the Supreme Court of Virginia, requests that the defendant [name] produce at the Law Offices of [name and address of plaintiff's counsel] on [date] the following documents for inspection and/or copying:

1. All of his (her) bank statements and canceled checks of each and every one of his (her) checking bank accounts, from January 1, [year], to the date of production, including individual accounts and those held in trust by him (her) or for his (her) benefit.

2. All statements of each and every savings account, money market account, mutual fund, stock and/or bond account, and any other account of value of [name of defendant] from January 1, [year], to the date of production, including individual accounts and those held in trust by him (her) or for his (her) benefit.

3. Documentary evidence of any and all business enterprises, including but not limited to, partnerships, corporations or syndicates, in which he (she) has or had a financial interest from January 1, [year], to the date of production.

4. A statement of all earnings of [name of defendant] for the period January 1, [year], to the date of production, whether by wages, dividends, interest or other income, whether reportable for income tax purposes or not.

5. Documentary evidence of all gifts received from any person, firm, corporation, trust or other entity for the period January 1, [year] to the date of production.

6. Signed copy of his (her) [year] federal income tax return.

[Signed by plaintiff's counsel]

CERTIFICATE OF SERVICE

I, the undersigned, hereby certify that a true copy of the foregoing Request for Production of Documents was mailed, first class postage prepaid, this [date] to [name and address of defendant's counsel], counsel for defendant.

[Signed by plaintiff's counsel]

Form 8. Notice of taking discovery deposition.

VIRGINIA:

IN THE CIRCUIT COURT FOR THE COUNTY (CITY) OF [NAME]

[Name of plaintiff])	
)	
v.)	In Chancery No. _____
)	
[Name of defendant])	

NOTICE OF TAKING DISCOVERY DEPOSITION

TO: [Name of defendant]
        c/o [Name and address of defendant's counsel]

PLEASE TAKE NOTICE that on the [day] day of [month], [year], at [time] o'clock a.m./p.m., at the offices of [name and address of plaintiff's counsel], the undersigned will, pursuant to Rule 4:5 of the Supreme Court of Virginia, take the discovery deposition of [name], defendant herein.

If said deposition is commenced but not concluded, the taking thereof shall be continued to such date and time as shall be mutually agreed by counsel for the parties.

[Signed by plaintiff's counsel]

CERTIFICATE OF SERVICE

This is to certify that a copy hereof was mailed, first class postage prepaid, to [name and address of defendant counsel], as counsel for defendant, on [date].

[Signed by plaintiff's counsel]

Form 9. Notice of motion for decree of reference.

VIRGINIA:

IN THE CIRCUIT COURT FOR [Jurisdiction]

[Name of plaintiff]   )
)
v.   )   In Chancery No. _____
)
[Name of defendant]   )

NOTICE OF MOTION FOR DECREE OF REFERENCE

TO: [Name of defendant]
       [Defendant's address]

PLEASE TAKE NOTICE that on the [day] day of [month], [year], at [time] o'clock a.m./p.m., or as soon thereafter as I can be heard, I will move in the Circuit Court of [Jurisdiction], that the court refer this case to one of the duly appointed commissioners in chancery. The commissioner will have the authority to hear the evidence I present and to report his or her findings and recommendations to the Court.

[Plaintiff's counsel, or Plaintiff if pro se]
[Counsel's address]

Form 10. Motion for decree of reference.

VIRGINIA:

IN THE CIRCUIT COURT FOR [Jurisdiction]

[Name of plaintiff]	)	
	)	
v.	)	In Chancery No. _____
	)	
[Name of defendant]	)	

MOTION FOR DECREE OF REFERENCE TO COMMISSIONER

On [month] [day], [year], I filed a Bill of Complaint for Divorce in this Court. A copy of this was duly served upon the defendant by the Sheriff of [Jurisdiction] on [month] [day], [year]. Defendant did not file an answer to the Bill of Complaint. More than twenty-one (21) days have passed since defendant was served. The cause is therefore ready to be heard.

I THEREFORE MOVE that this cause be referred to one of the duly appointed commissioners in chancery of this Court, to convene the parties, supervise the taking of evidence, and to report his/her findings and recommendations to the Court respecting the issues raised.

Made this [day] day of [month], [year].

I ASK FOR THIS:

_____
[Plaintiff's counsel, or Plaintiff, pro se]

Form 11. Decree of reference.

VIRGINIA:

IN THE CIRCUIT COURT FOR [Jurisdiction]

[Name of plaintiff]	)	
	)	
v.	)	In Chancery No. _____
	)	
[Name of defendant]	)	

DECREE OF REFERENCE TO COMMISSIONER

THIS CAUSE was heard based upon the Bill of Complaint for Divorce previously filed. A copy of this was duly served upon the defendant by the Sheriff of [Jurisdiction] on [month] [day], [year]. Defendant did not file an answer to the Bill of Complaint. More than twenty-one (21) days have passed since defendant was served. The cause is therefore ready to be heard. It is therefore, upon motion of the Plaintiff,

ADJUDGED, ORDERED AND DECREED that this cause be, and the same hereby is, referred to one of the duly appointed commissioners in chancery of this Court, to convene the parties, supervise the taking of evidence, and to report his/her findings and recommendations to the Court respecting the issues raised.

Entered the [day] day of [month], [year].

Form 12. Notice of pendente lite hearing.

VIRGINIA:

IN THE CIRCUIT COURT FOR THE COUNTY (CITY) OF [NAME]

[Name of plaintiff]	)	
	)	
v.	)	In Chancery No. _____
	)	
[Name of defendant]	)	

NOTICE OF PENDENTE LITE HEARING

TO: [Name of defendant]
       c/o [Name and address of defendant's counsel]

PLEASE TAKE NOTICE that on the [day] day of [month], [year], at [time] o'clock a.m./p.m., or as soon thereafter as she may be heard, the undersigned will, by her counsel, petition for the following Pendente Lite relief:

[1] Spousal support or maintenance.
[2] Child custody.
[3] Child support for minor children of the marriage.
[4] Support for a child who is under the age of nineteen and a full-time high school student.
[5] Health insurance coverage for plaintiff and the children of the parties.
[6] An order restraining the defendant from harassing plaintiff or from imposing any restraint on plaintiff's physical liberty.
[7] An award of the exclusive use and possession of the family residence.
[8] An order excluding defendant from the jointly owned (rented) family dwelling.
[9] An order restraining defendant from disposing of his (her) personal or the marital estate pending the suit for divorce, and to furnish security against disposing of the same.
[10] Preliminary counsel fees and court costs.
[11] Reimbursement for Clerk's and Sheriff's Fees.

[Signed by plaintiff's counsel]

CERTIFICATE OF SERVICE

This is to certify that a copy hereof was mailed, first class postage prepaid, to [name and address of defendant's counsel], as counsel for defendant, on [date].

[Signed by plaintiff's counsel]

Form 13. Pendente lite decree.

VIRGINIA:

IN THE CIRCUIT COURT FOR THE COUNTY (CITY) OF [NAME]

[Name of plaintiff])	
)	
v.)	In Chancery No. _____
)	
[Name of defendant])	

PENDENTE LITE DECREE

This cause came on this day to be heard on motion of the plaintiff for [specify applicable relief from Form 9, paragraphs 1-11] after notice duly and timely served upon the defendant, and after the taking of the sworn testimony of the parties.

UPON CONSIDERATION WHEREOF, and the Court having considered the evidence of both the plaintiff and the defendant, and being of the opinion that the plaintiff is entitled to the relief prayed for, it is accordingly adjudged, ordered, and decreed that the defendant pay to the plaintiff the sum of [amount] per [time period] as support for the [number] minor children of the parties, commencing on [date], and a like sum on [future installment information] until further decree of this Court, and it is further ordered, adjudged, and decreed that the defendant shall within [number] days pay to [name], counsel for plaintiff, the sum of [amount] as preliminary attorneys' fees and [amount], reimbursement of Clerk's and Sheriff's service fees.

ENTER:

DATE:

SEEN:

_____ p.q.

SEEN AND OBJECTED TO:

_____ p.d.

Form 14. Notice of entry of final decree.

VIRGINIA:

IN THE CIRCUIT COURT FOR THE COUNTY (CITY) OF [NAME]

[Name of plaintiff]	)	
	)	
v.	)	In Chancery No. _____
	)	
[Name of defendant]	)	

NOTICE OF ENTRY OF DECREE

TO: [Name of defendant]
    c/o [Name and address of defendant's counsel]

  PLEASE TAKE NOTICE that on the [day] day of [month], [year], at [time] o'clock a.m./p.m., or as soon thereafter as she may be heard, the plaintiff will, by counsel, move for entry of a Final Decree of Divorce, copy of which is attached hereto.

               [Signed by plaintiff's counsel]

I ASK FOR THIS:

_____ p.q.

SEEN AND NO OBJECTION:

_____ p.d.

Form 15. Decree of divorce.

VIRGINIA:

IN THE CIRCUIT COURT FOR THE COUNTY (CITY) OF [NAME]

[Name of plaintiff])
)
v.) In Chancery No. _____
)
[Name of defendant])

DECREE OF DIVORCE FROM BOND OF MATRIMONY

This cause came to be heard upon the bill of complaint, service of process upon the defendant, (*add as applicable:* defendant having neither appeared and answered nor otherwise responded, answer filed by the defendant, answer and cross-bill filed by the defendant, plaintiff's answer to the cross-bill, decree of reference appointing [name], Commissioner in Chancery, depositions taken before the same commissioner in chancery after due notice to defendant and the commissioner's report recommending that the plaintiff be awarded a divorce from the bond of matrimony from the defendant, upon a hearing *ore tenus,* upon depositions duly taken before [name], notary public, and was argued by counsel).

The court finds from the evidence, independently of the admissions of the parties in the pleadings or otherwise, that the plaintiff has been a bona fide resident of and actually domiciled in the Commonwealth of Virginia for more than six months next preceding the filing of this suit; that the defendant was a resident of [locality], Virginia when this suit was filed and that the parties last cohabited as man and wife in [locality], Virginia, and that this Court has jurisdiction to hear and determine this cause; that plaintiff and defendant were lawfully married to each other on [date], in [locality], and are both over the age of eighteen years and neither is a member of the Armed Forces of the United States; that [number] children were born of this marriage, and that the defendant [set out facts supporting grounds for divorce].

Accordingly, it is adjudged, ordered and decreed that plaintiff [name] be, and she (he) hereby is, granted a divorce from the bond of matrimony from the defendant [name] on the ground of [set out grounds for divorce]; [*add as applicable:* relief from Form 1, paragraphs 41-49]; that this cause be, and hereby is, transferred to the Juvenile and Domestic Relations District Court of the City (County) of [name] for such further proceedings as may be from time to time required on all matters pertaining to support and maintenance and to the care and custody of the minor children of the parties; that the Separation Agreement dated [date] by and between the parties hereto, and introduced into evidence as

Plaintiff's Exhibit A, be, and hereby is, affirmed, ratified and incorporated by reference in this decree, pursuant to § 20-109.1, Code of Virginia (1950), as amended.

And nothing further remaining to be done in this case, it is ordered stricken from the docket and filed among the ended causes.

ENTER:

DATE:

I ASK FOR THIS:

_____ p.q.

I HAVE SEEN THIS:

_____ p.d.

Form 16. Final decree for divorce (no answer).

VIRGINIA:

IN THE CIRCUIT COURT FOR [Jurisdiction]

[Name of plaintiff]	)	
	)	
v.	)	In Chancery No. _____
	)	
[Name of defendant]	)	

DECREE OF DIVORCE FROM BOND OF MATRIMONY

Plaintiff filed a bill of complaint, and served process upon the defendant. Since the defendant neither appeared, answered nor otherwise responded, the court issued a decree of reference appointing [name] as Commissioner in Chancery. After a hearing, the Commissioner's report recommended that the plaintiff be awarded a divorce from the bond of matrimony from the defendant. The court has considered these pleadings and the commissioner's report.

The court makes findings from the evidence independent of the admissions of the parties in the pleadings or otherwise. The court finds that the plaintiff has been a bona fide resident of and actually domiciled in the Commonwealth of Virginia for more than six months next preceding the filing of this suit; that the defendant was a resident of [town], when this suit was filed and that the parties last cohabited as man and wife in [town, Virginia], and that this Court has jurisdiction to hear and determine this cause. Further, the court finds that plaintiff and defendant were lawfully married to each other on [date] in [city, state], and are both over the age of eighteen years. On [date], the parties separated, and since then, and for a period in excess of six months, they have lived separate and apart, without any cohabitation and without interruption. No children were born of this marriage. On [date], the plaintiff and defendant entered into a separation agreement.

Accordingly, it is adjudged, ordered and decreed that plaintiff [name] be, and [he or she] hereby is, granted a divorce from the bond of matrimony from the defendant [name] on the ground of living separate and apart for a period in excess of six months; and that the Separation Agreement dated [date] between the parties, and introduced into evidence as Plaintiff's Exhibit A, be, and hereby is, affirmed, ratified and incorporated by reference in this decree, pursuant to § 20-109.1, Code of Virginia (1950) as amended.

Since nothing further remains to be done in this case, it is ordered stricken from the docket and filed among the ended causes.

s/_____
[Circuit Judge]

I ASK FOR THIS:

_____
[Name of plaintiff's counsel]

Form 17. Petition for custody and support.

VIRGINIA:

IN THE CIRCUIT COURT FOR THE COUNTY (CITY) OF [NAME]

[Name of plaintiff]   )
)
v.   )   In Chancery No. _____
)
[Name of defendant])

PETITION FOR CUSTODY AND SUPPORT

The plaintiff respectfully represents as follows:

(1) Plaintiff and defendant were married on [date] in [locality].

(2) [Number] children were born of this marriage, namely: [name, date of birth, and age of each child].

(3) Plaintiff and defendant are domiciled in and have been bona fide residents of the State of Virginia for more than six months next preceding the commencement of this suit and their minor children, now residing with plaintiff, are also domiciliary residents of the state.

(4) The parties hereto have been living separate and apart, since on or about [date], when defendant left the parties' home in [locality].

(5) Defendant has recently advised plaintiff that he (she) intends to move to [locality] and to take said children with him (her). Plaintiff wishes the children to remain with her (him), which she (he) considers to be in their best interest. Plaintiff feels that such a move would be detrimental to the children, who are happy and well adjusted residing with plaintiff.

WHEREFORE, plaintiff prays, pursuant to § 31-15, Code of Virginia (1950), as amended, that she (he) be awarded custody of the parties' minor children, [names of children], and support for said children, subject to rights of reasonable visitation with said children by defendant, a reasonable award of counsel fees and reimbursement for court costs and for such other and further relief as may seem just and equitable.

[Signed by plaintiff]

[Name and address of plaintiff's counsel]

Form 18. Decree for custody and support.

VIRGINIA:

IN THE CIRCUIT COURT FOR THE COUNTY (CITY) OF [NAME]

[Name of plaintiff]	)	
	)	
v.	)	In Chancery No. _____
	)	
[Name of defendant]	)	

DECREE FOR CUSTODY AND SUPPORT

THIS CAUSE came to be heard on [date] upon the bill of complaint, (*add as applicable:* service of process upon the defendant in person, maturity of the cause for hearing by the Court after defendant failed to file response in pleadings herein, upon due notice of said hearing served upon defendant in person by [name and address of process server], answer filed by the defendant, upon a hearing *ore tenus,* and was argued by counsel).

The Court finds from the sworn testimony of plaintiff and her (his) witnesses, and that of defendant, and his (her) witnesses, that plaintiff and the [number] minor children of the parties have been bona fide residents of, and actually domiciled in, the Commonwealth of Virginia for more than six months immediately preceding the filing of this suit; that the defendant was a resident of [locality], Virginia when this suit was filed and that the parties last cohabited in [locality], Virginia; that the parties hereto were lawfully married to each other on [date] in [locality]; and that the [number] minor children aforesaid were born of the marriage.

The Court further finds, from the evidence taken and considered, that the Court has jurisdiction of this cause, that all parties are properly before the Court, and that the plaintiff is entitled to the custody of and support from defendant for the [number] said minor children, subject to defendant's right to reasonable visitation with said children.

Accordingly, it is adjudged, ordered and decreed that the plaintiff [name] be, and hereby is, awarded custody of [names of children], the [number] minor children of the parties, that the defendant pay to plaintiff [amount] on [date] and on the 1st day of each month thereafter, as support for said minor children, until further decree of this Court, subject to reasonable visitation with said children reserved to defendant, at such reasonable times and places as the parties may from time to time mutually agree, and that defendant shall pay to plaintiff's counsel,

[name], the sum of [amount], on or before [date], as counsel fees due for said counsel's representation of plaintiff in this proceeding.

ENTER:

DATE:

SEEN:

_____ p.q.

Form 19. Petition for rule to show cause.

VIRGINIA:

IN THE CIRCUIT COURT FOR THE COUNTY (CITY) OF [NAME]

[Name of plaintiff]　)	
)	
v.　　　　　　　　)	In Chancery No. _____
)	
[Name of defendant]　)	

PETITION FOR RULE TO SHOW CAUSE

Comes now [name], plaintiff in the above action, by her (his) counsel, and in support of her (his) affidavit heretofore filed herein, petitions pursuant to § 20-113 et seq., Code of Virginia (1950), as amended, for the issuance of a rule to show cause, returnable [date], to be personally served upon the defendant herein, [name], to show cause, if any he (she) may, why he (she) should not be adjudged in contempt of this Court for his alleged failure to have complied with this court's decree entered on [date]. Plaintiff respectfully prays for:

(1) Issuance of a rule to show cause why defendant should not be held in contempt of this Court and for award of counsel fees and Court costs.

(2) Such other relief as to the Court may seem just and equitable.

[Signed by plaintiff's counsel]

[Name and address of plaintiff's counsel]

Form 20. Affidavit for rule to show cause.

VIRGINIA:

IN THE CIRCUIT COURT FOR THE COUNTY (CITY) OF [NAME]

[Name of plaintiff])	
)	
v.)	In Chancery No. _____
)	
[Name of defendant])	

AFFIDAVIT

STATE OF VIRGINIA

COUNTY (CITY) OF [name], to wit:

    I, [name], plaintiff herein, having been first duly sworn, upon oath depose and state that the defendant herein, [name], has failed and refused to abide by the Court's decree, entered herein on [date], in that he (she) has not paid plaintiff the sum of [amount] now due her (him) under the terms of said decree.

    WHEREFORE, plaintiff prays that a rule to show cause be issued, returnable [date], whereby said defendant is summoned to appear before this Court to show cause, if any he (she) can, why he (she) should not be adjudged in contempt of this Court for such nonpayment and for counsel fees and Court costs.

[Signed by plaintiff]

    Subscribed and sworn to before me on [date].

[Signed by notary public]
My commission expires:

[Signed by plaintiff's counsel]

Form 21. Rule to show cause.

VIRGINIA:

IN THE CIRCUIT COURT FOR THE COUNTY (CITY) OF [NAME]

[Name of plaintiff]	)	
	)	
v.	)	In Chancery No. _____
	)	
[Name of defendant]	)	

RULE TO SHOW CAUSE

This cause came to be heard upon the affidavit of plaintiff and plaintiff's petition for rule to show cause, and the Court that there is cause to grant the prayer of plaintiff's petition for rule to show cause, based upon her (his) affidavit filed herein.

Accordingly, it is adjudged, ordered and decreed that the defendant, [name], be, and hereby is, directed to appear before this Court on [date] to show cause, if any he (she) may, why he (she) should not be adjudged in contempt of this Court for his (her) alleged failure to comply fully with the terms of this Court's decree, entered herein on [date], and it is further adjudged, ordered and decreed that plaintiff cause to be served upon [name of defendant], whose last known address is [address], a certified copy of this rule to show cause.

ENTER:

DATE:

I ASK FOR THIS:

_____ p.q.

Form 22. Income and expense summary.

INCOME AND EXPENSE SUMMARY

MONTHLY INCOME:

Name:
Occupation:
Employer's name and address:
Pay period:
Rate of Pay:
Average gross pay per pay period:
Average net pay per pay period:
Other income (specify):
Average monthly net income:

MONTHLY EXPENSES: (Indicate self and/or children)

Household

    Mortgage/rent:
    Maintenance of residence and grounds (specify):
    Property taxes:
    Reserve for major repairs:
    Furniture/appliance repair/replacement:
    House cleaning:

Utilities

    Electricity:
    Fuel oil/gas:
    Telephone:
    Water/sewer:
    Garbage:
    Cable television:

Food

    Groceries:
    Lunches:

Automobile

Payment/depreciation:
Gas and oil:
Repair/maintenance/tires:
License tags/inspection/local registration:
Other transportation:
Personal property taxes:
Parking:
Reserve for replacement:

Insurance

Automobile liability:
Health:
Home owners:
Life:

Clothing and shoes

New:
Dry cleaning, laundry:
Special/uniforms:

Health expenses

Doctor:
Dentist:
Eye glasses:
Hospital:
Clinic membership:
Medicines, vitamins:
Other (specify):

Gifts

Church/charity:
Holidays/birthdays:

Entertainment/recreation

Vacations

Dues

    Professional:
    Social clubs:
    Pool:
    Other (specify):

Sundries

    Newspapers:
    Magazines:
    Personal grooming:
    Hair care:
    Other (specify):

Children's special expenses

    School supplies:
    Nursery school or day care:
    School tuition:
    Extended day fees:
    Lunch money:
    Allowance:
    Additional health insurance to provide coverage for children:
    Medical expenses not covered by insurance:
    Sports, musical, etc., equipment/supplies:
    Lessons-music, art, etc.:
    Special education:
    Transportation:
    Camp:
    Other (specify):

Pets

    Vet:
    Other (specify):

Miscellaneous

    Legal expenses:
    Taxes:
    Hobbies:
    Other (specify):

Fixed debts with interest

For each credit provide name and address, monthly payment amount, and balance due:

Current debts (over and above monthly expenses)

For each creditor provide name and address, minimum or usual monthly payment amount, and balance due:

MONTHLY EXPENSE SUMMARY:

Self and children:
Fixed debts:
Current debts:
    Total:

TOTAL AVERAGE MONTHLY NET INCOME:

TOTAL MONTHLY EXPENSE:

BALANCE (+ or –):

Signed:

Date:

Form 23. Assets and liabilities disclosure statement.

DISCLOSURE

Party Making Disclosure:

Separate property

ASSETS

Cash on hand:

Real property (describe; specify when and how acquired, source of purchase price, legal title and/or ownership interest; give estimated value and offset any liens to give net value):

Personal property (identify specific items and for each: specify when and how acquired, source of purchase price), title and/or ownership interest; give estimated value and offset any liens to give net value):

Marital property

ASSETS

Cash on hand:

Real property (describe; specify when and how acquired, source of purchase price, legal title and/or ownership interest; give estimated value and offset any liens to give net value):

Personal property (identify specific items and for each: specify when and how acquired, source of purchase price), title and/or ownership interest; give estimated value and offset any liens to give net value):

LIABILITIES

Joint debts (for each list name and address of creditor, amount currently due, date incurred, and purpose for incurring):

Separate debts of husband (for each list name and address of creditor, amount currently due, date incurred, and purpose for incurring):

Separate debts of wife (for each list name and address of creditor, amount currently due, date incurred, and purpose for incurring):

Form 24. Premarital agreement. (Va. Code § 20-147 et seq.)

NOTE: Like the Complaint for Divorce, the Premarital Agreement Form consists of a group of numbered paragraphs which may be selected as desired to fit the individual needs and desires of the client. Numbered paragraphs without brackets must be included in order to comply with Va. Code § 20-147 et seq. Those with brackets are optional, although the subjects of the suggested paragraphs are usually included in premarital agreements.

Numbering is according to subject matter, as follows:

01-09 *Recitals*
- 01   General purpose of agreement
- 02   Intent that agreement govern classification of property
- [03] Acknowledgement of property acquired prior to marriage
- [04] Acknowledgement that separate assets may increase in future
- [05] Acknowledgement of previous marriage and children by such marriage
- 06   Understanding of legal rights in property that would accrue absent agreement
- 07   Review by separate counsel
- 08   Acknowledgement of disclosure of property
- 09   Voluntary nature of agreement

10-19 *Separate property*
- [11] Separate property, income from, and appreciation of separate property
- [12] Control and disposition of separate property
- [13] Additions to separate property
- [14] Gifts, conveyances, and bequests between the parties

20-29 *Marital property*
- [21] Property titled jointly
- [22] Income earned through gainful employment during marriage
- [23] Contributions for spousal support from separate property
- [24] Support during marriage

30-39 *Individual obligations and liabilities*
- [31] Debts and tortious liability
- [32] Voluntary contributions to individual obligations or liabilities

40-49 *Disposition of property at death of spouse*
- [41] Release of marital interests in property that would otherwise accrue
- [42] Waiver of ability to claim against estate
- [43] Joinder in instruments needed by personal representative
- [44] Waiver of right to claim as beneficiary of life insurance

PREMARITAL AGREEMENT

THIS AGREEMENT is made and entered into between [name] and [name] (sometimes referred to as the parties) in contemplation of their marriage. It is to become effective upon their marriage to each other. The purpose of this agreement is to settle the rights and obligations of each of them, during their marriage, upon the death of either or both of them, or in case of dissolution of the marriage.

RECITALS:

01 [Name] and [name] have entered into this agreement through their mutual discussions. The parties desire to contract with each other concerning matters of the classification and disposition of the parties' property in the event of their death or divorce.

02 It is the intention of both parties that the classification of each other's property and estate during their lifetime, in the event of the death of either of them, or in the event of divorce, shall be determined solely by this Agreement.

03 Both parties as of this date are individually possessed of certain separate property, and both acknowledge that they played no role in the accumulation of the other's separate property.

[04] Each party understands that the assets of the other may be increased in the future by reason of inheritances, gifts, business profits, realized or unrealized appreciation, accumulated income, and other increases or additions, and each acknowledges that he or she is entering into this Agreement regardless of the value thereof.

[05] Each party has previously been married to another, and each party has children (and grandchildren) by that previous marriage, all of whom are each individual party's presumptive heirs-at-law.

06 Each party fully understands that, in the absence of this agreement, the law would confer upon him or her certain property rights and interests in the assets and property owned, received, or acquired by the other presently or in the future; and it is the intent of each party, by this agreement, to relinquish certain of such property rights and interests in such assets as specified herein.

07 This agreement has been reviewed by the separate legal counsel of each party.

08 Each party is aware of the nature and extent of their separate and joint income, real and personal property, and any outstanding debts or other liabilities. Both parties affirm that they have, in negotiating this agreement, fairly disclosed to the other all their respective incomes and expenses, assets and liabilities, all of which are set forth in the Appendices to this Agreement to the best of each parties' knowledge and ability.

09 [Name] and [name] have entered into this agreement freely and voluntarily. No coercion or undue influence has been used by or against either party in making this agreement.

AGREEMENT:

The parties agree as follows:

[11] The property currently belonging to each party and titled in his or her name shall remain his (her) separate property. All income, dividends, rents or profits from this property shall also remain separate property. All appreciation in value of the separate property, whether attributable to market conditions or the application of the skills or efforts of the owner thereof or any other party, shall be separate property. Any property purchased from the proceeds of the management or sale of such separate property shall also be considered separate property.

[12] Each party shall have the right to sell, rent, use, or otherwise manage and control this separate property, with the same effect as if no marriage had occurred between them. The other party hereby ratifies and consents on his or her part to any such management and control. Notwithstanding anything contained herein, each party agrees that, if asked by the other party or by any grantee or donee, he or she will join in any deed, mortgage, or other conveyance of such property by the other for the purpose of divesting any such rights, claims, or property interests, whether actual or apparent, or perfecting a clear record title to the property.

[13] Any property coming to either party during the marriage through gift, bequest, or inheritance shall be considered separate property and shall be treated as set forth above.

[14] Notwithstanding any other provision of this agreement, either party may, by appropriate written instrument, transfer, give, convey, devise, or bequeath any property to the other. Neither party intends by this agreement to limit or restrict

the right to receive any such transfer, gift, conveyance, devise, or bequest from the other.

[21] Assets titled in the names of both parties shall be classified as marital property, and shall be held as tenants in common unless expressly stated to be owned or titled as joint tenants or tenants by the entireties.

[22] The parties agree that income earned from the gainful employment of either of them shall be considered marital property, and shall be used to meet household and other expenses.

[23] Should this income be inadequate to meet household or other expenses, the parties agree that they shall contribute equally (or in some other proportion) to their joint account in order to meet these obligations.

[24] The parties agree that each is currently physically, emotionally, and financially capable of providing for his or her own support at an appropriate standard of living. The parties may contribute in agreed upon proportions to provide for their mutual support and the household in which they reside in the form of food, clothing, transportation, and other necessities consistent with a reasonable and appropriate standard of day-to-day living of the parties. The parties realize that they cannot abrogate the duty to support each other under Virginia law.

[31] All liabilities or obligations of any nature or description, including without limitation, those for torts, punitive damages, penalties, fines or forfeitures, which either party has incurred or hereafter incurs, including the parties' respective shares of liabilities or obligations which have been incurred jointly, either with each other or with third persons, shall be the individual liabilities and obligations of the incurring party as though he or she were an unmarried person. Unless prohibited by law, any such liability or obligation shall be satisfied exclusively out of the incurring party's separate property.

[32] Notwithstanding the foregoing paragraph, either party may, at his or her sole option, voluntarily contribute toward the payment of the individual liabilities or obligations of the other. However, such payment shall not constitute an assumption of the individual liabilities by the contributing party, nor shall such payment constitute an admission of liability therefore by the contributing party.

[41] Each party waives, discharges, and releases all rights, claims, or property interests, of whatever nature, which he or she might otherwise have in the event of the death of the other in or to all or any part of the separate property of the other under any law nor or hereafter in effect in the state of Virginia or in any other jurisdiction in which the parties may be domiciled, whether by way of homestead, curtesy, dower, election against the will, spousal allowances, intestate succession, marital property, community property, or otherwise.

[42] Each party agrees that he or she will not, in the event of the death of the other, make or assert any claim or ownership right of any kind whatsoever in or to the individual property, estate or assets of the other, other than for a bona fide debt. In the event that either party dies leaving any property, or estate, or assets

to be administered intestate, the same shall be inherited by and distributed to the heirs at law of the decedent (excluding the other party) with the same force and effect as if they had not been married.

[43] Each party shall join in the execution and filing of any instrument or conveyance, and in the taking of any other action necessary to abrogate or otherwise avoid the effect of the law of any jurisdiction conferring any such right or interest, if the legal representative or successor in interest of the other party so requests.

[44] Each party agrees that he (she) will make no claim as beneficiary of any insurance policy upon the life of the other.

[51] In the event of the dissolution of their marriage, a vinculo or a mensa, the parties acknowledge that this agreement constitutes a written agreement recognized and enforceable under Va. Code § 20-107.3(H). In the event of the dissolution of the marriage of the parties, each party waives, discharges and releases all rights, claims, or property interests, of whatever nature, which he or she might otherwise have in or to all or any part of the individual property of the other under Va. Code § 20-107.3; and each party agrees that he or she will not, in the event of the dissolution of the marriage of the parties, make or assert any claim or ownership right of any kind whatsoever in or to the separate property of the other, other than for a bona fide debt.

[52] Each party agrees that he (she) will make no claim for spousal support or maintenance in the event of the dissolution of their marriage.

[61] The parties will file a joint federal and state income tax return for each year in which filing such a joint return will result in less aggregate federal and/or state income tax obligations than would result from their filing separate returns. The federal and state income tax liability due with respect to any such joint return shall be allocated between the parties and paid by each of them out of his or her separate property in a manner such that the amount paid out by each shall bear the same ratio to the total tax payable with respect to such joint return as the federal gross income of each bears to the total federal gross income. Any additional assessments or costs of taxation by audit or other adjustment shall be similarly allocated between the parties.

[62] Any refund resulting from joint federal and state declarations and returns shall be shared between the parties in the same proportion as their respective contributions to the tax payments. The parties agree to consult and cooperate in obtaining any refund to which they may be entitled and agree to share the reasonable expenses of obtaining a refund in the same proportion as their respective contributions to the tax payments.

[71] Other matters, such as support of children of either of the parties from prior relationships; the payment of debts generated prior to the marriage; or personal rights and obligations, such as religious instruction of children that might be born to the marriage, plans for education of the parties or relationships with

friends or family of either party may be included here. [Note that such provisions must not be in violation of public policy or criminal statutes.]

81 The parties agree that this Agreement shall be governed by the laws of the state of Virginia [or other state]. This agreement shall at all times be construed in accordance with the laws of the state of Virginia, notwithstanding the establishment of a domicile elsewhere by either or both of the parties at any time subsequent to the execution of this agreement.

82 This agreement shall be amended only by a written agreement signed by both parties. No modification or waiver of any of the terms of this agreement shall be valid unless in writing and executed with the same formality as this agreement.

83 The parties intend this agreement to set forth their present understanding in its entirety. If any of the provisions of this agreement shall for any reason become invalid or otherwise cannot be enforced, the remainder of the agreement shall remain in full force and effect, unless an injustice would thereby result.

84 Each party represents that he or she understands the meaning of the various provisions of this agreement, and that the text does set forth the agreement in the manner they had intended. The parties acknowledge that this agreement is the free and voluntary act of each and that they each believe it to be fair, just, and reasonable.

IN WITNESS, [name] and [name] have signed this agreement below and have placed their initials in the lower left margin of each page.

[Signed by wife-to-be]

Subscribed and sworn to before me on [date].

[Signed by notary public]
My commission expires:

[Signed by husband-to-be]

Subscribed and sworn to before me on [date].

[Signed by notary public]
My commission expires:

Form 25. Separation agreement.

NOTE: Like the Complaint for Divorce, the Separation Agreement Form consists of a group of numbered paragraphs which may be selected as desired to fit the individual needs and desires of the client. Numbered paragraphs without brackets must be included in order to comply with Virginia law. Those with brackets are optional, although the subjects of the suggested paragraphs are usually included in separation agreements.

Numbering is according to subject matter, as follows:

01-09   *RECITALS*
    01   Marriage of the parties
    02   Children born to or adopted by the parties
    03   Separation of the parties
    04   Intent of agreement
    05   Competence of parties
    06   Disclosure of assets in attachments
    [07]   Intent that agreement be ratified and incorporated into any final decree
    [08]   Knowledge that if there is divorce, waiving right to equitable division of property and entitlement to or modification of spousal support
    09   Parties to lead separate lives

10-19   *CHILD CUSTODY*
    11   General welfare of children paramount; fostering of good relationship with both parents
    [12]   Joint legal and physical custody
OR
    [13]   Joint legal custody; primary physical custody in one parent; visitation
OR
    [14]   Shared physical custody
OR
    [15]   Sole custody in one parent; reasonable visitation
    16   Modification of custody and visitation arrangements
    [17]   Restriction to residence in Virginia
    [18]   Restriction to overnight visits without adult member of opposite sex present
    [19]   Religious or moral training of child

20-29   *CHILD SUPPORT*
    21   Child support payable by noncustodial parent; amount
    22   Modification of child support; circumstances
        [22.1]   change with consumer price index
or   [22.2]   change with age of child

SEPARATION AGREEMENT

THIS AGREEMENT is made and entered into to take effect on this [date], by and between [name] (referred to as wife) and [name] (referred to as husband).

RECITALS:

01 Husband and wife were married in [locality] on [date].

02 [Number] children were born of their marriage (adopted by the parties). Their names are [names, dates of birth].

03 Due to certain unhappy differences, the parties mutually agreed to separate. They in fact commenced a marital separation on [date] and are presently living separate and apart.

04 The parties are entering into this agreement to settle the rights and obligations of either or both of them (and especially to make provision for the care and support of their minor children).

It is expressly understood and agreed that this agreement is not executed for the purpose of the obtaining of a divorce from each other, nor is it an agreement or consent by either party for the other to obtain a divorce, yet it is here agreed and stipulated that the parties have separated by mutual consent and have agreed to live separate and apart because they feel that such is in their mutual best interests.

05 Each party is over the age of eighteen years, and is fully competent to make this agreement.

06 The parties have, to the best of their ability, fully and frankly disclosed all assets held by either or both of them to each other. These assets are listed in Schedules A to C.

[07] The parties intend that this agreement be presented to the court in the event either party brings an action for divorce, and that it be ratified, approved, and incorporated into any final decree of divorce.

[08] The parties acknowledge that by executing this agreement, they will waive any right to have a divorce court equitably distribute their property under Va. Code § 20-107.3. They further acknowledge that by executing this agreement and filing it with any divorce pleadings, the court will have no power to award spousal support or to modify spousal support except in accordance with the agreement.

09 The parties shall lead their separate lives and live separate and apart from each other as fully as though each were unmarried. Each may engage in any business or profession as each may choose, free from any influence from the other. Each may reside where he or she may choose, free from any restriction of the other. Each may choose his or her friends to associate with, whether they be of the same or the opposite sex, and the other shall not inquire as to the nature of the relationship, nor interfere with it in any way. The parties agree not to molest or harass each other at their respective places of employment, residence, on the streets or elsewhere.

WHEREFORE, for $1 and other good and valuable consideration, the parties agree and contract as follows:

11 Husband and wife share a concern for the welfare and best interests of their minor children, [names]. They each respect the other's parental role with the children and they agree that both of them are fit and proper parents. The parties agree to put no obstacle in the way of the maintenance of love and affection between each of them and the children. They will not belittle, berate, scorn, ridicule, or condemn the other in the presence of the children and each will actively attempt to generate a feeling of good will between the other parent and the children. Although their personal lives may take them in separate directions, they intend to cooperate in their shared parenting arrangements. They realize that they cannot relieve the court of the ability to determine the best interests of the children regarding matters pertaining to them.

[12] The children shall be in the joint custody of husband and wife. This means that important parental decisions affecting the children's growth and development shall be made jointly whenever possible. The parents agree to consider the children's best interests in making these decisions. They agree regularly to advise one another on all important matters related to the children, with the goal of adopting a harmonious policy regarding the interests of the

children. Each party agrees promptly to notify and to consult with the other with respect to any medical problems or illness of the children. Each party hereby agrees promptly to notify and to consult with the other with respect to any educational progress, education problems, and any change of schools or classes of the children. [Set forth arrangement of physical custody of children: weekday/weekend; school year/summer; alternating days; Monday through Wednesday/Thursday through Sunday are common arrangements.] The parents agree to confer from time to time in order to arrange a mutually convenient advance schedule, which shall be in writing if either parent so requests. Each parent also agrees to give thoughtful consideration to any request to the other for a change in the schedule to deal with unanticipated situations.

[13] The children shall be in the joint legal custody of [names]. This means that important parental decisions affecting the children's growth and development shall be made jointly whenever possible. The parents agree to consider the children's best interests in making these decisions. They agree regularly to advise one another on all important matters related to the children, with the goal of adopting a harmonious policy regarding the interests of the children. Each party agrees to promptly notify and to consult with the other with respect to any medical problems or illness of the children. Each party hereby agrees promptly to notify and to consult with the other with respect to any educational progress, education problems, and any change of schools or classes of the children.

[Names of children] shall have their principal residence with [name]. They shall spend reasonable amounts of time with [name]. This shall include a fair sharing of holidays and other special days. The children shall also be with [name] for certain additional times during the summer. In particular, they shall spend [set forth visitation schedule: every other weekend; one overnight and one evening per week are common]. [Name] shall assist with the care of the children on snow days, sick days and other times when the children are unexpectedly out of school.

The parties agree to confer from time to time in order to arrange a mutually convenient advance schedule, which shall be in writing if either parent so requests. Each parent also agrees to give thoughtful consideration to any request from the other for a change in the schedule to deal with unanticipated situations.

[14] [Names of children] shall have their principal residence with [name]. They shall spend reasonable amounts of time with [name]. This shall include a fair sharing of holidays and other special days. The children shall also be with [name] for certain additional times during the summer. In particular, they shall spend [set forth visitation schedule: every other weekend; one overnight and one evening per week are common.]

The parties agree to confer from time to time in order to arrange a mutually convenient advance schedule, which shall be in writing if either parent so requests. Each parent also agrees to give thoughtful consideration to any request from the other for a change in the schedule to deal with unanticipated situations.

15 [Name or names of child or children] shall have his (her)(their) principal residence with [name of first parent]. He (she)(they) shall spend reasonable amounts of time with [name of other parent]. This shall include a fair sharing of holidays and other special days. [Name or names of child or children] shall also be with [name of other parent] for certain additional times during the summer. In particular, he (she) (they) shall spend [set forth visitation schedule: every other weekend; one overnight and one evening per week are common].

[Name or names of child or children] shall have his (her) (their) principal residence with [name of other parent]. He (she) (they) shall spend reasonable amounts of time with [name of first parent]. This shall include a fair sharing of holidays and other special days. [Name or names] shall also be with [name of first parent] for certain additional times during the summer. In particular, he (she) (they) shall spend [set forth visitation schedule: every other weekend; one overnight and one evening per week are common.]

16 The parties agree to confer should circumstances change so that it appears to either or both of them that the best interests of a child or children may warrant a change in the custodial arrangement. Such circumstances might include a serious illness or accident on the part of one parent; an increase or decrease in employment; an employment prospect outside the state or at a great distance from the other party within the state; or a desire by one or more of the children for a change in the custodial situation. If the parties cannot reach a mutually satisfactory resolution of the situation, they agree to seek mediation (arbitration) (counseling with clergy or other professional).

[17] The parties agree that it is in the best interests of the children that both have regular and extensive contact with both parents, and that this necessitates both parents living in the state of Virginia. They therefore agree that neither will relocate outside the state of Virginia without the advice and consent of the other party.

[18] The parties agree that it is in the best interests of the children that there be no overnight visitation while [name of husband or wife] has an overnight adult guest (of the opposite sex) to whom he (she) is not related.

[19] The parties agree that it is in the best interests of the children that they be raised according to the principles of the [religious organization. Set forth any provisions regarding attendance at religious services; religious instruction; dietary restrictions, and so forth].

21 The parties acknowledge that they cannot divest the court of the power to set or modify the amount of child support in the best interests of the children. Nevertheless, they agree that [name] should pay [name of other party] for the support and maintenance of the children the sum of [amount] per [period]. These sums shall be payable [set forth arrangement, such as on the first and fifteenth days of each month].

[22.1] The amount of child support established in the preceding paragraph may be modified as circumstances change. Specifically, the parties provide that the amount of support shall be adjusted yearly, according to changes in the consumer price index.

[22.2] The amount of child support established in the preceding paragraph may be modified as circumstances change. Specifically, the parties provide that the amount of support shall be increased by [sum] as each child reaches the age of [state age or ages], to begin with the next calendar month following the child's birthday.

[22.3] The amount of child support established in the preceding paragraph may be modified as circumstances change. Specifically, the parties provide that the amount shall be increased by the sum of [state amount per period] as [name of party]'s income increases by [state amount]. The amount shall be decreased by [state amount by which reduced per period].

[22.4] The amount of child support established in the preceding paragraph may be modified as circumstances change. Specifically, the parties provide that the amount of support shall be adjusted by reducing the amount owed by [sum] as each child reaches the age of 18 or is otherwise emancipated, or physical custody is placed with [name].

22.5 In some circumstances, the needs and best interests of the children may warrant a change in the amount of child support. The parties agree to confer in good faith regarding such a proposed change. If the parties cannot reach a mutually satisfactory resolution of the situation, they agree to seek mediation (arbitration) (counseling with clergy or other professional).

[23] The parties agree that [name] shall be entitled to claim [name of child or children] as a dependent (dependents) for income tax purposes pursuant to I.R.C. § 1215.

[24] The parties agree to discuss with each other and with the children the appropriate college and higher education needs and desires of each of them. The parties agree that such decisions shall be made giving due consideration to the needs, wishes, and abilities of the child. The parties agree to share in the financial obligations of all such agreed-upon higher education, in direct proportion to their total gross incomes from the prior calendar year (or state some alternative).

[25] The parties agree that they shall share expenses for summer camps, music or athletic lessons, special education or tutoring equally (in the proportion of [state amount]).

[26] The parties agree that [name] shall be responsible for maintaining health insurance coverage for the children.

[27] The parties agree that they shall share major medical expenses not covered by insurance in the following way [state proportion, or who is to pay for such expenses]. This includes orthodontic or dental care, eyeglasses, and psychiatric or other counseling not covered by insurance.

[28] The parties agree that the child support established by this agreement shall continue until all children are emancipated. Should [name of party] die before

[names] reach the age of majority or complete college, the agreed upon amounts, as modified by paragraph 22, shall continue to be payable by the estate of [name].

[29] [Name] agrees to keep life insurance on his (her) life in the amount of [state amount] with [name of child or children] as beneficiaries until the children are emancipated (reach age 18) (complete a four year full-time college education).

31.1 [Name] shall pay to [name] the sum of [amount] per [period] for her (his) support and maintenance.

31.2 The parties expressly waive any claim either of them may have, now or in the future, to receive spousal support and maintenance (alimony) from the other. They release each other from any such claim after being advised of the provisions of Va. Code § 20-109. They are thus aware that any right which either of them might otherwise have to spousal support may never be revived, regardless of the circumstances.

32 The parties realize that under Va. Code § 20-109 the amount of spousal support and maintenance may only be modified as provided in this agreement. They therefore agree that spousal support may be modified as follows:

[32.1] After each full calendar year following the execution of this agreement, the parties shall obtain the consumer price index. The amount of spousal support established under paragraph 31 shall be adjusted according to the percentage increase or decrease of the consumer price index over that of the year of execution of this agreement.

[32.2] Before [date] of each year following the execution of this agreement, the parties agree to furnish each other with their federal income tax Form 1040 from the previous calendar year. The amount of spousal support established by paragraph 31 shall be increased or decreased based upon the proportionate change in the gross (taxable) income of [name or names].

[32.3] The parties agree that the amount of spousal support established by paragraph 31 shall be decreased by [amount] (terminated) after the expiration of [period] after execution of this agreement.

[32.4] The parties agree that the amount of spousal support established by paragraph 31 shall be decreased by [amount] (terminated) when [name] completes her (his) degree in [name of degree].

32.5 The parties agree that the amount of spousal support established by paragraph 31 may need to be adjusted due to changes in the circumstances of the parties. These include, but are not limited to, changes in the parties' employment, health, marital situation, custody arrangements for minor children, or modifications of the tax laws that affect the treatment of these payments. Should either party feel that an adjustment in the amount of spousal support is warranted, the parties agree to confer to attempt to resolve the situation amicably. Should they be unable to reach agreement, the parties agree to submit the matter to mediation (arbitration).

[33] [Name of payor] will pay [name] the sum of [amount] in lieu of spousal support and maintenance. Such payments will be made in installments of [amount]

per month, payable over [number] months. This amount shall be payable whether or not [name] remarries, and any unpaid balance shall constitute a lien against the estate of [name of payor], should he (she) die before all installments are paid.

[34] Payments made for spousal support and maintenance shall continue (terminate) upon the death of [name of payor spouse]. Future payments shall be made by [name of payor spouse]'s estate, and any arrearages shall constitute a debt owed by his (her) estate.

[35] Payments made for spousal support and maintenance shall continue (terminate) upon the remarriage of [name of recipient spouse].

[36] Payments made for spousal support shall terminate if [name of recipient spouse] cohabits with an adult member of the opposite sex to whom she (he) is not related by blood or marriage, or holds herself (himself) out as married to such person.

[37] The parties agree that payments for spousal support and maintenance under this agreement shall be treated as alimony for income tax purposes under I.R.C. § 71. That is, they will be deductible by [payor spouse] and taxable as income to [recipient spouse].

[38] The parties agree that [name] shall keep his (her) medical coverage for the benefit of [name of other spouse] unless or until the marriage ends in a final decree of divorce.

40 Except as otherwise here provided, each party hereby relinquishes and releases all statutory and common law rights which each may have or in the future may acquire to any property, real or personal, which the other now owns or may hereafter acquire, and each agrees that he or she will, upon the request of the other, execute and deliver such releases or assurances as may be desired by the other to indicate, demonstrate, or to carry out the release and relinquishment of such interests.

41 The parties agree that [name] is the sole and separate owner of certain property identified in Schedule A, and of the approximate value listed in that schedule. [Name] is the sole and separate owner of certain property identified in Schedule B and of the approximate value listed in that schedule.

42 The parties agree that the property identified and valued in Schedule C is marital property. The parties have agreed to divide the property as follows: [list which assets go to which spouse, with individual and total amounts].

[43] The parties jointly own as their marital residence the property located at [address]. They agree that [name], as primary custodian of the children, shall retain the exclusive use and possession of the marital home until such time as the last child becomes emancipated, by age or otherwise. At that time, the home shall be sold and the proceeds divided equally (or specify some other proportion). Until that time, [name or names] shall be responsible for mortgage payments, taxes, insurance, and utility payments for the home. [Name] shall be responsible for routine maintenance and upkeep of the home. [Name or names] shall pay for a major repair or maintenance of the home, defined as one which costs over [sum].

These expenses shall be incurred only after advance consultation, except for emergency repairs, but neither party may unreasonably withhold consent for repairs.

[44] The parties jointly own the home located at [address]. They agree that [name] will purchase the share of [name] for the sum of [amount], (or for one-half the appraised value, as established by a written appraisal of [realtors]). Such payment may be made [period] in the amount of [sum]. [Name] agrees to execute all necessary documents to enable [name] to obtain good title to these premises.

[45] The parties currently own the premises at [address] as their marital residence. They agree that it is to be sold after appraisal by [realtor or realtors]. The proceeds, net of the expenses of sale and the mortgage principal, are to be divided equally (or specify some other proportion).

(Until the property is sold, [name] shall be entitled to remain in the home. For this period, she (he) will be responsible for mortgage, insurance, utilities, routine maintenance and repairs) (making payments of [sum] per month to [name] in lieu of rent).

[46.1] The parties own real property located at [address]. They agree that this property is to be allocated to [name] and agree that all necessary documents related to such conveyance shall be executed by [name].

[46.2] The parties own real property located at [address]. They agree that this property is to be sold after valuation by [realtors] and that the proceeds, net of the expenses of sale and the mortgage principal, will be divided equally (or specify some other proportion).

47 The parties agree that the household furnishings listed in Schedule C shall be divided as follows: [specify method].

48 The parties agree that the [year, make and model of automobile] shall become [remain] the property of [name]. To the extent that the said automobile is not paid for, the remaining obligation shall be solely that of [name]. All documents necessary to effect these transactions shall be executed willingly and promptly by [name]. The parties agree that the [year, make and model of automobile] shall become (remain) the property of [name]. To the extent that the said automobile is not paid for, the remaining obligation shall be solely that of [name]. All documents necessary to effect these transactions shall be executed willingly and promptly by [name].

[49] The parties agree that in addition to the foregoing division of property, the sum of [amount] will be paid by [name] to [name].

51 The parties will file a joint federal and state income tax return for each year in which filing such a joint return will result in less aggregate federal and/or state income tax obligations than would result from their filing separate returns. The federal and state income tax liability due with respect to any such joint return shall be allocated between the parties and paid by each of them out of his or her separate property in a manner such that the amount paid out by each shall bear the same ratio to the total tax payable with respect to such joint return as the federal

gross income of each bears to the total federal gross income. Any additional assessments or costs of taxation by audit or other adjustment shall be similarly allocated between the parties.

52 Any refund resulting from joint federal and state declarations and returns shall be shared between the parties in the same proportion as their respective contributions to the tax payments. The parties agree to consult and cooperate in obtaining any refund to which they may be entitled, and agree to share the reasonable expenses of obtaining a refund in the same proportion as their respective contributions to the tax payments.

[53] The parties agree to furnish each other with copies of prior year's tax returns as soon as these become available, for use in establishing the amount of spousal or child support.

[61] The parties expressly agree to close any joint credit card or other accounts within 30 days of this agreement. This shall be accomplished by writing to each creditor requesting that the accounts either be closed or be converted into an account for the exclusive use and responsibility of one party.

[62] Except as otherwise set forth in this agreement, each party shall be solely responsible for his or her respective indebtedness incurred after the separation. Neither party may in the future incur any debts or liabilities, or make any contract, for which the other could legally be held responsible, except by mutual consent. If one party is required to make any payment for which the other is responsible under this agreement, the responsible party shall indemnify and hold harmless the party making that payment for all costs and damages incurred by that party, including attorney's fees and other costs.

[71] The parties realize that they may wish to modify this agreement at some time in the future, should some unforeseen contingency arise. Such a modification must be in a writing signed by each of the parties. The parties agree that if they are unable to agree on a modification of this agreement, they shall seek resolution of their differences by submitting the matter to mediation (arbitration).

[72] The parties intend for this agreement to be submitted to the court in which any divorce action is filed and for it to be ratified, incorporated, and made a part of any final decree of divorce. The parties each agree not to oppose such incorporation and they agree that subsequently, this Agreement shall be enforceable as part of said decree or independently as a contract between the parties. In addition, the parties agree that any amendments or modification to this agreement entered into after such incorporation into a divorce decree shall be incorporated into an amended decree in order that the court record reflect the intent and meaning of the parties' agreements.

The parties understand that such filing and incorporation will mean that the amounts payable for spousal support and maintenance cannot be modified except in accordance with this agreement (that neither party will ever be entitled to spousal support and maintenance). Further, they understand that because of such incorporation, provisions relating to spousal support and maintenance, custody, child support and visitation may be enforced as with any other divorce decree, under Va. Code § 20-79 et seq., including use of the court's contempt powers.

[73] The parties agree that they shall submit this agreement to any divorce court for its review and approval, but that it shall not be made a part of any final decree nor incorporated by reference therein. The parties realize that under Va. Code § 20-109, the amounts payable for spousal support and maintenance cannot be modified except in accordance with this agreement (that neither party will ever be entitled to spousal support and maintenance), but provisions regarding child custody, child support and visitation will be enforced as with any other divorce decree under Va. Code § 20-79 et seq., including use of the court's contempt powers.

[74] The parties intend that this agreement not be filed with any pleadings or other papers pertaining to an absolute divorce, and therefore that this agreement will not be incorporated by reference in any final decree of divorce. Any remedies under this agreement will be contractual in nature.

75 The parties agree that the immediate circumstances leading to their separation may not be used by either of them as the basis for a charge of desertion or constructive desertion against each other.

76 The parties intend this agreement to set forth their present understanding in its entirety. There are no binding written or oral promises between them which they presently wish to make, except as set forth in this agreement. If any of the provisions of this agreement shall for any reason become invalid or otherwise cannot be enforced, the remainder of the agreement shall remain in full force and effect, unless an injustice would thereby result.

77 The parties acknowledge that they each believe this agreement to be fair, just, and reasonable. The parties acknowledge that this agreement is the free and voluntary act of each.

78 The parties acknowledge that this agreement was reviewed by the separate and independent legal counsel of each prior to signing. Each party represents that he or she understands the meaning of the various provisions of this agreement, and that the text does set forth the agreement in the manner they had intended.

79 The parties intend that this agreement be interpreted and enforced under the laws of the Commonwealth of Virginia.

Form 26. Petition for adoption.

VIRGINIA:

IN THE CIRCUIT COURT OF THE COUNTY (CITY) OF [NAME]
In the matter of the adoption
of a child to be known as
[NAME] by
[Names of adoptive parents]

PETITION

Your petitioners, [names of adoptive parents], respectively represent as follows:

1. They are husband and wife and reside in [name of locality]. They desire to adopt a child to be known as [adoptive name of child] (Birth Certificate Registration No. [number], registered in the State of [name of state]), an infant child under the age of fourteen years, not theirs by birth. Said child was born on [date of birth], and was surrendered to the [name of agency] by her (his) natural parents or welfare department for placement for adoption by said agency.

2. Said [agency] has given its consent to the adoption of this child by petitioners. The consent of said agency is attached hereto as Exhibit "A" and made a part hereof.

3. The child was placed in the home of petitioners by the [agency] and has lived in petitioner's home since [date].

WHEREFORE, your petitioners pray for leave to adopt said infant and that said child's name be changed to [name] and that to this end all necessary and proper orders be entered.

DATE: _____   _____
                                        [Adoptive Parent]

                                        _____
                                        [Adoptive Parent]

By _____
         Of Counsel
[Address of counsel]

Form 27. Consent to adoption.

VIRGINIA:

IN THE CIRCUIT COURT OF THE COUNTY (CITY) OF [NAME]
In the matter of the adoption
of a child to be known as
[NAME] by
[Names of adoptive parents]

CONSENT TO ADOPTION

The [name of agency], a child placing agency, to whom a female (male) child to be named [name of child], born on [date of birth], at [locality], was surrendered for placement for adoption by her natural parents on [date of surrender], hereby gives consent to the adoption of said child by [names of adoptive parents], with whom said child was placed for adoption on [date of placement]. The required supervisory visits have been made, and the child has been placed in the adoptive home for the period required by law.

In witness whereof, the [name of agency] has caused this instrument to be signed by [its Director] this [date].

[NAME OF AGENCY]

By _____
                [Director]

STATE OF VIRGINIA
COUNTY (CITY) OF

Subscribed and sworn to before me this [date].

[Signed by notary public]

My commission expires:

Form 28. Order of reference for adoption.

VIRGINIA:

IN THE CIRCUIT COURT OF THE COUNTY (CITY) OF [NAME]

In the matter of the adoption
of a child to be known as
[NAME] by
[Names of adoptive parents]

ORDER OF REFERENCE

On this day [names of adoptive parents], petitioners, jointly filed their petition to adopt a child, not theirs by birth, and to have the child's name changed to [name].

And it appearing to the court that the petitioners reside at [address, City or County, Virginia, Zip Code], that the child is now living in the home of the petitioners, having been placed by [agency], and that this court has jurisdiction over this proceeding pursuant to § 63.1-221 of the Code of Virginia, it is therefore

ADJUDGED, ORDERED and DECREED that the clerk of this court forward a copy of the Petition and all exhibits with this order to the Commissioner of Social Services and to the Virginia State Welfare Department; and that said Virginia State Welfare Department shall make a thorough investigation of the matter in accordance with § 63.1-223(a) of the Code of Virginia, and shall report thereon in writing to this Court within sixty (60) days after the copy of the petition herein is forwarded to it, and shall cause a copy of said report to be served upon the Commissioner of Public Welfare in accordance with the aforesaid statute. And it is further

ADJUDGED, ORDERED and DECREED that the Commissioner of Public Welfare shall notify this Court within thirty (30) days of his receipt of the report of the Virginia State Welfare Department of his approval or disapproval thereof, stating reasons for any further action on the report that he deems necessary. And it is further

ADJUDGED, ORDERED and DECREED that copies of the reports of the Virginia State Welfare Department and the Commissioner of Public Welfare shall be furnished by the reporting agency to petitioners' counsel of record at the same time said reports are furnished to the Court, subject to the requirement that such reports be returned to the Clerk of this Court, without duplication, to be disposed of in accordance with § 63.1-236 of the Code of Virginia.

And this proceeding is continued, awaiting the filing of said report by the Virginia State Welfare Department.

Entered this _____ day of _____, 19___.

_____
JUDGE

I ASK FOR THIS:

_____

Form 29. Interlocutory order of adoption.

VIRGINIA:

IN THE CIRCUIT COURT OF THE COUNTY (CITY) OF [NAME]

In the matter of the adoption
of a child to be known as
[NAME] by
[Names of adoptive parents]

INTERLOCUTORY ORDER

ON the _____ st day of [month, year], petitioners [names of adoptive parents] appeared through counsel, and the Virginia State Welfare Department and the Commissioner of Public Welfare having filed their reports in this matter in accordance with § 63.1-223 of the Code of Virginia, and the Order of Reference of this Court dated [date];

And it appearing to the Court that all requirements of the applicable statutes have been complied with; that petitioners [names] are proper persons adequately to maintain, care for, and train the infant child to be known as [name of child], whose adoption is the subject of this proceeding; that the child is suitable for adoption and that the best interests of the child will be promoted by her (his) adoption by petitioners and by changing her (his) name to [name] as requested in the petition; it is therefore

ADJUDGED, ORDERED and DECREED that the infant child to be known as [name] (Birth Certificate Registration Number [number], registered in the State of [state]) born of [natural parents] on [date of birth] in the State of [name of state], henceforth, subject to the probationary period provided for by § 63.1-228 of the Code of Virginia, and subject further to the provisions of the Final Order of Adoption of this Court, will be, for all intents and purposes, the child of [names of adoptive parents], petitioners herein; and it is further

ADJUDGED, ORDERED and DECREED that upon entry of the Final Order of this Court herein, the name of said child shall be changed to [name]; and it is further

ADJUDGED, ORDERED and DECREED that the Clerk of this Court shall forward an attested copy of this Interlocutory Order to the Commissioner of Public Welfare and to the Virginia State Welfare Department.

Entered this _____ day of _____, 19___.

_____
                                                    JUDGE

I ASK FOR THIS:

_____

Form 30. Final order of adoption.

VIRGINIA:

IN THE CIRCUIT COURT OF THE COUNTY (CITY) OF [NAME]

In the matter of the adoption
of a child to be known as
[NAME] by
[Names of adoptive parents]

FINAL ORDER

On the [date of hearing], petitioners [names of adoptive parents] appeared through counsel, and the Virginia State Welfare Department and the Commissioner of Public Welfare having filed their reports in this matter in accordance with § 63.1-228 of the Code of Virginia, and more than six months having elapsed since the entry of the Interlocutory Order herein dated [date];

And it appearing to the Court that all requirements of the applicable statutes have been complied with; that petitioners [names] are proper persons to maintain, care for, and train said child, that said child is a suitable child for adoption by petitioners; that the Commissioner of Public Welfare recommends to the Court the entry of a final order of adoption of said child by petitioners [names]; and that the best interests of the child will be served by the entering of a Final Order of adoption herein, it is

ADJUDGED, ORDERED and DECREED that henceforth said child shall be, for all intents and purposes, the child of said petitioners, [names], and shall be entitled to all the rights and privileges, and subject to all the obligations, of a child of said petitioners born in lawful wedlock.

And it further appearing to the Court that the petition filed in this cause includes a prayer that the infant's name be changed to [name], it is further ADJUDGED, ORDERED and DECREED that henceforth said child's name shall be [name].

And it is further ORDERED that the Clerk of this Court shall forward an attested copy of this Order to the Commissioner of Public Welfare and to the Virginia State Welfare Department and shall make such reports of the adoption of this infant as are required by law.

Entered this _____ day of _____, 19___.

_____
JUDGE

I ASK FOR THIS:

_____

TABLE OF CASES

A

B

Babb v. Scott Co. Dept. of Soc. Services, 1996 Va. App. LEXIS 41 —
§ 7-12

Baby Doe v. John & Mary Doe, 15 Va. App. 292, 421 S.E.2d 913 (1992)
— § 4-7; § 7-6

Bacon v. Bacon, 3 Va. App. 484, 351 S.E.2d 37 (1986) — § 20-21

Baer v. Baer, 1996 Va. App. LEXIS 73 — § 22-13

Bailes v. Sours, 231 Va. 96, 340 S.E.2d 824 (1986) — § 7-12; § 24-2;
§ 24-9

Bailey v. Bailey, 12 Va. Cir. 67 (City of Norfolk 1987) — § 18-1

Bailey v. Bailey, 62 Va. (21 Gratt.) 43 (1871) — § 6-1; § 19-1; § 19-7;
§ 20-21; § 21-15

Bailey v. Bailey, 172 Va. 18, 200 S.E. 622 (1939) — § 24-3

Baker v. Nelson, 291 Minn. 310, 191 N.W.2d 185 (1971) — § 6-7

Banagan v. Banagan, 17 Va. App. 321, 437 S.E.2d 229 (1993) — § 22-6

Bandas v. Bandas, 16 Va. App. 427, 430 S.E.2d 706 (1993) — § 21-6

Bandas v. Bandas, 25 Va. Cir. 492 (City of Richmond 1991) — § 18-4;
§ 20-9

Bandas v. Bandas, 32 Va. Cir. 285 (City of Richmond 1993) — § 20-23

Barbee v. Barbee, 23 Va. Cir. 68 (Fairfax Co. 1991) — § 22-6

Barber v. Barber, 51 Cal. 2d 244, 331 P.2d 628 (1958) — § 22-4

Barbero v. Barbero, 23 Va. Cir. 301 (Fairfax Co. 1991) — § 20-3

Barden v. Barden, 1995 Va. App. LEXIS 200 — § 22-16

Barnard v. Barnard, 132 Va. 155, 111 S.E. 227 (1922) — § 19-11;
§ 20-21

Barnes v. Barnes, 16 Va. App. 98, 428 S.E.2d 294 (1993) — § 20-7;
§ 21-6; § 22-11

Barnes v. Barnes, 231 Va. 39, 340 S.E.2d 803 (1986) — § 18-1

Barnes v. Barnes, 1995 Va. App. LEXIS 319 — § 22-7; § 24-3

Barnes v. Craig, 202 Va. 229, 117 S.E.2d 63 (1960) — § 18-19; § 23-16

Barnett v. Barnett, 24 Va. Cir. 282 (Campbell Co. 1991) — § 23-16

Barnhill v. Brooks, 15 Va. App. 696, 427 S.E.2d 209 (1993) — § 23-17

Barrett v. Barrett, 470 Pa. 253, 368 A.2d 616 (1977) — § 23-21

Bartanus v. Lis, 332 Pa. Super. 48, 480 A.2d 1178 (1984) — § 24-21

Baskerville v. Baskerville, 18 Va. Cir. 487 (City of Richmond, 1990) —
§ 18-1

C

D

E

G

H

I

K

L

Lundeen v. Struminger, 209 Va. 548, 165 S.E.2d 285 (1969) — § 18-27; § 18-30; § 24-9; § 24-12; § 24-17
Lusby v. Lusby, 283 Md. 334, 390 A.2d 77 (1978) — § 8-3
Lutes v. Alexander, 14 Va. App. 1075, 421 S.E.2d 857 (1992) — § 24-20
Lyle v. Eskridge, 14 Va. App. 874, 419 S.E.2d 863 (1992) — § 7-14

M

M.I. v. A.I., 107 Misc. 2d 663, 435 N.Y.S.2d 928 (1981) — § 16-1
Mabe v. Mabe, 8 Va. Cir. 339 (Wise Co. 1987) — § 22-14
Mack v. Mack, 217 Va. 534, 229 S.E.2d 895 (1976) — § 18-18
Mackey v. Mackey, 203 Va. 526, 125 S.E.2d 194 (1962) — § 20-18
Mackie v. Hill, 16 Va. App. 229, 429 S.E.2d 37 (1993) — § 18-16
MacNelly v. MacNelly, 17 Va. App. 427, 437 S.E.2d 582 (1993) — § 18-9; § 18-12; § 21-25
MacNelly v. MacNelly, 1995 Va. App. LEXIS 496 — § 21-22; § 21-25
Mahnke v. Moore, 197 Md. 61, 77 A.2d 923 (1951) — § 8-3; § 15-2
Mahoney v. Mahoney, 91 N.J. 488, 453 A.2d 527 (1982) — § 22-8
Mains v. Mains, 1993 Va. App. LEXIS 362 — § 22-20
Major v. Major, 36 Va. Cir. 190 (Pittsylvania Co. 1995) — § 22-16; § 23-8
Mallery-Sayre v. Mallery, 6 Va. App. 471, 370 S.E.2d 113 (1988) — § 21-17; § 21-25
Malnak v. Yogi, 592 F.2d 197 (3d Cir. 1977) — § 16-2
Malpass v. Morgan, 213 Va. 393, 192 S.E.2d 794 (1972) — § 7-16
Marion v. Marion, 11 Va. App. 659, 401 S.E.2d 432 (1991) — § 22-16
Markley v. Markley, 145 Va. 596, 134 S.E. 536 (1926) — § 20-7
Marshall v. Baynes, 88 Va. 1040, 14 S.E. 978 (1892) — § 19-1; § 19-16
Martin v. Bales, 7 Va. App. 141, 371 S.E.2d 823 (1988) — § 21-32
Martin v. Martin, 166 Va. 109, 184 S.E. 220 (1936) — § 20-6; § 20-11
Martin v. Martin, 202 Va. 769, 120 S.E.2d 471 (1961) — § 20-7; § 20-21
Martin v. Martin, 205 Va. 181, 135 S.E.2d 815 (1964) — § 21-31
Marvin v. Marvin, 18 Cal. 3d 660, 134 Cal. Rptr. 815, 557 P.2d 106 (1976) — § 2-1
Mason v. Mason, 209 Va. 528, 165 S.E.2d 392 (1969) — § 20-29; § 21-16
Mason v. Moon, 9 Va. App. 217, 385 S.E.2d 242 (1989) — § 24-2
Mason v. Rostad, 476 A.2d 662 (D.C. App. 1984) — § 2-1, n. 4

P

Q

R

S

T

W

Y

Z

INDEX

A

ABORTION.
Sexual activities of minors, §16-4.

ABSOLUTE DIVORCE.
See DIVORCE.

ACTIONS.
Child custody.
  Who may seek custody, §24-2.
Child support.
  Standing to bring cause of action for support, §16-1.
  Types of actions available, §16-1.
Separation agreements.
  Who may sue to enforce, §18-10.

ADOPTION.
Adults, §7-31.
Age of adoptive parents, §7-27.
Care of children during trial period, §7-22.
Child support.
  Adopted children, §16-1.
Coercion.
  Revocation of consent, §7-4.
Compacts.
  Interstate compact on the placement of children, §7-8.
Consent.
  Blanket consent forms, §7-5.
  Consent of child, §7-30.
  Dispensing with consent, §7-15.
  Forms, Form 27.
  Minor parent, §7-11.
  Objection of natural parent.
    Adoption over objection, §7-16.
  Presumptive father of illegitimate child, §§4-2, 4-4.
  Revocation, §7-10.
    Fraud, duress and coercion, §7-4.
    Time for revocation, §7-5.
  State licensed agency, §7-17.
  Time for consent, §7-5.
    Revocation, §7-5.
  Unwed father, §7-14.

507

CHILD SUPPORT —Cont'd
Separation agreements.
  See SEPARATION AGREEMENTS.
Standard of living, §16-1.
Standing to bring cause of action, §16-1.
Taxation.
  Tax aspect of child support, §23-15.
Termination.
  Age of majority, §18-18.
Termination of parental rights and responsibility, §16-1.
Torts.
  Failure to provide support, §15-8.
Uniform reciprocal enforcement of support act.
  Foreign judgment of support, §23-20.
  Generally, §23-3.
Unwed parents.
  Natural children, §16-1.
What type of support due, §16-1.
Witnesses.
  Parent as witness, §23-14.

COERCION.
Adoption.
  Revocation of consent, §7-4.
Crimes involving spouses, §11-7.
Marriage.
  Annulment, §6-13.

COHABITATION WITHOUT MARRIAGE.
Contracts between unmarried cohabitants, §2-1.
Virginia law, §2-2.

COLLEGE EDUCATION.
Child support, §§16-1, 23-7.
Separation agreements, §18-19.

COMMON LAW MARRIAGE, §5-2.
Recognition, §2-1.

COMPACTS.
Adoption.
  Interstate compact on placement of children, §7-8.

COMPLAINTS.
Annulment of marriage, §6-4.
Divorce.
  Absolute divorce, §20-14.
    Answer, §20-16.
    Service, §20-15.

D

DEPOSITION.
Forms.
  Notice for taking discovery deposition, Form 8.
DESERTION.
Divorce.
  Absolute divorce.
    Grounds, §20-7.
  Bed and board.
    Justifiable desertion.
      Defense to action, §19-23.
DISABLED CHILD.
Child support, §16-1.
DISCIPLINE OF CHILD, §15-6.
Education.
  Duties of parent, §16-2.
DISCOVERY.
Divorce.
  Absolute divorce, §20-18.
Notice of discovery deposition, Form 8.
DISTRIBUTION OF PROPERTY.
See PROPERTY DISTRIBUTION.
DIVORCE.
Absolute divorce.
  Adultery.
    Consent to adultery.
      Defense to action, §20-11.
    Grounds for divorce, §20-6.
  Alimony, §20-29.
    Pendente lite, §20-13.
  Answer, §20-16.
  Attorneys at law.
    Fees, §20-23.
  Bed and board.
    Merger into absolute divorce, §19-14.
  Commissioner, §20-19.
  Complaint, §20-14.
    Answer, §20-16.
    Service, §20-15.
  Condonation, §20-11.
  Court costs, §20-23.
  Cruelty.
    Grounds, §20-8.
  Curtesy.
    Effect on, §20-25.

DIVORCE —Cont'd
Separation agreements —Cont'd
  General provisions.
    See SEPARATION AGREEMENTS.
Support and maintenance.
  See SUPPORT AND MAINTENANCE.
Taxation.
  Bed and board.
    Tax aspects, §19-22.
Tenancy by the entirety.
  Division of marital property and divorce, §10-6.
Venue.
  Absolute divorce, §20-3.
Witnesses.
  Absolute divorce.
    Corroboration requirement, §20-21.
    Effect on ability to testify, §20-26.
  Bed and board.
    Effect of divorce on testimony, §19-25.
  Privileged communications.
    Testimony following separation or divorce, §12-4.

DOMICILE.
Acquisition of separate domicile, §14-2.
Child support, §16-1.
Divorce.
  Absolute divorce, §20-3.
  Bed and board, §19-4.
Marriage.
  Jurisdiction in annulment cases, §6-3.
  Necessity for domicile, §5-6.

DOWER.
Conveyance of dower right, §10-9.
Divorce.
  Absolute divorce.
    Effect on, §20-25.
  Termination of dower right, §10-9.
Property distribution.
  Effect on, §22-21.
Property in marital relationship, §10-9.

DUE PROCESS.
Education.
  Suspension from public school, §16-2.

DURESS.
Adoption.
  Revocation of consent, §7-4.

DURESS —Cont'd
Divorce.
  Bed and board.
    Defense, §19-23.
  Marriage.
    Annulment, §6-13.

E

EDUCATION.
Child custody.
  School report, §24-8.
Child support.
  College education, §§16-1, 23-7.
Duties of parents.
  Compulsory education, §16-2.
  Controversial subjects in curriculums, §16-2.
  Curriculum, §16-2.
  Discipline, §16-2.
  Due process, §16-2.
  Home instruction, §16-2.
  Immunization, §16-2.
  Introduction, §16-2.
  Rights of students, §16-2.
Property distribution.
  Degree, §22-8.
  Earning potential, §22-18.
Separation agreements.
  College education, §18-19.

EMANCIPATION.
Child support, §23-10.
  Generally, §16-1.
  Independence, §16-1.
  Joining armed forces, §16-1.
  Marriage, §16-1.
  Reaching majority, §16-1.

EMERGENCY PLACEMENT OF CHILDREN.
Termination of parental rights, §7-12.

ENOCH ARDEN RULE.
Bigamist marriages, §6-8.

EQUITABLE ADOPTION, §7-18.

EQUITABLE DISTRIBUTION.
Property distribution.
  See PROPERTY DISTRIBUTION.

I

INTERSTATE FAMILY SUPPORT ACT (UIFSA), §21-5.
Child support, foreign judgments, §23-20.
Enforcement of foreign judgments, §21-29.
INTRAFAMILIAL IMMUNITY.
Torts, §15-2.
IN VITRO FERTILIZATION.
Children conceived through artificial means, §4-7.

J

JOINT TENANCY.
Divorce.
  Absolute divorce.
    Effect on property held as, §20-28.
JOINT TENANTS WITH RIGHT OF SURVIVORSHIP.
Restrictions on conveyances, §10-5.
JURISDICTION.
Annulment of marriage, §6-3.
Child custody, §§24-3, 24-4.
  Family courts, §24-3.
  Modification proceedings, §24-20.
  Uniform child custody jurisdiction act, §24-3.
Child support, §§16-1, 23-3.
  Enforcement, §23-19.
  Family courts, §23-3.
  Modification of support, §23-18.
Divorce.
  Absolute divorce, §20-3.
  Bed and board, §19-4.
Family courts generally.
  See FAMILY COURTS.
Marriage.
  Annulment, §6-3.
Medical care for children, §16-5.
Property distribution, §22-4.
Reciprocal enforcement of support act, §21-29.
Separate maintenance, §17-2.
Support and maintenance, §21-3.
  Child support. See within this heading, "Child support."
  Enforcement proceedings, §21-27.
    Reciprocal enforcement, §21-29.
  Modification of award, §21-19.

K

KIDNAPPING.
Enforcement of custody decree, §24-21.
Religious deprogramming, §15-5.

KIDNAPPING —Cont'd
Removal of child from state, §24-15.

L

LACHES.
Child support, §§23-1, 23-22.
Support and maintenance, §21-32.

LICENSES.
Marriage.
  Required, §5-4.

LIENS.
Separation agreements, §18-15.
Support and maintenance.
  Against property of obligor spouse, §21-35.

LIVING SEPARATE AND APART.
Divorce.
  Absolute divorce.
    Grounds, §20-10.

M

MAIDEN NAME.
Divorce.
  Absolute divorce.
    Resumption of use, §20-24.
Use, §14-1.

MARITAL PROPERTY.
General provisions.
  See PROPERTY IN MARITAL RELATIONSHIP.
Property distribution.
  See PROPERTY DISTRIBUTION.
Property settlements.
  General provisions.
    See SEPARATION AGREEMENTS.

MARITAL SEXUAL ASSAULT, §11-3.

MARRIAGE.
Adoption.
  Marriage of adopted children, §7-38.
Annulments.
  Bigamous marriage, §6-8.
  Complaint, §6-4.

MEDIATION.
Child custody.
  Agreements between parties, §24-14.
Child support, §23-3.
Property distribution, §22-4.
Separation agreements, §18-4.
  Divorce, §18-4.

MEDICAL CARE FOR CHILDREN.
Compulsory medical treatment, §16-5.
Decisions to forego therapy, §16-5.
Elective therapy, §16-5.
  Religious objection, §16-5.
Introduction, §16-5.
Jurisdiction, §16-5.
Life sustaining therapy, §16-5.
Life-threatening situation, §16-5.

MENTALLY ILL.
Marriage.
  See INSANITY.

N

NAME.
Child custody.
  Change of name, §24-18.
Maiden name.
  See MAIDEN NAME.

NECESSARIES.
Child support, §16-1.
Introduction, §13-1.
Necessity for valid marriage, §13-4.
Reimbursement from estate, §13-3.
What is necessary, §13-2.

NO-FAULT DIVORCE, §20-5.
Living separate and apart, §20-10.
Support and maintenance, §21-6.
  Ability to obtain support following divorce, §21-16.

P

PARENT AND CHILD.
Abortion.
  Sexual activities of minors, §16-4.

T

TAXATION.
Child custody.
Dependent minor children, §18-25.
Child support.
Tax aspect of child support, §23-15.
Divorce.
Bed and board.
Tax aspects, §19-22.
Property distribution.
Consequences of distribution, §22-20.
Separation agreements.
Child custody.
Tax exemptions, §18-25.
Child support.
Unitary payment, §18-17.
Property distribution.
Tax consequences, §18-32.
Spousal support.
Tax consequences, §18-11.
Support and maintenance.
Consequences of support award, §21-18.

TENANCY BY THE ENTIRETY.
Creditors.
Effect on, §10-4.
Divorce.
Absolute divorce.
Effect on property held as, §20-28.
Personalty, §10-3.
Real property.
Creation, §10-2.

TERMINATION AGREEMENTS.
Bankruptcy, §18-9.

TERMINATION OF PARENTAL RIGHTS.
Adoption.
Involuntary termination, §7-12.
Substantive standards, §7-13.
Termination of natural parents' rights, §7-2.
Child support, §16-1.
Family courts.
Bifurcated trials, §7-12.
Jurisdiction, §7-12.

THEFT.
Crimes involving spouses, §11-4.

U